Sixth Edition

LOCAL GOVERNMENT
in Canada

C. Richard Tindal and
Susan Nobes Tindal

THOMSON
━━✳━━
NELSON

Australia   Canada   Mexico   Singapore   Spain   United Kingdom   United States

THOMSON

NELSON

Local Government in Canada
Sixth Edition

By C. Richard Tindal
and Susan Nobes Tindal

Editorial Director and Publisher:
Evelyn Veitch

Executive Editor:
Chris Carson

Senior Marketing Manager:
Murray Moman

Senior Developmental Editor:
Rebecca Rea

Managing Production Editor:
Susan Calvert

Production Coordinator:
Helen Jager Locsin

Proofreader:
Edie Franks

Creative Director:
Angela Cluer

Cover Design:
Julie Greener

Cover Images:
Top: Todd Korol;
Bottom: Victor Last/Geographical
Visual Aids

Printer:
Webcom

**National Library of Canada
Cataloguing in Publication**

Tindal, C. R., 1943–
Local government in Canada /
C. Richard Tindal and Susan Nobes
Tindal.—6th ed.

Includes bibliographical references
and index.
ISBN 0-17-641409-6

1. Local government—Canada—
Textbooks. I. Tindal, S. Nobes,
1949– II. Title.

JS1708.T55 2003   352.14'0971
C2003-905758-5

About the Authors

C. Richard Tindal, Ph.D., has been teaching, researching, and writing about local government for close to 40 years. For much of that period, he was a Professor of Government at St. Lawrence College in Kingston, and was Head of its Centre for Government Education and Training until taking early retirement in 1998. He also has been an occasional Visiting Professor in the School of Policy Studies at Queen's University, and recently has been developing and teaching courses via the Internet for the University of Alberta and Dalhousie University. Dick has written a dozen professional training programs in municipal government as well as three books and numerous articles on government and management. As president of *Tindal Consulting Limited*, a firm established in the early 1970s, he has conducted local government restructuring studies in several areas of Ontario, designed and delivered training seminars across Canada, and continues to undertake varied municipal consulting projects.

Susan Nobes Tindal, M.Ed., LL.B., is a lawyer and teacher. She has taught courses in law and municipal government for two decades. She acts as legal counsel for a children's aid society in Eastern Ontario and is the other principal in *Tindal Consulting Limited*. Susan is a past president of the Lennox & Addington County Law Association and is a member of the Family Court Community Liaison Committee. Her community service activities include being a current member of the Board of Governors of Kingston General Hospital, past chair of the Kingston, Frontenac and Lennox & Addington District Health Council, past chair of the Kingston Local Architectural Conservation Advisory Committee, and past chair of the Frontenac Historic Foundation.

Table of Contents

viii

Preface

This edition continues to provide a straightforward, factual overview of municipal government developments across Canada. It retains an historical and institutional focus, but gives more attention to the broader economic and political context within which municipalities operate. The text also continues and extends its discussion of the importance and challenge of fulfilling the representative as well as the service delivery role of municipal governments. While the basic structure and organization of the book is similar to the previous editions, there are two new chapters – on local government finances (Chapter 7) and on municipal policy making (Chapter 10).

As with previous editions, we have benefited greatly from the encouragement and support provided by colleagues in the field. Lee Farnworth of Algonquin College, James Lightbody of the University of Alberta, Paul Prosperi of Langara College, and Terry Ross of Algoma University reviewed the 5th Edition of this book and offered many helpful suggestions concerning this new edition. We are also very grateful to a large number of people who provided information and/or reviewed draft chapters of the new edition. It is with much appreciation that we acknowledge the contributions of Caroline Andrew of the University of Ottawa, Robert Bish of the University of Victoria, Peter Boswell of Memorial University, Daniel Bourgeois of the city of Moncton, Joe Garcea of the University of Saskatchewan, Pierre Hamel of the University of Montreal, Harry Kitchen of Trent University, Christopher Leo of the University of Winnipeg, Edd LeSage of the University of Alberta, Donald Lidstone of Lidstone, Young, Anderson, Melville McMillan of the University of Alberta, Gary Paget of the government of British Columbia, Dale Poel of Dalhousie University, Louise Quesnel of the University of Laval, Andrew Sancton of the University of Western Ontario, David Siegel of Brock University, John Sinclair of the University of Alberta, Enid Slack of Enid Slack Associates, Patrick Smith and Kennedy Stewart of Simon Fraser University, Johnny St-Onge of the government of New Brunswick, and Paul Thomas of the University of Manitoba. In spite of this extensive assistance, we are solely responsible for any short-comings that remain in the book.

Thanks also to the staff of Nelson, especially Rebecca Rea, Chris Carson, Susan Calvert, Edie Franks, and Murray Moman. It continues to be a very positive and pleasant experience working with this company.

Richard and Susan Tindal
Inverary, Ontario
August 2003

Chapter 1
Whither Local Government?

As Canada enters the 21st century, local governments are also going through a momentous transition. What is not immediately apparent is whether they are going forward to the future or back to the past.

Introduction

Local governments appear to be in a state of crisis as the new century unfolds. New or expanded responsibilities put upward pressure on expenditures and, therefore, on municipal taxes. Cities struggle with housing and transportation problems. There are ethnic strains fuelled by the influx of immigrants. Water and sewer systems are overworked or nearing capacity, and there are concerns about pollution, environmental damage, and dangers to public health. Municipalities seem overwhelmed, unable to cope with the increased workload thrust upon them. Municipal politicians are seen by many as an impediment to efficient decision making. Advocates for the business community urge municipalities to embrace new approaches and to become more "business-like" in their operations.

Familiar as this scenario may be today, it actually describes conditions in Canadian local government 100 years ago. The challenges then seemed insurmountable, but municipalities survived, adapted, and even sometimes flourished over the intervening years. This admirable resiliency of municipal government will be sorely tested in the years ahead. Since many of the problems of today are so similar to those of 100 years ago, it perhaps is not surprising that the solutions being advocated by many are a repeat of a number of the reforms from a century ago. It was because of this parallel between present and past that the previous edition of this book began with the two sentences highlighted at the beginning of this chapter.

The direction in which local government is proceeding should become clearer as the book unfolds, but first some information is needed for those without much background in this subject matter.

What are local governments and municipalities (two terms used interchangeably so far), what do they do, and how well do they do it?

Municipal Government

Local government is a broad term that includes municipalities and a variety of local special purpose bodies often referred to as agencies, boards, and commissions or ABCs. Most people tend to equate local government with municipal government, and it is municipalities that are the main focus of this book,[1] so we begin with them.

A municipality is a corporation, a legal device that allows residents of a specific geographic area to provide services that are of common interest. It is also a democratic institution, governed by an elected council that exists as a vehicle through which local citizens can identify and address their collective concerns. The chief distinguishing features of a municipality are:

i)   its corporate nature
ii)   defined geographic boundaries
iii)   an elected council
iv)   taxing power

There are over 4600 municipalities in Canada, almost one-third of them in Quebec. Saskatchewan comes second, with over 800 municipalities, followed by Newfoundland with close to 500 and then Ontario and British Columbia at some 450 each. Determining precise numbers, however, means making arbitrary decisions about whether certain types of local government unit should be included as municipalities. For example, British Columbia's 450 municipalities include more than 250 improvement districts that are incorporated, exercise one or more responsibilities, and are governed by trustees elected in annual meetings. But these districts are excluded from the definition of municipalities in some publications on British Columbia.[2] Similarly,

---

[1] In spite of its title, this book deals mainly with municipal government to keep its length – and our research requirements – manageable.

[2] Robert L. Bish and Eric G. Clemens, *Local Government in British Columbia*, 3rd Edition, Richmond, Union of British Columbia Municipalities, 1999, p. 5, classifies improvement districts as local governments but not municipalities.

the nearly 500 municipalities in Newfoundland include almost 200 local service districts. These are governed by committees of five to seven members, elected for two year terms, and can provide a number of local services – but perhaps they should not be classified as municipalities either. As will be seen, this imprecision in terminology becomes even more pronounced when local ABCs are added to the mix.

The specific classifications of municipal government include cities, towns, villages, rural municipalities (also categorized as townships, parishes, and rural districts), counties (both single and upper tier), and regional and metropolitan municipalities. Many municipalities today are much less local (in terms of their scale of operations and physical proximity) than they were a decade or two ago – as a result of the mergers that have taken place in provinces such as Nova Scotia, Quebec and, especially, Ontario. The Halifax Regional Municipality is hardly a *local* government, given that it contains almost 40% of the population of Nova Scotia and over 10% of the area of the province. It is also striking to find that over one-third of Ontario's population is now found in just three municipalities: the cities of Toronto, Ottawa, and Hamilton. One long-time municipal practitioner cautions: "When the local order of government is expanded to a size where it approaches the size of a provincial government, it runs the risk of expanding its horizon to a point where it loses the proximity to citizens necessary to be an effective local government."[3]

Canada's large municipalities understandably attract attention, and how well or poorly they are governed directly affects a great many Canadians – and indirectly affects all Canadians through the impact on our Gross Domestic Product. But the vast majority of municipalities in Canada are still small and rural. Even after all the mergers in Ontario in the 1990s, for example, just under one-third of its municipalities still have populations under 2500 and over two-thirds have populations under 10 000.[4] In many ways, the small size and scale of operations of these municipalities mean that they more closely represent what most people think of when they refer to municipal government. Nor are these smaller municipalities inevitably incapable of discharging their responsibilities, struggling in vain until they are "saved" through amalgamation with other municipalities.

---

[3] André Carrel, *Citizens' Hall*, Toronto, Between the Lines, 2001, p. 92.

[4] According to information found in *Ontario Municipal Directory 2002*, Association of Municipal Managers, Clerks and Treasurers of Ontario.

Box 1.1 Westport's Winning Ways

Consider the example of the village of Westport, Ontario, population 650. It was deemed too small and slated for amalgamation in a report 30 years ago by some consultant named Tindal. It survived that threat as well as the recent rounds of municipal amalgamation that swept through Ontario. Nestled below Foley Mountain on the shore of Upper Rideau Lake, at the high point of the Rideau Canal that runs between Ottawa and Kingston, Westport is a very picturesque community that has become a popular destination point for tourists and shoppers. The municipality entered a public private partnership for new sewage treatment technology, has joint agreements with a neighbouring municipality with respect to fire and waste management services, and has sub-contracted for the provision of roads, parks, and the collection of garbage and recyclables. In addition to its municipal water and sewer system, Westport operates a municipal harbour, arena, museum, and library, and is a shareholder in a new local electric power distribution company. It is a financially viable municipality with a healthy assessment base featuring a high proportion of commercial assessment. At least one indication of public satisfaction with the way Westport is governed is found in the fact that the head of council is still the same person who held that position when Westport faced its amalgamation challenge some 30 years ago.

We submit that there are many other "Westports" across Canada – small municipalities providing efficient, effective and innovative government for their communities. Their contribution and importance must not be overlooked in the current focus on big city government.

Other Local Governments

In addition to municipalities, there are various other special purpose bodies at the local level that defy classification. There are about 8000 of these bodies across Canada.[5] In Ontario alone, where the use of such local bodies has been quite prevalent, it is estimated that there are at least 2000 of these bodies of 70 different types. Common examples include police commissions, regional health authorities, conservation authorities, parks boards, and school boards. A number of the larger bodies operating at the regional level are less part of local government than they are a form of decentralized provincial administration.[6] This

---

[5] Dale Richmond and David Siegel (eds.), *Agencies, Boards and Commissions in Canadian Local Government*, Toronto, Institute of Public Administration of Canada, Monograph No. 15, 1994, p. xv.

[6] For a discussion of developments in Western Canada, see Evan Jones and Susan McFarlane, *Regional Approaches to Services in the West: Health, Social Services and Education*, Canada West Foundation, February 2002.

is the case, for example, with the regional health authorities established in most provinces. While many local boards are long standing, there are also a number of new bodies that have been created to facilitate partnership arrangements amongst local governing bodies or to preside over entrepreneurial operations such as convention centres or arenas.

The Local State/Civil Society

An even broader perspective would encompass such notions as the civil society or the local state. Civil society has been described as "[t]he web of non-governmental and voluntary associations that deal with urban issues such as community development, land and housing, cultural identity, social service delivery, and human rights protection...".[7] Municipalities that extend their operations from government to governance (as discussed later in this book) develop partnerships with these organizations of civil society. The term local state is rather similar in conveying the notion that local government is but one part of a complex network of organizations and influences that shape local decisions and how they are carried out.[8] These extend to other governments, including senior level governments, local community groups, and private and not-for-profit organizations that are increasingly involved in the delivery of municipal programs and services. Also included, at least in some definitions of this term, would be the social and economic milieu in which local government operates – about which a good deal more will be said later in this chapter.

What Do Local Governments Do?

The most obvious answer to this question (but a dangerously limited one) is that local governments provide a very wide range of services, programs, facilities, and regulations that largely shape our day-to-day

---

[7] Scott A. Bollens, "Managing Urban Ethnic Conflict," in Robin Hambleton, Hank V. Savitch, and Murray Stewart, *Globalism and Local Democracy*, Houndmills, Palgrave Macmillan, 2002, p. 118.

[8] Warren Magnusson, "Urban Politics and the Local State," *Studies in Political Economy*, 1985, 16:111-142.

lives. According to Sancton, local governments in Canada generally exercise the following responsibilities:

> policing; fire protection; animal control; roads, including traffic control, parking, and street-lighting; public transit; water supply (and sometimes natural gas, electricity and telephones); sewage collection and treatment; solid waste collection and disposal; land-use planning and regulation; building regulation and inspection; economic development and promotion; public libraries; parks and recreation; cultural facilities, including museums, concert halls, and art galleries; business licensing; and emergency planning.[9]

In addition, Sancton mentions public education, provided by school boards that have lost much of their taxing and policy making authority to their provincial governments in recent years, and public health and welfare functions that are found at the local level in only a few provinces, notably Ontario.

Valuable as all of these services may be, they are not the only reason, or the most important reason, for local governments to exist. More specifically, they are not the main reason why *municipal governments* exist. That reason is to provide a mechanism for inhabitants of defined local areas to express, debate, and resolve local issues and concerns. In other words, municipal governments perform a political role. They provide local citizens with the opportunity to choose representatives who will make decisions which reflect, or at least respond to, the views and concerns of those local citizens. The municipality is an extension of the community, the community governing itself.[10]

Alleged Benefits of Municipal Government

There are a number of benefits or potential benefits of municipal government. It diffuses the power of government and involves many decision makers in many different localities. This "localness" of municipal government provides greater local knowledge of the situations

---

[9] Andrew Sancton, "Provincial and Local Public Administration," in Christopher Dunn (ed.), *The Handbook of Canadian Public Administration*, Toronto, Oxford University Press, 2002, p. 254.

[10] For a more complete examination of this concept, see various writings by John Stewart including "A Future for Local Authorities as Community Government," in John Stewart and Gerry Stoker, *The Future of Local Government*, London, Macmillan Education Ltd., 1989, and Michael Clarke and John Stewart, *The Choices for Local Government*, Harlow, Longman, 1991.

about which decisions are being made. This arrangement offers the possibility that there will be diverse responses to varying needs of particular localities, thereby allowing the provision of services that better fit local circumstances than would be the case under more distant decision makers. The experimentation that arises may also lead to improved and more efficient approaches than would be possible if only one central standard were to be accepted. This network of municipalities also greatly broadens the opportunities for citizen participation. Municipal governments are more accessible than senior levels of government and more exposed to the possibility of public influence.[11]

In our view, however, it is the combination and interaction of the political and administrative roles that can make municipal government so important and desirable. To restate these roles:

Box 1.2 Primary Roles of Municipal Government

1. To provide the means by which a local community can express and address its collective objectives; and
2. To provide various services and programs to local residents.

It is not just that there is a level of government close to the people, representing their views and affording the opportunity for public participation. It is not just that municipal government provides a number of important services. The key feature of municipal government is, or ought to be, the fact that the services provided are in accordance with the needs and wishes of the local residents. It is this flexibility, this capacity to respond to varying local preferences, which, if realized, makes municipal government especially attractive. It suggests a level of government that allows the inhabitants of a particular area to decide, through their elected council, which range and level of services is most appropriate for them.

If the political and administrative roles of municipal government are not interrelated in this manner, neither one appears to be nearly as valuable. Consider a situation in which services are provided without regard to local needs and wants, or in which citizens participate in a government which doesn't have the capacity to deal with the issues that concern them. In either case, much of the potential significance of municipal government is lost. The reality is that that these two fundamental roles have not been interacting effectively. Both legal

---

[11] These arguments are based partly on G. Jones and J. Stewart, *The Case for Local Government*. London. Allen & Unwin Inc.. 1985

and economic limits keep municipalities from being responsive to local needs and, indeed, the political and representative role of municipal government often has been ignored or discredited. Moreover, there are even differing views about the extent to which municipal government and democracy are compatible much less synonymous.

Municipal Government and Democracy: A Tenuous Link?

The democratic features of municipal government have been emphasized by various writers from de Tocqueville and John Stuart Mill to K. G. Crawford.[12] To some, such as Mill, municipal government constituted a training ground for democracy, wherein elected representatives would "learn the ropes" before going on to service at a more senior level, and local citizens would learn about exercising their democratic rights in the context of issues which were relatively simple and understandable. No better expression of this latter sentiment can be found than the Durham Report. Lord Durham was struck by the lack of municipal institutions in the colony in the 1830s, especially in the rural areas still governed by the Courts of Quarter Sessions. He expressed concern that "the people receive no training in those habits of self-government which are indispensable to enable them rightly to exercise the power of choosing representatives in parliament."[13]

Others, such as de Tocqueville, with his oft-quoted statement that "municipal institutions constitute the strength of free nations," saw municipal government's democratic role in a much more direct, fundamental light. Indeed, Crawford saw municipal government as far from just a training ground, but as the level at which the democratic ideal was most likely to be fulfilled. The citizen is more likely to understand the issues under consideration locally than the increasingly complex, technical matters that predominate at the senior levels of government. Moreover, because the results of local decisions (or

---

[12] See Alexis de Tocqueville's *Democracy in America*, J. S. Mill's *Considerations on Representative Government* and *On Liberty*, and *Canadian Municipal Government* by K. G. Crawford.

[13] Quoted in Engin Isin, *Cities Without Citizens*, Montreal, Black Rose Books, 1992, p. 132.

indecision) are readily apparent in the local community, citizens should be able to evaluate the effectiveness of their government and the degree to which councillors have fulfilled their campaign promises.

Not everyone shares this positive view of municipalities, however. A contrasting viewpoint is provided by Langrod, who viewed municipal government as "but a technical arrangement within the mechanisms of the administrative system, a structural and functional detail...."[14] Langrod not only rejected the assumption that municipal governments are vital to democracy, he also contended that they could be contrary to the democratic process.

> In some countries local government, with its structured anachronisms, the high degree of its internal functionalisation, the preponderance in practice of the permanent official over the elected and temporary councillor, its methods of work and its obstinate opposition to all modernization, can ... act as a brake on the process of democratisation.[15]

Whatever the merits of these various arguments, the fact is that in Canada the link between municipal governments and democracy has always been tenuous and the constraints on the political role of municipal government are substantial.

A Focus on Property Not People

Canadian municipal governments were never intended to be instruments of mass democracy. The bias in favour of the propertied class and the lack of participation by the masses is evident from the restricted franchise given to early municipal governments. Higgins observes that when Halifax was incorporated in 1841, its charter limited the vote to only about 800 people who could meet a property qualification, and restricted candidacy for office to a fraction of that number.[16] To take another example, Baker's study of St. John's,

---

[14] Georges Langrod, "Local Government and Democracy," in *Public Administration*, Vol. XXXI, Spring 1953, pp. 25-33. The oft-quoted Langrod and Panter-Brick exchanges on the subject of local government and democracy are reprinted in Lionel D. Feldman (ed.), *Politics and Government of Urban Canada*, Toronto, Methuen, 1981, Section A.

[15] *Ibid.*, pp. 5-6.

[16] Donald J. H. Higgins, *Local and Urban Politics in Canada*, Toronto, Gage, 1986, p. 39.

Newfoundland, notes that the incorporation of the city in 1888 was accompanied by strict property qualifications for both voters and candidates. He describes a number of measures to ensure that it was the merchants, lawyers, and shopkeepers who dominated – within the colonial legislature as well as within the city council.[17] Similarly, Artibise has shown that the municipal governments of the major cities of western Canada were dominated by a business elite, "partly because of a restricted franchise which effectively limited opposition."[18]

As Kaplan pointed out, "Local government cannot be both an experiment in mass participatory democracy and a corporation created by and for property owners."[19] While the franchise was gradually extended over the years, the influence of the propertied class and the business elites continues to prevail – a recurring theme in this text.

Responsible to the Province Not the People

For municipalities to function as democratic governments, they need to be accountable and responsible to those who elect them and on whose behalf they have been constituted. But when the British North America Act was passed to establish the country of Canada, there was no recognition of a system of municipal governments existing to serve and respond to local needs. Instead, local governments were only mentioned in this constitutional document as one of the responsibilities assigned to the provincial level. As a result, their functions, finances, governing structure – even their very existence – depend upon provincial authorization. It follows that municipalities have two key characteristics:[20]

I.   They are created at the pleasure of the legislature, and need not require the consent of the people in the affected locality. The act of incorporation is not a contract between the legislature and the local inhabitants; and

---

[17] M. Baker, "William Gilbert Gosling and the Establishment of Commission Government in St. John's, Newfoundland, 1914," *Urban History Review*, Vol. IX, No. 3, February 1981, pp. 37-39.

[18] Gilbert Stelter and Alan Artibise (eds.), *Shaping the Canadian Landscape: Aspects of the Canadian City-Building Process*, Ottawa, Carleton University Press, 1982, p. 21. See also the Artibise article on pp. 116-147.

[19] Harold Kaplan, *Reform, Planning and City Politics: Montreal, Winnipeg, Toronto*, Toronto, University of Toronto Press, 1982, p. 63.

[20] Isin, *Cities Without Citizens*, p. 2.

2. The authority conferred on the corporation is not local in nature but derives from the provincial government.

As will be evident from ensuing discussions, notably with respect to intergovernmental relations (Chapter 6) and local finances (Chapter 7), municipalities operate within a very restricted legislative and financial framework that often constrains their ability to act on behalf of their local citizens – although these chapters also note some encouraging changes that may bring more municipal autonomy and flexibility.

The Prevalence of Economic Over Political Forces

While the legal limitations on municipal government have tended to receive the most attention, it is also the case that municipalities are very much constrained by economic forces, as will be evident from a brief examination of some of the theories that attempt to explain how these governments operate and how decisions are made.

Perhaps the best known theories about local decision making are the community power studies of the 1950s and 1960s centred on the research of Hunter and Dahl.[21] Hunter's study of reputed influentials in Atlanta led him to conclude that power was concentrated in the hands of a socio-economic elite that dominated local decision making. In contrast, Dahl's study of issues in New Haven led him to conclude that numerous individuals and groups had influence, which they might exercise depending on the issue involved, but not with respect to all issues. Dahl's pluralist model saw decisions arising from the interplay of various organized groups, while conceding that business interests were particularly well organized and influential.

Critics have argued that the approaches of both studies were flawed – Hunter's from asking those reputedly influential if they were, and Dahl's by selecting certain issues and not others and by ignoring those matters that were kept from the policy agenda and didn't even get to a decision. Their different findings could be explained, it has been argued, on the grounds that "what you see depends on how you look at it."[22] Whatever the merits of the two approaches, however,

---

[21] Floyd Hunter, *Community Power Structure*, New York, Anchor Books, 1953 and Robert Dahl, *Who Governs?*, New Haven, Yale University Press, 1961.

[22] This explanation is discussed in E. Barbara Phillips and Richard T. LeGates (eds.), *City Lights: An Introduction to Urban Studies*, New York, Oxford University Press, 1981, Chapter 12.

they both suggested that "local power is concentrated in the hands of a relative few, be it some socio-economic elite (as the elitists argued) or a series of elites with different resource bases (as the pluralists argued).[23]

The alleged economic limits on local government are even more evident in public choice theory,[24] which takes as its starting point the view that the best mechanism for allocating goods and services is the market and the worst is elected governments supported by large bureaucracies. To offset the natural tendency to over-production inherent in governments, public choice advocates support a fragmented local government structure, one in which multiple suppliers of goods and services at a variety of tax levels provide choice for local consumers. Critics of public choice question the extent to which local consumers have knowledge of the choices available to them and have the mobility to act upon this information. Such mobility is certainly not available to the poor and disadvantaged.

But this mobility is available to many businesses, increasingly so in today's world. As a result, local governments feel pressure to accommodate the interests of businesses or risk losing them to other locales (and even other countries). This idea has been taken to its limits, one might say, by Peterson,[25] who argues that the policies adopted by a city will be constrained and shaped by how those policies affect the city's overriding objective of promoting economic growth. In particular, he contends that redistributive policies (those that involve income transfers from higher to lower income segments of the population) will be avoided by cities as much as possible, lest they prompt businesses to respond to the extra tax burden by relocating.

Scope for Political Action Remains

Brief as the above summary has been, it conveys the widespread view that economic forces severely constrain political activity. But this view fails to give enough credit to political forces. In Mollenkopf's words:

---

[23] Harold Wolman and Michael Goldsmith, *Urban Politics and Policy: A Comparative Approach*, Cambridge, Blackwell Publishers, 1992, p. 13.

[24] See Charles M. Tiebout, "A Pure Theory of Local Expenditure," *Journal of Political Economy* 64, No. 5, October 1956 and Vincent Ostrom, Robert Bish, and Elinor Ostrom, *Local Government in the United States*, San Francisco, Institute for Contemporary Analysis, 1988.

[25] Paul Peterson, *City Limits*, Chicago, University of Chicago Press, 1981.

> By themselves, economic factors explain relatively little. They are
> necessarily mediated through, and influenced by, the political system.
> The classic market approach fails to see that political actors and
> government intervention help determine the relative costs of
> different locations, promote some sectors of the economy over
> others, and guide location decisions for new investments. It is blind
> to the fact that noneconomic, political factors strongly enter into
> such decisions. [26]

The reality is that local governments, indeed governments at
all levels, are not as passive and helpless in the face of economic forces
as they are portrayed, and they could be a good deal more forceful
with sufficient political will. Nor are developments the inevitable
result of the operations of the free market; indeed, the "free" market is
a myth – which is one of the fundamental flaws of the public choice
perspective.[27] It is governments that establish the regulatory and legal
framework that makes it possible to have functioning markets. The
housing market in urban areas has been largely shaped by government
policies that have long favoured single family dwellings. As Chapter 3
will make clear, government policies also underlie the pattern of
urbanization and urban sprawl that has evolved in Canada.

While local governments must obviously be mindful of
economic forces, they do have choices about how they respond to
these forces, as Leo demonstrates through an examination of planning
in Vancouver and Edmonton in the 1970s and 1980s. He concludes
that economic limits are not all encompassing and that they leave
"substantial space for community action and for the forging of unique
community identities through political action."[28] Leo contrasts
Edmonton's willingness to accommodate business interests in the
redevelopment of the city with Vancouver's determination to maintain
strict controls over development. He suggests that the approach
followed by Edmonton was less a result of objective economic circumstances than a "panicky misreading of its economic situation," which

---

[26] John H. Mollenkopf, *The Contested City*, Princeton, Princeton University
Press, 1983, p. 8.

[27] Peter Dreier, John Mollenkopf, and Todd Swanstrom, *Place Matters:
Metropolitics for the Twenty-First Century*, Lawrence, University Press of
Kansas, 2001, p. 98.

[28] Christopher Leo, "The Urban Economy and the Power of the Local State," in
Frances Frisken (ed.), *The Changing Canadian Metropolis: A Public Policy
Perspective*, Vol. 2, Toronto, Canadian Urban Institute, 1994, p. 663.

led it to conclude that it had to give in to the demands of the business community to bring about an economic revival.[29] While the economic context is important, Leo contends that attempts to explain any city's performance must also take into account the particular circumstances of that city, "including local political cultures and the political forces that comprise the local state and control the direction it takes."[30]

The external environment of local government will never be far in the background as we proceed to examine the structure and operations of local government in the ensuing chapters. Many decisions made by local governments influence and shape the external environment. In addition, forces in the external environment, especially those associated with business interests, influence and shape many of the decisions that are made by local governments. This symbiotic relationship is evident in many of the discussions in later chapters, including:

> The previously cited example of urbanization, discussed in Chapter 3;
> The way municipal amalgamations (discussed in Chapters 4 and 5), by combining city and suburbs, can alter the balance of power within the new government;
> The power shifts implicit in a move from election by ward to election by general vote (examined in Chapter 8); and
> The way that municipal taxes and other charges (outlined in Chapter 7) not only generate revenues but also influence the pattern of growth and development, especially in the direction of urban sprawl.

Political Role Denied and Decried

Not all constraints on the democratic nature of municipal governments have been imposed by economic forces or by the Canadian constitution. Some of them are self-imposed and arise from a misguided (in our view) perception of the role of municipal government. A major setback for municipal governments as instruments of local democracy occurred 100 years ago during the municipal reform movement of that era, as described in the next chapter. Advocating

---

[29] *Ibid.*, p. 693.

[30] *Ibid.*, p. 694.

more efficient administration and the removal of all corruption, reformers called for the exclusion of politics from municipal government. Decisions should be made on objective, rational grounds. Municipal administrators should be free to provide municipal services without political interference from the elected representatives. In their misguided zeal, the reformers substantially undermined the very system of municipal government that the Loyalists in Ontario and others had fought so hard to obtain only half a century earlier! From the reform era came not only a number of structural changes (including the establishment of separate boards and commissions) designed to reduce the influence of the politician and to elevate the role of the appointed expert, but also the lingering notion that politics has no place in local government.

Yet the efforts of reformers to remove politics from municipal decision making were really designed to remove the political influence that could now be exercised by growing city populations. In this respect, the reformers were quite undemocratic or anti-democratic. As Plunkett and Betts describe the situation:

> ... their intention was not to try to halt the process of making deci-
> sions on public policy at the local level. Their intention, rather, was
> to exclude various groups from the process.... The reformers were
> interested in restoring the efficiency and effectiveness of municipal
> service delivery. At the same time, they were plainly concerned with
> restricting the influence of the cities' burgeoning population of
> working people upon the conduct of municipal affairs.[31]

This latter viewpoint reflected the fact that many of the reformers were middle-class merchants and businessmen who had little sympathy for the democratic aspects of local government. In their minds, the solution was to run local government more like a business. Of course, this also meant that citizens should elect more businessmen to councils, an argument that revealed the self-interest of reformers.

The actions of the reformers in denying any political role for municipal government was misguided and harmful. The fact is that politics inevitably exists in every society because humans have wants and needs that must be satisfied from resources that are scarce and insufficient. As a result, competition and conflict arise, and the central purpose of governments is to resolve these disputes by deciding who gets what resources and how equitably they are distributed.

---

[31] T. J. Plunkett and G. M. Betts, *The Management of Canadian Urban Government*, Kingston, Queen's University, 1978, p. 27.

Governments possess legal authority that provides the foundation for their allocation decisions.

It follows that politics is an integral part of local government operations. It is no less true at this level that decisions must be made about allocating scarce resources. Competition and conflict are equally prevalent. Divisions arise on such questions as urban and rural interests, city and suburban, haves and have-nots, for and against development, and ethnic and racial issues. Since municipalities are governments, not just vehicles for service delivery, it is their role to mediate among the diverse interests, to build consensus where possible, to make choices, and to answer for them. "Politics, like sex, cannot be abolished. It can sometimes be repressed by denying people the opportunity to practice it, but it cannot be done away with because it is in the nature of man to disagree and to contend."[32]

Unhelpful Pressures and Adaptations

As Chapter 3 makes clear, the transformation of the economy and society of Canada during the 20th century placed many pressures on local government. These pressures and, in many cases, the responses to them, also served to limit the ability of municipalities to function as democratic governments.

The industrialization and urbanization of Canada, especially following the Second World War greatly increased the service demands placed upon municipalities – much as had happened with the urbanization at the beginning of the 20th century. These service demands were met, but often at a price for local municipalities. Some services shifted upward until they found a jurisdiction large enough to handle them effectively. For example, local services moved to the county level or to inter-municipal boards, or even to the provincial level. Services that stayed local often came under provincial requirements intended to ensure minimum standards. The municipal financial squeeze was eased by provincial grants, but most of these were conditional and imposed further provincial requirements. The net result of these developments was that municipalities became increasingly entangled with the operations and policies of their provincial governments and were correspondingly less able to respond to local needs and preferences.

---

[32] Edward Banfield and James Q. Wilson, *City Politics*, New York, Random House, 1963, pp. 20-21.

Chapter 3 also discusses the concerns that have been raised about the way that the pattern of urbanization itself has adversely affected the political and democratic role of municipal government. In particular, the built environment of urban areas, with their separate land uses regulated by zoning, does not facilitate the contact between individuals and commitment to community that arises from greater physical diversity. Suburban living, with its lengthy commutes, is also felt to discourage public involvement in community affairs.

As Chapters 4 and 5 make clear, the municipal government restructuring initiatives introduced in most provinces over the past 40 years have done little to enhance the link between municipal government and democracy. For the most part, these reforms have been preoccupied with improving the service delivery role of municipalities. Most of the reforms introduced in the 1960s and 1970s paid very little attention to its more important political role. The end result was new municipal government structures that were often perceived as more bureaucratic and less accountable. The reforms of the 1990s have in many ways been even more one-sided and neglectful of the political role of municipalities. This is especially evident in Ontario, where the province very aggressively promoted widespread amalgamations. Provincial press releases accompanying each restructuring note approvingly the efficiency gains that were expected and the number of municipal politicians reduced.

Municipalities in the New World Order

Municipal government has also been affected by fundamental changes affecting the world economy and the perceived role of governments therein. A key characteristic of this new economic era is what amounts to the internationalization of economic activity. Multinational corporations have becoming transnational corporations with no particular or permanent home base or domestic market. Modern technology allows them to deploy their resources spatially in whatever manner best serves their bottom line. The result is that most mass production, labour intensive work is shifted to low-wage regions of the world. As these corporations become more mobile, national governments are pressured to accommodate their interests or run the risk of losing them to other jurisdictions.[33]

The result has been a profound shift in the role of government, with significant implications for the municipal level. That role had become very prominent in the period following the Second World War. There was widespread acceptance of the view that governments could make a major contribution to the betterment of the human condition. Between the 1940s and the 1970s, a variety of new programs were introduced (especially at the federal level) that constituted a social safety net for Canadians and that also reinforced the expansionary fiscal policies of the government. Provincial and municipal governments also expanded their activities throughout this period, largely – as previously noted – in response to the servicing needs of a rapidly growing population. These government initiatives received widespread approval, both for addressing the needs of society and for contributing to economic growth.

Today, however, governments are portrayed as the cause of most of society's problems, not the solution to them. Social programs are no longer viewed as valuable contributors to economic policy through enhanced consumer spending. Instead, they are criticized as excessively expensive entitlements that breed dependence, create labour market rigidities, and inhibit Canadian competitiveness. The new global economy, we are told, requires the removal of all barriers that might inhibit the effective performance of Canadian companies or cause a flight of investment capital. Many of these "barriers" are found in the government programs and government regulations that were developed in earlier decades in support of a more civilized society. The prevailing ideology, usually referred to as neoconservatism or neo-liberalism, now calls for a much reduced role for government and a corresponding increase in activity for the private sector.

In response to these dictates of the global economy, Canada (along with a number of other Western nations) has been dismantling the social safety net – either directly through curtailing programs or indirectly by undermining the programs through expenditure cuts. The last decade of the 20th century saw a process in which the federal

---

[33] See, among others, Murray Dobbin, *The Myth of the Good Corporate Citizen*, Toronto, Stoddart, 1998, and John Shields and B. Mitchell Evans, *Shrinking the State: Globalization and Public Administration "Reform,"* Halifax, Fernwood Publishing, 1998.

government cut transfer payments and shifted responsibilities to the provincial level that, in turn, cut transfer payments and shifted responsibilities to the local level. At the bottom of the pile in this new form of "fend-for-yourself federalism," municipalities, as usual, were adversely affected by the actions of the senior levels of government.

As discussed in Chapter 6, municipalities in some provinces (notably Ontario and Nova Scotia) faced the combined impact of reduced provincial transfer payments and increased responsibilities arising from provincial downloading. How are municipalities to cope with this increased revenue squeeze they face? Not by increasing the property tax, and especially not by increasing property taxes on business, if we are to believe those who preach the new gospel. If taxes can't be raised, then expenditures must be cut, leaving municipalities with the same pressure to reduce or abandon public services that the senior levels of government have been experiencing.

(Re)Ascendancy of the Corporate Agenda

In the face of these pressures, enhancing municipal democracy doesn't receive much attention. Instead, municipalities are told to become more efficient and business-like. They are encouraged to redefine their core business, and are told to develop business plans, to set measurable targets, and to demonstrate improved service to their customers. They are encouraged to pursue alternative service delivery strategies, including joint ventures with other local government bodies, public private partnerships, and even outright privatization. In a move which is consistent with the new public management initiatives which have been occurring at the senior levels of government in a number of countries, municipalities are also being encouraged to separate their service delivery activities from those which involve policy making and to hive off these activities into separate agencies which – freed from the strictures of the traditional bureaucracy – can demonstrate improved customer service and greater entrepreneurship.

One hundred years after the turn of the century movement that denigrated politics, deplored interference by politicians, and called for municipalities to operate in a more business-like fashion, we find history repeating itself. Political "interference" from councillors is cited as a barrier to expeditious and thoughtful decisions. There are frequent suggestions that ward elections be replaced by elections at large and that the size of council be reduced to produce a body suited to more expeditious decision making.

Because of these developments, municipalities have become less like governments. Instead of being representative bodies that reflect democratic decision making at the local level, municipalities are viewed as vehicles for service delivery, focused on the preparation of business plans and the pursuit of whatever alternative delivery options are most economical. It is our position that this focus misses the primary purpose and benefit of municipal government. Local citizens should be the focus, and their active involvement and participation in municipal government should be the objective. We agree with Carrel: "A municipal council's obligation to engage citizens in democratic governance is far more important than its obligation to manage the services delegated to it by the provincial government."[34]

A Tale of Two Futures

If local governments are at a crossroads, as stated at the beginning of this chapter, what is the prognosis for their future? In the words of that well-known "political scientist" Charles Dickens, in his classic *Tale of Two Cities*, local governments face the best of times and the worst of times.[35] A brief summary of the basis for these optimistic and pessimistic perspectives should help to clarify the challenges currently facing local governments – and to introduce many of the issues to be examined in this book.

The Best of Times

A majority of the provinces passed new municipal legislation during the 1990s, giving their municipalities greater flexibility for taking action and often providing a commitment to greater provincial consultation. The prospect of more autonomy and discretion to act locally has also been supported by some recent decisions of the Supreme Court of Canada – notably in the pesticide case involving the

---

[34] Carrel, *Citizens' Hall*, p. 108.

[35] Charles Dickens, *Tale of Two Cities*, London, Chapman and Hall, 1859.

municipality of Hudson, Quebec.[36] More financial support, at least for our largest cities, may be on the horizon, as a result of numerous reports from diverse sources that emphasize the critical importance of cities to Canada's present prosperity and future growth. Reform and restructuring during the 1990s, especially in Ontario, Quebec, and Nova Scotia, created new much larger municipalities that are more capable of handing the challenges facing them. While globalization imposes constraints on the actions of national and provincial governments, it is allegedly increasing the importance of cities.

The optimistic view of all these developments is that larger municipalities, working within more flexible provincial legislative frameworks, bolstered by increased financial support – especially from the federal level – will be able to capitalize on the opportunities they have in a world that now recognizes that cities and city-regions are the key to a country's economic prosperity.

The Worst of Times

The pessimistic view is that municipalities remain under threat and under the thumb of their provincial governments. The ultimate expression of that threat is the complete elimination of municipalities as has happened in hundreds of instances during the restructuring of the 1990s. In Ontario alone, almost 400 municipalities (or 45%) of them) disappeared as a result of amalgamations, and only a minority of them went willingly or happily. Municipalities also remain at risk because provincial governments continue to impose changes without sufficient appreciation of, or concern for, their adverse local impact.

As discussed in Chapter 6, the new legislative framework provided for municipalities has, at best, uncertain potential, and provides no real protection against capricious provincial initiatives. Nor can supportive court rulings be assured, given the surprising position taken by the Alberta Court of Appeal with respect to the

---

[36] 114957 *Canada Ltée et al v. Town of Hudson et al (2001)*, 200 D.L.R. (4d) 419. The Court upheld a municipal by-law prohibiting the use of pesticides, except for enumerated uses, throughout the municipality, a by-law enacted on the basis of the "omnibus" provision in the municipal legislation authorizing by-laws to secure peace, order, good government, health and general welfare in the community. Such omnibus provisions have rarely been relied upon successfully in the past as an independent source of authority for municipal actions.

municipal legislation generally regarded as setting the standard.[37] As far as financial salvation for municipalities, sympathetic words from the federal government about the plight of Canada's cities are a far cry from cold, hard cash – and not much of that has yet been committed. There are also reasons to be concerned that globalization forces may prove as constraining for municipalities as they will be for the senior levels of government, and that international trade agreements will intrude upon municipal decision making.

Most of all, there is reason for pessimism when municipal governments remain preoccupied with ways of enhancing service delivery rather than ways of enriching local democracy.

Concluding Comments:
What's Past Is Prologue

To at least some extent, the answer to the question about the future prospects of local government lies in the past. More than is commonly appreciated, the structure of local government in many parts of Canada, its internal organization and governing machinery, and much of its operating philosophy, is a reflection of its historical evolution. A surprising number of current issues and themes can also be found at the forefront in much earlier periods. Before we speculate further on the future prospects of Canada's local governments, it is important to understand the legacy of the past, and how the system has evolved into its present state.

---

[37] *United Taxi Drivers' Fellowship of Southern Alberta v. Calgary (City of), 2002*, ABCA 131, as found at www.albertacourts.ab.ca. The Alberta Court of Appeal quashed a Calgary by-law that limited the number of taxi licences. The court found that while the old legislation had expressly conferred a power to limit the number of taxi licences, this power was not found in Alberta's landmark 1994 legislation, and Calgary's by-law, therefore, lacked specific authorization. So much for the notion that municipalities should be able to take action within broad spheres and not require specific authorization for every action taken.

Chapter 2
The Legacy of the Past

The local government systems found in Canada in the early 21st century retain many classifications of municipality originally created some 150 years ago and internal governing structures and governing philosophies established a century ago.

Introduction

The earliest municipal governments in Canada evolved in response to the settlement of the country. As the population increased, and particularly as it became concentrated in the limited urban centres of the early years, it was necessary to administer a growing variety of programs and regulations. With pockets of population scattered in a vast area, and with very rudimentary forms of transportation and communication, the responsibilities could not be handled directly by a centralized colonial government. While some form of local administration was inevitable for quite practical reasons, therefore, the particular form that did evolve was strongly influenced by the political values and traditions of the settlers of this country and the beliefs that they held or developed about municipal government. In this connection, the extent to which this country was settled through immigration was a significant factor, especially because of the belief in local self-government held by many of the United Empire Loyalists who entered this country in the years during and after the American War of Independence.

We begin our historical survey with developments in Central Canada because a comprehensive system of municipal government was first established there (in Ontario), and this system influenced the municipal institutions subsequently created in a number of the other provinces. No standard time frame is employed; rather, developments in each province are described up to the point where the basic municipal structure was established.

Central Canada

Local government made its first, although rather brief, appearance in Canada under the French regime in the settlements of Montreal, Quebec, and Trois Rivières. As early as 1647 a mayor, councillors, and syndics d'habitations (who made representations on behalf of local residents to the provincial authorities) were elected in Quebec. This practice was strongly discouraged by the very authoritarian and centralized home government in France, which felt that it was a dangerous innovation, and in 1663 the mayor and aldermen of Quebec resigned. The whole issue of local self-government then lapsed for 100 years – until 1760 and the advent of British rule.

The British vested all government in the military and then in a Governor and an appointed council. In 1763 a proclamation was issued which promised to introduce English law and the English system of freehold land grants in Quebec, in order to encourage English settlement. In the following year the Governor established the ancient English system of local justices of the peace meeting in the Courts of Quarter Sessions for the three districts around Montreal, Quebec, and Trois Rivières for the trial of unimportant matters.

Despite the rule by British Governors and the promise of the benefits of English law, little occurred to interrupt the traditional running of the affairs of Quebec. There was little interference with the Roman Catholic Church, the Court of Common Pleas continued to administer French civil law, and land was still granted through the feudal French system, "en fief et seigneurie." The Quebec Act of 1774 formally recognized this situation and extended Quebec's boundaries west to the Great Lakes and Mississippi River and north to Labrador.

The Loyalist Influx

The American Revolution broke out soon after and precipitated a flow of United Empire Loyalists to Nova Scotia and western Quebec.[1] The peak years of the influx were 1782 and 1783, when 10 000 arrived in the Saint John area of the Bay of Fundy, 25 000 arrived in Nova Scotia, and 20 000 arrived in the unsettled areas around Lake Ontario, particularly around present day Kingston, Toronto, and Niagara.

---

[1] The figures that follow are from K. G. Crawford, *Canadian Municipal Government*, Toronto, University of Toronto Press, 1954, p. 21.

These immigrants came chiefly from New York and the New England colonies, where they had enjoyed some degree of local self-government. They brought with them the tradition of municipal government through the town meeting. Under this system, selectmen (councillors) were elected at the annual town meeting by those residing within one-half mile of the meeting house. These selectmen were to oversee the affairs of the town between meetings. In theory their appointment and actions were to be approved by the Governor but, in practice, they operated independent of the central authorities.

Upper Canada (Ontario)

Needless to say, these Loyalists were unhappy under French civil law, especially the system of land grants under the seigneurial system and the limited local autonomy. There soon were numerous petitions from the Loyalists around Lake Ontario for some form of local courts and administration, English civil law, and separation from that area of Quebec that was east of Montreal.

Because of population growth pressures, but much against their better judgment, the British acquiesced and in 1787 passed an ordinance which divided the western settlements, previously a part of the district of Montreal, into four new districts with various appointed officials including justices of the peace who constituted the Courts of Quarter Sessions. The Quarter Sessions assumed judicial, legislative, and administrative responsibilities including maintaining the peace, regulating domestic animals running at large, the conduct of licensed taverns, the appointment of minor officials, and the superintending of highways.[2] As new problems arose, the Quarter Sessions, which were the only official agency dealing with local matters, were simply given more powers to deal with them.

However, this new system proved to be unworkable under the French feudal laws and institutions which had been established with the Quebec Act and pressure continued for a separate province with English civil law and an English system of land tenure. This continuing pressure finally culminated in the Constitutional Act of 1791 (also known as the Canada Act). Its main provisions included:

1. The creation, from the province of Quebec, of the provinces of Upper and Lower Canada, with the Ottawa River roughly as the dividing line.

---

[2] *Ibid.*, p. 23.

2. The provision of a government for each province consisting of a British
    Lieutenant Governor, an appointed executive council and legislative council,
    and an elected legislative assembly.
3. The use of English law and land tenure in Upper Canada.

J. G. Simcoe, the first Lieutenant Governor of Upper Canada, strongly discouraged any form of local government. This stance reflected the prevailing view of the Colonial Office, which was haunted by the prospect of another colonial rebellion. Municipalities were distrusted on the grounds that they were breeding grounds for dissent and disloyalty.[3] When the first townships on the upper St. Lawrence were surveyed in 1783, the authorities directed that they be called royal seigniories and not townships, and that they be numbered and not named as was customary, to discourage any strong attachment to a particular place. However, even before the Constitutional Act was passed, the Loyalists had already set up town meetings and designated their settlements townships. In an imaginative act of defiance, they named the townships after King George and members of his family.

The Loyalists, who constituted most of the population of the province, felt that they had proven their loyalty to the Crown by fleeing the rebellious colonies and therefore deserved to have local self-rule. The first bill introduced in the first session of the legislative assembly of Upper Canada was "to authorize town meetings for the purpose of appointing divers parish officers." It was passed in 1793 as the Parish and Town Officers Act. The Act permitted annual town meetings to appoint a town clerk, assessors, a tax collector, road over-seers and fence viewers, a pound-keeper, and town wardens. The town wardens were to represent the inhabitants in the Quarter Sessions of the district in which the town(ship) was located. The only legislative authority the town meeting[4] had was to fix the height of fences and to regulate animals running at large. An act dealing with assessment was also passed in 1793 to provide for raising money to pay for the costs of court and jail houses, paying officers' fees, and building roads.

The end of the War of 1812 in North America and the Napoleonic Wars in Europe saw the beginning of a new wave of immigration from the British Isles. About 800 000 came to British

---

[3] This point is made by Engin Isin, "The Origins of Canadian Municipal Government," in James Lightbody (ed.), *Canadian Metropolitics: Governing Our Cities*, Toronto, Copp Clark Ltd., 1995, pp. 60-61.

[4] In Ontario, town meetings were actually township meetings.

North America between 1815 and 1850, the great bulk of whom settled in Upper Canada. This population growth magnified the existing urban problems and petitioning continued for some form of municipal government. In 1828 Belleville applied to be incorporated as a town. The Legislative Council rejected this application, saying:

> Since men do not like to be forced, they are pretty certain to elect only such persons as will not make effective rules or adequately enforce them; hence in the interest of efficient administration, such innovations must be discouraged.[5]

Despite this setback for Belleville, in 1832 the legislature capitulated and created a distinct corporate body in the president and board of police of the town of Brockville. This body was essentially the first form of elected council and it took over the local government functions previously undertaken by the Quarter Sessions, with the justices of the peace retaining only their judicial functions within Brockville. This movement to representative local government proved to be popular. In 1834 York was created the self-governing city of Toronto and by 1838 there were eight police towns and two cities.

One should not overstate the significance of this development, however.[6] Only members of the boards of police were incorporated, not the town inhabitants. The qualifications to be a member of the board required that a town inhabitant be a freeholder or a householder paying a certain amount of rent per annum for his dwelling. A governing elite was formed whose obligation was to govern the town. The qualification to be a voter in the election required that the town inhabitant be a male householder, a subject of the King, and possessing a freehold estate. "These qualifications for board membership and voting demonstrate the calculated restrictions that were put upon participation in town politics."[7]

While the urban areas of Upper Canada were gaining more local self-government, the magistrates of the Quarter Sessions remained in almost total control in rural areas. Reform newspapers of the time charged that many magistrates were unfit, intemperate, and ready to stir up the mob against reformers. The magistrates decided which local

---

[5] Shortt, *op. cit.*, p. 19.

[6] See Engin F. Isin, *Cities Without Citizens*, Montreal, Black Rose Books, 1992, pp. 112-114, on which this discussion is based.

[7] *Ibid.*, p. 113.

works were to be carried out, often ignoring areas in which they had no personal interest, and how much tax revenue was to be raised.[8] The growing unrest culminated in the 1837 Rebellion in Upper and Lower Canada.

Durham Report

In response, the Earl of Durham was appointed to investigate the insurrection particularly and the general state of government in all of the provinces. Durham produced a comprehensive report dealing with the conditions in British North America, and of particular importance for our purposes are his recommendations dealing with local government. He wrote that "municipal institutions of local self-government ... are the foundations of Anglo-Saxon freedom and civilization."[9] He also stated: "The latter want of municipal institutions giving the people any control over their local affairs, may indeed be considered as one of the main causes of the failure of representative government and of the bad administration of the country."[10]

Durham recommended that the two Canadas be reunited and that local matters should be looked after by municipal bodies of a much smaller size than the province. Governor General Sydenham, who replaced Durham in 1840, recognized the importance of these recommendations and he wrote to the Colonial Secretary:[11]

> Since I have been in these Provinces I have become more and more satisfied that the capital cause of the misgovernment of them is to be found in the absence of Local Government, and the consequent exercise by the assembly of powers wholly inappropriate to its functions.

Sydenham sent the Colonial Secretary a draft bill for union of the Canadas that incorporated Durham's recommendations. But at the time, Durham had fallen into personal unpopularity and the principle of responsible government and the clauses on local government were dropped from the Union Act passed by the English Parliament. One

---

[8] Fred Landon, *Western Ontario and the American Frontier*, Toronto, McClelland and Stewart Limited, 1967, p. 223.

[9] Gerald M. Craig (ed.), *Lord Durham's Report*, Toronto, McClelland and Stewart Limited, 1963, p. 60.

[10] *Ibid.*, p. 67.

[11] Landon, *Western Ontario*, p. 223.

cannot overstate the importance of this omission. Had the Union Act contained clauses providing for a system of municipal government, then such a separate and distinct provision might well have been reproduced in the British North America Act which brought Canada into existence. Had this happened, municipalities would have gained the constitutional recognition that has always eluded them.

District Councils Act

Lord Sydenham persuaded the new Canadian legislature to pass an act in 1841 to establish elected district councils to take over the administrative authority formerly exercised by the Quarter Sessions in rural areas. There were no drastic changes in the general way that local government was carried on; the annual town meeting still elected various officers and passed town laws. But it also elected one or two district councillors from each township. The head of the district council, the warden, was appointed by the Governor General, although subsequently the councils were given the right to choose their own warden. The councils were given responsibility for roads, municipal officers, taxing, justice, education, and welfare. Their expenses could be met by tolls or taxes on real or personal property or both. The Governor General could disallow any by-laws and could dissolve any or all of the district councils.

The District Councils Act is perhaps even more important than any succeeding act because it was the first real break with the system of local government by Courts of Quarter Sessions and preceded by almost 50 years the abandonment of this system in England.[12] While it was too radical for conservative elements in the legislature and not radical enough for the reformers, it did provide for a transition period in the rural areas between no local self-government and full local self-government. The central authorities retained much power because it was genuinely felt that local people would not be able to manage their own affairs.

Despite initial fears, the first district councillors apparently were fairly capable people who were able to stimulate the development of their townships because of their knowledge of local needs. By far the most important functions were the construction and repair of roads and bridges and the laying out and creating of school districts.

---

[12] Crawford, *Canadian Municipal Government*, p. 31.

The councils were hampered, however, by problems with assessment, provincial control, and scarce finances – problems that persist to this day. It has been written of the revenues available to district councils:[13]

> These were paltry sums for the needs of large districts, and it is quite certain that the very light direct taxation on which Canadians long prided themselves was a rather important factor in the backward condition of the country for so many years.

Baldwin (Municipal) Act

In 1843 the Municipal Act was introduced, but because of a rupture with the Governor General it was not passed (as the Municipal Corporations Act) until May 1849. Its major purpose was to combine all municipal legislation under one measure. It built upon, and extended, the powers of the District Councils Act. The Baldwin Act differed *in two major respects*: (1) the county rather than the district became the upper tier of municipal government, and (2) for the first time townships were recognized as a rural unit of municipal government.

As well, the act established villages, towns, and cities as urban municipal units. Cities and separated towns were not a part of the county for municipal government purposes. This municipal system established in 1849 has endured to the present in many areas of Ontario. Moreover, as will be discussed in Chapter 4, many of the reformed structures introduced in the second half of the 20th century were essentially modified county systems.

Box 2.1 Robert Baldwin: Father of the First Municipal Act
Baldwin was a Toronto lawyer who was called to the bar in 1825 and first elected to the Assembly of Upper Canada in 1830. He twice formed a government with La Fontaine from Lower Canada, the second time from 1848 to 1851. Baldwin's most significant contributions during this second mandate were the reform of the judiciary of Upper Canada, the creation of the University of Toronto, the granting of amnesty to the participants in the 1837-38 rebellions, and – of course – the reform of municipal institutions via the Municipal Act of 1849. Something of a romantic, Baldwin preferred poetry to politics, and never recovered from the death of his wife in 1836. His later life was plagued by depression and ill health and he died in 1858, at the age of 54.[14]

---

[13] Adam Shortt and Arthur G. Doughty (gen eds.), *Canada and its Provinces: A History of the Canadian People and Their Institutions*, Toronto, Glasgow, Brook and Company, 1914, Vol. XVIII, p. 437.

[14] Information at National Library of Canada site, www.nlc-bnc.ca, accessed March 15. 2003.

Lower Canada (Quebec)

In Lower Canada, as in Upper Canada, government by justices of the peace grew to be very unpopular, and there were frequent demands for improved administration. But it was not until 1832 that Quebec and Montreal were granted charters that enabled the citizens to elect a mayor and two aldermen per ward. According to Isin,[15] the long delay since the 1785 incorporation of Saint John reflected the caution and hesitancy of colonial and British authorities about the use of this legal device. Indeed, the Quebec incorporations were limited to a four year term, and were not renewed until after 1840 because of the political turmoil caused by the 1837 Rebellion.

In 1840, under the guidance of Lord Sydenham, an ordinance was passed that provided for a system of local government that in many respects resembled the district councils established soon after in Upper Canada. Lower Canada was divided into districts that were to be governed by an elected council and an appointed warden. Another ordinance passed at the same time provided for the election of a clerk, assessors, tax collector, surveyors, overseers of roads and the poor, fence viewers, drain inspectors, and pound-keepers. Townships and parishes with sufficient population were constituted corporate bodies and elected two councillors each to the district councils. Although the district councils were given the power of taxation, much of the real power remained with the Governor.

Both of the 1840 ordinances were unpopular in Lower Canada. The execution and deportation of rebels of the 1837 Rebellion caused resentment and mistrust and the people were especially wary of Lord Sydenham and his motives. The Union Act itself was unpopular and local government was seen as another means of oppression. But perhaps the most unpalatable measure was the power of taxation which, but for customs duties, had previously been unknown in Lower Canada. Therefore, it is not surprising that in 1845 an act was passed which repealed both ordinances and constituted each township or parish a body corporate with an elected council with most of the duties of the district councils.

In 1847 a county system roughly based on the district councils was established. This system lasted until 1855 when the Lower Canada Municipal and Road Act was passed which became the foundation of

---

[15] Isin, *Cities Without Citizens*, p. 142.

Quebec municipal institutions. It established parishes, townships, towns, and villages, while retaining the county as an upper tier unit. The heads of the local councils sat on the county council and chose their own warden. Each level could appoint the officers it felt were necessary and could levy taxes. Cities continued to be provided for by special charters rather than being incorporated under the provisions of the general act. This system remained in effect with minor changes until the beginning of the 20th century.

Atlantic Provinces

The development of municipal institutions in the Atlantic provinces initially paralleled that in Ontario. In the early 1700s the area known as Acadia was ceded by France to Britain. The area soon became known as Nova Scotia and gradually people from New England spread north and settled in the new province. They brought a tradition of local government through town meetings, but officially local government was to be carried on by the Quarter Sessions and a grand jury.

After the American Revolution, a wave of Loyalists migrated to the area, this time less from New England than from New York, New Jersey, Pennsylvania, and the South. The Southern Loyalists brought with them a different tradition of local government based on the classed society of the American South in which the Courts of Quarter Sessions discharged local government functions and the Governor appointed local officials. Because of anti-American feelings caused by the Revolution, the New England Loyalists were unsuccessful in promoting local self-rule. Despite dissatisfaction with corrupt practices of certain magistrates, the system of the Courts of Quarter Sessions was to prevail for over 100 years.

At this point, developments in the Atlantic provinces proceeded on a different course from those in Ontario. Far from fighting for local municipal institutions, many Loyalists actively discouraged their development. Many reasons have been suggested for this attitude. They include the feeling that the town meeting had contributed to the revolutionary tendencies of the Americans, a fear of increased taxation, a concern that local officials would lose patronage, and public apathy. In addition, the compactness of the area and the availability of cheap water transportation rendered road construction, one of the major municipal functions, less important. Developments in each province will now be briefly examined.

Nova Scotia

Early local government in Nova Scotia was provided by Courts of Quarter Sessions established by the British authorities around 1750. A wave of immigration from New England at the beginning of the 1760s brought settlers accustomed to the town meeting form of local government. The colonial authorities were unwilling to consider such a democratic approach, especially after the American War of Independence. It wasn't until 1841 that the first municipal incorporation took place, with the granting of a charter to Halifax.

After the introduction of responsible government in 1848 the authorities showed more willingness to allow local government. Legislation permitting the incorporation of counties was enacted in 1855, and the following year the incorporation of townships was authorized. Ironically, now that the right to local government was finally granted, Nova Scotians did not exercise it. According to Higgins, the early enthusiasm waned with the realization that incorporation would bring with it higher taxation.[16] However, the provincial government was determined to shift some of the financial burden for local services on to local residents. The result was the 1879 County Incorporation Act.

> That Act was conceived in secrecy at the provincial level and it was the direct offspring of the financial difficulties of the provincial government. The then Attorney General, J.S.D. Thompson, who later became Prime Minister of Canada, frankly stated that the main object of the Act was "to compel Counties to tax themselves directly to keep up their roads and bridges."[17]

Under the Act, the rural areas of the province were incorporated as counties or districts, single tier municipalities governed by a warden and an elected council. Urban areas were dealt with in the Towns Incorporation Act of 1888. It stipulated geographic and population requirements which would enable a town to apply for a charter of incorporation. (Eight such towns had already been

---

[16] Donald J. H. Higgins, *Local and Urban Politics in Canada*, Toronto, Gage, 1986, pp. 39-40.

[17] A. William Cox, Q.C., in a 1989 paper, "Development of Municipal-Provincial Relations," quoted in *Task Force on Local Government*, Report to the Government of Nova Scotia, April 1992, Briefing Book, p. 13.

incorporated by charter prior to the passage of the statute.) Provisions for separate rural and urban municipalities continue to this day.

Prince Edward Island

In 1769 Prince Edward Island separated from Nova Scotia. Two years earlier the island had been divided into counties, parishes, and townships for judicial purposes and for the election of representatives to the provincial legislature, but these areas were never used as municipal units. Indeed, there wasn't any obvious need for municipal government, or even for a decentralization of the colonial administration, given the small size and tiny population of Prince Edward Island.

The first municipal government appeared in 1855 with the incorporation of Charlottetown as a city. In 1870 an act was passed which enabled the resident householders of a town or village to petition the provincial authorities to allow the election of three or more wardens who could appoint local officers and pass by-laws with regard to finance and police matters. Summerside was incorporated as a town in 1875 but, presumably because of the very small population of most settlements, only six more towns had been incorporated by the time the procedure fell into disuse, in 1919.

New Brunswick

Fifteen years after Prince Edward Island separated from Nova Scotia, New Brunswick followed suit, with the break being precipitated by an influx of United Empire Loyalists. The following year, 1785, Saint John was incorporated as a city, preceding by almost 50 years the creation of cities in the rest of Canada. Elsewhere in the colony, however, local government was carried on by the Courts of Quarter Sessions and a grand jury. The local citizenry, according to Higgins, seems to have been largely indifferent to the idea of local self-government.[18] This attitude has been partly attributed to the smaller population of Loyalists who came from New England and had thus experienced local government. Whalen, however, rejects this viewpoint, contending that only about 7% of the Loyalists came from the Southern Colonies with their system of Quarter Sessions and that, in any event, even the Loyalists from New England made little demand

---

[18] Higgins, *Local and Urban Politics in Canada*, p. 40.

for more democracy at the local level.[19] Nor did the province's French population, with its tradition of centralism, make such demands.

Interestingly, much of the impetus for the incorporation of municipalities came from the central authorities who were concerned about "reducing the time consumed on endless debates and squabbles over parish and county issues in the legislature" and anxious to shift a growing expenditure burden.[20] Finally, in 1851 an act was passed for the incorporation of counties, but its provisions were permissive and only six counties were established over the next three decades. However, the Municipalities Act of 1877 made county incorporation mandatory, thus bringing the entire population and area of the province under municipal government. The county system was two-tiered like that in Ontario, but differed in that councillors from the rural areas were directly elected to county council while all urban areas, except Fredericton, were represented at the county level, usually by ex-officio members.

During this period a number of urban communities sought corporate status. Fredericton had received its charter in 1848, over 60 years after the first urban incorporation in Saint John. By 1896 nine towns had been established by separate charter. In that year the Town Incorporation Act was passed providing for a uniform system for the creation of towns with an elected council consisting of a mayor and aldermen. The basic municipal system of New Brunswick was established in this 1896 statute and the 1877 Counties Act. Cities each have their own charter of incorporation and a 1920 act provided for the incorporation of villages.

Newfoundland

The development of municipal institutions in Newfoundland was a slow and arduous process, attributed to several factors.[21] The settlements that developed in the early years were numerous but geographically isolated from each other, generally quite limited in population, and financially unable to support any form of local government. Moreover, since Newfoundlanders only gained the right

---

[19] H. J. Whalen, *The Development of Local Government in New Brunswick*, Fredericton, 1963, Chapter Two.

[20] *Ibid.*, p. 20.

[21] Higgins, *Local and Urban Politics in Canada*, pp. 33-34.

to own property in 1824, they jealously guarded this right against the taxation that would inevitably come with local government.

Newfoundland, because of its geographic isolation, was not influenced by the development of municipal government elsewhere; nor did its early settlers have prior experience with such a system. There was little apparent need for municipal government in much of the province, since transportation needs were partly served by water and the central government provided local services such as roads.

After some unsuccessful attempts, St. John's was created a town in 1888, but once again the impetus was not the demand for local democracy but the desire of the colonial authorities to shift some of their expenditure burden. As Higgins explains, municipal status for St. John's was imposed partly to facilitate costly improvements to the sewerage and street systems and partly to be a mechanism whereby the privately owned and heavily in debt St. John's Water Company would become the financial responsibility of the City – a Water Company in which the Premier of Newfoundland and other prominent government supporters and business people were shareholders![22]

No other municipalities were formed for 50 years. Acts authorizing incorporation were passed in 1933 and 1937, but without any response. A new approach was then attempted, which offered subsidies and any taxation form a municipality desired if it would incorporate. Twenty municipalities had been incorporated by special charter by 1948 and only five of these imposed the real property tax.[23]

Western Provinces

The provinces of Manitoba, Saskatchewan, and Alberta were part of the original Hudson's Bay Company land grant and later of the Northwest Territories. For most of their early history these provinces were governed by the Company, which had complete judicial, legislative, and administrative authority. In 1869 the Company's rights in Rupert's Land and the Northwest Territories were acquired by the newly created Dominion of Canada. It was not until late in the 19th century that a substantial amount of settlement occurred in the Prairie

---

[22] *Ibid.*, pp. 34-35.

[23] Crawford, *Canadian Municipal Government*, p. 41.

provinces. This growth, and accompanying service demands, called for a local government system, and it was only logical for these provinces to look to their nearest eastern neighbour, Ontario, for a model. But because of the different physical characteristics of the West, the Ontario model was modified to suit local needs.

Manitoba

In 1870 Manitoba was created a province separate from the Northwest Territories. The first provincial legislature provided for a system of local government by a grand jury and Courts of Sessions that were to administer a County Assessment Act and a Parish Assessment Act. As well, the judges of the Sessions chose local officers such as treasurers, assessors, highway surveyors, pound-keepers, and constables from lists presented by the grand jury.

The first municipality was established in 1873 with the incorporation of Winnipeg as a city – although not without a struggle. Apparently the Hudson's Bay Company and four other property owners, who together owned over half of the assessable property in Winnipeg, had opposed the incorporation and the resultant taxation of that property.[24] In that same year, general legislation was also passed which provided for the establishment of local municipalities upon petition of the freeholders within a district. Only six areas were incorporated during the decade that this act was in force.

This permissive approach was dropped in 1883 when the Manitoba government decided to introduce a municipal system for the whole province modelled on the two tier county system of Ontario. The new act established 26 counties with councils composed of the heads of both rural and urban local (lower tier) municipal councils. The county council elected a warden from among its own members. This Ontario county system proved to be ineffective, however, because of the large areas covered, the often sparse and scattered population, and the local objections to a two tier system. It was abandoned after only three years and the province was divided into smaller rural municipalities.

In 1902 a general act established cities, towns, villages, and rural municipalities as the basic units of local government, although Winnipeg was given its own special charter. This system has continued

---

[24] Higgins, *Local and Urban Politics in Canada*, pp. 50-51.

to the present, except for major changes in the structure of government for the Winnipeg area discussed in a later chapter.

Saskatchewan

Like Manitoba, Saskatchewan had been part of the lands granted to the Hudson's Bay Company. It was taken over by the Canadian government in 1870 and administered essentially as a colony until it gained provincial status in 1905. The territorial council first provided for municipal government in 1883 by enacting a municipal ordinance that was patterned on the previously cited Manitoba legislation of that year which, in turn, had been modelled on the 1849 Municipal Act of Ontario. The ordinance provided for either rural municipalities or towns depending on area and population and on whether local citizens petitioned for municipal status. Regina received town status that very year and four rural municipalities were organized in 1884, but little initiative was evident thereafter. By 1897 only one additional town had been created and two rural municipalities had dropped their municipal status. One major problem was that the vast area and small, scattered population made it difficult to generate the financial base needed to support municipal government.

However, since some form of local organization was necessary to provide roads and protection against prairie and forest fires, an ordinance was passed allowing the creation of "statute labour and fire districts" in areas not organized as rural municipalities. By 1896 these local improvement districts, as they were now called, were made mandatory and the following year legislation was passed which allowed for elected committees to administer the districts. In 1903 the districts were reorganized into larger units made up of four of the former districts, each with one elected councillor on a municipal district council. Meanwhile, a revision of municipal ordinances in 1894 authorized the incorporation of cities, towns, and rural municipalities.

Throughout this period the federal government strongly encouraged Western settlement and large numbers of settlers arrived from Europe and from Eastern Canada, the latter bringing previous experience with municipal government. The impetus that these developments gave to the creation of municipal institutions is evident from the fact that when Saskatchewan became a province in 1905 there were already 4 cities, 43 towns, 97 villages, 2 rural municipalities, and 359 local improvement districts.[25]

Alberta

Since Alberta was also part of the federally administered Northwest Territories from 1870 until 1905, its municipal background resembles that of Saskatchewan. The first municipal government was introduced in 1884 in Calgary, established as a town under the 1883 ordinance noted above. Incorporation efforts were initially thwarted by large landowners – among them the CPR – opposed to the prospect of property taxes.[26] Two more urban municipalities were created over the next decade (Lethbridge in 1891 and Edmonton in 1892), but because of the sparse, scattered rural population, there were no petitions for the creation of rural municipalities under the ordinance. As in the area that became Saskatchewan, the main form of local government was the statute labour and fire district or local improvement district.

Toward the end of the century, however, the large influx of settlers began to stimulate the creation of local governments. When Alberta became a province in 1905, its population was 170 000 (compared to 18 000 in 1881) and it had 2 cities, 15 towns, and 30 villages. By 1912 a new municipal system was established with cities, towns, villages, and local improvement districts. The latter could be established as rural municipalities on reaching a specified population, but few incorporations were requested because of fears about tax increases.

British Columbia

The area of what is now British Columbia was also initially under the jurisdiction of the Hudson's Bay Company – until 1849 in the case of Vancouver Island and 1858 in the case of the mainland. The physical characteristics of British Columbia played a significant role in the development of municipal institutions in the province. Because of the mountainous terrain, early settlements were scattered and isolated. New Westminster, the capital of the mainland colony, became a municipality in 1860, and two years later Victoria, the capital of the

[25] Horace L. Brittain, *Local Government in Canada*, Toronto, Ryerson Press, 1951, p. 179.

[26] *Ibid.*, p. 54.

Vancouver Island colony, was incorporated as a town. Shortly after gaining provincial status in 1871, British Columbia enacted the Consolidated Municipal Act providing for local petitions for municipal incorporation, but by the end of 1874 there were still only five municipalities in the province. Vancouver, originally known as Granville, was a small logging community with only about 300 residents at the time of its incorporation in 1886, but its future had been assured when the CPR chose it (in 1884) as the western terminus of the transcontinental railway.[27]

In 1892 the Municipal Clauses Act was passed, governing all new municipalities formed and providing for a system similar to that in Ontario, but without a county level. Municipalities were either cities with a mayor and council or rural districts with a reeve and council. By 1900 there were some 52 of these municipalities. In 1920 a Village Municipalities Act was passed, allowing smaller urban areas to incorporate with limited powers.

Northern Territories

The area of the Yukon and Northwest Territories was controlled by the Hudson's Bay Company until acquired by the federal government in 1870.[28] Its territory was reduced that year by the establishment of Manitoba as a separate province, reduced in 1905 when Saskatchewan and Alberta became provinces, and again in 1912 when the northern boundaries of Ontario, Quebec, and Manitoba were extended north to their present positions. The discovery of gold in the Klondike in 1896 sparked a rapid increase in the population of the Yukon and in 1898 it was established as a separate territory. A third territory, Nunavut, was established in the Eastern Arctic effective April 1999.

Dawson City was incorporated as the first municipality in 1901, but its charter was revoked in 1904 and provision of local services reverted to the territorial administration for a number of years. Also in 1901, a provision was made for the establishment of unincorporated towns upon petition. But these units were not full municipal governments since residents could only elect one official and only a very limited range of services could be provided. In any event, the one

---

[27] Higgins, *Local and Urban Politics in Canada*, pp. 57-58.

[28] The description in this section is partly based on *ibid.*, pp. 59-60.

unincorporated town created was disbanded when its population subsequently declined. This often temporary nature of northern settlements added to the problems caused by the extremely small, scattered population. Therefore, while both the Northwest Territories and the Yukon had municipal ordinances authorizing municipal governments, very few units were created until the last couple of decades. As late as 1964 there were only three incorporated municipalities – the towns of Yellowknife and Hay Bay and the village of Fort Smith.

Prior to 1960, virtually all real government within the Northern Territories came from Ottawa. With the relocation of the Territorial Council from Ottawa to Yellowknife in 1967, however, new municipal structures were introduced which allowed for more decision making at the local level. The category of city was introduced in 1969, with Yellowknife becoming the first city. Another change has been a growing emphasis on the passing of authority down from the territorial government to local governments, along with an attempt to strengthen the political role of the municipalities. One government study claimed that "[In] the NWT the importance of the local level of government is of particular magnitude because of the cultural diversity and the vast distances between communities."[29]

While only a very small portion of the vast area of the Northern Territories is organized municipally, the organized portion contains three-quarters of the population. The few villages, towns, and cities, which contain most of the population, are basically modelled upon the structure of municipal government found in Southern Ontario. In addition to these tax-based municipalities, there are some 40 non-tax-based municipalities (mostly hamlets) with more limited powers. Of particular interest is a relatively new form of municipal unit called the charter community, whose specific features depend on what is spelled out in the charter establishing it. This flexibility is especially useful in areas where band councils have provided the traditional leadership in the community. Natives have tended to view municipalities as "foreign" structures. The charter community approach allows the creation of a new governing arrangement that can combine elements of the band council structure and of municipalities.

In addition to these municipal structures, a large number of local boards and special purpose committees are found in the Northern

---

[29] *Constitutional Development in the Northwest Territories, Report of the Special Representative* (Drury Report), Ottawa, 1980.

Territories.[30] Many of these bodies were established to obtain feedback from the local communities, to compensate for the fact that there were few elected members of the territorial council (legislative assembly) and few elected municipal councils. Even though municipal councils are now more widespread, these special purpose bodies have proven difficult to eradicate – a problem also experienced in Southern Canada.

Summary: Lessons of History

As the table below makes clear, the establishment of municipal institutions essentially spread westward across Canada, consistent with the opening and settlement of the country.

Table 2.1 Historical Landmarks	
1782-83	Influx of United Empire Loyalists
1785	Saint John, New Brunswick incorporated as a city
1793	Parish and Town Officers Act in Upper Canada (Ontario)
1832	First Board of Police (elected council) in Brockville, Ontario
1832-36	Quebec City and Montreal granted charters
1837	Rebellion, followed by Durham Report
1841	District Councils Act, Upper Canada
1841	Halifax, Nova Scotia received charter
1849	Baldwin (Municipal Act), Upper Canada
1851	Legislation authorizing counties in New Brunswick
1855	Municipal and Road Act, Lower Canada
1855	City of Charlottetown, first municipality in PEI
1873	City of Winnipeg, first municipality in Manitoba
1873	General Municipal Act, Manitoba
1877	Municipalities Act, New Brunswick
1879	General Municipal Act, Nova Scotia
1884	Calgary incorporated as a town
1886	Vancouver incorporated
1888	St. John's, Newfoundland established as a town
1892	Edmonton incorporated
1892	Municipal Clauses Act, British Columbia
1901	Dawson City, first municipality in Yukon
1908	City, Town, and Villages Act, Saskatchewan
1912	Alberta established general local government system
1949	Newfoundland passed general local government legislation
1969	Yellowknife became first city in Northwest Territories

---

[30] See Report of the Project to Review the Operations and Structure of Northern Government, *Strength at Two Levels*, November 1991.

The development of full municipal systems in the Maritime provinces was slowed by the compactness of the area and the availability of cheap water transportation. The small, scattered population of Newfoundland and the strong opposition to the introduction of the real property tax slowed the development of a municipal system even longer in this province. Because municipal systems in Central Canada were in place by the mid-19th century, the Western provinces initially used these as a model as they began to develop their own systems.

By the beginning of the 20th century, most provinces had in place, or were in the process of establishing, a system of municipalities. The major exception was the Northern Territories where the development of municipal institutions was much slower because of the small, scattered, and largely migratory population and the concentration of government in Ottawa until the mid-20th century. All of the municipal systems were fairly similar, in large part because of the influence of the Ontario model established in 1849. The systems generally consisted of cities, towns, and villages as urban units; a rural unit variously known as a township, municipal district, or rural municipality; and sometimes an upper tier county unit. Councils were for the most part directly elected, with the notable exception of the county level in Ontario, Quebec, and, to some degree, New Brunswick. An Assessment Act was usually passed, providing the main source of municipal revenue.

There were three key features of these municipal systems that were quite appropriate for the conditions of the time. These were:

1. a differentiation between urban and rural municipal classifications;
2. an expectation that municipalities would provide a quite limited range of services, primarily services to property; and
3. an assumption that the property tax would be both appropriate and adequate to finance the cost of these services.

However, the primarily agricultural and rural nature of the economy and society in which these municipal systems were established was to undergo a fundamental change over the next 50 to 100 years – in ways that made the traditional municipal systems increasingly inadequate.

Over the years, a romantic notion has developed concerning the long, bitter struggle waged by our ancestors to wrest local self-government from an unsympathetic and paternalistic regime both in the colonies and in Britain. This vision is used to defend the status quo whenever change threatens "historic" boundaries. Yet the true record of how the municipal systems originated is considerably less stirring. While something approaching this chain of events did take place in

Ontario, municipal government was less warmly received in Quebec where it was viewed as simply another means of oppression because of the power of taxation. In the Atlantic provinces, this fear of the property tax prompted strong opposition to the introduction of municipal government. An editorial in the *New Brunswick Courier* in 1843 about a proposed municipal bill stated that had the bill been passed, "it would have cut loose that many-headed monster, Direct Taxation and its Myrmidon, the Tax-Gatherer, into the happy home of every poor man throughout the land."[31] Resistance to municipal incorporation because of opposition to property taxation was also noted in the Western provinces, not only from local settlers but also from wealthy landowners like the Hudson's Bay Company.

It is also noteworthy that where the provincial authorities did encourage or ultimately impose municipal governments on their populace, it was not because of any apparent belief in the values of local democracy. Rather, it was motivated by a desire on the part of the provincial administrations to shift at least some of the growing burden of expenditures to the local level. This pattern is evident in the historical developments in the Atlantic and Western provinces – and there are some fascinating parallels with developments today.

It is clear that municipal governments were mainly established in response to population growth and consequent service demands. Even in Ontario where pressure for local self-government was most pronounced, an important factor in the creation of municipal institutions was the inability of the Courts of Quarter Sessions to deal with growing urban problems. As will be seen, an increase in urbanization and urban problems at the end of the 19th century precipitated changes that continue to reverberate today.

Turn of the Century Reform Era

By the onset of the 20th century Canada was at the end of 25 years of industrialization and in the midst of large-scale immigration. During this period of unprecedented economic and population growth, Canadians developed a "boom" mentality and municipal councils were no exception. They began to compete with each other for the location

---

[31] Quoted in Whelan, *The Development of Local Government in New Brunswick,* pp. 20-21.

of industry, population growth, and new residential and commercial construction. An indication of the extent of this growth is the fact that the number of real estate agents in Halifax, Saint John, Montreal, Vancouver, Ottawa, Toronto, London, Winnipeg, Regina, Calgary, Edmonton, and Victoria increased from 506 in 1901 to 4250 in 1913.[32]

This surge of development brought with it not only prosperity but also new servicing demands and problems. Chapter 3 describes how the physical nature of this development changed the urban environment and the human interaction taking place there. In the remainder of this chapter we will examine the impact that this growth had on Canadian municipal institutions and on the operating philosophy of municipal government.

Urban Problems Develop

Between 1901 and 1911 Canada led the Western world in population growth. Much of this growth was due to immigration, with the foreign-born population of Canada increasing by over 2 000 000. While many of these immigrants were in Canada as temporary labour, a significant number were permanent arrivals seeking employment in urban centres. For example, Calgary and Edmonton multiplied their populations 40 times and changed almost overnight from villages to cluttered cities. Winnipeg, which had already shown an impressive increase in population from 1800 to 40 000 between 1874 and 1899, surged to 150 000 by 1913. The bulk of this increase came from immigration, and by 1911 no other city in Canada had as high a proportion of European-born residents. The problems of assimilation that resulted led to what Artibise called a "Divided City."[33]

Even without these ethnic and cultural strains, however, the sheer numbers involved generated greatly increased service demands. The years 1900-1913 saw a tremendous jump in urban land values that was accompanied by extensive land speculation. In 1913 an English

---

[32] John C. Weaver, *Shaping the Canadian City: Essays on Urban Politics and Policy 1890-1920*, Toronto, Institute of Public Administration of Canada, Monographs on Canadian Urban Government, No. 1, 1977, p. 12. This monograph provides an excellent insight into the reform era and is a partial basis for the discussions in this section of the chapter.

[33] Alan F. Artibise, "Divided City: The Immigrant in Winnipeg Society, 1874-1921," in Gilbert A. Stelter and Alan F. Artibise (eds.), *The Canadian City: Essays in Urban History*, Toronto, McClelland and Stewart, 1977.

traveller wrote of the Victoria land boom that in two and one-half years values increased 900%.[34] The increase in land values precipitated a change in downtown land use from that of a mix of small businesses and residential housing to high-rise office towers. This change in land use and higher real estate prices also served to push the working class out to the suburbs. These new settlement patterns continued to unfold throughout the 20th century, with disturbing results that are discussed in the next chapter. Despite a building boom accompanied by large-scale land assembly and suburban development, all major Canadian cities were soon faced with a serious housing shortage and the subsequent development of ghettos and slums.

Besides a scarcity of housing, Canadian cities were confronted with other new servicing problems. To accommodate immigrant workers, inferior housing units were hastily built, often without sanitary conveniences. Families frequently shared accommodation and overcrowding became a strain on already overworked municipal water and sewer systems. In 1910 in Canada, 57 systems of inland water were receiving raw sewage from 159 municipalities, and 111 water supply systems were obtaining their water from bodies of water into which raw sewage had been discharged. These factors produced a serious health hazard that became only too apparent in the early 1900s with an alarming increase in the number of epidemics. During this period, one of every three deaths was caused by tuberculosis, and typhoid and flu epidemics produced more casualties than World War One.[35]

Other major problem areas were transportation and the provision of utilities. The overcrowding of the downtown district plus the increased numbers commuting from the suburbs created the need for new modes of transportation or, at the very least, the construction of more roads and sidewalks. By 1913 most cities had electrified street-car systems, which were often privately owned monopolies, and at the same time municipalities were being pressured into providing municipal electric power plants. The mayor of Medicine Hat proclaimed, "The municipal ownership town is in a better position to deal with industrial institutions.... Municipal ownership (of utilities) and

---

[34] J. B. Thornhill, *British Columbia in the Making*, London, Constable and Company, 1913, pp. 126-127, quoted in Weaver, *Shaping the Canadian City*, p. 13.

[35] The figures on pollution and health are from Alan H. Armstrong, "Thomas Adams and the Commission on Conservation," in L. A. Gertler (ed.), *Planning the Canadian Environment*, Montreal, Harvest House, 1968, pp. 20-22.

industrial progress go hand in hand."[36] These new and expanded services in turn meant increased costs and therefore higher municipal taxes. Wickett pointed out in 1907 that:[37]

> The annual expenditure of Winnipeg clearly exceeds that of Manitoba; Montreal's that of the province of Quebec; and until the present year Toronto's that of the province of Ontario.

These growth pressures resulted in the development of various reform movements throughout Canadian society that were also part of a larger international movement common to most industrialized nations. At this time groups such as the Women's Christian Temperance Union, YMCA, YWCA, Salvation Army, and White Cross Army were founded to help stamp out crime, vice, and poverty – evils associated with the emergence of the wicked city. In response to the servicing and financial pressures facing municipal governments, groups were formed such as the Civic Art Guild of Toronto, City Improvement League of Montreal, Union of Canadian Municipalities, Good Roads Association, and the Civic Improvement League of Canada. The goals of these various groups included social justice, a healthy and beautiful city, regulation of utilities, and the restructuring of municipal government. Two movements of particular note were those that encouraged municipal planning and municipal government reform.

Development of Municipal Planning

There were three main forces that affected the development of municipal planning. The first to emerge was the civic enhancement or "city beautiful" movement that was often embraced by civic boosters. While city beautiful had supporters who wanted to improve the city for its own sake, councillors and businessmen frequently regarded it as simply another means of attracting industry and growth.[38] The central

---

[36] Mayor Foster, "Development of Natural Resources Under Municipal Ownership," *Canadian Municipal Journal*, II, April 1906, p. 133, quoted in Weaver, *Shaping the Canadian City*, p. 38.

[37] Quoted in P. Rutherford, "Tomorrow's Metropolis: The Urban Reform Movement in Canada, 1880-1920," in Stelter and Artibise, *The Canadian City*, p. 376.

[38] Alan J. Artibise, "In Pursuit of Growth: Municipal Boosterism and Urban Development in the Canadian Prairie West, 1871-1913," in Gilbert Stelter and Alan Artibise (eds.), *Shaping the Urban Landscape: Aspects of the Canadian City-Building Process*, Ottawa, Carleton University Press, 1982, p. 124.

belief of the boosters was the desirability of growth and the importance of material success. Their views were very influential, partly
because not to be a booster suggested a lack of community spirit and
business sense. "Good citizenship and boosterism were synonymous."[39]
    The city beautiful movement was embraced by Canadian archi-
tects, engineers, and surveyors unhappy with the squalor and the ugly
environment developing in Canadian communities with the rapid
urbanization of the time. Their objective was the achievement of civic
grandeur through the development of civic centres featuring monu-
mental public buildings grouped around a public square and a broad
tree-lined avenue leading to it.[40] The grand designs provoked criticism
of the city beautiful movement as "mere adornment" and extravagance
that failed to address the real problems of city housing and sanitation.[41]

City Healthy Movement

A second force that influenced planning resulted from the deteriorating health conditions in urban areas. For example, Fort William
tripled its population between 1896 and 1905 as the result of railroad
expansion. In the winter of 1905-1906 a sewer that emptied into the
city's water supply caused some 800 cases of typhoid.[42] This and other
similar situations gave rise to the "healthy city" movement, with
public health advocates pressing for better public water supplies and
sewer systems and for the eradication of slums.[43]
    People became convinced that housing conditions were related
to public health. Toronto's Medical Officer of Health described slums
as "cancerous sores on the body politic, sources of bacteria spreading
disease, crime, and discontent throughout the city."[44] The middle and
upper classes were continually warned that disease did not respect
social standing and they pressed for measures which expanded the
powers of health and building inspectors and legislated housing

---

[39] *Ibid.*, p. 125.

[40] Gerald Hodge, *Planning Canadian Communities*, 2nd Edition, Scarborough,
Nelson Canada, 1991, p. 53.

[41] *Ibid.*, p. 56.

[42] Weaver, *Shaping the Canadian City*, p. 28.

[43] Hodge, *Planning Canadian Communities*, p. 83.

[44] Rutherford, "Tomorrow's Metropolis," p. 375.

standards. J.J. Kelso, an Ontario lobbyist for children's aid, advocated a form of urban renewal:

> Rear houses and those built in the notorious alleys and lanes of the city should be pulled down. There should be a by-law that every dwelling must front on a forty or sixty foot street and that only one dwelling should be created to each 20 by 100 foot lot.[45]

Unfortunately, because many dwellings were subsequently condemned, these measures only served to make the existing housing shortage worse.

The early public health movement was to have a very significant effect on the development of municipal government. The prevention of illness called for municipal action on a wide range of matters. Municipal public works departments grew out of the public health movement, and so did urban planning, parks, housing, and social service functions.[46] As the 20th century advanced, however, advances in medicine shifted the emphasis of health from prevention to the treatment of sickness and from municipal government preventive programs to massive expenditures on hospitals and doctors. It is only recently, through the revival of a "healthy communities" movement, that we are rediscovering the links between the services provided by municipalities and the maintenance of a healthy population.

The two reform themes we have been discussing, those of city beautiful and city healthy, were brought together with the creation in 1909 of a federal Commission for the Conservation of Natural Resources. The impetus for its establishment was the recognition that "industrial processes were consuming natural resources at an alarming rate, often leaving in their wake waste and pollution."[47]

Thomas Adams was appointed Advisor on Town Planning to the Commission in 1914. He proceeded to draft local plans and model provincial town planning acts based on the British Act, and by 1916 only British Columbia and Prince Edward Island did not have a planning statute of Adams' making in force.

---

[45] *Labour Gazette*, July 1910, p. 128, quoted in Weaver, *Shaping the Canadian City*, p. 33.

[46] Trevor Hancock, "From Public Health to the Healthy City," in Edmund P. Fowler and David Siegel (eds.), *Urban Policy Issues: Canadian Perspectives*, 2nd Edition, Toronto, Oxford University Press, 2002, p. 257.

[47] Hodge, *Planning Canadian Communities*, p. 86.

Box 2.2 Thomas Adams: Planning Leader in Three Countries

A native of Scotland, Adams had studied law and then been attracted to the Garden City Movement in Britain, which aimed to disperse the population and industry of a large city into smaller concentrations and to create more amenable living conditions in what we would now call "new towns" or "satellite towns." He had served on the board that administered the British Town Planning and Housing Act and when he arrived in Canada he already had a reputation as "an eloquent author and speaker on the Garden City Movement, on agricultural land use and on town planning and housing as aspects of local government."[48] His influence also extended to the United States where he was one of the founding members of the American City Planning Institute and taught at Harvard and MIT.

The model created by Adams featured a separate honorary planning board, influenced by American prototypes, with the mayor as the only elected representative. He also assisted many Canadian municipalities in the preliminary stages of local planning and promoted the creation of provincial departments of municipal affairs in Ontario and Quebec.

City Efficient Movement

A third force, and one which also influenced municipal structural reforms, was the "city efficient" movement. In this movement the goals of city beautiful and city healthy – that is beauty, order, convenience, and health – were interpreted as economy and efficiency. Planning became a rational scientific process in which experts would provide technical solutions. As one speaker explained, "if all the facts can be collected ... then a solution of any town planning problem becomes comparatively simple."[49] This point of view was consistent with, and reinforced by, the new ideas of "scientific management" which were becoming popular at this time. Its disciples claimed that there was only "one best way" to run any organization, to be discovered by rational inquiry.

Although most reformers claimed that they were working to improve the plight of the slum dwellers, a certain amount of self-interest can be detected in reforms actually implemented. Zoning by-laws were often passed to protect middle-class and upper-class property values and neighbourhoods since, according to one of the

---

[48] *Ibid.*, p. 50.

[49] Gilbert Stelter and Alan Artibise, "Urban History Comes of Age: A Review of Current Research," *City Magazine*, vol. 3 no. 1, September-October 1977, p. 31.

supporters of the Manitoba Tenement Act of 1909, tenement houses "may ... to a large extent spoil the appearance of a neighbourhood."[50]

Development of Municipal Reform Movement

By 1900 urban reformers were advocating changes in the structure of local government as a means of eliminating corruption and improving efficiency. Structural reforms had first been popularized by newspapers covering the corruption of the Tammany Society in New York City (and other American political machines) and subsequent American efforts at municipal reform. In fact, much as American immigrants had influenced the original development of Canadian municipal government, Americans also exerted a strong influence on Canadian reforms at the turn of the century. But while the corruption of municipal government had reached crisis proportions in the United States, the situation in Canada was somewhat less severe.

Canadian municipal politicians were not immune, however, to the opportunities presented by the sudden urban growth and get-rich mentality.[51] In Toronto, corporations bidding on contracts and franchises complained that aldermen were "shaking them down" and precipitated an inquiry in which only a few were found guilty but the entire council was tarnished by association. It was also soon after discovered that the Montreal Police Commission was running a protection racket, the Toronto zoo keeper was stocking his own kitchen with food meant for the animals, and Regina city councillors were being given unusually low assessments and utility bills. These revelations and others left the public disillusioned and prompted calls for action.

In the forefront of the municipal reform movement were middle class merchants and businessmen. Many of these people had little sympathy for the democratic aspects of local government. They were mainly concerned with expanding local services in order to attract more growth (often on land they owned) which in turn would expand the local tax base to help pay for new services. To these business people, most of whom were part of the boosterism discussed

---

[50] John C. Weaver, "Tomorrow's Metropolis Revisited: A Critical Assessment of Urban Reform in Canada, 1890-1920," in Stelter and Artibise, *The Canadian City*, p. 407.

[51] The examples that follow are from Weaver, *Shaping the Canadian City*, pp. 56-59.

above, local government was just a tool to serve personal and community prosperity. "It was merely a device to be used for the benefit of the people who managed to gain political power or influence."[52] It was business people who gained control and used it for their ends.

As the labour movement developed, working people tried to exert influence as a counterbalance to the strength of business interests. The Industrial Workers of the World (I.W.W.), later known as the One Big Union (O.B.U.), was a force to be taken in earnest in the second decade of the 20th century – pledged to the overthrow of the capitalist system. By the end of World War One, it had begun to attract allies in several countries, including Canada.[53] With the end of the war, returning soldiers swelled the labour force, jobs were scarce, and many workers were dissatisfied with their wages and their hours. On May 13th, 1919, the growing labour unrest in Canada exploded in a general strike in Winnipeg, leaving Canada's third largest city half paralyzed. Sympathy strikes broke out in a dozen other cities, including Toronto, Vancouver, Edmonton, and Calgary, but not with the same intensity. Gradually, the civilian authorities reasserted their authority and, more than a month after it began, the strike was ended with the arrest of its alleged leaders. This polarization of business and labour contributed to ongoing clashes between these two interests for control of council in Canada's major cities, as described in Chapter 9.

Businessmen were not prepared to accept any responsibility for the problems caused by urban expansion since this growth was perceived as only allowing nature to follow its own course. Instead, they blamed corrupt local politicians and inefficient municipal governments for the situation. While the initial purpose of municipal reforms was to eliminate corruption, a second important purpose was to improve efficiency. The obvious solution, to business at any rate, was to take the politics out of municipal government and to run it on business principles. In Hamilton, reform mayor Captain McLaren ran on the slogan that "civic business is not politics."[54]

The business community was not alone in its perception of municipal government as a business venture that should be run on business principles. Many contemporary newspapers felt this way and

---

[52] Stelter and Artibise, *Shaping the Canadian Landscape*, p. 128.

[53] The description that follows is based on Ralph Allen, *Ordeal By Fire*, Toronto, Doubleday, 1961, p. 175.

[54] Weaver, "Tomorrow's Metropolis Revisited," p. 42.

often carried editorials promoting municipal reform. Typical of this
view is this comparison of a municipality and a joint stock company:

> If we could only manage our business as private corporations
> manage theirs we certainly would not have such a queer lot of
> directors – aldermen as we call them – or make presidents – mayors
> as we call them – out of men who have never proven themselves as
> good businessmen.[55]

Business people were also concerned about the power and
narrow focus of ward-based politicians who failed to understand the
importance of municipal reforms and hindered their implementation.
In many cities these ward politicians were elected from areas where
foreigners constituted most of the electorate and as Winnipeg's Mayor
Sharpe stated: "The city's many foreigners could not comprehend civic
issues and hence the role of the wards which gave them a degree of
influence should be reduced in any new system."[56]

Much of the reform fervour was also due to a certain amount
of enlightened self-interest since many businessmen stood to gain
financially through municipal actions. Winnipeg's Mayor Sharpe was a
wealthy contractor who specialized in sidewalks. In Regina the reform
candidate was known as "the Merchant Prince." He claimed that he
paid $3 out of every $100 of local taxes. In Montreal the leaders of the
business community, including the president of the Street Railway
Company, privately financed a plebiscite on structural reforms.

The reforms advocated by the business community really only
served to give it a greater hand in municipal affairs. Businessmen had
ambitions to have certain public works undertaken, but they found
that in municipal politics they were only one of many competing
interests, including newly enfranchised lower classes. Since they were
"unwilling to fully accept the realities of political pluralism they
worked to scupper the rules of the game,"[57] as outlined below.

The Reforms

The American schemes of municipal reform that were to influence
Canadian reformers had two main thrusts: first, to give more power to
the mayor and, second, generally to separate legislative and executive

---

[55] *Saturday Night*, 1899, quoted in Weaver, *Shaping the Canadian City*, p. 41.

[56] *Ibid.*, p. 62. The examples in this section are drawn from pp. 62-63.

[57] *Ibid.*, p. 64.

powers. The reforms actually implemented in Canada seemed to have been tempered by British traditions and the main concession made toward obtaining a strong mayor was the move to "at large" elections for the head of council. But there was a greater acceptance of the need to remove certain responsibilities from the control of council and in effect create separate executive and administrative bodies.

Changes to the Electoral Process

One of the structures most under attack was the council-committee system that seemed to allow ward aldermen a great deal of power in specific areas and thus "opened the door to corruption." In a move to reduce this power, reformers called for the complete abolition of the ward system in favour of at large elections for all of council. One of the more convincing arguments for abolishing wards was that they fostered a parochial view of municipal issues instead of a broader view of city wide concerns. This situation frequently resulted in "back scratching" and "log rolling," or "I'll give you what you want in your ward if you'll give me what I want in mine." An editorial in the *Financial Post* in 1912 stated that the ward system was one of the dominant evils of municipal life and that "all aldermen should hold their seats by the vote of all the electors and should represent all the city at all times."[58]

Of course, at large elections, plus a concurrent move to raise the property qualification for voters, would reduce the influence of foreign-born and slum residents. As early as 1857 Montreal changed from aldermen choosing their mayor to the mayor being elected at large and in 1873 Toronto followed suit. In 1891 Toronto reduced the number of wards and in 1894 both Saint John and Fredericton abolished wards completely. In Toronto and Montreal an unsuccessful attempt was made to extend the right to vote to companies.

Board of Control

Another reform, the establishment of a board of control, was directed at strengthening the executive at the expense of council. The board of control made its first appearance in Toronto in 1896 in response to a water and sewer crisis. It was influenced by local business models and

---

[58] *Financial Post*, February 10, 1912, as quoted in Weaver, *Shaping the Canadian City*, p. 67.

by the commission system popular in the United States. Only one Canadian city, Saint John, New Brunswick, specifically adopted the commission system. In 1912 its council was abolished and provision made for the election at large of a five member commission. Each commissioner was responsible for a particular field or department, thereby gaining expertise in that area. Democratic control features of the commission system included public recall of councillors, the initiative, and the referendum – which are discussed in Chapter 9.

The Canadian board of control differed significantly from the American commission system in that it retained a council. The members of the board of control were initially chosen by the councillors from among themselves but subsequently they were elected at large. The purpose of the board of control was to take important executive functions out of the control of council by allowing the board to prepare the budget, appoint and dismiss department heads, and award all contracts. Board decisions could only be overturned by a two-thirds vote of council, and this was difficult to accomplish since council included the board of control members.

This form of executive committee proved to be popular in Ontario where it became mandatory for municipalities of 100 000 population and over. It also spread to other provinces and in 1906 was adopted by Winnipeg, in 1908 by Calgary where it was called a commission, and in 1910 by Montreal. The Montreal board of control, which was actually part of a more comprehensive reform that also cut the size of council in half, was seen as a managing commission whose powers were subject to the majority approval of council.

In Western Canada most politicians were reluctant to adopt the extreme measures of the American commission system or even the somewhat more democratic board of control. Instead, Western cities adopted a system of appointed commissioners who would specialize in specific fields and act as administrators, without any formal role in policy making. Edmonton was the first city to implement this system in 1904; Regina, Saskatoon, and Prince Albert followed in 1911-1912.

Chief Administrative Officer

Another American reform adopted by many Canadian municipalities was the city manager (also known as council manager) system. This was especially popular in Quebec after 1920. The system entailed the appointment of a chief administrator who was to coordinate and supervise all of the departments and affairs of the municipality. The system was premised on the assumption that policy making, which was to be the exclusive concern of a small elected council, could be completely separated from policy implementation. This system was appealing to reformers because it appeared to be one step closer to the corporate model. In 1919, Guelph adopted the system and the city clerk described the organization as similar to a joint stock company with the aldermen as directors and the mayor as president.[59]

> The city manager through his different departments, plans the work, submits same to council for their approval. When approved, it is up to the city manager to carry it out in a business-like manner, without interference from the aldermen.

In some cities it was even suggested that the elected council be abolished, with local affairs managed by an appointed executive. In London, Ontario, it was proposed that this appointed executive should be composed of representatives of special interest groups such as Rotary clubs, ratepayers associations, and the Board of Trade. In Montreal it was intended to retain the council with the mayor, two members elected by council, one by the Board of Trade, and one by the Chambre de Commerce as the executive committee. While most of these proposals were not adopted for councils, in the 1940s Montreal did have a council consisting of a mayor and 99 councillors, of whom 66 were elected and 33 were appointed by public associations.[60] The idea of special interest group representation also became a popular plan when establishing special purpose bodies.

Boards and Commissions

In a further effort to reduce council's control, reformers advocated the creation of various boards and commissions that would oversee activity in a specific area and thus remove it from the political arena. Although these special purpose bodies were not a new phenomenon, Ontario having had police commissions and boards of health as early

---

[59] Frank H. Underhill, "Commission Government in Cities (1911)," in Paul Rutherford (ed.), *Saving the Canadian City: The First Phase 1880-1920*, Toronto, University of Toronto Press, 1974, p. 68.

[60] Paul Hickey, *Decision Making Processes in Ontario's Local Governments*, Toronto, Ministry of Treasury, Economics and Intergovernmental Affairs, 1973, p. 203.

as the 1850s, they flourished between 1890 and 1920. To some extent this is understandable. The pressures of urban growth and new technological developments made municipal government more complex. Municipalities now faced decisions in areas relating to sewers, pumping stations, streetcars, power systems, street and sidewalk paving, building codes, assessments, department budgets, tenders, debentures, and sinking funds.

Goldwin Smith, a member of a Toronto municipal reform group, summed up the general attitude in 1890 when he said that in the past city government was a proper setting for debates on principles, but now "a city is simply a densely peopled district in need of a specially skilled administration."[61] The age of the experts or the professionals had arrived and their coming was seen as the panacea for urban problems. The creation of a committee of experts was that much better.

Another argument in favour of creating special purpose bodies was that a commission could attract "the services of bright, able men who have not the time to serve in the council."[62] What this also meant was that business people were more likely to serve in an appointed position than they were to engage in an election contest and, if successful, to endure the tedious task of attending to constituents' requests. In any event, lobbying for appointed commissions increased; in Toronto for a parks commission, fire commission, hydro commission, and transportation commission; in Montreal for a parks commission; and in Vancouver for a water works commission. As previously discussed, the impetus for town planning also included the creation of a separate planning board or commission. As well, when municipalities took over the operations of street railway systems in the name of efficiency, they usually established a separate body to oversee the administration of this very important function.

By 1917 the proliferation of special purpose bodies was causing concern over the amount of decentralization and fragmentation that had resulted. The October issue of *Municipal World* that year carried an article with the following statement:[63]

---

[61] Weaver, *Shaping the Canadian City*, p. 72.

[62] Mayor Bethune, Vancouver (1907), quoted in *ibid.*, p. 70.

[63] S. M. Baker, "Municipal Government Reform," *Municipal World*, Vol. 27, October 1917, p. 154, in Weaver, "Tomorrow's Metropolis Revisited," p. 411.

> Decentralization has been carried too far. Town Planning
> Commissions, Suburban Road Commissions, Railway Commissions,
> Police Commissions, Boards of Education, Hospital Trusts, Utilities
> Commissions have usurped Council powers. The Council today is
> little more than a tax-levying body with little or no control.

Summary: The Legacy of the Reform Era

Each of the reform movements had its vision of what tomorrow's city
should be like: [64]

> ➤ a city beautiful, filled with parks, trees, boulevards, and stately
>   buildings;
> ➤ a nation of Garden Cities in which development was
>   controlled to ensure all the basic amenities of life;
> ➤ the Canadian city converted into a Christian community
>   where poverty, crime, and vice were eliminated; or
> ➤ an orderly community with a municipal government run on
>   principles of economy and efficiency.

While many of the reformers undoubtedly were sincere in
their efforts, others had less noble motives behind their reform
proposals. C. S. Clarke, an opinionated Torontonian, denounced those
crusaders who wanted to purify city life as "a small group of pious
fanatics who bothered the respectable and terrorized the weak."[65] In
only slightly more generous terms, Kaplan states that "the reform
doctrine was self-congratulatory, contemptuous of outsiders, and thus
highly vulnerable to charges of hypocrisy,"[66] especially since, as
indicated above, its main advocates were prominent businessmen
seeking to expand their influence.

Keating describes the concern of the business community and
also much of the professional middle class about the demands of an
increasingly assertive working class, armed with the franchise.[67] These

---

[64] Rutherford, *Saving the Canadian City*, p. xvii.

[65] Rutherford, "Tomorrow's Metropolis," p. 371.

[66] Harold Kaplan, *Reform, Planning and City Politics: Montreal, Winnipeg,
Toronto*, Toronto, University of Toronto Press, 1982, p. 173.

[67] Michael Keating, *Comparative Urban Politics*, Aldershot, Edward Elgar,
1991, pp. 43-46.

demands had produced "machine politics" in the United States and a socialist movement centred mainly in Western Canada. Both of these troubling developments (in the minds of the business community) could be curtailed by limiting the role of the poor and working class in local politics through institutional reform and by reasserting the ideology of non-partisanship and good government. As Keating points out, "attacks on politics or partisanship often mask objections to the use of political power to counteract inequalities in the social or economic spheres. Non-partisanship thus tends to be a conservative rallying cry."[68] This bias will become evident with the examination of activities of local political parties in Chapter 9.

The reforms pertaining to municipal government were partly meant to eliminate corruption and to improve efficiency. The primary method of achieving this was to remove powers from council control by decreasing the number and importance of ward politicians, by increasing the power of a small executive through the board of control, by increasing the powers of the administration through the commissioner and city manager systems, and, finally, by creating separate special purpose bodies to take over completely certain important functions which could not be entrusted to politicians. Municipal government was regarded less as a level of government and more as a business. The right to vote was viewed as less important than ensuring a well-run municipal organization that would provide services efficiently. As Goldwin Smith said of the municipal franchise:[69]

> What is the power which we now exercise, and which is largely illusory so far as the mass of us are concerned, compared with our health, our convenience, and the rescue of our property from the tax-gatherers?

The net result of the reforms was a more complex, less accountable municipal government, more responsible to economy and efficiency than to the voters. But as early as 1899 there was some recognition that structural reforms had not eliminated waste and corruption. There were also complaints about evasion of responsibility, with a *Toronto Star* editorial claiming that council and the board of control were playing "a game of shuttlecock and battledore."[70] In

---

[68] *Ibid.*, p. 43.

[69] Weaver, *Shaping the Canadian City*, pp. 45-46.

[70] *Ibid.*, p. 70.

1909 the Fort William-Port Arthur Utilities Commission had to admit that service was poor. In 1913 Calgary's commissioners purchased a $5000 car with special paint and a special siren horn for their use,[71] perhaps not the most efficient use of public funds. The problem, of course, was that even businessmen and experts were as prone to self-interest and corruption as those municipal officials they had previously chastised. In 1895 the *Telegram* observed that "the fault is not with the system but with the people,"[72] an insight that today's proponents of structural change might keep in mind.

Concluding Comments

There is a striking similarity between the challenges and problems of 100 years ago and those of today. Common to both periods are concerns over the adequacy of the municipal infrastructure, housing shortages and resistance to low-income housing; concerns about rapid consumption of resources and environmental degradation, the promotion of preventive health programs, conflict of interest and corruption charges surrounding municipal councillors; and a feeling that structural changes make little difference if people and their practices remain unchanged.

The legacy of the reform era is evident in the continued existence of many of the structural reforms from the early 1900s and in the continued denial of the relevance of politics at the local level. Indeed, there has been a resurgence in the criticism of politics and politicians as we proceed today through another turn of the century era. Once again, municipalities are told to embrace business principles and practices as the key to their survival. Cities pursue with great vigour the coveted title of being "the best city for business," often at the expense of more balanced policies and practices. Economy and efficiency are once again the touchstones of a well run municipality. If it is true that "those who don't learn from history are condemned to repeat it," today's municipal leaders need to pay more attention to the lessons from their past.

---

[71] *Ibid.*, p. 72.

[72] *Ibid.*, pp. 72-73.

Chapter 3
Pressures of Growth and Change

To many observers, the problems that faced local government as the 20th century advanced derived from the process of urbanization. They were the result of misguided policies of the federal and provincial governments and an inevitable consequence of the capitalist mode of production.

Introduction

The foundations of Canada's municipal system were laid as long as 200 years ago. They were developed for a small and scattered population comprising a primarily agricultural and rural society. Over the past century the population of Canada increased from 5 million to 31 million, and that much larger population has been concentrated in rapidly growing cities and their suburbs and particularly in a few major metropolitan areas discussed herein. Over this same period, we have gone through industrialization to an information economy. Advances in technology, instantaneous communications, agreements that facilitate the free movement of goods and services around the world, have all contributed to an increasingly integrated world economy, one in which the autonomy of individual national governments seems to be diminished.

These developments significantly altered the nature of Canadian society and our interactions with government. They constrained the roles and responses of government, even as they were influenced in turn by the policies pursued by governments at all levels. This chapter explores the nature and impact of Canada's urban and economic changes and the way that these developments have affected, and been affected by, the actions of our governments. Particular attention, of course, is given to causes and consequences of urban sprawl, the role that governments played in the creation of sprawl, and the role they could play in responding to this settlement pattern.

The Urbanization of Canada

Sir John A. Macdonald has been credited with (or accused of) many things, but it may seem surprising to cite him as a key player in determining the pattern of urban development in Canada. Yet, his "national policy" of 1879, and especially its emphasis on high tariffs to protect the new domestic manufacturing industries of central Canada, was to lead to the early (and continuing) concentration of manufacturing in a central corridor extending from Quebec City to Windsor. This development, in turn, contributed to the growth of a number of cities in this area, and to the dominance of the Montreal and Toronto areas.

The transformation was described by the Economic Council of Canada in its *Fourth Annual Review*, a document that helped to focus attention on the problems of urbanization.

> ... economic change in Canada has thus been marked by a relative shift in the focus of employment and output from on-site exploitation of the natural resource base to the processing of materials, to manufacturing and advanced fabrication, and to the provision of a rapidly widening range of modern private and public services. Inevitably this change has implied a shift in the location of economic activity away from the rural area and its small service centres towards the larger urban centre.[1]

The Canadian economy has been going through a pronounced economic restructuring over the past couple of decades – not only in response to the free trade agreements signed with the United States and Mexico but, more fundamentally, in response to the globalization of the economy, and the opportunities and challenges that this process brings. One result of this restructuring is that cities in the Windsor-to-Quebec industrial heartland have found themselves at a disadvantage compared with cities in the peripheral regions such as Atlantic Canada and the Western provinces.[2] The shift in growth momentum was reflected in more rapid growth in western centres such as the Calgary and Vancouver regions. The economic downturn of the early 1990s was particularly severe in Ontario and in the Toronto area. As a result, Courchene contends that Toronto and the GTA have had no choice

---

[1] Economic Council of Canada, *Fourth Annual Review*, Ottawa, 1967, p. 181.

[2] John Marshall, "Population Growth in Canadian Metropolises, 1901-1986," in F. Frisken (ed.), *The Changing Canadian Metropolis: A Public Policy Perspective*, Toronto, Canadian Urban Institute, 1994, Vol. 1, p. 45.

but to make the transition "from a national economic capital with a significant economic reach to a full-blown global city intimately tied to NAFTA's emerging geopolitical reality."[3] One need not accept fully his interpretation of events to recognize how global forces are altering the prospects for Canada's cities.

Figures on both overall population growth and the growth in urban populations mirror the developments in the Canadian economy. The early years of the 20th century saw rapid population growth. Almost half of this growth was caused by the extensive immigration of this period. The rate of increase in population then slowed during each successive decade, reaching a low of only 10.9% during the intercensal decade of 1931 to 1941. During this period of the "Great Depression" there was not only a decline in immigration but also a marked reduction in the movement of rural populations to urban centres. With jobs hard to find in the cities, many able-bodied adults who had migrated to urban areas moved "back to the land," where they might hope for regular meals.[4] After 1941 population growth again accelerated to a near-record expansion rate of 30.2% between 1951 and 1961. In subsequent periods the rate of increase steadily declined, largely because of the reduction in birth rates. Indeed, the population increase of only 4% between 1996 and 2001 was the slowest experienced except during the Depression of the 1930s and the period between 1981 and 1986 – a time of exceptionally low levels of immigration.[5]

Of particular interest is the classification of the population as between urban and rural. Statistics Canada defines as urban those places with a population of 1000 or more, although "in most analyses the urban designation is limited to places over 10 000 population."[6]

---

[3] Thomas J. Courchene, "Ontario as a North American Region-State, Toronto as a Global City-Region: Responding to the NAFTA Challenge," in Allen J. Scott (ed.), *Global City-Regions*, Oxford, Oxford University Press, p. 159. See also Courchene and C. R. Telmer, *From Heartland to North American Region-State: The Social, Fiscal, and Federal Evolution of Ontario*, Toronto, Faculty of Management, University of Toronto, 1998.

[4] *Ibid.*, p. 49.

[5] Statistics Canada, *2001 Census Analysis Series – A Profile of the Canadian Population: Where We Live*, available at www.statcan.ca, accessed May 1, 2003.

[6] Larry S. Bourne, "Urban Canada in Transition to the Twenty-First Century: Trends, Issues, and Visions," in Trudi Bunting and Pierre Filion, *Canadian Cities in Transition*, 2nd Edition, Oxford University Press, 2000, p. 26.

Using the minimum definition, Canada was an urban nation as early as 1921, and even if we define urban places as those with populations over 10 000, Canada was urban by the mid-20th century. By the 1976 census, Canada's urban growth since the end of the Second World War had exceeded that of any Western industrial nation, with three-quarters of our population concentrated on less than 1% of its land area.[7] The results of the 2001 census indicate that more than 80% of the country's population (and employment and wealth) is now concentrated in the 139 urban places with populations of 10 000 or more that make up Canada's urban system.[8]

Even greater concentration of population is evident if we look at the growth of Canada's census metropolitan areas (census areas comprised of at least two adjacent municipal entities, each at least partly urban, with an urbanized core of 100 000 or more). There were only 6 of these CMAs in 1921, but by 1971 there were 19 such areas containing over half of Canada's population. The 2001 census identified 27 CMAs, containing 64% of the country's population. Most of the recent population growth of the country has been in the CMAs.

Compounding this urbanization and its attendant pressures has been the mushrooming growth within just four areas of Canada. According to the 2001 census results, Ontario's extended Golden Horseshoe, Montreal and adjacent region, British Columbia's Lower Mainland and southern Vancouver Island, and the Calgary-Edmonton corridor contain half of Canada's population. The table below shows the significance of these areas within their provinces and the country.[9]

Table 3.1 Canada's "Big Four"		
Area	% of Provincial Population	% of Canadian Population
Ontario's Golden Horseshoe	59%	22%
Montreal and adjacent region	52%	12%
Lower Mainland of B.C.	69%	9%
Calgary-Edmonton corridor	72%	7%

---

[7] Len Gertler and R. W. Crowley, *Changing Canadian Cities: The Next 25 Years*, Toronto, McClelland and Stewart, 1977, p. 41.

[8] Larry S. Bourne and Jim Simmons, "New Fault Lines? Recent Trends in the Canadian Urban System and their Implications for Planning and Public Policy, *Canadian Journal of Urban Research*, Volume 12, Issue 1, Summer 2003, p. 25.

[9] Statistics Canada, *2001 Census Analysis Series*, pp. 6-7.

Canada's largest cities are also of great economic significance as indicated by their percentage contribution to the GDP (Gross Domestic Product) of their respective provinces, summarized in the accompanying table.[10] As usual, Jane Jacobs describes this economic reality forcefully.[11]

Economic Engines	
Toronto	44%
Montreal	50%
Vancouver	53%
Calgary-Edmonton	64%
Winnipeg	64%

Without Vancouver, Calgary, Toronto, Montreal and Winnipeg – without these cities – Canada would be so poor it would qualify as a third world country. The federal and provincial income and consumption taxes that businesses and residents in these five cities pay are what make federal and provincial programs and activities financially possible.

The Nature and Impact of Urbanization

Urbanization involves much more than the concentration of population and economic activity. It arises from, and gives rise to, fundamental changes in the nature of our economy and society. As noted above, it was industrialization, and especially the development of mass production, which encouraged the concentration of population in cities. With this shift in population, other changes occurred. The movement from farm to factory created growing numbers of workers who were dependent upon industrial employment and its attendant uncertainties instead of being relatively self-sufficient by living off the land. They increasingly turned to government to provide them with some protection and security, and gradually the "positive state" evolved with its elaborate range of services and programs designed to ensure all citizens a minimum standard of living conditions. All levels of government were affected by this development, and the resultant increase in services demanded of local government represented a heavy burden for most municipalities.

The shortage, expense, and inadequacy of urban housing led to greater government involvement by all levels. The concentration of

[10] Figures from Conference Board of Canada, as summarized in Toronto Dominion Bank, *A Choice Between Investing in Canada's Cities or Disinvesting in Canada's Future*, April 2002, p. 5.

[11] Remarks at C5 meeting of big city mayors, May 25-26, 2001, as reported in *Ideas That Matter*, Volume 2, Number 1, p. 4, accessed March 12, 2003 from www.ideasthatmatter.com.

low income families in inner city neighbourhoods strained the social service system. The loss of spacious country living, for those who had moved to the city, led to growing demands for parks and recreational facilities. The higher living standards and leisure time of a techno-logical society accentuated this demand. Transportation and traffic movement required increasing government attention, as did the provision of an adequate supply of water and the disposal of domestic and industrial waste. Governments had to deal with air pollution concerns, in large part because of the exhaust from the concentration of motor vehicles. New problems of subdivision control and urban renewal and redevelopment also claimed the attention of the urban municipality. Population overspill caused the conversion of land from agricultural production to urban uses and government action was needed to protect against developments that had an undesirable impact on the natural environment.

Rural municipalities also experienced new servicing pressures, largely because of the influx of the non-farm rural population. Improved road maintenance and fire protection were demanded and such urban amenities as sidewalks and streetlights were expected in many hamlets. New recreational facilities were requested. Extensive cottage development on scenic lakes and rivers and excessive residential development on unsuitable soil often caused pollution problems requiring government action. When these problems arose in a concen-trated area, the municipality often faced the very heavy financial burden of a water supply and sewage treatment system. Residential development and farming activities proved an uneasy mix and the resulting friction provided one more example of the need for land use planning policies and controls in rural areas. New intensive farming operations – the so-called factory farms – presented additional environmental challenges and a potential threat to the quality of the groundwater on which rural development depends. Municipal efforts to restrict the development and operation of such farming operations have not always been successful when challenged in the courts.

The Issue of Urban Sprawl

Of all the issues and problems associated with urbanization and settle-ment patterns, there is little doubt that urban sprawl heads the list. What is this phenomenon, how has it occurred, and why is it so problematic?

In spite of the currency of the term, there is no single, universally accepted definition of urban sprawl. After reviewing the literature, Gillham offers the following general definition.[12]

Box 3.1 Urban Sprawl

Sprawl (whether characterized as urban or suburban) is a form of urbanization distinguished by leapfrog patterns of development, commercial strips, low density, separated land uses, automobile dominance, and a minimum of public open space.

There is ample evidence of urban sprawl within Canada. One study found that during the 1980s, "almost 60 per cent of the net growth in Canada's CMAs and almost 50 per cent of Canada's net growth was located in the CMAs' fringe areas beyond the urbanized core, and CMA fringe areas account for an increasingly large share of CMA population."[13] In 1996, as many as 19 of the then 25 CMAs had more than one-quarter of their populations living in the suburbs and fringe areas and the cities surrounding most CMAs have had significant population increases.[14] Between 1996 and 2001, the combined population of the city centres of the four largest CMAs grew by only 0.9% per year, compared with a 2.3% growth per annum in the suburban and outlying areas.[15] Emerging economic centres or "edge cities" beyond the urban core are becoming important sources of growth and prosperity. One study[16] identified over 200 edge cities dotting the urban landscape of America. This pattern is also evident in Canada, with Toronto facing a challenge from cities like Mississauga and Oshawa, and Montreal confronted by Laval.[17]

---

[12] Oliver Gillham, *The Limitless City: A Primer on the Urban Sprawl Debate*, Washington, Island Press, 2002, p. 8.

[13] Christopher Bryant and Daniel Lemire, *Population Distribution and the Management of Urban Growth in Six Selected Urban Regions in Canada*, Toronto, Intergovernmental Committee on Urban and Regional Research, 1993, p. 14.

[14] Gerald Hodge and Ira M. Robinson, *Planning Canadian Regions*, Vancouver, UBC Press, 2001, p. 241.

[15] Toronto Dominion Bank, *Investing or Disinvesting*, p. 8.

[16] J. Garreau, *Edge City: Life on the New Frontier*, New York, Doubleday, 1991.

[17] Katherine A. Graham, Susan D. Phillips, and Allan M. Maslove, *Urban Governance in Canada*, Toronto, Harcourt Brace & Company, Canada, 1998, pp. 75 and 79.

While sprawl is associated with rapidly-growing population centres, Lennon and Leo demonstrate that it is also found in the Winnipeg area which has been characterized by slow growth. This sprawl is reflected in reduced density of development and loss of agricultural land and open spaces. It is also found in a declining inner city population of Winnipeg coupled with a growth rate in municipalities bordering the city of more than 10% and even more than 20%, over a five year period[18] – although the small population base in these outlying areas means that even modest growth translates into sizeable percentage increases.

While critics see urban sprawl as the result of badly managed urban growth, others argue that it is simply a process of cities expanding outward, as they have done for centuries, with the resulting development pattern reflecting the operation of economic markets for land and the choices made by individuals as to where they want to live and locate their business.[19] Indeed, proponents of markets contend that over time economic forces will resolve the concerns raised by sprawl through a process of infill housing and commercial development in the empty spaces that had been created by leapfrog development. There are even benefits attributed to sprawl in the form of cheaper housing, more private open space, shorter commuting time for those who live and work in the suburbs, and easier access to public open space.[20]

Problems With Sprawl

Lithwick sees the situation very differently and argues that the process of urbanization inherently gives rise to sprawl and associated problems. As he explains, the growth of cities produces competing demands for the one feature that they share – scarce urban space – thus driving core prices upward and households outward. He suggests that transportation, pollution, and poverty problems flow from this.

---

[18] Richard Lennon and Christopher Leo, *Stopping the Sprawl: How Winnipeg Could Benefit from Metropolitan Growth Strategies for a Slow-Growth Region*, Canadian Centre for Policy Alternatives, January 2001, p. 9.

[19] Paul G. Thomas, "A Layman's Perspective on Urban Sprawl," November 2001, accessed January 18, 2003 from the web site of the Capital Region of Winnipeg at www.gov.mb.ca/ia/capreg.

[20] Anthony Downs, "Some Realities About Sprawl and Urban Decline," *Housing Policy Debate*, Fannie Mae Foundation, 1999, 10 (4), p. 962.

Moreover, he argues that because of these interdependencies, efforts to deal with each problem in isolation have inevitably failed.

> Housing policy has added to the stock of urban accommodations, but has led to urban sprawl and fiscal squeeze for the municipalities. Transport policies have moved people faster initially, but have led to further sprawl, downtown congestion, pollution, and rapid core deterioration.[21]

Fowler is very critical of the process of urbanization pursued in North America, the urban sprawl and suburban development, and the extensive transportation network criss-crossing the landscape. He describes how we ended up with cities "where we sleep en masse in huge residential complexes and work en masse in huge retail or industrial developments – and spend our lives travelling between them, from living room to kitchen, so to speak."[22] He is even more critical of the built environment of our cities and its lack of physical diversity. He cites the proliferation of large-scale projects, the deconcentration and decentralization of development (not just with respect to low-density residential development, but also affecting office and factory space), and the homogeneity of architecture and of land use. In his view, we are squandering billions of dollars in North America because of the built environment in our urban areas that has "an extravagant transportation system, life-threatening levels of pollution, a needlessly large infrastructure of utilities such as water mains and trunk sewers, and significantly more expensive housing and consumer goods."[23]

The servicing costs associated with sprawl have also been documented in the Canadian context. For example, a study of the GTA estimated that a more compact and efficient development pattern could save $12.2 billion over a 25 year period, or roughly 22% of the capital investment required to sustain existing development patterns.[24] It also found that another $200 million could be saved in costs relating to air pollution, health care, and policing associated with automobile accidents. After factoring in lower congestion, parking and land

---

[21] N. H. Lithwick, *Urban Canada: Problems and Prospects*, Ottawa, Canada Mortgage and Housing Corporation, 1970, p. 15.

[22] Edmund P. Fowler, *Building Cities That Work*, Kingston, McGill-Queen's University Press, 1992, p. 31.

[23] *Ibid.*, p. 69.

[24] Report of the GTA Task Force, *Greater Toronto*, 1996, p. 111.

acquisition costs, the study concluded that the savings were in the order of $1 billion annually.

Quite apart from the higher servicing costs, there are other negative economic impacts from urban sprawl. The time spent by individuals in long commutes along clogged artery roads and the time taken by trucks to transport products from place to place both represent economic waste and lost production.[25]

Urban sprawl may also have an adverse impact on the economic prospects for our cities. This view is based on a growing awareness that in today's knowledge-based economy businesses are attracted to areas that have a talent pool, which, in turn, means that places that can attract talented people will enjoy economic success.[26] To do so, they must offer vibrant neighbourhoods, lots of after-hours activity, ample recreational facilities and activities, and an atmosphere that welcomes and nurtures creativity and diversity. Indeed, Richard Florida's research indicates that metropolitan areas that score high on the BoHo index (for Bohemian, as in home to lots of writers, designers, musicians, actors, painters, dancers and the like) enjoy success in attracting "high tech" firms. But culturally vibrant neighbourhoods are not associated with the suburban areas of many cities, a fact that may hamper their ability to attract young knowledge workers. It is in this way that urban sprawl may undermine a city's competitiveness.[27]

Urban sprawl also adversely affects the environment in several ways, from the air pollution caused by the concentration of automobiles, to the loss of good farmland, which, unfortunately, is often located adjacent to our large cities. There is no better example than the fact that 42% of the GTA is classified as farmland, and the vast majority of it is considered part of the 5% of the Canadian landmass

---

[25] Liam Stone, with Roger Gibbins, *Tightening Our Beltways: Urban Sprawl in Western Canada*, Canada West Foundation, October 2002, pp. 3-4, a discussion paper available from the Foundation web site at www.cwf.ca, accessed March 14, 2003.

[26] A leading proponent of this view is Professor Richard Florida. His publications include *The Economic Geography of Talent*, Pittsburgh, Carnegie Mellon University, 2001, *The Rise of the Creative Class*, New York, Basic Books, 2002, and *Technology and Tolerance: The Importance of Diversity to High-Technology Growth*, Washington, The Brookings Institution, June 2001.

[27] This is a concern with respect to cities in Western Canada, according to Stone and Gibbins, *Tightening Our Beltways*.

that is designated as prime agricultural land.[28] Low density suburban growth also threatens the natural renewal of water reservoirs located under or adjacent to our cities. Parking lots and roads cause precipitation to enter the storm sewer systems as runoff rather than filtering into underground aquifers, thus slowing their replenishment.[29]

The environmental impact of the concentration of people and businesses in cities has been described as follows:[30]

> ...cities are massive consumers of non-renewable resources and producers of solid wastes not easily disposed of or broken down. As such, they confront major environmental challenges in air and waste pollution, waste management, destruction of agricultural lands, and disruption of ecosystems.

There is a growing recognition of the fact that our cities as they currently operate are not sustainable. In response, we are urged to embrace sustainable development, growth management, smart growth, and/or the new urbanism – all of which advocate fairly similar approaches as discussed later in this chapter.

Urban sprawl can also have a negative social impact. In a pattern that has been more pronounced up until now in the United States than in Canada, middle class families – and increasingly businesses as well – move to the suburbs. Those left behind in the central cities include the homeless, the mentally ill, transient unemployed youth, those on fixed incomes, the elderly, immigrants, and single mothers with children.[31] Income polarization is increasing within our urban areas, challenging efforts to maintain the quality of life in central cities, as documented by recent surveys by the Federation of Canadian Municipalities. The second survey, in 2001, found that poverty and income inequality had continued to expand in large urban communities since the first survey in 1999.[32]

---

[28] Pamela Blais, *Inching Toward Sustainability: The Evolving Urban Structure of the GTA*, Report to the Neptis Foundation, March 2000, pp. 23-24.

[29] Stone and Gibbin, *Tightening Our Beltways*, p. 3.

[30] Neil Bradford, *Why Cities Matter: Policy Research Perspectives for Canada*, CPRN Discussion Paper F\23, June 2002, Canadian Policy Research Networks, available at www.cprn.org, accessed February 20, 2003.

[31] Bourne, "Urban Canada In Transition," p. 39.

[32] Federation of Canadian Municipalities, *Quality of Life in Canadian Communities 2001 Report*, available at web site www.fcm.ca, accessed May 2, 2003.

Lee also found higher poverty rates in the central cities of Canada than in their adjacent suburbs – often much higher – and an increased geographic concentration of poor families. The number of neighbourhoods in Canada with high concentrations of poverty increased between 1980 and 1995. Aboriginal people, who are an increasing presence in urban centres, have a poverty rate of 55.6%, compared to an average rate among all city residents of 24.5%.[33]

Some inner city neighbourhoods are characterized by delinquency and higher crime rates. In response, those who are mobile depart, leaving those who remain with fewer resources to cope with their situation. In the words of one report:[34]

> A vicious cycle has been launched – where movement away from the urban core places downward pressure on residential and industrial densities and tax bases, forcing municipalities to hike downtown property taxes and other tax levies, which in turn prompts more urban flight. Making matters worse, stagnant or shrinking tax bases have made it difficult for downtown municipalities to address the very social problems that drove businesses and individuals to outlying areas in the first place.

Different kinds of negative social impact and exclusion are experienced by those living beyond the central city. Those without vehicles (the young and the elderly) can feel isolated and trapped in the suburbs. Conversely, suburban commuters have little time, or opportunity, for interaction and participation in local community events. Theodore Lowi goes so far as to suggest that the suburbs represent a failure of citizenship.[35]

> We have removed ourselves not only from the responsibilities of civic participation but also from the challenges of social relations by zoning poor families out of our neighbourhoods. The social and political skills of adults have declined; we have lost the ability, at a personal level, to say how we feel, to negotiate, to solve problems creatively – in short, to be publicly responsible individuals.

According to Jacobs, the physical diversity that has been disappearing from our cities made contact among neighbours more likely and encouraged people to care about what went on in their

---

[33] Kevin K. Lee, *Urban Poverty in Canada: A Statistical Profile*, Ottawa, Canadian Council on Social Development, 2000, p. xv.

[34] Toronto Dominion Bank, *Investing or Disinvesting*, p. 8.

[35] Theodore Lowi, *The End of Liberalism*, 2nd Edition, New York, W. W. Norton, 1979, p. 267.

neighbourhood.[36] The mixture of workplaces and residences ensured the presence of many people throughout the day. Short blocks maximized the number of corners and therefore meeting places. The result was streets filled with activity and under constant observation.

Box 3.2 Jane Jacobs: The Planning Visionary

Without any training as a professional planner, but with astute observation and much common sense, Jane Jacobs turned conventional views of planning on their head with the 1961 publication of her book *The Death and Life of Great American Cities*. She embraced the crowded streets filled with mixed land uses so distasteful to traditional planning. She demonstrated that this density and diversity are essential to healthy city life. Jacobs moved with her family to Toronto in 1968 and almost immediately became involved in that city's battle to block the construction of the Spadina expressway. She has written several other books, including *Cities and the Wealth of Nations* and *Systems of Survival*. In recent years she has lent her voice and her intellect to the demands by Canada's five largest cities (the C5) that their needs must receive more recognition and support from the provincial and federal governments.

Fowler takes a similar position in arguing that the physical characteristics of the post-war urban environment have an adverse impact on our social behaviour, including our political activities. What he terms "authentic politics" is, he contends, only possible in small-scale, diverse spaces where a variety of casual face-to-face interactions occur naturally – a development pattern disappearing as our cities have been rebuilt in the post-war period.[37] Fowler and Layton point to a direct relationship between traffic and neighbourhood vitality, arguing that increased reliance on cars means that streets are now used almost exclusively as thoroughfares rather than as public meeting places. They go so far as to suggest that the reduction in healthy street level contact contributes to the present distrust of government and the erosion of the public sector.[38]

With all of the problems attributed to sprawl – economic waste, reduced competitiveness, environmental degradation, social problems, and a weakened sense of community and citizenship – much attention has been directed to the causes of this settlement pattern.

---

[36] Jane Jacobs, *The Death and Life of Great American Cities*, New York, Random House, 1961.

[37] Fowler, *Building Cities That Work*, p. 132.

[38] Edmund P. Fowler and Jack Layton, "Transportation Policy in Canadian Cities," in Edmund P. Fowler and David Siegel, *Urban Policy Issues*, 2nd Edition, Toronto, Oxford University Press, 2002, p. 125.

Looking for Causes:
The Government or the Market?

There are two main explanations offered for the pattern of urbanization and sprawl, and its associated problems. One view attributes these developments to actions taken by governments, while the other points to underlying forces in the marketplace. As will become clear, both influences played a major part.

It's the Government

When asked to identify the most important influences on the American metropolitan areas since 1950, leading urban scholars singled out the overwhelming impact of the federal government and particularly its policies that intentionally or unintentionally promote suburbanization and sprawl.[39] Because the impact of many of the federal policies is indirect or unintentional, they have been referred to as "stealth urban policies."[40]

Banfield was an early and influential proponent of this viewpoint.[41] He writes that from the New Deal onward, the flight to the suburbs was encouraged, albeit inadvertently, by the federal government through its transportation and housing policies and programs. Indeed, he contends that these two programs account for 90% of the federal government expenditure for the improvement of the cities, that neither is directed toward the really serious problems of the cities, and that both make the problems worse![42] The improvement of transportation serves to encourage further movement of industry, commerce, and relatively well-off residents (mostly white) from the inner city. Federal housing programs have subsidized home building on a vast scale by ensuring mortgages on easy terms, mostly for the purchase of new homes that were being built in the suburbs. Urban renewal initiatives have also been harmful, forcing hundreds of

---

[39] Peter Dreir, John Mollenkopf, and Todd Swanstrom, *Place Matters: Metropolitics for the Twenty-First Century*, Lawrence, University Press of Kansas, 2001, p. 93.

[40] *Ibid.*, p. 102.

[41] Edward C. Banfield, *The Unheavenly City*, Boston, Little, Brown and Company, 1968.

[42] *Ibid.*, p. 14.

thousands of low-income people out of low-cost housing to make room for luxury apartments, office buildings, hotels, civic centres, industrial parks, and the like.[43]

Far from being productive, Banfield demonstrates that these federal programs actually work at cross-purposes. The expressway program and the housing mortgages in effect pay the middle-class whites to leave the central city for the suburbs; at the same time, the urban renewal and mass transit programs pay them to stay in the central city or to return.

A rather similar pattern is evident in Canada, particularly with respect to federal housing and urban renewal initiatives. Since the 1935 Dominion Housing Act, and especially since the establishment of the Central (now Canada) Mortgage and Housing Corporation (CMHC) in 1946, federal financial assistance for single-family dwellings has reinforced low density sprawl. The actions of the CMHC also contributed to neighbourhood dislocations and attendant problems because of what has been described as a bulldozer approach to urban renewal. It is evident that in Canada, as well as in the United States, urban growth became a prime instrument of public policy to stimulate and maintain high levels of economic activity.[44] After studying federal housing policy, Fallis concludes that it is mainly influenced by federal macroeconomic policy and he observes: "the federal government has always used housing programs as instruments of fiscal policy."[45]

Leo describes how all three levels of government became involved in a massive program of government support for suburban development, pursuing policies that not only reinforced the rapidly growing popular preference for the private automobile over public transportation, but also gave it free reign and entrenched it.[46] He notes that this state action was quite consistent with the demands of the public at the time. These demands, to a large extent, were a function of

---

[43] *Ibid.*, p. 16.

[44] Michael Goldrick, "The Anatomy of Urban Reform in Toronto," in Dimitrios Roussopoulos (ed.), *The City and Radical Social Change*, Montreal, Black Rose Books, 1982, p. 264.

[45] George Fallis, "The Federal Government and the Metropolitan Housing Problem," in Frisken, *Canadian Metropolis*, p. 376.

[46] Christopher Leo, "The State in the City: A Political-Economy Perspective on Growth and Decay," in James Lightbody (ed.), *Canadian Metropolitics*, Toronto, Copp Clark Ltd., p. 31.

changing demographics. The baby boom following World War Two meant families of young children in search of the back yard and the quiet street that were to be found by commuting to the suburb.[47] But Leo points out that the state was also responding by its actions to "the demands of E. P. Taylor and other development magnates, to the professional biases of bureaucrats in the Department of Finance and the CMHC, to the sensitivities of Liberal Party contributors, and to the interests and concerns of a variety of other parties."[48] It was these influences that led to the specific government response found in Canada, as opposed to, for example, the situation in Europe where suburban development has been less automobile-dominated. According to Leo, the costs of Canada's form of suburban development are evident in deteriorating transit systems, inner city decay, and crumbling infrastructure.[49]

Indeed, one can be very critical of the widespread disruption (some would say destruction) of the city through government policies designed to meet the needs of the private use of automobiles without anything like this degree of support for public transit. Indeed, public transit services have been struggling to maintain ridership, hesitating to increase fares which would likely lose more riders, yet faced with growing deficits and, traditionally, very little financial support from the senior levels of government. According to the Science Council of Canada's report, Cities for Tomorrow, "it appears that barely one-half of the cost incurred by the automobile is returned to different levels of government in gasoline taxes and license fees."[50]

Not only do public transit services face unfair competition because of this subsidy, but too little consideration is given to the broad social benefits that they bring – and the social costs of our devotion to the automobile. It is true that provincial governments played a key role in the development of urban mass transit systems in

---

[47] This point is well developed in David K. Foot, Boom, Bust & Echo, Toronto, Macfarlane Walter & Ross, 1996, Chapter 7, who also explains how the aging population has brought about a decline in public transit ridership and a growth in the suburbs and the reliance on cars.

[48] Leo, "The State in the City," p. 32.

[49] Ibid., p. 33.

[50] Quoted in Boyce Richardson, The Future of Canadian Cities, Toronto, New Press, 1972, p.130.

the Toronto, Montreal, and Vancouver areas in the 1970s and 1980s,[51] but the level of government support remains far below that which has already been provided for the automobile. For example, one study found that private cars in the Vancouver area enjoy public subsidies of $2700 a year each, seven times the subsidy for public transit.[52] What makes these government policies even more shortsighted is that transit investments pay off at the rate of 9 to 1 for every dollar spent.[53]

Lorimer contends that "most of the development of Canadian cities in the three boom decades from the Forties to the Seventies was a direct consequence of the economic development strategy chosen by Ottawa for Canada."[54] In his view, this strategy had two principal components – the exploitation of natural resources for use mainly by the major metropolitan economies, and the expansion of a branch-plant secondary manufacturing industry in Southern Ontario. Local government's primary role was to provide the physical services needed to support growth and development. The result, according to Lorimer, is that local governments became servants of the development industry that they were supposed to regulate.[55]

Bradford describes the period between 1940 and 1970 as one of "cities in the shadows of Keynesian space,"[56] referring to the economic policies of John Maynard Keynes then being pursued by the federal government. Central to those policies was government spending as a stimulus to the economy, both through an expanding network of social programs and through the construction of housing to accommodate the rapidly growing population – fuelled by baby boomers and immigrants. Local governments were expected to do their part, in return for increased tax revenues and jobs.

---

[51] F. Frisken, "Provincial Transit Policy-Making in the Toronto, Montreal, and Vancouver Regions," in Frisken, *Canadian Metropolis*, p. 528.

[52] Foot, *Boom, Bust, and Echo*, p. 133.

[53] Joseph Hall, "Commuter Corner," *Toronto Star*, April 10, 2000.

[54] James Lorimer, "The post-developer era for Canada's cities begins," in *City Magazine Annual 1981*, Toronto, James Lorimer and Company, 1981, p. 7.

[55] See, for example, *The Real World of City Politics*, Toronto, James Lewis and Samuel, 1970; *A Citizen's Guide to City Politics*, Toronto, James Lewis and Samuel, 1972; *The Developers*, Toronto, James Lorimer, 1978; and *After the Developers* (with Carolyn MacGregor), Toronto, James Lorimer, 1981.

[56] Bradford, *Why Cities Matter*, pp. 16-19.

Magnusson describes the federal government's efforts to support the housing market to ensure an expansion of the economy.[57] But, he also notes that the provinces were just as concerned as the federal level about removing any possible checks on growth, which was one of their reasons for increasing conditional grants for improving public facilities in the cities. He also suggests that provincial legislation on planning and zoning was based on the assumption that urban development would be undertaken through private initiative, with municipalities playing a regulatory role, but one that facilitated private enterprise.[58]

An analysis by Slack, discussed in more detail in Chapter 7, contends that municipal governments must also accept some responsibility for the pattern of urban sprawl and its attendant costs because their taxing and financing policies support and encourage such development. She points out that higher property taxes provide an incentive for less dense projects and these lower densities mean that development expands outward rather than upward. Since property values are highest in the central core of our cities, property taxes are higher there than in outlying areas, even though the cost of services is relatively lower in the central core.[59]

It's the Market

Some blame the problems in our cities not on government actions but on insufficient government intervention and on the excesses of private decision making.[60] Those who hold to this viewpoint have numerous examples to support their contention. Perhaps the most blatant example is the land speculation in and around our cities. The extension of services, at public expense, often brings windfall profits to the private speculator who purchased and held land against such an eventuality. Escalating land costs then push the cost of housing beyond the reach of more and more Canadians.

---

[57] Warren Magnusson, "Introduction," in Warren Magnusson and Andrew Sancton (eds.), *City Politics in Canada*, Toronto, University of Toronto Press, p. 27.

[58] *Ibid.*

[59] Enid Slack, *Municipal Finance and the Pattern of Urban Growth*, Commentary No. 160, C. D. Howe Institute, February 2002, pp. 9-10.

[60] See, for example, Richardson, *The Future of Canadian Cities*, on which this section is based.

Private enterprise has also been deficient in providing adequate and appropriate housing for the varied needs of the Canadian population. Here again, the forces of urbanization have played a part by making land very scarce and therefore very valuable. As land prices increase, it becomes necessary to have buildings that will generate a large income for the landowner. As Richardson describes the process:

> ... poor houses inhabited by poor people must be swept away, their occupants with them; new places go up, let at high rents; young men and women, married couples, or the rich, move in where poor people lived before; the poor people just "disappear" – most of the time we don't even take the trouble to find out where they go.[61]

While Richardson's analysis of the shortcomings of private decision making may seem quite critical, to some it is far too tame. A more radical viewpoint is that such "problems" as too many cars in the streets, insufficient affordable housing, lack of green space, and environmental pollution are but symptoms of more fundamental causes.[62] According to this view, "it is impossible to understand both the urban sprawl which passes for development and the urban conflict it has produced unless one recognizes the determining power of the capitalist mode of production which governs these processes."[63]

Rather than being haphazard and random, city growth is seen as intimately linked with the changing needs of the economic system. "The city is developed, redeveloped and moulded over time according to long term cycles in how profits are made and investment decisions taken."[64] As Western nations emerged from the depression of the 1930s, they faced the need to stimulate consumption to sustain the capitalist system. The response was to introduce a series of policies to facilitate urban growth. By shifting the focus of capital from production to consumption and by emphasizing urban development as a key vehicle to achieve it, these actions effectively changed the function of cities from that of workshops to "artifacts of consumption."[65] The impact of the resulting urban development has already been noted.

---

[61] Richardson, *The Future of Canadian Cities*, pp. 155-156.

[62] Dimitrios Roussopoulos, "Understanding the City and Radical Social Change," in Roussopoulos, *The City and Radical Social Change*, p. 61.

[63] M. Castells, as quoted in *ibid.*, p. 111.

[64] Goldrick, "The Anatomy of Urban Reform in Toronto," p. 263.

[65] *Ibid.*, pp. 264-265.

The chief beneficiaries have been the property development industry, including developers, financiers, real estate companies, construction companies, and property managers.

At some stage it becomes pointless to argue over whether government or the market is to blame for the problems in our urban and suburban areas. Both are responsible. However, the chances of changing government policies to be more helpful are certainly greater than getting the market to behave in any fundamentally different way.

Looking For Solutions

To the extent that the problems described above arise from urban sprawl, they will not easily be overcome. Most of the population overspill into suburban and rural areas reflects strongly held values about what constitutes a superior quality of life. Unless and until these values change, suburbanites are likely to use their political muscle to protect their lifestyle, sprawl and all.[66]

Managing Growth

However, many of the actions needed to counteract urban sprawl are fairly obvious and they have been spelled out in a number of closely related movements or reform initiatives. The following table attempts to provide a brief summary of these various initiatives and their links. The common thread is managing growth so that more desirable settlement patterns result.

Box 3.3 Approaches to Managing Growth	
Sustainable Development	Promoted by the 1987 World Commission on Environment and Development Report to the United Nations (Bruntland Report), which argued that it was possible to have economic development while protecting the environment.
Growth Management	Also known as regional growth management (RGM), this concept has been around for at least 50 years. Originally focused on limiting growth, it now has broader goals to accommodate new development in ways that preserve communities and the environment and limit new infrastructure investment.[67]

---

[66] Stone and Gibbins, *Tightening Our Beltways*, p. 9.

[67] Gillham, *The Limitless City*, p. 155.

Box 3.3 (continued)	
Smart Growth	This term was apparently coined in the United States in the 1990s as a neutral phrase that would allow for necessary growth and development but in ways that were less wasteful of resources and would be less likely to encounter opposition.[68] It incorporates many of the techniques of growth management and, indeed, the two terms are often used interchangeably.[69]
The New Urbanism	Since the late 1980s, the new urbanists have called for the development of compact neighbourhoods containing community facilities and stores, with transit close by. But it was more than 40 years ago that Jane Jacobs set out the rationale for this form of development.[70]

Bradford provides an excellent summary of the primary objective of these related concepts and the main methods of achieving them.[71]

> A sustainable city is dedicated to reducing its impact on the bio-region by shrinking the size of the ecological footprint. The strategies are by now well known and involve government deploying a host of policy instruments and fiscal incentives to embed ecological factors into the decision making processes of citizens and governments. Familiar goals are substituting brownfield conversions for greenfield development, and higher density housing complexes for detached single family lots; ensuring local waste management and reuse rather than exporting it to distant landfill or incineration sites; limiting private automobiles; and protecting natural heritage sites or expanding green spaces.

Reforming Municipal Structures

While some of these growth management strategies are gradually receiving attention in Canada, the primary response to the problems of urban growth and sprawl has been to focus on alleged shortcomings in the local government system – and then to introduce reforms and restructuring as described and analyzed in the next two chapters. To set the stage for that discussion, this section summarizes the main problems attributed to local structures, functions, and finances.

---

[68] Canadian Urban Institute, *Smart Growth in Canada*, March 2001, p. 3.

[69] As they are in Lennon and Leo, *Stopping the Sprawl*.

[70] Jacobs, *The Death and Life of Great American Cities*.

[71] Bradford, *Why Cities Matter*, p. 45.

Structural concerns centred on the fact that there were a number of separate municipalities operating within most urban areas. For example, within the 18 metropolitan areas identified in the 1961 census, "there were some 260 separate municipal government jurisdictions, together with an additional unknown number of semi-independent single purpose special authorities such as school boards, water boards, transit and utility commissions, and sewerage districts."[72] To most observers, such a fragmented structure made concerted action to deal with urban problems both difficult and unlikely. Trapped in an "iron cage" of jurisdictional competition, central cities could not provide adequate public services within their boundaries, or pursue redistributive policies (to address inequities), without putting their economic position at risk.[73] There was a need for mechanisms that could facilitate intermunicipal or regional coordination. While many such mechanisms exist, the preferred approach in Canada – especially in Central and Atlantic Canada – was to amalgamate municipalities.

The ability of municipal governments to respond to urban problems was complicated by the fact that a number of traditionally local responsibilities "outgrew" the local level in terms of their significance, importance, and impact. The result, in fields such as health, education, and welfare, was a gradual shift of responsibility to the senior levels of government and an increasing sharing of responsibilities between two or more levels of government. At the same time, a parallel but reverse trend was under way in which senior governments launched new initiatives but delegated responsibility to the local level for at least some aspects of program delivery. This pattern was evident in such areas as housing, urban renewal, and environmental protection. The combined result was that municipal operations became increasingly intertwined with those of the senior governments.

In many traditional areas of local competence, provincial supervision, regulation or outright control have been deemed the acceptable solutions.... Their overall effect has incorporated municipal affairs more completely in the broader contexts of provincial and federal public administration. Indeed, local autonomy in all but a few ... areas is extinct.[74]

---

[72] Economic Council of Canada, *Fourth Annual Review*, p. 210.

[73] Dreir et al, *Place Matters*, pp. 206-207.

[74] H. J. Whalen, *The Development of Local Government in New Brunswick*, Fredericton, 1963, p. 90.

Disentanglement initiatives were launched in several provinces over the past several decades (as described in Chapter 6) but with mixed results. A more significant impact on municipal operations came from the change in provincial and federal government policies following the abandonment of Keynesian economics during the economic downturn of the 1970s. Bradford refers to this era, still underway, as "cities in the shadow of neo-liberal space."[75] Instead of managing rapid growth and ensuring an equitable distribution of its benefits, the attention of governments turned to ways of restoring national competitiveness in a less forgiving international environment. By the 1990s, the federal government's preoccupation with deficit and debt reduction led to substantial cuts in spending and activity in urban areas, with respect to such matters as housing, immigration services and transportation. Provinces, in turn, took steps to shift responsibilities and costs to the local level. They also turned to amalgamations again, creating larger municipalities that were presumably expected to be able to handle better the downloaded responsibilities and costs.

Concluding Comments

The local government system was established in the 19th century, with characteristics appropriate to the agricultural economy and rural society of the time. It featured a very large number of relatively small municipalities, largely organized on the basis of a differentiation between urban and rural units. The system was predicated on the assumption that municipalities would provide a limited range of services, mainly services to property, and that a tax on property would be both an appropriate and adequate means of financing these services.

During the 20th century, Canada changed from a rural society to a highly urbanized one and from an agricultural base to industrial production and then to the knowledge-based economy of today. As these changes unfolded, population growth and overspill outstripped municipal boundaries. With this sprawl came increasing concerns about a growing concentration of poverty in inner city neighbourhoods, harmful intermunicipal competition, the high cost of servicing scattered, low density development, the loss of farmland and a variety

---

[75] Bradford, *Why Cities Matter*, p. 23.

of environmental concerns, and a weakened sense of community and citizenship.

It is important to remember that municipalities are hardly the sole cause (or even, arguably, the primary cause) of the problems increasingly concentrated in their places and they cannot, on their own, be expected to find ways to resolve these problems.[76] Yet the response to urban problems in many provinces was to blame them on a fragmented municipal structure and to encourage or impose municipal amalgamations as the solution. The next chapter attempts to provide a summary of the widespread amalgamation and restructuring activities. The following chapter (Chapter 5) will then assess the validity of these reforms and will provide further insights into the other approaches that might have been taken.

---

[76] *Ibid.*, p. 12.

Chapter 4
Local Government Restructuring

While the mass amalgamations that created enlarged cities in places such as Montreal, Quebec City, Toronto, and Ottawa have attracted most of the attention, there has been quite a variety of restructuring initiatives across Canada. The approach to reform, as between locally generated agreements and provincially imposed changes, also varies widely.

Introduction

As the previous chapter made clear, the pressures of growth and change brought many challenges, especially in relation to rapid urbanization and extensive sprawl. This chapter examines one particular response to these challenges, that of municipal reform and restructuring. Some other relevant responses occurred – such as new municipal legislation, initiatives to disentangle and realign provincial and local responsibilities, and limited changes affecting municipal revenue sources – and they are discussed in Chapters 6 and 7. Many other responses could have been introduced, as will be evident from discussions in the next chapter. But it was particularly through municipal amalgamation and restructuring that most provinces attempted to address perceived local problems and, as will become clear, dealing with just this one type of response makes for a full chapter all by itself.

The description of the reforms in this chapter must inevitably be quite brief,[1] and any major analysis of the reforms and their strengths and shortcomings is reserved for the following chapter. That chapter will also offer some examples of the many other responses that could have been introduced – responses that arguably would have been more effective than restructuring in addressing the areas of concern.

---

[1] Considerably more detail on local government reforms up to the end of the 1990s can be found in Chapters 5 and 6 of the previous edition of this book.

The reforms have featured the enlargement of municipalities (and school boards) through amalgamation, the creation or strengthening of upper tier regional municipalities, and the creation of intermunicipal joint servicing bodies. These reforms have been unfolding for at least 50 years and have altered the local government system in virtually every province, although to markedly varying degrees. A strict chronological outline of developments would involve jumping back and forth among provinces, and even returning to the same municipality more than once in those instances where there have been repeated reforms. Instead, developments will be described by province, followed by a summary of the results of the reforms. Since the examination of the historical foundations of local government in Chapter 2 essentially travelled east to west as did the settlement of the country, we will reverse course in this chapter and travel west to east. Following such a sequence will also serve to highlight the quite different approach to reform taken in the Western provinces.

British Columbia

British Columbia's approach to local government reform has been very pragmatic and directed to specific problems as perceived by the provincial government. To a large extent these problems were related to the absence of a municipal structure over much of the province. In 1966 only 2870 out of 266 000 square miles in British Columbia were within organized municipalities.[2] The remainder of the province, containing one-sixth of its population, received some services (mainly policing and roads) directly from the provincial government. It also received services from improvement districts, most of which provided at least water and fire protection. The organized municipalities also faced problems, with small, financially weak areas finding it difficult to provide necessary services and some municipalities suffering from sprawl and poor land use. The need for a joint approach to the provision of services in the Greater Vancouver area had already prompted the establishment of a number of regional special purpose agencies for such matters as drainage, water, health, planning and parks.

---

[2] The figures are from D. W. Barnes, "The System of Regional Districts in British Columbia," in Advisory Commission on Intergovernmental Relations, *A Look to the North: Canadian Regional Experience*, Washington, 1974, p. 110.

Creation of Regional Districts

The British Columbia government's response was to provide for the creation of regional districts that could administer functions over wide areas, including unincorporated territory. In marked contrast to the imposition of municipal reforms that will be evident in the experiences of a number of other provinces, British Columbia created boundaries for 30 districts covering the entire province, but left it up to the local governments within these areas to decide if they wanted to incorporate, and did not assign any functions to these districts initially.[3] The specific objectives of this initiative were not made clear but that may have been deliberate since one analysis contends that the province was especially interested in the potential of these regional districts in the two major urban centres of Vancouver and Victoria and used a strategy of "gentle imposition" to implement structures capable of becoming significant regional governments for these areas.[4]

Whatever the motives, 29 regional districts have been set up since the enabling legislation was passed in 1965, covering the province except the very lightly populated northwest corner. As a result of amalgamations in the Fraser Valley, there are currently 27 regional districts. They vary greatly in area and population, from the 2 million in Greater Vancouver to just over 4000 in the Central Coast. Each district is governed by a board of directors comprising councillors appointed by and from the councils of incorporated municipalities within its boundaries and representatives elected from the population of the unorganized areas. Differences in the numbers represented by the board members is reflected in a weighted voting system[5] that applies for budgetary matters and when decisions are being made about the provision of services to particular areas within a district. Only representatives from the affected areas vote in these latter instances.

[3] Robert L. Bish, "Evolutionary Alternatives for Metropolitan Areas: The Capital Region of British Columbia," *Canadian Journal of Regional Science*, Special Issue, Spring 2000, p. 75.

[4] Paul Tennant and David Zirnhelt, "Metropolitan Government in Vancouver: the strategy of gentle imposition," *Canadian Public Administration*, Spring 1973, pp. 124-138.

[5] For details on the voting system, see Robert L. Bish and Eric G. Clemens, *Local Government in British Columbia*, 3rd Edition, Richmond, Union of British Columbia Municipalities, 1999, pp. 46-47.

In the 40 years since their establishment, the province has mandated very few functions for the regional districts. They act on behalf of municipalities in dealings with the Municipal Finance Authority, from whom all municipalities must obtain their long term borrowing (except Vancouver, which nonetheless borrows extensively from the Authority on a voluntary basis). The regional districts are responsible for preparing comprehensive plans for managing solid waste, and while they no longer serve as hospital boards (since regional health authorities were set up in 1997), they are responsible for financing the local share of the capital costs of new hospitals.

In 1983, the districts lost their mandatory responsibility for regional planning that required compliance by local municipalities, but continued to undertake some planning on a voluntary basis. Regional planning powers were restored by the Growth Strategies Act of 1995, but on a voluntary basis. Four regional districts have adopted regional growth strategies, and a further two are close to adoption at the time of writing.[6] The districts also provide a wide range of other services to various combinations of municipalities within their jurisdiction – averaging, for example, 15 functions in 1989, most of them provided to only part of a district.[7] It is these widely varied servicing arrangements, determined by the local governments themselves that are seen by some as a particular strength of the regional district model.

The regional districts do not levy taxes. They send to each municipality a separate requisition for each service, which includes the appropriate share of the administrative costs – and the municipality must pay.[8] In the case of services provided to unincorporated areas, the requisition goes to the province, which in turn collects property taxes from inhabitants of those areas.

A Regional District Review Committee set up by the province in 1977 cited several problems with the regional districts, including:[9]

---

[6] Communication from Gary Paget, British Columbia Ministry of Community, Aboriginal, and Women's Services, June 23, 2003.

[7] Bish and Clemens, *Local Government in British Columbia*, p. 43.

[8] Allan O'Brien, *Municipal Consolidation in Canada and its Alternatives*, Toronto ICURR Press, May 1993, p. 53.

[9] Regional District Review Committee, *Report of the Committee*, Victoria, Ministry of Municipal Affairs and Housing, 1978.

> public concerns that the districts were inaccessible, dictatorial, and a secretive organization;
> insufficient effort by the districts to explain their responsibilities and to encourage public involvement; and
> heavy-handed treatment of the districts by the provincial government.

Provincial interventions continued during the 1980s, including the previously cited 1983 legislation removing the right of regional districts to plan for their regions as a whole, and 1985 legislation centralizing the transit function at the provincial level. According to Oberlander and Smith,[10] the loss of the planning function resulted from continuing conflict between the Greater Vancouver Regional District (GVRD) and the provincial government, especially after the Social Credit party returned to power and showed a willingness to release land from agricultural designation so that it could be developed.

The legislation governing the regional districts was revised in 1989. For the first time the local services that potentially fall within regional district jurisdiction were listed in the statute. Regional districts were authorized to make such service decisions by by-law, rather than having to go through the province to revise letters patent, as had formerly been the case.[11]

A further Regional District Review was carried out in 1999, and identified only limited problems relating to the need for a better balance between voting strength and financial contributions with respect to service delivery and the lack of public awareness of the regional districts and how they functioned.[12] The following year, the province passed Bill 14, the Local Government Statutes Amendment Act, 2000, which provided for more flexible service arrangements for

---

[10] H. Peter Oberlander and Patrick J. Smith, "Governing Metropolitan Vancouver," in Donald Rothblatt and Andrew Sancton (eds.), *Metropolitan Governance: American/Canadian Intergovernmental Perspectives*, Berkeley, Institute of Governmental Studies Press, 1993, pp. 361-363.

[11] O'Brien, *Municipal Consolidation*, p. 52.

[12] Robert L. Bish, *Regional District Review – 1999: Issues and Interjurisdictional Comparisons*, prepared for the Ministry of Municipal Affairs, published by the Local Government Institute, University of Victoria and available at http:/web.uvic.ca/lgi_pub.htm.

the regional districts and new processes for reviewing the terms and conditions of existing service arrangements.[13]

It is difficult to assess the overall impact of the regional district initiative. Much of the analysis has focused on the GVRD, but Bish contends that it is in some respects the least important of the districts, because many of its member municipalities are sizeable and have pursued only limited sharing of services.[14] It is in the less populated areas of the province that the districts have played an important role, by providing a flexible structure for addressing servicing needs in unorganized areas and across municipal boundaries. Existing municipal units are allowed to continue under this structure, thereby contributing to the preservation of an existing sense of community, allowing for diversity within the regional area, and helping to ensure accessibility and responsiveness in the municipal system.[15] At the same time, the services provided by the regional districts have promoted the common interests of area municipalities, and the fact that these regional services have been assigned by the area municipalities means that they are determining their common interests rather than having this definition imposed from above. On the other hand, it appears that the structure of the regional districts and the indirect election of a portion of the board members has contributed to the very limited public discussion of board activities and an insulated decision making process.

Smith has expressed concern about the extra responsibilities being given to the regional districts, such as the shift of public transit from the province to the Greater Vancouver area, effective April 1, 1999. He and Stewart conclude[16] that a municipal accountability crisis is looming, in part because of the way that the regional boards are

---

[13] A number of pamphlets describing these changes are available at the Ministry's web site at www.mcaws.gov.bc.ca/lgd/advice_index.htm#regional, accessed April 22, 2003.

[14] Communication from Robert Bish, June 17, 2003.

[15] This point and the subsequent ones in this paragraph are based on Lionel D. Feldman Consulting Ltd. and the Institute of Local Government, Queen's University, *Evaluation of Alternative Structures and a Proposal for Local Governance in the Edmonton Region*, January 1980, especially pp. 37-42.

[16] Patrick J. Smith and Kennedy Stewart, *Making Accountability Work in British Columbia*, Report for the Ministry of Municipal Affairs and Housing, June 1998.

chosen, and they call for direct election of a Greater Vancouver authority to replace the GVRD. Artibise also believes that reform of the GVRD is necessary. He argues that its mandate is too limited, since it is delegated to the district by member municipalities and "changes with the fortunes of the regional interest at the local ballot box."[17] Because all of the board members are part time regional politicians, no one speaks out forcefully and consistently for the region and, as a result, the staff of the GVRD have too much influence. Artibise also points to what he terms a complex and confusing system of weighted voting.

On the other hand, Bish concludes that the present governing arrangements are beneficial in that they do not engender competition and rivalry between elected councillors at the local and regional levels. This problem was very much in evidence in Ontario when it introduced directly elected upper tier councils within a number of its regional government systems. He also points out that only a small percentage of services are provided across the whole area of a district. As a result, it is not inappropriate to have a structure that gives priority to local citizens' interests rather than some concept of a regional interest.[18]

The regional district model is now the most enduring of the forms of restructuring introduced in Canada, approaching 40 years in existence. As will be discussed more in the next chapter, it also provides a striking contrast to the municipal consolidations or mergers that have been so prevalent in other parts of the country.

Before leaving British Columbia, it should be noted that some municipal restructuring has been occurring as a result of local initiatives. Some 35 municipalities were the subject of a substantial municipal restructuring between 1985 and 2000, including the amalgamation of the districts of Abbotsford and Matsqui to form the city of Abbotsford in 1995.[19]

---

[17] Alan F. J. Artibise, *Regional Governance Without Regional Government*, background report prepared prepared for the Regional Municipality of Ottawa-Carleton, April 1998, p. 23.

[18] Robert L. Bish, *Accommodating Multiple Boundaries for Local Services: British Columbia's Local Governance System*, paper presented at Indiana University, Bloomington, October 21, 2002, p. 16.

[19] For an analysis of this amalgamation and four others, see Igor Vojnovic, *Municipal Consolidation in the 1990s: An Analysis of Five Canadian Municipalities*, Toronto, ICURR Press, 1997.

Alberta

The Alberta government has taken an approach similar to that of British Columbia, leaving restructuring largely to the decision of the local governments. The rapid population increase that accompanied the development of the petroleum industry in the period after World War Two led to a number of changes in municipal boundaries in the Calgary and Edmonton areas, as discussed first. The province began to encourage the notion of amalgamation more actively in the mid-1990s, but the choice was still left to the local level, and few changes resulted. Local needs have been addressed mainly by joint servicing arrangements and intermunicipal collaboration. In addition, municipalities were given broader and more flexible governing powers through pioneering Alberta municipal legislation discussed in Chapter 6.

The Calgary and Edmonton Areas

A Royal Commission recommended in 1956 that the boundaries of Edmonton and Calgary be enlarged to encompass their full metropolitan areas,[20] but no action was taken on this proposal. Instead, there were frequent annexations of adjacent territory (notably some 19 separate annexations involving Edmonton between 1947 and 1980), usually at the initiative of landowners and developers wishing an extension of services. But his piece-meal approach proved frustrating for both cities. Concern arose when the Alberta government, between 1974 and 1976, unilaterally imposed restricted development areas (RDAs) around both cities. While intended as utilities and transportation corridors, the RDAs were seen as barriers to future expansion.

Edmonton's response took the form of a March 1979 application to the Local Authorities Board for a massive annexation, including the City of St. Albert and the entire county of Strathcona (an application that would add some 467 000 acres to the city's existing 80 000). After complex and expensive Board hearings that lasted almost a year, the outcome was a compromise solution. While the Board approved a very large expansion of Edmonton's boundaries, the Cabinet revised this order and gave the city 86 000 acres of land but

---

[20] *Report of the Royal Commission on the Metropolitan Development of Calgary and Edmonton* (McNally Commission), Edmonton, Queen's Printer, 1956.

not its dormitory suburbs. According to Feldman, there weren't really any winners or losers and none of the protagonists was severely harmed. "Edmonton got land on which to expand, but possibly not the lands and assessment it really wanted. St. Albert ... lost no territory. Strathcona saw 54 000 acres ... go to Edmonton."[21]

Attempting to reform municipal structures this way presents a number of problems besides the extensive cost involved. It is at best a piecemeal, fragmented approach that does not consider the overall needs of the entire urban area, but instead focuses on particular territories affected by proposed annexations, and in an invariably confrontational atmosphere. Moreover, the relentless pace of urban sprawl makes frequent annexations necessary in an attempt to keep up. Lightbody notes that as a result of the aggressive annexation efforts of Calgary it still has over 90% of its regional population within its boundaries, whereas Edmonton finds itself ringed by four cities and four urbanizing rural municipalities.[22] "For the past 20 years Edmonton has been involved in never-ending annexation and amalgamation battles with its surrounding municipalities."[23]

There have been two initiatives over the past decade designed to provide some form of broader, regional jurisdiction that could deal with intermunicipal issues affecting the Edmonton area. The Alberta Capital Region Forum was created in March 1995, comprising 14 municipalities and relying on voluntary funding, especially from Edmonton. One analysis found that during its short life the Forum was unsuccessful either in land use planning or in developing any coherent regional economic strategy.[24] It was replaced at the beginning of 1999 by the Alberta Capital Regional Alliance, comprising the City of Edmonton and 19 surrounding communities.

At that time, the Minister of Municipal Affairs also set up a formal review of municipal operations in the Edmonton census metropolitan area. The result was the Alberta Capital Region Governance

---

[21] Lionel Feldman, "Tribunals, Politics and the Public Interest: The Edmonton Annexation Case – a Response," *Canadian Public Policy*, Summer 1982, p. 371.

[22] James Lightbody, *The Comparative Costs of Governing Alberta's Metropolitan Areas*, Edmonton, Western Centre for Ecnomic Research, Information Bulletin Number 48, January 1998, p. 4.

[23] Susan McFarlane, *Building Better Cities: Regional Cooperation in Western Canada*, Canada West Foundation, October 2001, p. 13.

[24] *Ibid.*, p. 14.

Review report, released in February 2002. It made a number of recommendations for improving cooperation and sharing services across the area. However, the province rejected its call for a new body (the Greater Edmonton Partnership) to which all area municipalities would have to belong. For now at least, it appears that progress will depend upon the voluntary cooperation of the municipalities in the area. Progress may be slow in that regard, especially since many of the participating municipalities view with suspicion joint servicing proposals from Edmonton. A case in point is Edmonton's suggestion that it provide policing, firefighting, and ambulance service for the entire metro area, in return for a sharing of the tax revenues from the industries located in surrounding municipalities. Those municipalities fear that sharing services will eventually lead to amalgamation and the loss of their identity.[25]

Intermunicipal Agencies and Agreements

Reliance on joint service agreements and agencies has long been a prominent feature of Alberta local government. There is also a Calgary Regional Partnership comprising representatives from 13 municipalities, including the city of Calgary, and promoting improved service delivery through intermunicipal initiatives. There have also been a number of intermunicipal agencies and boards, as illustrated next.

Regional planning commissions were originally authorized in 1929, although the first of them (in the Edmonton area) wasn't established until 1950. Eventually 10 commissions were set up, covering 70% of the area of the province.[26] Their most important function was to prepare a regional plan with which the plans of all member municipalities were expected to conform. The commissions were governed by elected representatives from the councils of the member municipalities. While the larger municipalities were given multiple votes, they were still underrepresented on these commissions, and this provided a source of ongoing friction.[27] The commissions were abolished by the province in 1994, supposedly as an economy measure. While the local

---

[25] Roy Cook, "Mayor's idea to share services doesn't fly," *Edmonton Journal*, February 13, 2003.

[26] O'Brien, *Municipal Consolidation*, p. 60.

[27] Jack Masson, with Edward LeSage Jr., *Alberta's Local Governments: Politics and Democracy*, Edmonton, University of Alberta Press, 1994, p. 422.

level has gained more responsibility for planning as a result, there is now a lack of broader regional planning except where municipalities collaborate on intermunicipal plans.[28]

Another intermunicipal agency in Alberta is the regional services commission, authorized by 1981 legislation to provide water, sanitary and storm sewerage, and waste management services (or any of them) with respect to more than one municipality. There are now 41 of these commissions,[29] governed by representatives from the councils of the member municipalities.

Regional service delivery is also evident with respect to health and social services programs. Alberta established 17 regional health authorities (RHAs) in 1994, with responsibility for hospitals, continuing care, community health services, and public health programs. There were between 7 and 16 members on each board, with two-thirds of them being elected.[30] The 17 health regions were amalgamated into 7 effective April 2003, and mental health services are being integrated into the operations of the new health authorities, whose boards no longer include elected members. There were also 18 regional Child and Family Services Authorities established in 1994 (including one authority covering the 8 Métis Settlements in Alberta). Of all Western provinces, Alberta has gone the farthest in devolving decision making to regional authorities, raising questions about the possible overlap of responsibilities between local governments and these regional authorities and about the extent to which these authorities are becoming political actors in their own right.[31]

Yet another example of the intermunicipal activity in Alberta is found in the more than 500 agreements through which

---

[28] Edward C. LeSage, *Municipal Reform in Alberta: A Review of Statutory, Financial and Structural Changes Over the Past Decade*, paper presented at the Canadian Political Science Association annual meeting, Quebec City, May 28, 2001. Much of this paper has been incorporated into the Alberta chapter of Joseph Garcea and Edward LeSage (eds.), *Municipal Reforms in Canada: Dynamics, Dimensions, Determinants*, forthcoming publication.

[29] According to information at the Alberta Municipal Affairs web site www.gov.ab.ca/ma, accessed August 3, 2003.

[30] Evan Jones and Susan McFarlane, *Regional Approaches to Services in the West: Health, Social Services and Education*, Canada West Foundation, February 2002, p. 3.

[31] *Ibid.*, p. 10.

municipalities purchase and sell municipal services to each other. The services most commonly subject to these arrangements are fire protection, ambulance service, recreation facilities, garbage disposal, libraries, family and community support services, airports, roads, and disaster services.[32]

Saskatchewan

Municipal restructuring has been limited in Saskatchewan, mainly taking the form of small scale annexations. According to O'Brien, as urban places have grown, they have usually been able to annex land required for urban development, partly because rural municipalities haven't approved of suburban fringe development within their boundaries. Writing in 1993, he notes that there had been 315 annexation and incorporation initiatives in Saskatchewan since 1979, of which 280 were approved, and that 12 of these were annexations to Regina and Saskatoon.[33] As a result, these two single tier cities cover, respectively, 94% and 87% of their census metropolitan areas.[34] Intermunicipal agreements have also been common in Saskatchewan, especially for fire protection and road maintenance, and single purpose intermunicipal agencies are used for economic development, planning, and water.

The provincial government introduced legislation in 1996 to provide for service district boards modeled on British Columbia's regional districts and the regional service commissions in Alberta. No action was taken on this matter in the face of strong local opposition. However, there is extensive regionalization in the province, including health boards, regional tourism boards, and regional agriculture and development boards. Regional cooperation in the Saskatoon area is facilitated by the Saskatoon District Planning Commission and the Saskatoon Regional Economic Development Authority. There is also a Regional Economic Development Authority for the Regina area.[35]

---

[32] O'Brien, *Municipal Consolidation*, p. 60.

[33] *Ibid.*, p. 58.

[34] Data from the 2001 Census, as summarized on StatsCan Community Profiles page, found at www12.statcan.ca/English/profil01/PlaceSearchForm1.cfm, accessed May 12, 2003.

[35] McFarlane, *Building Better Cities*, pp. 12-13.

The provincial government established a *Task Force on Municipal Legislative Renewal* in 1998, and its interim report contemplated a dramatic reduction in the number of municipalities from 1000 to about 125. The local response was very negative, highlighted by referendums held in 145 rural municipalities in which 98% of participants opposed forced amalgamations.[36] The final report of the task force[37] emphasized that it had not proposed forced amalgamations in its interim report but had envisaged a continuum with voluntary amalgamation at one end where local preference would be quite extensive and mandated amalgamation at the other end where local preference would be relatively limited. No action was taken on the amalgamation recommendations, but the Municipal-Provincial Roundtable and Northern Municipal Roundtable were formed in 2000, and their deliberations identified a number of financial and legislative impediments to voluntary municipal restructuring in Saskatchewan, which were removed in legislation passed in 2001.[38]

Saskatchewan continues to function with a large number of very small municipalities. The northern half of the province faces particularly pressing problems.[39] It contains approximately 60 communities, some under municipal governments and some under First Nation governments. There is a need for improved municipal infrastructure and community services but northern municipalities lack the financial resources and professional staff to respond effectively.

Manitoba

The opportunity for a comprehensive reform of the overall system of local government in Manitoba was presented by a Royal Commission report in 1964. It offered a new delineation of provincial and municipal responsibilities, fairly similar to the services to people versus services

---

[36] Saskatchewan Association of Rural Municipalities, *News Release*, May 2, 2000.

[37] Task Force on Municipal Legislative Renewal, *Municipal Governance for Saskatchewan in the 21st Century, Options 2000: A Framework for Municipal Renewal – Summary of Final Report*, August 2000, p. 11.

[38] McFarlane, *Building Better Cities*, p. 12.

[39] Task Force on Municipal Legislative Renewal, *Municipal Governance*, p. 64.

to property distinction used in New Brunswick and discussed later in this chapter. The report also called for the division of Manitoba into 11 administrative regions, each governed by councillors from municipalities within the region, and the amalgamation of the existing 106 municipalities in Manitoba to form 40 or 50 units.[40]

In the face of strong opposition to the creation of larger municipal units, the province moved instead to formalize a system of single purpose districts for joint municipal services.[41] The system involved a combination of both intermunicipal and provincial-municipal services for rural residents on a more affordable basis than a single municipality could deliver. Examples included planning districts, conservation districts, regional development corporations, community round tables, weed control districts, veterinary services districts, and a recreational opportunities program.

The municipal government structure outside of Winnipeg was reviewed again in the early 1990s, through a process of public consultations conducted by a panel established by the Minister of Rural Development. A major issue identified was the need for better coordination in service delivery, given that there were nearly 300 special purpose bodies along with over 200 municipalities beyond the boundaries of Winnipeg – most of them very small and financially weak.[42] However, with the power base of the ruling Conservative party largely in rural Manitoba, the provincial government had every reason to "tread lightly."[43] Accordingly, the panel's report avoided any suggestion that amalgamations would be mandated, leaving the desired coordination of services to be achieved through local initiative.

Restructuring in the Winnipeg Area

Local government reform activities in Manitoba have focused on Winnipeg, which, as the provincial capital and the centre for over half

---

[40] *Report of the Manitoba Royal Commission on Local Government Organization and Finance* (Michener Report), Winnipeg, Queen's Printer, 1964.

[41] This section is based on O'Brien, *Municipal Consolidation*, p. 31.

[42] Province of Manitoba, *Final Report: Meeting the Challenges of Local Government*, 1995, pp. vi-vii.

[43] Mark Piel and Christopher Leo, "Governing Manitoba's Communities: Legislative Reform in the 1990s and Beyond," in Garcea and LeSage, *Municipal Reforms in Canada*.

of the population and three-quarters of the economic activity, understandably dominates the local government scene. Population growth after the Second World War brought the usual urban problems. Expenditures soared, notably in education, while the revenues were distributed unevenly and there were wide variations in property assessment. There was inadequate sewage disposal for the area and water rationing became common. A number of intermunicipal special purpose bodies operated in the Greater Winnipeg Area and, while they enjoyed some success, their very existence was seen as evidence of the need for area-wide government.

A Greater Winnipeg Investigating Commission report in 1959 called for the establishment of a two tier system of metropolitan government. Apparently the Commission was strongly influenced by the Metropolitan Toronto system and had frequently consulted with its chair, Fred Gardiner.[44] However, the reform introduced by the province in 1960 was more modest than the Commission's recommendations and differed from Toronto in significant respects.

Metropolitan Winnipeg

The two tier system established in 1960 had 10 municipalities within the jurisdiction of the new Metropolitan Winnipeg metropolitan government and 9 more partly within and partly in the outlying "additional zone" over which Metro Winnipeg had planning authority. The metro government was given full authority over all planning, zoning, and issuing of permits as well as such operating functions as assessment, civil defence, flood protection, sewage disposal, and water (excluding local distribution). Many responsibilities that had previously been exercised by separate special purpose bodies were vested directly in the metro council.

The 10 members of the metropolitan council were directly elected from special pie-shaped districts that included both central and suburban areas. Moreover, metro councillors could not hold local office. It was hoped that this type of district and method of representation would encourage an area-wide perspective. This it did, but almost too successfully! The metro council contained a strong core of metro supporters and with more specific, parochial demands being

---

[44] T. Axworthy, "Winnipeg Unicity," in Advisory Commission on Intergovernmental Relations, *A Look to the North*, p. 90.

directed at lower tier councils, they were able to take the broader view. However, in their enthusiasm they were rather aggressive in their initiatives and insufficiently sensitive to the concerns of local councils. Adding to the problems was the extent of opposition to the new metro system. While some negative reaction had been expected, "[W]hat occurred instead was a virtual municipal insurrection, an assault on metro far exceeding anyone's expectations. During its ten year history, but especially in 1961-65, metro lived under a state of siege."[45]

The attack on the metro system was led by Stephen Juba, the long time mayor of Winnipeg, and was "conducted without restraint or let-up in the mayor's characteristically strident, affectively charged, assaultive style.[46] Attacks on the system subsided somewhat after 1965 when the Premier of the province reaffirmed his support for it. The election of an NDP government in 1969, however, led to a whole new approach to the governing of the Winnipeg area.

Winnipeg Unicity

As its name implies, Unicity replaced the two tier metro system with one enlarged city government. But much more than amalgamation of municipalities was involved, and the administrative centralization for efficiency in service delivery was to be offset by various provisions for political decentralization. In sharp contrast to most other reform initiatives, then and now, Unicity was not created with the objective of reducing governments or cutting costs; it was intended to increase the capacity of municipal government to control and shape urban development and to promote greater social and economic equality.[47]

The representative role of local government and the importance of citizen access and participation was a central feature of the new system, reflected in the provision for an unusually large council of 50 members (plus the mayor), each elected from a separate ward. In addition, the Unicity legislation established 13 community councils, each covering a number of wards and consisting of the

[45] Harold Kaplan, *Reform, Planning and City Politics: Montreal, Winnipeg, Toronto*, Toronto, University of Toronto Press, 1982, p. 554.

[46] *Ibid.*, p. 562.

[47] Andrew Sancton, "Why Unicity Matters: An Outsider's View," in Nancy Klos (ed.), *The State of Unicity – 25 Years Later*, Winnipeg, Institute of Urban Studies, 1998, p. 4.

councillors from these wards. These committees were intended to maintain close two-way communications between Unicity and its residents and to have responsibility for preparing budgets for services with a local orientation (and variation). To advise and assist each committee, the legislation also provided for the election of a resident advisory group (RAG). These arrangements signified the intention "to weaken the alliance between public officials and land-based business by promoting the formation of alternative governing coalitions."[48]

A second significant feature of the new system was the attempt to build in the elements of the parliamentary model of government, particularly in terms of a separate executive responsible for providing leadership and answering to the elected council. A key provision of this model, proposed in the White Paper but deleted from the legislation, was the stipulation that the mayor be chosen by and from the members of council. Through this process, mayors could provide leadership on council because of majority support. At the same time, they would remain in this position only so long as they retained the confidence of the councillors. It was envisaged that the members of the executive committee would be chosen in the same way and, with the mayor as chair, this body would be akin to the cabinet in the parliamentary system. An important element of this system, of course, was the existence of organized political parties. Some form of political party activity had been evident in Winnipeg since 1919, but it was hoped that a more formalized party system would evolve to complement the new structure.

Unfortunately, the actual performance of Unicity has been rather disappointing – perhaps inevitably so, given the innovative and ambitious objectives that had been initially set for the system. A Committee of Review appointed in 1975 found that a number of the primary objectives of the new structure had not been realized. It laid much of the blame on the fact that the mayor was directly elected rather than chosen from council (as originally intended), thereby removing the focus of leadership and accountability central to the parliamentary model. This lack of strong political leadership was especially significant given the large size of the council and the potentially fragmented outlook inherent in election by ward. As a result, considerable attention was directed to the securing of public services

---

[48] Paul G. Thomas, "Diagnosing the Health of Civic Democracy: 25 Years of Citizen Involvement With City Hall," in Klos, *The State of Unicity*, p. 47.

for particular wards – often taking the form of a city/suburbs division, rather than the establishment of overall policies for the Winnipeg area. After reviewing the new system, Plunkett and Brownstone concluded that "city policy making has not been altered drastically, and that is has only been improved slightly from what it seems likely to have been if the former structure had remained unchanged.[49]

In June 1977 the Manitoba government adopted a number of amendments to the Unicity structure but, ironically, these changes did little to resolve the weaknesses identified and, in some cases, intensified them. The 1975 Committee of Review had recommended that the mayor be elected from within the council and that the mayor appoint the chairs of the standing committees. These chairs and certain other specified members would constitute the executive and would be given the powers necessary to function as a cabinet. The Committee further recommended that the mayor and executive committee should be confirmed or replaced in their positions annually by a vote of council and that a chief critic should also be elected annually by councillors not voting for the mayor. While it could not legislate a party system, the Committee expressed the hope and conviction that such a system would evolve "under the influence of the parliamentary characteristics of our model."

Instead, however, the revised legislation removed the mayor from the board of commissioners, and he was also replaced on the executive policy committee by a council-elected chair. These changes, together with the continuation of direct election of the mayor, seemed intended to reduce the position to the largely ceremonial role found in most Canadian municipalities. A further change saw the reduction in the size of council from 50 to 29. The number of community commit-tees (12 since 1974) was reduced to 6 and their vague and limited powers were further reduced. They dealt only with libraries, parks and recreation, and some planning functions,[50] a reflection of the growing trend toward centralization in program design and service delivery. Moreover, with greatly increased areas and with populations of about 100 000, the community councils and RAGs lost the close contact and familiarity with local issues which had been their main (and just about

---

[49] M. Brownstone and T. J. Plunkett, *Metropolitan Winnipeg: Politics and Reform of Local Government*, Berkeley, University of California Press, 1983, p. 173.

[50] Feldman Consulting Ltd., *Evaluation of Alternative Structures*, p. 67.

only) strength. Overall, the changes made in 1977 "essentially kept a weak-mayor political system, but strengthened the professional administration through centralizing power in their hands at the expense of the Community Committees and the Standing Committees."[51]

Another review committee was appointed in 1984 and its 1986 report recommended strengthening the position of mayor and increasing the planning powers of the community committees. Once again, however, the government's response[52] seemed designed to prevent the mayor from exercising the kind of strong leadership intended. While it did agree to increase the planning powers of the community councils, the potential of this change was limited by the fact that no additional financial resources were allocated to the councils.

The NDP government was replaced by the Conservatives at the end of the 1980s, and it introduced legislation in 1992 that reduced the Unicity council from 29 to 15 members. This change was supposed to reduce parochialism and encourage the council to take a broader, city-wide approach to planning. It was also expected to streamline and speed up the decision making process. The result was to be a smaller and more cohesive group to manage city hall.[53] But Gerecke and Reid argue that this change also meant that there were now only three members from the inner city, leaving the old city of Winnipeg as "nothing more than three wards on the rump of a suburban council."[54]

Other changes in the 1992 legislation saw the community committees further reduced in number from six to five, and the RAGs abolished outright. The bold experiment in citizen participation launched in 1972 was all but gone 20 years later!

Much urban-related development has been taking place beyond the Unicity boundaries in recent years. Over the period from 1971 to 1991, Unicity's population increased a modest 15.2%, while the

[51] Greg Selinger, "Urban Governance for the Twenty-First Century: What the Unicity Experience Tells Us," in Klos, *The State of Unicity*, p. 90.

[52] Ministry of Urban Affairs, *Discussion Paper*, "Strengthening Local Government in Winnipeg: Proposals for Changes to the City of Winnipeg Act," February 27, 1987.

[53] O'Brien, *Municipal Consolidation*, pp. 31-32.

[54] Kent Gerecke and Barton Reid, "The Failure of Urban Government: The Case of Winnipeg," in Henri Lustiger-Thaler (ed.), *Political Arrangements: Power and the City*, Montreal, Black Rose Books, 1992, p. 127.

population in the surrounding municipalities increased by 69.4%.[55] Between 1991 and 1996, the city's population growth was 0.3%, while municipalities bordering Winnipeg grew at a rate of more than 10% and even more than 20% in some instances.[56]

In 1989 the Manitoba government established what became known as the Capital Region Committee, comprising three provincial ministers and the heads of council for Winnipeg and 15 surrounding municipalities. In the early years, the committee's limited meetings focused mainly on developing a strategy for sustainable development.[57] Since each municipality was given one member on the committee, this meant that Winnipeg had the same representation as the other 15 municipalities that averaged 5000 in population. Moreover, most of the fringe municipalities had an incentive to build their tax revenues through low density urban development. Not surprisingly, the committee made little progress in tackling urban sprawl.[58]

In June 1998, the Manitoba government announced the creation of an independent Capital Region Panel "to provide an avenue for better cooperation and understanding between Winnipeg and its neighbours." According to the announcement, "a more coordinated approach in areas such as land use planning or delivery of services will benefit all concerned."[59] The Panel's final report acknowledged that there was little support for further amalgamations in the Winnipeg area, but that some form of regional association was desirable to address the growth and development now occurring beyond the boundaries of Unicity.

In January 2001 the province introduced a 10 point action plan for improved planning of Manitoba's capital region. This plan included the appointment of a Regional Planning Advisory Committee (RPAC) to provide advice on regional planning issues and to stimulate public

---

[55] Institute of Urban Studies, University of Winnipeg, *Prairie Urban Report*, Issue No. 1, Volume 1, May 1996.

[56] Richard Lennon and Christopher Leo, *Stopping the Sprawl: How Winnipeg Could Benefit from Metropolitan Growth Strategies for a Slow-Growth Region*, Canadian Centre for Policy Alternatives, January 2001, p. 9.

[57] Andrew Sancton, *Governing Canada's City Regions: Adapting Form to Function*, Montreal, Institute for Research on Public Policy, 1994, pp. 27-28.

[58] Piel and Leo, "Governing Manitoba's Communities."

[59] Manitoba Government News Release. June 17, 1998.

discussion and participation in the process.[60] The Committee's interim report in April 2002 emphasizes that capital region municipalities should act in unison to attract business opportunities from outside the province and should not compete excessively or inappropriately for economic advantages. While sharing of services and perhaps even taxes are under consideration, the committee is unlikely to recommend amalgamations or a new government over the capital region. The province has shown no willingness to introduce either of these measures in the absence of local support for them – which does not exist.

Table 4.1 Restructuring Highlights – Western Provinces	
British Columbia	Upper tier regional districts
Alberta	Calgary and Edmonton annexations Intermunicipal board in Edmonton area (Capital Region Forum and now Capital Regional Alliance) Various regional bodies re planning, hard services, social services
Saskatchewan	Many small scale annexations Intermunicipal agencies for economic development, water, planning
Manitoba	Two tier Metropolitan Winnipeg system Winnipeg Unicity through amalgamation of all municipalities Intermunicipal board in Winnipeg area (Capital Region Committee and now Capital Region Panel)

Ontario

The experiences in Ontario provide a marked contrast to those of Western Canada. Municipal restructuring began 50 years ago with the establishment of the Municipality of Metropolitan Toronto, continued with the creation of a series of two tier regional government systems in the 1960s and early 1970s, and then resumed with a vengeance over the past decade during which the number of municipalities was almost cut in half. Not only has the restructuring been much more widespread, but also it has been largely imposed or induced by the provincial government.

---

[60] Information on this initiative and a variety of background reports is available at the capital region web site at www.gov.mb.ca/ia/capreg/reports, accessed May 12. 2003.

Metropolitan Toronto

With the post-war "population explosion," the rapid growth of a number of municipalities surrounding the city of Toronto produced serious servicing difficulties. Most pressing were the problems of water supply and sewage treatment facilities, arising from the fact that only 6 of the 13 municipalities involved had direct physical access to Lake Ontario. Arterial road development could not keep pace with the rapidly increasing volume of traffic. Public transportation and the existing highway network were poorly integrated. There was a desperate need for new schools. Many of the outlying municipalities were particularly ill-equipped to finance these service demands since, as dormitory suburbs, they lacked industrial assessment to help relieve the tax burden on the residential taxpayer.

The city of Toronto also faced serious economic and social problems, with a large backlog of public works because of the disruption of the depression and war years, and a greatly increased demand for welfare services. There was growing traffic congestion because of the extent of commuter population, and urban renewal and redevelopment needs were increasingly obvious. With each municipality seeking capital funds on its own credit, borrowing by the burgeoning suburbs became more and more difficult as interest rates rose.

In response to these problems, a federated form of government embracing the city of Toronto and the 12 surrounding municipalities was introduced, effective January 1, 1953. As the lower tier in a two tier structure, these 13 municipalities retained their existing boundaries and continued to exercise a wide range of responsibilities. In addition, an upper tier unit, the municipality of Metropolitan Toronto, was established with the responsibility for such major functions as assessment, debenture borrowing, water supply and trunk mains, sewage treatment works and trunk sewers, and designated metropolitan roads. A number of responsibilities were also to be shared between the two levels of government. The fact that the metropolitan council was indirectly elected, that is, composed of individuals elected initially to designated positions on the lower tier councils, made the new structure similar to Ontario's century-old county system. The major differences were the inclusion of the city in the metropolitan system and the much stronger powers given to the upper tier council.

In its early years, Metropolitan Toronto was substantially successful in combating the servicing problems facing the member municipalities, particularly as regards sewers, water supply, education, and general financial stability. To a considerable extent, these early successes have been attributed to the forceful, skilled leadership of the first chair of the Metro council, Fred Gardiner, who held this position from 1953 to 1961. Gardiner's personal philosophy was clearly consistent with the founding objectives of the new metropolitan system, to develop the servicing infrastructure needed to accommodate the growth pressures.

But Colton notes that there were concerns even before Gardiner retired.[61] Yes, there was a massive expansion of housing, but primarily in the form of high-rise apartment construction that was accompanied by an increasing concentration of power in the development industry. Toronto enjoyed a boom in downtown development but fears mounted about an excessive growth mentality and the disruption of established neighbourhoods – as reflected in the activism of citizens and citizen groups in the 1960s. This activism was also reflected in a growing anti-expressway sentiment culminating in the "Stop-Spadina" (expressway) movement.

Quite apart from these changing public attitudes, Kaplan offers some interesting explanations for the decline in Metro Toronto's momentum after the first few years.[62] He emphasizes the significance of the indirect election of Metro councillors, noting that they stood, succeeded, or failed largely on the basis of their records in their lower tier council, only referring to Metro when it was politically expedient to blame it for not delivering enough for the local municipality in question. Ironically, according to Kaplan, it was this parochialism of councillors that helped to explain Metro Toronto's initiatives and successes in the early years. Gardiner astutely avoided issues that would threaten local municipalities, and councillors were largely indifferent to everything else and prepared to accept Gardiner's persuasive leadership. However, when Metro turned to the more complex issues of the 1960s, especially under the less forceful chairs who succeeded Gardiner, the limitations of this passive support became increasingly apparent. Noting that Metro Toronto's main achievements were between 1953 and 1957, Kaplan contends that "in retrospect, the early burst of activity was the aberration and the

---

[61] Timothy J. Colton, *Big Daddy*, Toronto, University of Toronto Press, 1980, pp. 177-178.

[62] Kaplan, *Reform, Planning and City Politics*, pp. 685-690.

subsequent prolonged retreat a more accurate expression of the system's character."[63]

A Royal Commission was established in 1953 to examine Metro's first decade. Its 1965 report[64] endorsed continuation of the two tier system. The main change, introduced effective January 1, 1967, was a consolidation of the original 13 municipalities at the lower tier into 6. In addition, the Metro council was increased to 32 members, with 20 of these coming from the 5 suburban municipalities in recognition of their much greater population growth since the system was established. A few responsibilities, notably waste disposal and social assistance, were transferred from the lower tier municipalities to Metro Toronto, continuing a trend that had been evident throughout the 1950s. As Kaplan observed, however, there was little in these reforms to revive Metro.[65] While the suburban municipalities now enjoyed a majority position, they had no regional aspirations on which to use their power. They had received the necessary expansion of their basic services during the first decade. Now it was the city of Toronto that needed Metro more – to help finance the renewal of aging facilities. But Kaplan concludes that with a complacent suburban majority, Metro Toronto was even less inclined to blaze new trails.

Major changes in the election of the Metro council were introduced at the time of the 1988 municipal elections. While the mayors of the 6 lower tier municipalities continued to serve as members, the remaining 28 were directly elected, and did not hold seats on the lower tier councils. Provision was also made for the chair of Metro to be chosen by the Metro council from among the directly elected members. These changes appeared to reflect a belated concern by the Ontario government for the representative role of municipal government and its accountability and responsiveness.

By this time, the area of urban development that Metropolitan Toronto had been established to embrace and to stimulate had long since expanded beyond its boundaries. Just as the population growth of the city of Toronto failed to keep pace with that of the suburban lower tier municipalities within Metro, so too did Metro itself fall behind the rapid pace of growth of areas adjacent to it. It found itself "hemmed

---

[63] *Ibid.*, p. 694.

[64] *Report of the Royal Commission on Metropolitan Toronto* (H. Carl Goldenberg, Commissioner), Toronto, Queen's Printer, 1965.

[65] Kaplan, *Reform, Planning and City Politics*, p. 697.

in" on all sides by four regional governments (discussed below) and by Lake Ontario. Until 1971 Metro Toronto absorbed the bulk of the new population growth in this area – now known as the Greater Toronto Area (GTA) – but since then its growth has dropped off sharply. In fact, Metro's share of the population of the GTA had fallen from 77% in 1961 to 54% by 1991.[66]

The growth pressures in the GTA and the lack of coordination in managing this growth led in 1988 to the creation of the Office of the Greater Toronto Area (OGTA), reporting directly to a provincial cabinet minister. The OGTA did not have any legislative mandate, but defined its role as one of fostering communication among government bodies, seeking solutions to immediate problems that no single government could solve on its own and helping governments in the area to develop a consensus on what the GTA should look like in the future.[67] Gradually, however, the view developed that a new governing body was needed for the GTA. A major impetus for this approach came from the 1996 "Golden Report," which proposed replacing the five existing regional governments with a single, streamlined Greater Toronto Council and giving lower tier municipalities added powers and responsibilities to deliver a wider range of services.[68] This proposal was endorsed later that year by the *Who Does What* panel headed by David Crombie.[69] Thus, the stage seemed set for the abolition of the regional governments in the GTA, including Metro.

Toronto Megacity

Given these developments, most were caught off guard when the province announced in late 1996 that all six lower tier municipalities and the metropolitan government would be combined to form a new city of Toronto embracing some 2.4 million people, thereby creating a municipality more populous than five of Canada's provinces. The main rationale for this about-face seemed to be the savings that would

---

[66] Frances Frisken, "Planning and Servicing the Greater Toronto Area," in Rothblatt and Sancton, *Metropolitan Governance*, p. 157.

[67] *Ibid.*, p. 161.

[68] Report of the GTA Task Force, *Greater Toronto*, (Anne Golden, Chair) January 1996.

[69] The panel was established "to ensure the very best service delivery by reducing waste, duplication and the overall cost of government...."

supposedly be generated by amalgamation. In addition, however, it may be that the Conservative government hoped and expected that submerging the old city of Toronto into a larger municipality where its elected representatives were outnumbered by members from the suburbs would result in a reining in of what the province saw as the free spending ways of the old city. In that regard, the motivation for amalgamation was mainly ideological – the imposition of the values of the ruling Conservatives upon the more left-leaning council of the old city of Toronto.[70]

Opposition to the creation of the megacity was very strong, highlighted by the large majority voting against it in referenda held in all six of the lower tier municipalities. But the province pushed ahead, endured an opposition filibuster, and passed the legislation in April 1997. Effective January 1, 1998, the area previously under a two tier metropolitan government system became one municipality, governed by of a council of 57 members elected by ward (subsequently reduced to 44), plus the mayor elected at large. Perhaps the most striking thing about this reform – apart from the fact that there was no previous rationale for it, either in restructuring studies or in the Conservative Party's past positions – is that it created a municipality with boundaries both too large and too small. Its massive size, at least in the Canadian context, presents major challenges for representation and local democracy. Yet its creation did nothing to address the need for an overall governing body for the GTA.

The Greater Toronto Services Board (GTSB)

To respond to this latter need, the government established a Greater Toronto Services Board in January 1999. It was initially given only one specific power, the control of GO Transit (the provincially established commuter train system that operated across the bottom of the GTA). In addition, the Board was to provide a forum for promoting better coordination and integration of interregional services in the GTA. Every GTA municipality was represented on the Board (plus one representative from the adjacent municipality of Hamilton-Wentworth

---

[70] For an analysis of the possible explanations of the megacity decision, see Neil Thomlinson, "When Right is Wrong: Municipal Governance and Downloading in Toronto," in Mike Burke, Colin Mooers, and John Shields, *Restructuring and Resistance: Canadian Public Policy in an Age of Global Capitalism*, Halifax, Fernwood Publishing, 2000, pp. 226-260.

but only with respect to GO Transit matters), and there were weighted voting provisions to achieve representation by population.

During its short-lived existence, the Board attempted, without success, to get agreement from the member municipalities that coordination of growth and development was a prerequisite to effective action on any of the other intermunicipal issues facing the GTA. It faced strong resistance from a number of municipalities that feared that any expansion of the Board's role would be at their expense. The Board carried out a number of useful studies of the GTA and the issues facing it, but in 2001 the province announced that it would be dissolved at the end of that year. With responsibility for GO Transit going back to the province, from which it had been downloaded as part of the service reallocation that followed the previously cited *Who Does What* exercise, it was claimed that the GTSB had lost is job.

But the need to address issues across the GTA continues, and is unlikely to be addressed by the Smart Growth Advisory Panels appointed in 2001, one of them covering the GTA. Members of these panels are appointed by the province and are to represent the province, municipalities, the private sector, and non-governmental agencies/associations. The main function of these new bodies is to develop smart growth plans that provide a long term vision for economic growth along with strategies to improve the quality of life and protect the environment in each area.[71] But if the Central Ontario panel, the one covering the GTA, attempts to extend its mandate beyond its strictly advisory role, it is likely to encounter the same municipal resistance that blocked the Greater Toronto Services Board.

The Other Regional Governments

The ongoing developments in the Toronto area are by no means the only municipal restructuring activities that have occurred in Ontario. The original Metro Toronto was really the first of the regional governments and within a decade it had been transplanted to a dozen other areas. While Metro has been characterized as an ad hoc response to specific servicing problems, the broader regional government program developed, at least officially, from an overall government policy. That policy recognized the need to provide not only efficient delivery of

---

[71] Web site www.smartgrowth.gov.on.ca, accessed May 27, 2003, provides more details on the Smart Growth panels.

services but also adequate access and effective representation of local views and concerns. It called for regional governments based on such criteria as community of interest, an adequate financial base, and sufficient size to generate economies of scale. The policy also proposed varied structural approaches including both two tier and one tier government and the direct or indirect election of the upper tier councillors in the former instance.[72]

While the policy was potentially quite broad and imaginative, in practice the reforms introduced were all two tier regional government systems closely resembling Metro Toronto. As such, they can best be described as a modification of the traditional county system in Ontario. The regional boundaries followed the boundaries of one or more counties, with minor exceptions. Election to the regional councils closely resembled the indirect election of county councils, but with limited and increasing exceptions as direct election was introduced or expanded over the years. The costs of regional services were apportioned to lower tier municipalities according to their assessment in essentially the same manner as under the county system. All or major municipal responsibility for such functions as welfare, roads, water supply, sewage disposal, planning, and capital borrowing were vested in the regional level, making it more powerful than county governments. The other main difference is that the lower tier units in the regional governments were formed by an amalgamation of constituent municipalities and included cities and separated towns, previously not part of the county system.

In the decade from the commissioning of the first local government reform study (of Ottawa-Carleton) in May 1964 to the coming into operation of the Regional Municipality of Haldimand-Norfolk in April 1974, 11 regional governments were established,[73] covering over one-third of the population of Ontario. If we add the prototype, Metro Toronto, and the Restructured County of Oxford (described below), we had 13 regional governments in Ontario, containing two-thirds of its population. As the unpopularity and political cost of the reforms

[72] The Honourable John Robarts and the Honourable W. Darcy McKeough, *Design for Development Phase Two*, statements to the Legislature of Ontario, November 28 and December 2, 1968.

[73] These were Ottawa-Carleton, Niagara, York, Waterloo, Sudbury, Peel, Halton, Hamilton-Wentworth, Durham, Haldimand-Norfolk, and Muskoka, with the latter being known as a District Municipality.

became increasingly apparent, however, the government announced that it was winding up the program, which, it claimed, had served its purpose.

In its place, a County Restructuring Program was announced early in 1974. Very little action was taken on the local studies carried out under this program, and the prolonged period of minority government in Ontario in the latter part of the 1970s forestalled any new provincial initiatives. Ironically, the one restructured county in Ontario, Oxford County, was created prior to this program being announced. County government reform resurfaced at the end of the 1980s, with several provincial reports calling for restructuring based on the amalgamation of lower tier units and the expansion of county powers. As with the program 15 years earlier, virtually no action was taken on the studies carried out.

New Wave of Restructuring

A few ad hoc annexations and amalgamations continued to occur, notably in Sarnia-Lambton county, in Simcoe County, and around the city of London. But by the 1990s attention was shifting away from structural changes to process improvements. Various books and presentations on *In Search of Excellence* and *Reinventing Government*[74] stimulated interest in the way governments carry out their responsibilities, how they measure and reward performance, how they take care of their customers, and how innovative and entrepreneurial they are. The attention of the Ontario government was increasingly focused on matters of function (disentanglement) and finance (deficit reduction). No new regional governments had been established for more than 20 years, and it began to look as if major municipal restructuring activities were a thing of the past. But then June 1995 brought the election of the Conservatives, led by Mike Harris – and the municipal world was in for a shock.

Within a few months of taking office, the Conservatives introduced a number of legislative provisions (in the Savings and Restructuring Act) that they claimed were intended to make it easier for municipalities to implement annexations and amalgamations. These

---

[74] Tom Peters and Robert Waterman Jr., *In Search of Excellence*, New York, Penguin Books, 1982, was the first of a series of writings on excellence authored or co-authored by Peters. David Osborne and Ted Gaebler, *Reinventing Government*, New York, Penguin Books, 1993.

provisions essentially laid out a two-pronged approach to municipal reform, clearly constructed in such a way as to put enormous pressure on municipalities to act. Reform could be achieved by reaching local agreement, provided that the change had the support of a majority of the affected municipalities containing a majority of the population and, where applicable, a majority of the members of the upper tier council as well. If no local agreement could be reached, however, and if even only one municipality so requested, the minister could appoint a commission with total authority to determine the new structure for the municipal area defined by the minister. This two stage process, coupled with various statements made by the province about reducing the number of municipalities in Ontario, created an atmosphere in which municipalities felt great pressure to pursue amalgamation.

Two dramatic events added significantly to this pressure. When the province forced through the amalgamations in Toronto, most smaller municipalities understandably wondered what chance they had to resist if the wishes of such a large population area were ignored. Events in Kent County were even more threatening. A commission was appointed and recommended the amalgamation of all municipalities within the county, the county government, and the separate city of Chatham – against the wishes of 22 of the 23 munici-palities affected! The message for municipalities in the rest of the province was that there was no telling what might happen to them if a commission was appointed. Better to make changes yourself, however unpalatable, than to have more drastic changes imposed upon you.

The high-pressure campaign pursued by the province was quite effective in achieving the substantial pace of restructuring it desired. The term of municipal office following the November 1997 municipal elections began with 200 fewer municipalities than the 815 that existed prior to the elections. All but 7 were dissolved by ministerial or commission orders issued under the Savings and Restructuring Act. Those 7 were the Toronto municipalities merged by legislation to form the megacity.

Following the re-election of the Conservative government, the pace of municipal restructuring increased again dramatically – this time with particular focus on a number of the regional government areas that had not been covered by the Savings and Restructuring Act. The province appointed Special Advisors who were given 60 days to consult and prepare final reports for restructuring in Ottawa-Carleton, Hamilton-Wentworth, Sudbury, and Haldimand-Norfolk. In all but the last instance, the reports led to the establishment of one amalgamated city replacing both existing upper and lower tier units. A modified version of this approach was introduced in Haldimand-Norfolk, with one amalgamated city covering Haldimand and a second one covering Norfolk. A number of other amalgamations were also introduced prior to the November 2000 municipal elections, one of the most dramatic being the creation of the City of Kawartha Lakes through the amalgamation of all municipalities within the former Victoria County, following the recommendations of a provincially-appointed Commission.

In early 2001, the province let it be known that it would proceed with amalgamations in the future only on the basis of strong local support. Queen's Park sources were quoted as saying that the major savings expected from amalgamation had failed to materialize, that implementation costs had been a drain on the provincial budget, and that the political costs of forced amalgamation were too high.[75] By this time, however, the number of municipalities was down to 446, almost 100 fewer than the 539 that existed in Ontario at Confederation.

No clear explanation has ever been offered for the aggressive program of municipal amalgamations pursued by the Conservatives in the second half of the 1990s. Siegel and Hollick suggest that the province felt that municipalities would be better able to handle the additional services being downloaded to them (as a result of the *Who Does What* exercise) and the reduction in provincial transfer payments, if they were amalgamated.[76] According to LeSage, the Alberta government was also concerned about how its municipalities would be able to handle reduced provincial grants and the planned downloading of provincial responsibilities – but its response was to legislate a new Municipal Act rather than to impose restructuring.[77]

The Ontario government never provided a set of policy guidelines for municipal restructuring, along the lines of the *Design for Development* policy that applied to the earlier regional government reforms. It did offer restructuring principles, but rather than

---

[75] See James Rusk, "Province plans to stop forcing cities to merge," *Globe and Mail*, February 2001.

[76] Thomas R. Hollick and David Siegel, *Evolution, Revolution, Amalgamation: Restructuring in Three Ontario Municipalities*, London, University of Western Ontario, Local Government Case Studies No. 10, 2001, p. 29.

[77] Garcea and LeSage, *Municipal Reforms in Canada*.

explaining how a new system should be designed, these principles focused on what the outcome of restructuring should be – in the form of less government, fewer municipal politicians, lower taxes, less bureaucracy, and more efficient service delivery. As Siegel and Hollick observe, the emphasis of the restructuring principles made it sound as though "one consolidation is as good as another."[78]

Quebec

Municipal restructuring efforts have proceeded on several fronts, some more successfully than others. The largest urban areas in Quebec, and especially the Montreal area, have been the focus of considerable restructuring activity, involving the establishment of two tier metropolitan or regional systems and then, quite recently, the merging of these systems into individual enlarged municipalities. A network of upper tier municipalities has also been introduced across the province in place of the old county governments. But, as discussed first, progress has been very slow in reducing the number of very small municipalities that are so prevalent in the Quebec municipal system.

Small and Rural Consolidations

The 1960 election of the Liberal Government of Jean Lesage, and the launching of the "Quiet Revolution," ushered in a series of reforms aimed at modernizing Quebec and many of its institutions. At that time, over 90% of Quebec's 1600 municipalities had less than 5000 population and nearly 50% had less than 1000 population.[79] Hamel and Rousseau suggest[80] that the close links that had existed between the rural elite and the Duplessis regime that ruled Quebec for the preceding 20 years gave the Lesage government added incentive to

---

[78] Hollick and Siegel, *Evolution, Revolution, Amalgamation*, p. 97.

[79] Jean Godin, "Local Government Reform in the Province of Quebec," in Advisory Committee on Intergovernmental Relations, *A Look to the North: Canadian Regional Experience*, Washington, 1974, p. 50.

[80] Pierre Hamel and Jean Rousseau, "Revisiting Municipal Reforms in Quebec and the New Responsibilities of Local Actors in a Globalising World," a paper prepared for the Municipal-Provincial-Federal Relations Conference, Institute of Intergovernmental Relations, Queen's University, May 9-10, 2003, pp. 3-6.

reform municipalities that it regarded as not only too small but also as likely opponents of its new vision of an urban and industrial society for Quebec.

The government's response was the Voluntary Amalgamation Act of 1965, which allowed two or more municipalities to amalgamate following a council's resolution to that effect. Not surprisingly, this voluntary approach was ineffective, with fewer than 100 municipalities abolished between 1965 and 1971. While new legislation in 1971 gave the Minister of Municipal Affairs more power to force amalgamations where he felt it was desirable, this power was little used because of opposition and because (as will be seen) the government was by then preoccupied with metropolitan reforms. According to O'Brien,[81] the peak period for municipal consolidations was between 1971 and 1975, when the number of municipal units was reduced by 84. A limited number of voluntary consolidations (and a few forced ones) continued over the next couple of decades – although provincial government financial policies that gave larger subsidies to smaller municipalities than to larger ones certainly did not encourage the consolidations. Two examples from this period were Lévis and Lauzon (located across the river from Quebec City), which after amalgamation were joined by adjacent St. David, and – in 1992 – the city of Sorel and the parish of St. Pierre de Sorel.[82]

In the 1990s, the Quebec government began to take an increasingly tough stand with respect to amalgamations, partly out of a desire to create municipal institutions to which responsibilities could be downloaded. The Liberal budget of April 1990 outlined the downloading of about $400 million in responsibilities to municipalities, mostly in the area of public transit and police services and local roads in rural areas. The Minister, Claude Ryan, did not deny accusations that these measures were designed to pressure municipalities into combining and acknowledged that such a consequence would not be unwelcome.[83]

---

[81] O'Brien, *Municipal Consolidation*, p. 39.

[82] Details on these consolidations are provided in *ibid.*, pp. 41 and 46.

[83] Robert Cournoyer, "Municipal Amalgamation in the Nineties in Quebec," in Klos, *The State of Unicity*, p. 58.

The Parti Québécois took power in 1994 and in 1996 it introduced a new municipal amalgamation program.[84] It first targeted 400
municipalities with populations under 10 000, offering them financial
assistance for amalgamation studies. To provide further incentive to
restructure, the Minister announced that failure to participate would
result in a reduction in provincial funding for municipal programs
starting in 1997. However, implementation of the amalgamation
program was twice postponed in the face of strong municipal
opposition and the April 1999 report of the Bedard Commission
(discussed below) repeated the need for amalgamations. This process is
still alive, but proceeding very slowly, on a case-by-case basis. The slow
progress is evident from the fact that in 1998, more than 30 years after
the municipal consolidations were first attempted, Quebec still had
1400 municipalities, with fewer than 10% having populations of 10 000
or more and only 5 of them having populations over 100 000.[85]

Regional County Municipalities

Another restructuring initiative was the 1979 Land Use Planning and
Development Act) established a network of 95 new upper tier units
called regional county municipalities or RCMs. These new units
replaced all the former 72 county municipalities, which had consisted
entirely of rural units and had exercised very limited responsibilities.

Municipalities were grouped together to form these RCMs on
the basis of "affinity" – a criterion that was similar to the community
of interest concept specified (but almost never applied) in Ontario's
regional government program. Under the provisions of the legislation,
cities (which had been politically separate from their surrounding
counties) had to become part of the new RCM system, just as
Ontario's cities became part of the regional governments established in
that province. Each RCM had to adopt a regional land use plan, and
was also to take over the functions of the old counties, at least for the
mainly rural areas in which counties had been operating.[86]

---

[84] The description of the program that follows is based on Louise Quesnel,
"Municipal Reorganization in Quebec," *Canadian Journal of Regional Science*,
Special Issue, Spring 2000, pp. 119-120.

[85] *Ibid.*, p. 117.

[86] Louise Quesnel, "Political Control over Planning in Quebec," *International
Journal of Urban and Regional Research* 14, 1990, pp. 25-48.

Each RCM is governed by a council composed only of the head of council (or representative) of each member municipality. In Sancton's view, the message was clear: "a new source of elected political authority was *not* being established."[87] The RCMs were to represent existing municipalities acting together – nothing more. Tomalty's assessment supports this interpretation.[88] He finds that the RCMs failed to become a political forum of action independent from the local municipalities. Their ineffectiveness as regional planning agencies he attributes in part to the fact that they do not have responsibility for providing infrastructure, such as roads and sewage treatment, and thus have little leverage with local municipalities. He also cites the indirectly elected governing councils and elaborate voting arrangements as further constraints.

Concerns about the adequacy of the representation arrangements have increased as the expenditures of the RCMs have grown. Costs are shared by municipalities in proportion to their share of the area's taxable assessment. Cities with a healthy assessment base are, not surprisingly, critical of the fact that their voting strength on council is not nearly as large as their expenditure burden. In response, the province amended the legislation in 1987 to provide new options for voting arrangements within the RCMs.

The RCMs differ from Ontario's county governments in several key respects. First, negotiations leading up to the establishment of the RCMs led to boundaries quite different from the old counties, something Ontario has been unable to achieve even with its restructured counties and regional governments. Second, cities are included within the RCMs, but cities remain separate from the unreformed county systems still found in Ontario. Third, for better or worse, RCMs are designed as flexible mechanisms through which the province and the existing municipalities can better perform their assigned responsibilities, not as genuine political institutions. In that regard, they are probably closer to the regional districts of British Columbia than to Ontario's county and regional governments.[89]

---

[87] Sancton, *Local Government Reorganization*, p. 16.

[88] The discussion that follows is based on Roy Tomalty, *The Compact Metropolis: Growth Management and Intensification in Vancouver, Toronto and Montreal*, Toronto, ICURR Press, 1997, p. 159.

[89] Sancton, *Local Government Reorganization*, p. 23.

Some expansion of the role of RCMs may occur as a result of the amalgamation policy introduced in the mid-1990s. The third phase of this policy is focused on the 700 or so municipalities that are referred to as base communities, three-quarters of them with populations of less than 1500 people. To support these municipalities, the government has proposed that the power of the RCMs will be reinforced to enable them to provide the municipalities with adequate technical and administrative services.[90] On the other hand, a number of RCMs have recently been disbanded, in those urban areas of the province in which new enlarged cities have been created, as discussed below.

Government of Urban Centres

As the main cities in Quebec grew and spilled over their boundaries, the by now familiar challenges arose. Annexations were used early and often in response to problems of urban sprawl in the Montreal area. The need for a vehicle to address intermunicipal problems in the area led to the establishment of the Montreal Metropolitan Corporation in 1959. It was authorized to exercise a number of important functions including sewers, water distribution, arterial roads, planning, mass transit, major parks, and all other services considered as intermunicipal by agreement among the municipalities or by decision of the Corporation. Its jurisdiction extended over the city of Montreal and 14 island municipalities and its governing body comprised 14 representatives from the city, 14 from the suburbs, and a chair appointed by the province. This arrangement ensured the vigorous opposition of Montreal's Mayor Jean Drapeau, who, as Sancton notes, was like most central city mayors (remember Stephen Juba of Winnipeg) in resisting any form of metropolitan government that he could not control. But Sancton adds that another and unique reason for Montreal's opposition was the concern that any metropolitan government, by extending to the suburbs and their high proportion of English-speaking citizens, would decrease the influence of the French.[91] Montreal's refusal to cooperate effectively sabotaged the Corporation, which was never a major force in spite of its impressive terms of reference.

---

[90] Vojnovic, *Municipal Consolidation in the 1990s*, p. 54.

[91] Andrew Sancton, "The Impact of Language Differences on Metropolitan Reform in Montreal," in Lionel D. Feldman, *Politics and Government of Urban Canada*, Toronto, Methuen, 1981, p. 372.

Three New Urban Community Governments

In June 1969, the Union Nationale government that had replaced the Liberals announced plans to introduce a new governing structure for the Montreal area (and for Quebec City and Hull as well). The Montreal Urban Community (MUC) came into existence on January 1, 1970. The new structure had a governing council made up of the mayor and councillors of the city of Montreal and one delegate from each of the other 29 municipalities under its jurisdiction. The city was also given 7 of the 12 seats on the powerful executive committee and provided the first chair in the person of Lucien Saulnier, who had been Mayor Jean Drapeau's chief lieutenant.

The sudden introduction of the MUC resulted from the devasting police strike that hit Montreal on October 7, 1969. A prompt end to that strike was engineered by none other than Saulnier, whose strategy was "in essence, to promise to pay the police what they wanted and then to force the suburbs and the provincial government to finance the increases." The vehicle for this redistribution of funding was the new MUC, "organized such that in many ways it was a mere extension of the city of Montreal."[92]

By January 1972, all of the police forces on the island had been unified into the MUC police department, and the new upper tier government gradually became involved in several other areas of activity. In financial terms, the main initiatives were with respect to subways and sewers, but the effectiveness of the MUC was hampered by a city-suburb split and by the fact that while Montreal had a majority of the votes on the council, a motion could only pass if supported by at least half of the suburban delegates present. An analysis by Sancton concludes that the original hopes that the MUC would evolve into a genuine metropolitan government were never realized.

While the original legislation contemplated that internal boundary adjustments would be made, any such changes would involve some merging of French-speaking and English-speaking populations – a task no politician wanted to tackle. The principle that a double majority (city and suburb) was needed before action could be taken meant that often no decision was made. As a result, the province increasingly took the initiative, especially after the Parti Québécois

---

[92] *Ibid.*

came to power in 1976, and the MUC's role became a passive one of accepting provincial money and implementing provincial decisions.[93]

The December 1969 legislation that created the Montreal Urban Community also provided for an urban community for Quebec City and for a similarly constituted regional government for Hull and environs known as the Regional Community of Outaouais. The latter municipality faced municipal opposition on the grounds that the reform was introduced without sufficient prior consultation. A primary motivation for its establishment was apparently the perceived need to provide a counterweight to the adjoining Regional Municipality of Ottawa-Carleton in Ontario, and to represent the area's interests to the National Capital Commission. A somewhat more positive attitude was evident in the Quebec Urban Community where more consultation with local leaders had occurred.

The fact that the Outaouais Urban Community contained major portions of rural as well as urban territory resulted in an uneasy partnership that placed strains on the organization. Following a ministerial statement and a study (the Giles Report) in 1990, two new structures were put into place effective January 1, 1991 – a new regional county municipality covering the rural areas and a modified Outaouais Urban Community confined to the urban areas of Gatineau, Hull, Aylmer, Buckingham, and Masson. These latter five have recently been merged into a single municipality as one of a number of reforms that accompanied recent restructuring in Montreal, to which we now turn our attention.

Governing the Montreal Area

Changing population patterns presented new problems and challenges for the Montreal Urban Community. With the suburbs growing at a much faster rate than the city of Montreal, adjustments had to be made in the voting arrangements within the MUC and the make-up of its executive committee. Even greater growth was taking place in the outer suburbs, beyond the MUC, making its boundaries increasingly irrelevant.[94] While the MUC had contained 71% of the population of the Montreal census metropolitan area in 1971, that proportion was

[93] The assessment in this paragraph is based on Andrew Sancton, "Montreal's Metropolitan Government," Hanover, *Quebec Studies*, No. 6, 1988.

[94] Sancton, *Canada's City Regions*, p. 84.

down to 57% by 1991. Yet expansion of the MUC boundaries seemed unlikely, since the adjacent areas were governed by regional county municipalities – leaving Montreal hemmed in much the way Toronto had been with regional governments surrounding it.

In response, the province appointed a Task Force on Greater Montreal (chaired by Claude Pichette) that reported in December 1993 and recommended that a Montreal Metropolitan Region be established, "the territory of which would correspond exactly to that of the CMA and which would automatically be adjusted to match future CMA boundary changes."[95] The Task Force did not recommend any amalgamations of the more than 100 municipalities within the CMA but instead proposed the creation of four Intermunicipal Service Agencies or ISAs, each covering a group of municipalities, with authority to borrow money and to assume responsibilities as delegated by their member municipalities. This rather unwieldy structure that seemed to suggest three levels of municipal government for the Montreal area was an attempt to find a compromise between the city and the suburbs. It failed in the face of strong opposition from suburban mayors who feared that an overall metropolitan government would prevent them from competing with the municipalities of the MUC and would, therefore, undermine their plans for growth. They were also opposed, especially the mayors on the north shore, to taking on a share of Montreal's financial burden.

In 1996, a Minister for the Montreal Region was designated, who recommended a single metropolitan region covering the whole Montreal area. The provincial government had strong support from the south and north shores, and little support from within the MUC, so its rejection of this proposal was not surprising.[96] The government did pass legislation in mid-1997 to establish a 40 member commission de développement pour la métropole (CDM). It was to be presided over by the Minister for the Montreal Region, with the remaining 39 members to be elected councillors (two-thirds) and appointed representatives of socio-economic groups (one-third). All existing municipalities, including the MUC, were to remain in place, but the

---

[95] *Ibid.*, p. 88.

[96] Tomalty, *The Compact Metropolis*, p. 164. This situation paralleled that found in Ontario during the same period, with the Conservative government enjoying strong support from the suburban areas (the so-called 905 area, known for its telephone area code) and much less support within Toronto.

new CDM was supposed to make recommendations "for streamlining this remarkably cumbersome set of municipal structures."[97] However, the government did not implement this new arrangement.

April 1999 saw the release of yet another report, this one from the Bedard Commission on local finances and taxation. The Commission had been set up by the province to placate the municipal level which was hit with an annual $375 million levy for the period 1997-2000, as the municipal contribution to the province's fiscal efforts.[98] While the report did deal extensively with financial matters, it also put forth a number of recommendations for municipal restructuring – much to the dismay of the municipal level. Of particular note was its recommendation that the municipalities in the greater Montreal area should be amalgamated, into no more than 20, with a maximum of 5 covering the island of Montreal. It also called for the creation of metropolitan structures in the Montreal and Quebec City metropolitan areas, with directly elected governing bodies possessing autonomous taxing powers.

Opposition to the report was strong and widespread. Since the report recommended that provincial grants relating to public transit, roads, and social housing be cut, it seemed to promote the downloading of provincial responsibilities and costs to enlarged municipalities, in much the same way as had been happening in Ontario. Concerns were also expressed about the impact of a number of the reforms on the rights of Quebec Anglophones, since the proposed amalgamations would absorb predominantly English-speaking areas into new municipalities with a majority of French-speaking residents. Of particular concern was the fact that 14 of the 28 municipalities to be merged on the island of Montreal enjoyed a bilingual status under the province's language charter.[99]

---

[97] Andrew Sancton, "The Municipal Role in the Governance of Cities," in Trudi Bunting and Pierre Filion (eds.), *Canadian Cities in Transition*, 2nd Edition, Toronto, Oxford University Press, 2000, p. 438.

[98] Discussion of the Commission is based on Quesnel, "Municipal Reorganization in Quebec," pp. 121-123. This downloading of costs is rather similar to action taken by the Ontario government earlier in the decade, when its Social Contract and Expenditure Control Program effectively shifted close to $300 million a year to the municipal level.

[99] *Ibid.*, p. 128. However, the Quebec government subsequently confirmed that the bilingual designations would remain.

New Urban Structures

In March 2000, the Minister of Municipal Affairs issued a reorganization plan for Quebec local government. Particular attention was focused on the three urban communities or regional governments (in Montreal, Quebec, and Hull-Gatineau) that were established in 1970 and where 70% of the Quebec population is found. Advisory committees were set up for the three areas to make recommendations about services, tax sharing, and municipal amalgamations. Municipalities and their associations condemned the plan and argued that fiscal problems should be solved before structural changes were considered. Referenda in the suburban areas brought voter turnout of between 10% and 35%, who rejected amalgamation by 90%.[100]

Nonetheless, in November 2000 the government introduced legislation (Bill 170) to merge the municipalities within the Montreal, Quebec City, and Hull-Gatineau areas – including the upper tier urban communities covering these areas – and to replace them with three single tier cities. Amalgamations were also introduced to create enlarged cities for Lévis, Longueuil, Trois-Rivières, Sherbrooke, Saguenay, Shawinigan, and Saint-Jérôme.

Community councils (conseils d'arrondissement) have been established in five of these new cities.[101] In the case of Montreal, 27 boroughs have been delineated, with boundaries closely conforming to those of the urban neighbourhoods of old Montreal and the old suburban municipalities. City councillors elected from within each borough make up the borough councils (except for some councils in the suburbs that have elected members serving only at the borough level). The boroughs have a variety of administrative and consultative responsibilities, but no separate taxing power, and very limited independence from the city administrations of which they form part. One local government observer, however, considers that these boroughs have been given more legal authority over local services than similar bodies set up in other amalgamated jurisdictions such as Toronto and Halifax.[102]

---

[100] Quesnel, "Municipal Reorganization in Quebec," pp. 125-127.

[101] Communique from Louise Quesnel on March 5, 2003.

[102] Andrew Sancton, "Why Municipal Amalgamations? Halifax, Toronto, Montreal," a paper prepared for the Municipal-Provincial-Federal Relations Conference, Queen's University, Institute of Intergovernmental Relations, Queen's University, May 9-10, 2003.

In addition to the borough councils below the level of the new cities, the province also established two new metropolitan communities, covering the new, enlarged municipalities of Montreal and Quebec City and other surrounding municipalities. In the Gatineau-Hull area (the last of the three areas that had been governed by upper tier urban communities), just a planning coordinating commission was created, given the fact that the area now consists only of one large city and one regional county municipality.[103]

Taking the Montreal Metropolitan Community (MMC) as an example, it covers the entire area of the Montreal census metropolitan area (CMA) and its population of over 3 million. The council is composed of representatives chosen among the elected representatives of the 64 municipalities (including the new city of Montreal) within the CMA. The MMC is responsible for such matters as metropolitan planning and economic development, social housing, planning for public transit and solid waste disposal, the mitigation of air and water pollution, and various metropolitan facilities.[104] The result of all these changes is that residents of Montreal now find themselves governed by three levels of urban administration.

Table 4.2 Restructuring Highlights – Central Canada	
Ontario	Two tier Metropolitan Toronto system Single Toronto municipality through amalgamation Intermunicipal board for Greater Toronto area (Greater Toronto Services Board) Network of other two tier regional governments Single cities through amalgamation of regional governments in Ottawa, Hamilton, Sudbury, and Haldimand-Norfolk areas Widespread amalgamations across municipal system
Quebec	Limited amalgamation of small municipalities Montreal Metropolitan Corporation as upper tier board Upper tier governments for Montreal, Quebec City, Hull Single cities through amalgamation for Montreal, Quebec City, Hull-Gatineau, Levis, Longueuil Upper tier governments (regional county municipalities) replacing former county municipalities Metropolitan communities for Montreal and Quebec City areas

---

[103] *Ibid.*

[104] Andrew Sancton, "Canadian Cities and the New Regionalism," *Journal of Urban Affairs*, 2001, volume 23, Number 5, p. 552.

New Brunswick

Comprehensive local government reform initiatives were undertaken in New Brunswick in the 1960s as a result of the report of the *Royal Commission on Finance and Municipal Taxation*. The emphasis on fiscal matters evident in the title reflected the difficulties facing local governments in the province at the time. Service standards varied widely (especially in education), there were marked inequities in municipal taxation and high tax arrears, municipalities were finding it difficult to finance their servicing needs, and three of the single tier rural counties were virtually bankrupt.

The recommendations of the Byrne Commission (as it came to be known, after its chair, Edward Byrne) were designed to provide all citizens with an equal opportunity to access and benefit from minimum standards of service regardless of the financial resources of their local municipalities. To this end, it proposed that the province take over full responsibility for a number of services to people to ensure uniformity, leaving municipalities responsible for more localized services to property. The Commission also recommended that the provincial government take over the provision of local services in the rural areas of the province.

Equal Opportunity Program

The New Brunswick government responded with an equal opportunity program in 1967 under which the main recommendations of the Byrne Commission were implemented. The province took over responsibility for the administration of justice, welfare, and public health, and also financial responsibility for the provision of education. Property assessment and collection of property taxes became provincial responsibilities. The 15 single tier counties that had governed the rural areas of New Brunswick were abolished, and the provincial government took over the provision of services to these areas through new local service districts (discussed in more detail below) established for the purpose. Some 90 villages were established, in partial compensation for the loss of the county governments.

The reforms were successful in bringing about a substantial improvement in the quality of such services as education, justice, and welfare – although this benefit was achieved through the municipal level losing all or partial responsibility for these functions to the province. Where the reforms failed (or were incomplete) was in relation to the municipal government structure. The need for boundary changes in urban areas was not addressed. As the urban population overspilled existing boundaries, the fact that municipal governments had been eliminated in rural areas became increasingly problematic. In addition, the fact that two-thirds of the municipalities in New Brunswick still have populations of 2000 or less make it very difficult for them to provide an appropriate range and level of services at acceptable tax rates.[105]

Governing Urban New Brunswick

A December 1992 government report[106] acknowledged that the equal opportunity reforms had not addressed the problems of urban centres, seven of which had populations of 20 000 or more. The urban sprawl occurring around these centres was obviously on a small scale, but problems were magnified by the lack of municipal institutions in the surrounding rural areas. The report noted that a variety of ad hoc regional bodies had been established (as discussed below) to deal with the provision of services, but that these bodies added to the fragmentation of the local government structure and weakened accountability. It proposed that each of the centres be studied with a view to possible restructuring.

In April 1994, reports appeared on the first two areas chosen, Moncton and the Miramichi.[107] The latter report led to the amalgamation of all 11 communities in the study area (only 5 of which were incorporated municipalities) into one municipality, making Miramichi the fourth largest municipal government in the province.

In contrast, the Moncton report ruled out amalgamation of Moncton, Dieppe, and Riverview, primarily on the issue of language. While Dieppe is predominantly French, the report pointed to the lack of bilingual operations in Moncton, especially with respect to police

[105] *Report of the Minister's Round Table on Local Governance*, June 2001, p. 20.

[106] Ministry of Municipalities, Culture and Housing, *Strengthening Municipal Government in New Brunswick's Urban Centres*, December 1992.

[107] Local Government Review Panel, *Greater Moncton Urban Community: Strength Through Cooperation* and Miramichi Local Government Review Panel, *Miramichi City: Our Future – Strength Through Unity*, both 1994.

and fire protection.[108] Instead, a joint services board was established, which became known as the Commission of the Three Communities (CTC). It was comprised of appointed and elected officials from the three municipalities, and was to facilitate the shared provision of various municipal services among the three municipalities and to coordinate the regional bodies administering some of these services. The CTC operated for three and one-half years but was hampered by municipal turf wars and resistance to service sharing and by conflicting directives from provincial departments. It also suffered from the fact that it was not given decision making power but could only recommend actions to the three municipal councils. As a result, it was limited to being a think tank on the regionalization of services.[109]

In 1996, studies were launched of the urban areas of Greater Saint John, Greater Campbellton, Madawaska, and Greater Dalhousie. There was strong opposition in the outlying areas to the possible merger of all nine municipalities in the Saint John area to form a single city. While that merger was the preferred option of the Commission's report on this area, the province responded to political pressures[110] by adopting a compromise solution. Effective January 1, 1998, the eight suburban municipalities were consolidated into three, with the boundaries of Saint John remaining the same. In addition, a Regional Facilities Commission was established to integrate the financing of major facilities in Saint John that benefited the region. Three municipalities and a portion of a local service district were amalgamated with the city of Edmundston.

Intermunicipal cooperation rather than amalgamation was proposed by the study of the Dalhousie area, once again through the vehicle of a joint services board. The province decided (based on the expressed willingness of municipal leaders) to create an inter-community forum for the Dalhousie region to pursue the regionalization of services, but no such forum was established and no new municipal services have been regionalized. The study of the

[108] Communication from Daniel Bourgeois, June 18, 2003.

[109] See *Final Report of the Commission of the Three Communities on the Implementation of the 27 Recommendations Made by the Robison-Malenfant Panel*, September 17, 1999, on which this discussion is based.

[110] At least that is the interpretation of George M. Betts, "Municipal Restructuring, New Brunswick Style: The Saint John Experience," *Municipal World*, September 1997, pp. 3-8.

Campbellton area recommended the amalgamation of three munici-palities (Campbellton, Atholville and Tide Head), but the province instead encouraged cooperative action through a joint services board. Such a body was established and reached agreement on sharing the operation and costs of the Memorial Civic Centre owned by Campbellton. However, the province's efforts to establish a water and wastewater commission to own and operate the existing facilities of the three municipalities were not successful.[111]

Governing Rural New Brunswick

As already mentioned, the abolition of county governments left the rural areas of New Brunswick without municipal governments. About 100 local services districts were established initially, to provide local services to unincorporated areas according to local preference, and there are now 269 such LSDs.[112] A 1976 report[113] identified a number of problems, including the lack of elected councils to represent the people, inequities in the financing of services, and difficulties imple-menting services such as community planning. However, no action was taken on the report's recommendation that the local service districts be replaced by 11 new rural municipalities. A 1993 report[114] also found numerous problems, including conflicting land uses, sprawl, and unmanaged development just outside major centres. It called for rationalization of local service districts into rural communities with elected councils. One pilot community (Beaubassin East) was created in 1995, but no others have followed.

The unincorporated rural areas comprise 80% of the land mass of New Brunswick (about half of which is Crown Land) and about 40% of the province's population, and these areas are outpacing

---

[111] Information about Dalhousie and Campbellton was provided in a communi-cation from Johnny St.-Onge, New Brunswick Department of Environment and Local Government, May 5, 2003.

[112] *Final Report of the Select Committee on Local Governance and Regional Collaboration*, January 2003, Executive Summary, p. 16. The report is available at www.gnb.ca/legis/business/committees, accessed March 24, 2003.

[113] *Report of the Task Force on Nonincorporated Areas in New Brunwsick*, Fredericton, Queen's Printer, 1976.

[114] Government of New Brunswick, *The Commission on Land Use and the Rural Environment: Summary Report*, April 1993.

growth within municipalities – aggravating the problems already identified.[115] Municipalities and unincorporated areas do not have a framework or vehicle that would allow them to address common issues. A provincial levy of 65 cents per $100 of assessment is charged to owner-occupied residential properties in unincorporated areas, but this levy is not directly related to the cost of the transportation, policing, administration, and dog control services provided by the provincial government, and since this levy has not changed in 20 years, it is estimated that its proceeds fall at least $22 million short.[116]

A report of a Minister's Round Table in June 2001[117] outlined several options for new municipal structures in the rural areas, including models similar to British Columbia's regional districts and Quebec's regional county municipalities. A Select Committee of the Legislature was then established to conduct public consultations with respect to these and other recommendations arising from the Round Table exercise, and its January 2003 final report[118] disclosed little public support for new structures. Interestingly, many residents in unincorporated areas are apparently concerned that incorporation would bring increased taxation[119] – echoing the concerns that delayed the original introduction of municipal institutions in several provinces, as discussed in Chapter 2. The Committee's report was a cautious, politically sensitive document that encouraged various locally initiated changes (with respect to such things as the boundaries of local service districts and more joint provision of services by regional bodies), but did not propose any provincially-imposed restructuring in rural areas.

Reliance on Local Boards

A distinctive feature of local government in New Brunswick has been the creation of single purpose boards to deliver services that transcend political boundaries. Some 300 of these bodies have been established, to handle such regional services as economic development, sewage,

---

[115] *Report of the Minister's Round Table*, p. 10.

[116] *Ibid.*, p. 14.

[117] *Ibid.*

[118] Final Report of the Select Committee on Local Governance and Regional Collaboration, *Executive Summary*.

[119] *Report of the Minister's Round Table*, p. 10.

transit, hospitals, ambulance service, emergency planning, pest control, libraries, and solid waste management.[120] Many of these boards have representation from both local service districts and municipalities. The Minister appoints representatives from unincorporated areas, which raises concerns about local accountability.

It would appear that the boards will continue to play an important role in New Brunswick's local government system according to the recommendations of the previously cited Select Committee report. It calls for the extension of District Planning Commissions to serve all local service districts and municipalities throughout the province, proposes some changes in the composition of these Commissions and Solid Waste Commissions, and recommends that all Commissions be required to adopt a multi-year service plan and to conduct an annual review of that plan in consultation with participating municipalities and local services districts.

Nova Scotia

Local government reform initiatives in Nova Scotia have come in two main waves, almost 20 years apart. A comprehensive report and recommendations appeared in the early 1970s, and led gradually to some changes over the ensuing decade. The 1990s brought restructuring in a few urban areas, but there have not been any since.

Graham Commission: Too Much At Once?

The Royal Commission on Education, Public Services, and Provincial-Municipal Relations in the Province of Nova Scotia (chaired by Professor John F. Graham) lived up to its lengthy title by releasing a massive report in June 1974. Like the Byrne Commission in New Brunswick a decade earlier, the Graham Commission report concluded that the province should be responsible for such general services as education, health, social services, housing, and the administration of justice, and that it should provide such support services to municipalities as capital borrowing, assessment, tax collection, water and sewer user billing and collection, and the administration of municipal pension funds. The Graham Commission also recommended that the

---

[120] *Miramichi City*, p. 4.

existing rural municipalities, towns, and cities be replaced by 11 one tier counties covering the province.

Informal discussions involving representatives from the Union of Nova Scotia Municipalities and the Department of Municipal Affairs evolved into what became known as the Task Force on Municipal Reform. Its deliberations culminated in a February 1978 White Paper entitled *New Directions in Municipal Government in Nova Scotia*, which mainly called for various reforms to the provincial-local financial relationship – most of which were gradually implemented over the ensuing years.

Annexations and Amalgamations

While the province-wide restructuring of municipalities recommended by the Graham Commission was not pursued, a number of boundary changes did take place through more localized annexations and amalgamations. These included major expansions to Dartmouth and Halifax and the creation of the Town of Bedford – all involving lands taken from Halifax County. The increasingly intertwined relationships between these four municipalities led to the establishment of the Metropolitan Authority of Halifax,[121] which was originally set up to operate a regional jail and gradually took on the operation of a regional transit system and a sanitary landfill operation. The authority was governed by a 12 member board comprised of elected representatives from the councils of each of the member municipalities. But it was hampered by internal wrangling over the financing of its work and different views of its priorities,[122] and was ineffective in pursuing regional planning and in dealing with such challenges as the environmental cleanup of Halifax harbour.

Task Force on Local Government

The impetus for further restructuring (in the Halifax area and elsewhere) came as a result of a 1992 report of a task force established by the Minister of Municipal Affairs. As in New Brunswick and

---

[121] Andrew Sancton, *Local Government Reorganization in Canada Since 1975*, Toronto ICURR Press, 1991, p. 35.

[122] Katherine A. Graham, Susan D. Phillips, and Allan M. Maslove, *Urban Governance in Canada*, Toronto, Harcourt Brace & Company, 1998, p. 83.

elsewhere, the fact that rural development was outpacing growth in the established urban centres was a cause for concern. In addition to recommendations for a significant realignment of functions between the provinces and municipalities – rather similar to the proposals arising from the disentanglement process unfolding in Ontario during this same period – the report also called for a major restructuring of municipal governments in the five most urbanized counties in the province (including Halifax County) that together contained 67% of the Nova Scotia population. It stated that one tier amalgamated municipalities would be the preferred restructuring model.[123] The following year saw reports from municipal reform commissioners for Cape Breton County and Halifax County.

Cape Breton Regional Municipality

Previous reports had recommended amalgamations for the Cape Breton area and there was growing criticism of the complex network of special purpose bodies in the area. The Cape Breton Commissioner, Charles Campbell, called for amalgamation of all eight municipalities including the county. A provincial election that replaced the Conservatives with a Liberal government caused a delay in action, but the new municipality commenced operations on August 1, 1995. The limited resistance to this change probably reflected the widespread recognition of the financial difficulties facing a number of the municipalities, and public hope and expectation that savings would result from the restructuring. The Commissioner had estimated annual savings of $13.8 million, $7.3 million of which were to come from the realignment of provincial and municipal services that had been introduced across Nova Scotia. Instead, the service swap resulted in an additional cost of $5 million a year, contributing to the $15 million shortfall that the new municipality faced in its initial, 1995-1996 operating budget.

Halifax Regional Municipality (HRM)

In contrast with Cape Breton, there was considerable opposition to the amalgamation of the cities of Halifax and Dartmouth, the town of Bedford and the surrounding county of Halifax, which took effect on

---

[123] Report to the Government of Nova Scotia, *Task Force on Local Government*, April 1992, p. 33.

April 1, 1996. The new municipality is huge, covering 6000 square kilometres or almost 10 times the area of Metropolitan Toronto (now the amalgamated City of Toronto). It contains 40% of the population of Nova Scotia, with only a very small proportion of that population in its substantial rural area. In this case as well, substantial savings were supposed to result from amalgamation ($10 million annually) but the early years saw cost increases instead, resulting in a deficit budget for the municipality in each of its first three years. According to a 1999 survey, most citizens did not have a favourable assessment of the amalgamation or the performance of their council (which exhibited "dysfunctional parochialism"), did not see the geographic, social, and economic diversity of the enlarged municipality as a strength, and – except for solid waste management – did not link amalgamation in a positive way with service improvements.[124] A study of police services found that amalgamation is associated with higher costs, lower numbers of sworn officers, lower service levels, no real change in crime rates, higher workloads for sworn officers, and a public perception that police services have declined.[125]

It appears, however, that the province wanted to have the amalgamation for reasons other than possible cost savings. One objective was to eliminate what was seen as excessive and harmful economic competition between the business and industrial parks of the municipalities and the other was to avoid a financial (and political) problem being generated by the service swap then underway in the province.[126] The new service alignment would have had a very adverse financial impact on Halifax County while significantly benefiting the other three municipalities. The amalgamation removed, or at least concealed, this discrepancy.

A third amalgamation during this period, which merged the county of Queens and the town of Liverpool to form the Region of Queens municipality, was locally initiated. It was intended to improve

---

[124] Dale H. Poel, "Amalgamation Perspectives: Citizen Responses to Municipal Consolidation," *Canadian Journal of Regional Science*, Special Issue, Spring 2000, pp. 43-44.

[125] J. C. McDavid, "The impacts of amalgamation on police services in the Halifax Regional Municipality" *Canadian Public Administration*, Winter 2002, pp. 538-565.

[126] Dale H. Poel, "Municipal Reform in Nova Scotia," in Garcea and LeSage, *Municipal Reforms in Canada*.

services, achieve some economies of scale, and recognize the community of interest between the areas brought together. It has apparently been a successful amalgamation in terms of improved financial capacity, financial management, and the provision of services.[127]

The revised Municipal Government Act of 1999 outlines a process for amalgamating all municipalities within a county to create a single regional municipality but it also specifies (in section 372) that any such change requires a plebiscite in which a majority of those voting support the proposed amalgamation. There have been no further amalgamations of this nature since the three above were established a decade ago.

Prince Edward Island

The need for municipal reform in Canada's smallest province as raised in a 1990 report of the *Royal Commission on the Land*, which described the by now familiar problem that municipal boundaries had not been adjusted to keep up with population overspill. It gave particular attention to the Charlottetown area, where nine suburbs and the city had struggled with what the Commission termed the "Herculean" task of achieving a coordinated approach voluntarily. The Commission felt that the limited collaboration that resulted had not been as cost-effective, efficient, or rational as the coordination that could be achieved under one unified jurisdiction.[128]

A June 1993 *White Paper on Municipal Reform* called for restructuring in both the Charlottetown and Summerside areas, which it found overgoverned. It considered several options and expressed a preference for amalgamation. A Commissioner was appointed and his December 1993 report[129] called for three sets of amalgamations in the Charlottetown area, including an enlarged city of Charlottetown. It also recommended the complete merger of the five municipalities in the Summerside area, along with some unincorporated territory.

---

[127] *Ibid.*

[128] The summary of the Commission's position is based on O'Brien, *Municipal Consolidation*, pp. 27-30.

[129] Prince Edward Island, *Report of the Commission on Municipal Reform (Charlottetown and Summerside Areas)*, December 1993.

Legislation implementing these changes was passed in 1994 and the new cities began operations the following year.

Newfoundland and Labrador

Within a few years of joining Confederation in 1949, Newfoundland experienced rapid growth and the number of municipalities had risen to almost 300 by the early 1970s when the province set up a royal commission chaired by H. G. Whalen. Its 1974 report called for the gradual creation of as many as 20 regional governments with upper tier units similar to, but stronger than, British Columbia's regional districts. It also recommended tightening up incorporation procedures, the introduction of the property tax because of the poor financial conditions in most municipalities, and a new system of provincial grants. The latter recommendations were gradually incorporated into revisions to the Municipalities Act.

Municipal Consolidations

Shortly after the election of the Liberal government headed by Clyde Wells in 1989, the province launched an ambitious program of municipal consolidations. One hundred and ten candidates for amalgamation were chosen on the basis of physical proximity and a combined population of 1250, and the declared objective was to reduce these to 43.[130] But for a variety of reasons, including strong local opposition, many of the proposed amalgamations were not pursued. By the time the consolidation program was put on hold in 1992, to allow for a review of the process and its accomplishments, 33 former communities had been reduced to 13.

The main changes occurred in the Northeast Avalon area, which included the city of St. John's and about 20 smaller surrounding municipalities largely dependent on St. John's for employment and retail services.[131] There had been a number of earlier studies calling for

---

[130] Donald Peckham, "Amalgamation Program Undertaken in the Province of Newfoundland and Labrador," *Boardroom Files*, Halifax, Maritime Municipal Training and Development Board, Spring/Summer 1993, p. 15.

[131] Peter Boswell, "Regional Government for St. John's?" *Urban Focus*, Institute of Local Government, Queen's University, January-February 1979.

restructuring in this area, including the Henley Commission, which recommended in 1977 that a two tier system of regional government be established for the area. Draft legislation was introduced twice (without success), but the 1979 Municipalities Act authorized the establishment of regional governments anywhere in the province.

A St. John's Metropolitan Area Board was created in 1963, as a result of the first study of this area. In the absence of action on boundary changes, this board continued to grow and evolve. It spent its first six years developing a municipal plan. It then began to supply urban services in a number of subdivisions outside the towns and city. In 1978 the board took over responsibility for administration of the regional water supply on behalf of the province. [132] During the 1980s, the board had nine members appointed by the province, two of whom represented the city of St. John's and one the town of Mount Pearl, a major suburb of the city.

As a result of the previously cited municipal consolidation program, the number of municipalities in the St. John's area was reduced to 13, effective January 1, 1992, with the city absorbing two municipalities and most of the area previously under the Metropolitan Area Board which was abolished at the same time. The new arrangement also gave St. John's new regional responsibilities for public transit, solid waste management, water supply, fire protection, and secondary processing of sewage. [133] In effect, it became a regional service provider with respect to these responsibilities, a role that it has not welcomed.

St. John's claims that it is paying a disproportionate share of regional costs and is carrying neighbouring municipalities. It would prefer to see its boundaries extended "to incorporate the majority of the surrounding urban and suburban development." [134] Since the province has repeatedly indicated that it will not amalgamate the municipalities except in response to local requests, St. John's can expect to continue in this role of acting as a regional service provider. To the extent that its claims of unfair financial burden are valid, these can presumably be addressed through increasing the costs charged to

[132] This summary is based on O'Brien, *Municipal Consolidation*, p. 24.

[133] Andrew Sancton, Rebecca James, and Rick Ramsay, *Amalgamation vs. Inter-Municipal Cooperation: Financing Local and Infrastructure Services*, Toronto, Intergovernmental Committee on Urban and Regional Research, 2000, p. 42.

[134] March 1997 submission by St. John's, quoted in *ibid.*, p. 44.

the municipalities buying services from it. Such arrangements represent a means of addressing intermunicipal servicing issues without amalgamation or the imposition of a regional body.

The Regional Alternative

The provincial government continued to be concerned about the number of municipalities and began to give more attention to the possibility of a regional focus for service delivery. The province was divided into 20 economic zones to facilitate economic development, as a result of a report on Community Economic Development. In the fall of 1996 the government released a consultation document, *Reforming Municipal Government in Newfoundland and Labrador*, which stated that municipalities could be expected to play a greater role in economic development in their respective regions, and which suggested that the boundaries of the new economic zones might logically be used to delineate new regional groupings of municipalities.

A Task Force was appointed the following spring, to follow up on these matters. Its September 1997 report called for the establishment of a regional county services board in each of the 20 economic zones, to be governed by a board of directors comprised of both elected and appointed members representing unincorporated areas and municipalities, respectively. The Task Force recommended few initial powers for these boards, but proposed that they take on additional functions as required and approved by the board of directors and that municipalities and unincorporated communities be allowed to opt in and opt out of the services provided.[135] The proposed boards appear to be quite similar to British Columbia's regional districts, but the recommendations have not been acted upon to date.

Resistant or Realistic?

In spite of a number of reports, recommendations, and government initiatives, little progress has been made with respect to municipal consolidation or regionalization. At first glance, it appears that local resistance to change and lack of political will at the provincial level have left Newfoundland and Labrador saddled with far too many municipalities. But Boswell makes an interesting alternative case. He

---

[135] Newfoundland and Labrador, Department of Municipal and Provincial Affairs, *Final Report, Task Force on Municipal Regionalization*, 1997, p. 9.

suggests that the need for widespread municipal reform is not as great in Newfoundland as in other parts of Canada and that many of the province's nearly 300 municipalities are very small and often operate quite efficiently with minimum staff and expense. He points out that some voluntary sharing of resources is occurring and more formal joint arrangements are being considered. In Boswell's view, it is possible that the existing structure of many small municipalities is the most cost-effective way of delivering services while providing democratic representation.[136]

Table 4.3 Restructuring Highlights – Atlantic Provinces	
New Brunswick	Miramichi formed from amalgamation of 11 communities Eight suburban municipalities into three in Saint John area Some 300 boards to deliver services, often on behalf of municipalities and unincorporated areas
Nova Scotia	Halifax and Cape Breton regional municipalities formed from amalgamation of municipalities in their areas
PEI	Charlottetown and Summerside enlarged by amalgamation
Newfoundland	Amalgamation program produced few results, mostly in St. John's area

Concluding Comments

There are several distinctive features of municipal reform and restructuring in Western Canada. The scale of restructuring has been modest and, with very few exceptions, has occurred as a result of local agreement, not provincial imposition. Winnipeg's Unicity model is the main exception, but there is certainly no indication that further restructuring will be imposed upon the Manitoba capital region. British Columbia's regional districts were established under enabling legislation, but were allowed to develop gradually on the basis of local decisions in what was earlier referred to as a strategy of gentle imposition. A Saskatchewan report that contemplated widespread provincially initiated amalgamations of small and rural municipalities was not acted upon. A Manitoba report that also focused on the servicing challenges facing small and rural municipalities eschewed

---

[136] This discussion is based on Peter Boswell, "Municipal Renewal in Newfoundland: A Tradition of Cautious Evolution," in Garcea and LeSage, *Municipal Reforms in Canada*.

amalgamation in favour of calls for local cooperation and coordination. Indeed, such local collaboration, through intermunicipal agreements and intermunicipal service boards, is a primary feature of the local government system in Western Canada.

Municipal restructuring in the West has included annexations and amalgamations, especially to address urban growth and sprawl, such as in the areas surrounding Calgary and Edmonton. Restructuring has also introduced two of the most original and interesting models in Canada – the venerable regional districts of British Columbia and the much-heralded and much-maligned city of Winnipeg structure.

Unlike the experience in Western Canada, the provincial governments in Ontario and, to a much lesser extent, Quebec have been quite prepared to impose municipal restructuring – sometimes in the face of very strong opposition. These two provinces have also followed a similar path in terms of the types of restructuring undertaken. They have amalgamated many of the small and rural municipalities (Ontario more so than Quebec) and they have gone through two stages of urban restructuring. The first stage involved the establishment or strengthening of two tier systems for the major urban areas of each province – headed up by regional governments and urban communities. In the second stage, only recently completed, many of these two tier systems have been eliminated through the creation of enlarged cities that cover all of the area formerly under various regional governments and urban communities.[137]

Restructuring experiences in Atlantic Canada reflect a mixture of Western and Central Canada experiences – both in the provincial posture on reforms and in the kinds of changes introduced. While restructuring has been imposed in some instances, there has also been a good deal of support for the status quo or for very incremental change, proceeding only to the extent that local support is evident. Amalgamations to create enlarged cities has been the most common form of restructuring, but addressing intermunicipal issues through joint servicing agreements and service boards is also very much an alternative in Atlantic Canada.

---

[137] Although, in the case of the Montreal and Quebec City areas, a form of two tier system has been perpetuated through the establishment of as yet weak upper tier metropolitan communities.

Chapter 5
The Limits of Local Restructuring

Municipal restructuring efforts in Canada have been limited in several respects – in the reforms actually carried out; in the overemphasis on amalgamation (especially in recent years); in the alternative approaches to reform that have received too little attention; in the broader, external changes that should occur and often haven't; and in the internal changes and innovations that have been relatively neglected because of the preoccupation with boundary changes.

Introduction

To keep its length manageable (barely), the preceding chapter concentrated on describing, without analysis, the reforms made to the structure of local governments in Canada over the past 50 years. The primary objective of this chapter is to evaluate that restructuring experience, including the validity of the underlying rationale for the reforms and the effectiveness and potential of the resulting structures.

It is beyond dispute that the local government structure in Canada faced growing challenges over the past half century, many of them related to the pressures of growth and change described in Chapter 3. That chapter documented the problems arising from urbanization and demonstrated the need for broad-based action to deal with economic, environmental, and social costs associated with urban sprawl. But it is open to debate whether boundary changes through municipal amalgamation have to be – or should be – the principal instrument for addressing these changes and challenges. Some alternative responses will become evident as we examine the Canadian experience with restructuring and as we compare a number of different approaches found in the United States.

Recapping the Reforms

The approaches to restructuring and reform can be grouped, somewhat arbitrarily, in three main categories as described and illustrated below.

1. The establishment of intermunicipal boards to provide a forum for addressing issues that cross municipal boundaries and/or for providing particular services (such as planning, economic development, water and sewer systems, and transit).

Table 5.1 Intermunicipal Boards	
Metropolitan Authority of Halifax	Originated in 1962 as Halifax-Dartmouth Metropolitan Authority, and over the years gained responsibility for operating a regional jail, regional transit, and a regional landfill site. Abolished when the Halifax Regional Municipality was established in 1996.
St. John's Metropolitan Area Board	Established in 1963, for planning, then provided a number of urban services. Abolished in 1992, with the newly enlarged municipality of St. John's becoming a regional service provider in its place.
Commission of Three Communities (Moncton, Dieppe, Riverview)	Set up in 1996 as an alternative to amalgamation, and charged with regionalizing common services including fire, police, water treatment, cultural facilities, industrial parks, economic development, urban planning, public transportation, solid waste, and emergency measures. Disbanded in 2000.
Montreal Metropolitan Community (MMC)	Set up in 2001 with representatives from all municipalities in the Montreal CMA. Duties include metro planning and economic development, social housing, and planning for urban transit and solid waste disposal.
Greater Toronto Services Board (GTSB)	Established in 1999 with representation from all municipalities in the Greater Toronto Area, but with responsibility only for the GO Transit commuter train system. Dissolved at the end of 2001.
Manitoba Capital Region Committee	Set up in 1989 with heads of council for Winnipeg and 12 (now 15) surrounding municipalities, and focused on developing a strategy for sustainable development. Replaced by Capital Region Panel in 1998, to provide a more coordinated approach in areas such as land use planning and delivery of services.
Alberta Capital Region Forum	Created in 1995 with representatives from 14 municipalities, including Edmonton. Had little success in land use planning or developing a coherent regional economic strategy and was replaced in 1999 by the Alberta Capital Regional Alliance comprising Edmonton and 19 surrounding communities.

2. The establishment of a regional or metropolitan two tier system of municipal government, with the upper tier unit responsible for addressing the cross-boundary issues and lower tier municipalities (enlarged through amalgamation or not) providing the more localized services.

Table 5.2 Two Tier Systems	
Ontario	Metropolitan Toronto, 1953-1997
	Regional Governments, established during 1969-1974
Manitoba	Metropolitan Winnipeg, 1960-1971
British Columbia	Regional Districts, 1965
Quebec	Urban communities in Montreal, Quebec City, and Hull, 1970
	Regional county municipalities, 1979

3. The amalgamation of two or more (often many more) municipalities to create one unified jurisdiction.

Table 5.3 Amalgamated Single Tier Municipalities	
St. John's, Newfoundland	Effective January 1992, with St. John's combining with two municipalities and most of the area formerly under the Metropolitan Board.
Summerside, PEI	Five municipalities merged in 1995.
Charlottetown	The city, a town, and five communities merged in 1995.
Cape Breton, NS	Eight municipalities merged, effective August 1995.
Halifax	Four municipalities, including Halifax county, April 1996.
Miramichi, NB	Merger of 11 communities (five incorporated municipalities) effective 1995.
Montreal, Quebec	Merger of 28 municipalities, including an upper tier urban community, to form enlarged city of Montreal, effective 2002.
Quebec City	Merger of 13 municipalities, including an upper tier urban community, effective 2002.
Gatineau-Hull	Merger of 5 municipalities, including an upper tier urban community, effective 2002.
Longueuil	Merger of 8 municipalities, effective 2002.
Lévis	Merger of 10 municipalities, effective 2002.
Toronto, Ontario	Merger of 7 municipalities, including upper tier metro government, effective Jan. 1998.
Chatham-Kent	Merger of 23 municipalities, including upper tier county government and separated city, effective Jan. 1998.
Kawartha Lakes	Merger of 17 municipalities, including county, Jan. 2001.
Ottawa	Merger of 12 municipalities, including regional government, Jan. 2001.
Hamilton	Merger of 7 municipalities, including region, Jan. 2001.
Sudbury	Merger of 8 municipalities, including region, Jan. 2001.
Haldimand-Norfolk	Merger of 7 municipalities, including region, to form two towns, Jan. 2001.
Winnipeg,, Manitoba	Merger of 13 municipalities, including metro government, Jan. 1972.

The Impact of the Three Types of Reform

The figure below places the three types of response on a spectrum from least intrusive to most intrusive, in terms of how much they affect the existing municipal structures.

Figure 5.1 Gradations of Restructuring

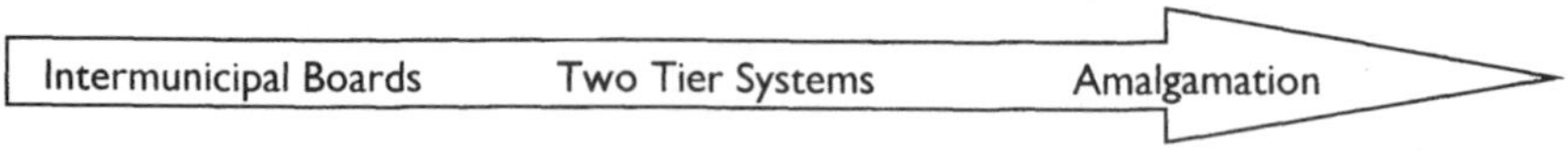

Intermunicipal Boards	Two Tier Systems	Amalgamation

When intermunicipal boards are established, all municipalities usually continue to exist. When metropolitan and regional government systems are established, lower tier municipalities continue to exist, although usually with some amalgamations. With the third option, full amalgamation, all previously existing municipalities are subsumed within a single enlarged municipality.

Deciding where a particular structure fits along this spectrum, however, is not always straightforward. For example, does the new Montreal Metropolitan Community really belong in Table 5.1 above, or should it be classified as a two tier system and placed in Table 5.2? In Quesnel's view the MMC is more than a forum or intermunicipal board.[1] Hamel and Rousseau contend that it has few powers or resources and is not fully a regional government.[2] At this point, it is simply too soon to tell how the MMC will evolve and whether it will become a significant level of government.

If there is any pattern apparent with respect to the three types of response distinguished above, it appears to be that amalgamated single tier municipalities are now the preferred model, especially in comparison with two tier systems. Most restructured two tier systems were created 40 to 50 years ago, and even the most recent such systems (Quebec's urban communities and regional county municipalities) were set up in the 1970s. Moreover, many of these two tier systems have been abolished in the past few years as part of the amalgamations that have created large single tier municipalities. Gone are Quebec's

---

[1] Communication from Louise Quesnel, July 2, 2003.

[2] Pierre Hamel and Jean Rousseau, "Revisiting Municipal Reforms in Quebec and the New Responsibilities of Local Actors in a Globalising World," a paper prepared for the Municipal-Provincial-Federal Relations Conference, Institute of Intergovernmental Relations, Queen's University, May 9-10, 2003, p. 11.

urban communities[3] and half of Ontario's regional governments; long gone (since 1972) is Winnipeg's metropolitan system. The most enduring two tier system (now 40 years in existence) is that of British Columbia's regional districts, their longevity no doubt partly attributable to their modest scale and flexible nature of their operations. Indeed, some would probably place the regional districts in the first category above – as an intermunicipal board rather than as an upper tier government. Their hybrid nature is part of what makes the regional districts distinctive.

Should We Shed a Tier?

The recent actions to eliminate two tier municipal systems in Canada merit further examination, especially since this move seems to be contrary to most expert opinion on this subject. According to Stephens and Wikstrom, the establishment through amalgamation of one municipality covering an entire metropolitan area was popular among scholars during the first half of the 20th century but has virtually no support in the scholarly community today. Instead, "most present-day scholars of urban affairs predisposed toward metropolitan government reform endorse a federative, two tier type of metropolitan governmental structure."[4]

The Case for a Two Tier System

A report recommending a two tier system for the Hamilton area at the end of the 1960s offered the following justification.[5]

> The Commission believes that the two tier system for the area offers the best opportunity of reconciling the two main aspects of municipal government – efficiency and access. The larger administrative unit would provide a greater chance for efficiency, but the sheer size, number of people and volume of business would mean

---

[3] Although it could be argued that the two tier model has been continued in the form of the new Montreal Metropolitan Community and the similar body established for the Quebec City area – depending, as already noted, on how these new bodies evolve.

[4] G. Ross Stephens and Nelson Wikstrom, *Metropolitan Government and Governance*, Oxford, Oxford University Press, 2000, p. 29.

[5] The Hamilton-Burlington-Wentworth Local Government Review, *Report and Recommendations*, November 1969, p. 72.

> that the elected council of the metropolitan community would have
> difficulty in hearing all persons wishing to express aspects of local
> concern. There are many functions that are not of overall concern
> but are of extreme local importance. These functions may be more
> readily dealt with by the lower tier council who will have the
> knowledge of local conditions.

The report went on to explain that a two tier system of municipal
government allows different decisions to be made and different levels
of service to be provided in various areas of the region to best meet the
desires and needs of its inhabitants.

Sharpe makes a similar point when noting that some find an
inherent logic in the two tier model of municipal government "since it
can help resolve the eternal conflict within local government between
the values of participation, access and local identity on the one hand
and functional optimality and production efficiency on the other."[6] He
also states that the unitary type is not an option that works for the
very largest cities, simply because of scale.[7]

Kitchen offers several benefits from the existence of both
lower tier and upper tier municipalities.[8] The first is that the larger
geographic area of the region can better address and control spillovers
(positive or negative externalities) that might arise if some services
were provided by lower tier municipalities. As an example of a
negative spillover, he cites the problem that could arise if solid waste
disposal were a lower tier responsibility and if a solid waste disposal
site were opened by one municipality near the boundary of an adjacent
municipality, generating negative impacts on the residents of that
neighbouring municipality.

A second benefit of a regional level is ensuring consistent
standards in the provision of certain services. If, for example, social
welfare assistance were administered at the lower tier, and if support
differed among lower tier municipalities, there would be an incentive
for recipients to relocate to those municipalities offering the highest
level of support. Until changes introduced in the late 1990s, this
pattern was evident in those areas of Ontario without a county welfare

---

[6] L. J. Sharpe, *The Government of World Cities: The Future of the Metropolitan
Model*, Chicester, John Wiley & Sons, 1995, p. 18.

[7] *Ibid.*

[8] Harry Kitchen, "Does Amalgamation Really Produce Cost Savings?" paper
presented to Municipal Amalgamation Conference, Halifax, April 25, 1995.

system where cities, with their wider range of services and programs, carried a disproportionate share of the welfare burden.

A third benefit of the two tier system, according to Kitchen, is that where spillovers are not prevalent and uniform standards are not required, local preferences can be reflected in the quantity and quality of services provided by lower tier municipalities. In addition, the existence of a number of separate municipalities looking after these services generates a competitive atmosphere that provides a stimulus for improved service delivery.

Bird and Slack[9] also find merit in the two tier system, partly as a way of getting around the fact that each urban service will likely achieve the lowest per unit cost at a different scale of production.

> ...the optimum form of government will likely turn out to be a two tier or multi-tier structure where some services are provided by the upper tier – either a province or a regional government – and some by the lower tier or tiers. Indeed, since most government activities consist of a cluster of functions, what appears to be unnecessary overlap of government functions may sometimes represent a rational solution to the spillover problem.

The Case for a One Tier System

In spite of this impressive list of potential benefits, two tier systems have come under increasing attack in Canada and many of them were eliminated in the extensive restructuring of the 1990s. Typical of the criticisms of the two tier model were these comments of the commissioner who recommended the amalgamation that created the Halifax Regional Municipality:[10]

> A two tier structure is more expensive: there are more elected officials, more administrators, and more facilities. It is more confusing to the taxpayer, since there are always questions about which of the two tiers is responsible for what. As a result, it is less responsive.

One of the most difficult challenges faced by two tier systems is often the relationship between the upper and lower tier. Depending on the area and population covered by the system, there are often

---

[9] Richard M. Bird and N. Enid Slack, *Urban Public Finance in Canada*, 2nd Edition, Toronto, John Wiley & Sons, 1993, p. 35.

[10] Nova Scotia, *Interim Report of the Municipal Reform Commissioner, Halifax Metropolitan Area*, July 8, 1993, p. 39.

complaints about city or suburban domination. Where the upper tier councillors are chosen by indirect or double direct election – in that they hold their positions by virtue of being selected by lower tier councils or by being elected to councils at both levels – the concern is that they are too focused on the interests of the local municipalities from whence they come. However, when upper tier councillors are directly elected, as was the case with Metropolitan Winnipeg in the 1960s and Metropolitan Toronto (for the most part) and Regional Ottawa-Carleton in the 1990s, the result is to sharpen the clash between upper and lower tier.[11] Lower tier municipalities complain that they lack representation on the upper tier council. For upper tier councillors, direct election gives them a sense of greater legitimacy and a better opportunity to direct their attention to region-wide issues, but it also tends to make them less sensitive to local views and concerns. The result is usually growing conflict and confrontation, which becomes one of the justifications for the provincial governments to eliminate the two tier systems in these areas.

In contrast to these alleged defects of two tier systems, pro-ponents of a one tier system claim that it is simpler, avoids duplication, is more efficient and therefore saves money, and provides clearer lines of accountability.

Reviewing the Rationale for the Reforms

Among the reasons advanced, to a greater or lesser extent in Canada, to justify municipal restructuring are the following:

1. To generate savings
2. To ensure equity (or at least less inequity)
3. To eliminate intermunicipal clashes and turf wars
4. To compete more effectively in a global world
5. To reduce bureaucracy and have less government

[11] Andrew Sancton discusses this problem in two of his recent writings: "The Municipal Role in the Governance of Cities," in Trudi Bunting and Pierre Filion, *Canadian Cities in Transition*, 2nd Edition, Toronto, Oxford University Press, 2000, pp. 437-438, and "Signs of Life? The Transformation of Two-Tier Metropolitan Government," in Caroline Andrew, Katherine A. Graham, and Susan D. Phillips (eds.), *Urban Affairs: Back on the Policy Agenda*, Kingston, McGill-Queen's University Press, 2002, pp. 180-181 and 187.

A closer examination of these justifications indicates that some of them appear to have much more validity than others. Ironically, it is the least valid reasons that have often been advanced most forcefully by a number of provincial governments.

Generating Savings

Especially in recent years, proponents of municipal amalgamation or consolidation have emphasized the need to overcome fragmentation, reduce duplication, and generate savings. Every news release from Ontario's Ministry of Municipal Affairs announcing an amalgamation repeated the standard statement: "Municipalities across Ontario are eliminating waste and duplication and providing better service at lower cost, through local restructuring." The municipal mergers introduced in Nova Scotia, New Brunswick, and Quebec over the past decade were also preceded by predictions of savings. Opponents of amalgamation responded, among other objections, by disputing the savings predictions. The efforts of newly amalgamated municipalities, not surprisingly, have been largely devoted to the pursuit of the promised savings – with, at best, mixed results – and evaluations of the success of the new structures have also focused primarily on how well they have held the line on expenditures and taxes.

It is felt that this issue has unduly monopolized attention, to the neglect of other considerations that are at least as important in judging the merits of amalgamation versus fragmentation. However, it is examined first because it has loomed so large in discussions.

Those who anticipate savings from amalgamation seem to proceed from three main assumptions.

i)   That economies of scale will result from providing services over larger areas;

ii)   That reducing duplication means substantial staff reductions that will account for the bulk of the anticipated savings; and

iii)   That the existing range and level of services will continue largely unchanged within the new municipality.

Economies of scale arise where the per unit cost of delivering a service falls as the quantity of the service provided increases. However, each municipal service is likely to achieve these economies at a different scale of production. The optimum size of government may be different for fire services than for roads or police. For example, studies by Kitchen have shown that the lowest cost per gallon of water supplied existed in municipalities in the range of 25 000 to 35 000, whereas the least expensive delivery systems for solid waste collection were found in municipalities under 5000, with per capita costs then rising until municipalities reached about 325 000 residents.[12] According to Bish, most research indicates that "approximately 80 percent of local government activities do not possess economies of scale beyond relatively small municipalities with populations of 10 000 to 20 000."[13]

If one wants to achieve economies of scale, amalgamation is a problematic choice, because while the larger municipality that results may be more efficient for delivering some municipal services, it will also be less efficient for delivering others. As already noted, a better alternative is for municipalities to come together in a variety of combinations for different services, or even for different aspects of the same service. For example, there are many different activities within the policing function, each with a different optimum scale of operation. A detailed study of production arrangements for policing in Standard Metropolitan Areas in the United States found that police patrols are best handled by very small detachments, while dispatching systems, detention facilities, crime labs, and training facilities are best handled over successively larger areas.[14] From this perspective, the best arrangement isn't a single amalgamated municipality *or* a two tier system; it is a large number of separate municipalities. Such a structure not only allows for flexible service production, as needed, but also provides a competitive atmosphere because of the multiple service producers.

The second assumption, that savings would arise from a substantial reduction in staffing, has also proven to be elusive. Staff layoffs or buyouts result in increased costs in the early going because of the severance packages that must be paid. Before long, municipalities often found that they had downsized too much and had lost too much experience and expertise – leading to increased costs as the staff complement was expanded again. Savings that have been sustained

---

[12] Kitchen, "Does Amalgamation Really Produce Cost Savings?"

[13] Robert L. Bish, *Local Government Amalgamations: Discredited Nineteenth-Century Ideals Alive in the Twenty-First*, Commentary No. 150, C. D. Howe Institute, March 2001, p. 14.

[14] Discussed in *ibid.*, pp. 13-14.

have usually arisen from the introduction of more efficient work processes, but it is arguable that such improvements could have been made (and were in numerous municipalities) without amalgamation.

Savings on staffing costs are hard to achieve because there are strong upward pressures on these costs after an amalgamation. There is pressure to standardize services by moving to the highest level previously prevailing – that is, by levelling up, not levelling down. There is pressure to standardize salaries and wages, by levelling up to the highest remuneration that previously existed. Additional staff may need to be hired because of a loss of volunteer activity associated with the previous, smaller municipalities. The new municipality may also face demands for additional levels of supervisory personnel, more support staff, or new specialized positions.

Partly because of these pressures, the substantial savings that are claimed by amalgamation proponents have not usually materialized. Sancton makes this point on the basis of examples drawn from Britain, the United States, and Canada. He notes that numerous studies in the United States have shown that larger municipalities spend more money per capita on most services than do smaller ones, and that the federal government's Advisory Commission on Intergovernmental Relations had reversed its position by 1987 and no longer advocated municipal consolidation.[15] A study on the determinants of municipal expenditure in Ontario found that within a regional government structure, the larger the municipality, the higher the per capita expenditures.[16]

Vojnovic's preliminary analysis of the effects of five amalgamations of Canadian municipalities[17] demonstrates the futility of trying to establish a precise link between amalgamation and costs, and also debunks the third assumption listed above – that services and service levels continue unchanged after amalgamation. In some instances where costs decreased, it was because provincial grants were provided to smooth and sweeten the transition process. In other

---

[15] Andrew Sancton, "Reducing costs by consolidating municipalities: New Brunswick, Nova Scotia and Ontario," *Canadian Public Administration*, Fall 1996, p. 272.

[16] J. Kushner, I. Masse, T. Peters and L. Soroka, "The determinants of municipal expenditures in Ontario," *Canadian Tax Journal* (1996), vol. 44, no. 2.

[17] Igor Vojnovic, *Municipal Consolidations in the 1990s: An Analysis of Five Canadian Municipalities*, Toronto, ICURR Press, 1997.

instances, costs went up significantly, but at least partly because of provincial downloading, increased service standards, or other factors not directly related to the act of amalgamation. Poel's assessment of restructuring in Nova Scotia leads to the same conclusion. He points out that the amalgamation in Cape Breton can't be blamed for the area's economic problems related to the loss of fishing, coal mining, and a steel industry any more than the Halifax amalgamation can be given credit for economic growth derived from off-shore gas and oil developments.[18]

Rather than amalgamation saving money, followers of public choice theory argue that it is fragmented municipal structures that generate savings because such structures most closely approximate the market place, allowing individuals to make choices about services and taxes. As already noted, the presence of several municipalities offering services creates a competitive atmosphere among individuals and among the bodies providing services. This view reflects the contribution of Tiebout,[19] who equates municipalities with firms and local citizens with consumers. Municipalities attempt to provide the services desired by their populations at minimum cost, while individuals shop around for that jurisdiction that provides the combination of services and tax level that meet their preferences. The more municipalities there are, the more choices, the more competition, and the more pressure for each one to be efficient.

Focus On Savings Misplaced

There is some logic in these public choice arguments, and a number of studies do indicate lower per capita costs for municipal services within fragmented structures. But as Keating points out, just because smaller jurisdictions have lower costs does not mean that they are more efficient. "It might equally reflect the tendency for the American

---

[18] Dale H. Poel, "Municipal Reform in Nova Scotia," in Joseph Garcea and Edward LeSage (eds.), *Municipal Reforms in Canada: Dynamics, Dimensions, Determinants*, forthcoming publication.

[19] Charles Tiebout, "A Pure Theory of Local Expenditures," *Journal of Political Economy*, Vol. 64, 1956, pp. 416-424. Bish, cited earlier, is another exponent of public choice theory. His publications include *The Public Economy of Metropolitan Areas*, Chicago, Markham/Rand McNally, 1971 and (with Vincent and Elinor Ostrom) *Local Government in the United States*, San Francisco, Institute for Contemporary Studies, 1988.

middle classes to retreat into small, homogeneous communities which do not face the high costs of areas with more social stress or central place functions, and to provide more services privately."[20]

By emphasizing the savings that were to result from municipal amalgamations, provincial governments created a situation in which opponents of amalgamations could claim that the reforms had failed when the savings did not materialize. But a fragmented municipal structure gives rise to a number of considerations other than the cost of services and failure to take these into account leaves incomplete any assessment of the effect of reforms to that structure. This misplaced focus has been expressed as follows:[21]

> Instead of highlighting the political advantages of metropolitan integration in terms of information, equity in service provision, and democratic control, supporters of consolidation all too often make insupportable claims about economies of scale that shift the terms of the debate to the wrong issues.

Central to public choice is the notion of a number of different municipalities offering different combinations of services and tax levels, and thus providing locational options for residents and businesses. But many residents are not mobile and can't easily shift locations even if they have information that suggests more attractive alternatives. The poor and disadvantaged are especially lacking in mobility, and a fragmented municipal structure can give rise to policies that reinforce this reality. Urban sprawl has traditionally included the movement of middle class families to suburbs where they could pursue their objective of having single family homes on large lots, free of the congestion and crime associated with the inner city. By practising "exclusionary zoning,"[22] suburban municipalities attempt to keep out the poor and (often) racial minorities. The more these groups become concentrated in the central city, the more the suburbs attempt to dissociate themselves from the city and its social problems, which they usually try to blame on inefficient and spendthrift city administrations.

---

[20] Michael Keating, "Size, Efficiency and Democracy: Consolidation, Fragmentation and Public Choice," in David Judge, Gerry Stoker, and Harold Wolman, *Theories of Urban Politics*, London, Sage Publications, 1995, p. 125.

[21] W. E. Lyons, D. Lowery, and R. H. deHoog, *The Politics of Dissatisfaction: Citizens, Services and Urban Institutions*, Armonk, M. E. Sharpe, 1992, p. 192.

[22] David Rusk, *Inside Game Outside Game*, Washington, Brookings Institution Press, 1999, p. 8.

As a result, local government fragmentation (especially in suburban America) "is largely a mechanism for preserving racial and social segregation and protecting private property values."[23]

Ensuring Equity/Reducing Inequity

It follows that a fragmented municipal structure can give rise to serious concerns about equality and equity. In fact, such a structure tends to perpetuate, and even accentuate, inequalities in income, economic opportunity, and quality of life. Not only do those in the suburbs avoid the social costs of the inner city as much as they can, but also – in a cruel irony – inner city residents are called upon to subsidize those in the suburbs, to the extent that they pay through their taxes to finance the very expensive extension of road, water and sewer lines, and other major infrastructure investments that facilitate the suburban development. After studying 165 metropolitan areas in the United States, Rusk found that those that had created metropolitan governments by annexation or consolidation were less segregated by race and class, economically healthier, and more equitable for their residents.[24]

The problems outlined above have been more pronounced in the United States than Canada, which may help to explain why the issue of equity has scarcely been mentioned in the Canadian context, at least until recently. It is instructive to examine briefly the solutions that have been advocated by observers of the American scene. Apart from Rusk, cited above, most of the others writing about this issue have largely ignored the issue of boundaries and have encouraged various mechanisms that would enable municipalities in a metropolitan area to cooperate with each other.[25]

Myron Orfield has done more than observe the urban scene in the United States; he has meticulously documented the spread of urban poverty from inner city to inner suburb and the rise of affluent outer ring suburbs. By so doing, he managed to split the normal suburban alliance against the city and forged a new one between the declining central city and older, threatened blue collar suburbs – leading to a

---

[23] Keating, "Size, Efficiency and Democracy," p. 128.

[24] David Rusk, *Cities Without Suburbs*, Washington, Woodrow Wilson Centre Press, 1993.

[25] Andrew Sancton, *Merger Mania*, Kingston, McGill-Queen's University Press, 2000, pp. 80-81.

number of intermunicipal collaborations in the Minneapolis-Saint Paul area.[26]

Orfield calls for seven reforms to address the problems facing America's urban areas.[27] The first three – fair housing, property tax sharing, and reinvestment in infrastructure – are needed to deconcentrate poverty, provide fiscal equity, and support the physical rebuilding needed to bring back the middle class and restore the private economy. He also calls for broader land use planning, an expansion of transit, and a combination of welfare reform and job creation centred on local public works projects, all designed to provide growth that is balanced socioeconomically, accessible by transit, economical with government resources, and sensitive to the environment. Finally, he suggests that the previous six reforms can be most effectively administered and sustained by an elected metropolitan coordinating structure.

Two things about Orfield's list come immediately to mind. The first is that structural reform, which has received so much attention in Canada over the past decade, is but one of seven reforms that he advocates. The second is that the other six proposals on his list all relate to policies and programs that can be introduced without any municipal restructuring, especially since many of these policies are best provided by higher levels of government. Ironically, Canada already had most of these policies in place to some degree, but has been abandoning them somewhat at the same time that provinces have been pushing restructuring.

Policies That Address Equity

Equity issues can be addressed in a number of ways besides restructuring. In fact, while the existence of a number of separate municipalities within one urban area can give rise to problems of coordination in the provision of services and of equitable sharing of costs, restructuring doesn't necessarily help to alleviate interjurisdictional externalities. This is particularly the case where urban and rural municipalities with widely varying service standards are brought together. Vojnovic points

---

[26] Myron Orfield, *Metropolitics: A Regional Agenda for Community and Stability*, Washington, Brookings Institution Press, 1997, is his personal account of the battle he waged to bring about regional collaboration.

[27] *Ibid.*, pp. 11-12, on which the following discussion is based.

out that if differences in levels and standards of service among the merging municipalities are not recognized in the design of the tax structure, externalities may actually be exacerbated after amalgamation, with some people unknowingly paying for services from which they get no benefits.[28]

Provinces can provide unconditional grants to bolster the assessment base of assessment-weak municipalities (in much the same way as the federal government has long provided equalization payments to the have-not provinces). A majority of the provinces have had such programs, but not on a scale that suggested that equalization was a major priority.[29] Provinces can also promote a more equitable distribution of public housing throughout an urban area to offset the fact that lower-priced housing is associated with higher levels of demand for publicly funded social services and education. The Ontario Housing Corporation was established in 1964 to access federal funding for public housing and had considerable success in dispersing public housing throughout the Metropolitan Toronto area.[30] However, the federal government abandoned the public housing field in the 1990s (only recently to return on a smaller scale) and the Ontario government turned what is now usually termed "social" housing over to the private sector (without much take-up) upon assuming power in 1995. Subsequently, the province downloaded responsibility for social housing to municipalities in what must be considered a backward step in terms of the equity concerns under discussion.

Ontario's withdrawal was part of a fairly widespread cutback evident in most provincial jurisdictions as they struggled to combat deficit and debt problems that had been made worse by cuts in the transfer payments that they received from the federal government. Any such reduction in provincial support, however, leaves munici-

---

[28] Igor Vojnovic, "Municipal Consolidation, Regional Planning and Fiscal Accountability: The Recent Experiences in Two Maritime Provinces," *Canadian Journal of Regional Science*, Special Edition, Spring 2000, pp. 49-72.

[29] The discussion in this section is largely based on Frances Frisken, "Jurisdictional and Political Constraints on Progressive Local Initiative," in Timothy L. Thomas (ed.), *The Politics of the City*, Toronto, ITP Nelson, 1997, pp. 163-166.

[30] Frances Frisken, L. S. Bourne, Gunter Gad, and Robert A. Murdie, "Governance and Social Sustainability," in Mario Polese and Richard Stren (eds.), *Social Sustainability of Cities: Diversity and the Management of Change*, Toronto, University of Toronto Press, 2000, p. 85.

palities more vulnerable to inequities and social problems. A study of the Greater Toronto Area[31] finds such features as:

- a deepening city-suburban split;
- an increasing polarization of income and social status;
- a relative decline of parts of the older mature suburbs;
- the continued geographical concentration of low income and socially disadvantaged households; and
- the intense separation of social groups with non-traditional social and cultural backgrounds.

A study of the Montreal area notes that social programs from the provincial and federal level have helped to ensure its social sustainability and questions whether this sustainability will be undermined by the cutbacks in social programs since the mid-1990s.[32]

Transit is another example in which provincial government grants have played a positive role, only to be cut back as part of the retrenchment of the 1990s. Ontario's actions were again quite dramatic, with the province withdrawing from all funding for municipal transit systems and transferring to the municipal level the cost of an intermunicipal train service across the Greater Toronto Area known as GO Transit. Saner heads prevailed eventually, and the province recently took back responsibility for GO Transit and also introduced grant payments covering 33% of transit operations (well down from the 75% that it used to subsidize). As Chapter 7 describes, provinces such as British Columbia and Alberta provide support for public transit by sharing a portion of their fuel taxes with their major cities. But Chapter 7 also documents the very limited federal financial support for public transit, as compared with the situation in the United States.

Another approach that provinces can pursue is to take over or fully fund particular local services as a way of ensuring uniformity of service delivery. New Brunswick's equal opportunity program is the most dramatic example of this approach, under which that province assumed full responsibility for the administration of justice, welfare, public health, and educational finance. Paradoxically, the Ontario government has moved in the opposite direction, shifting downward

---

[31] Larry Bourne, *People and Times: A Portrait of the Evolving Social Character of the Greater Toronto Region*, Toronto, Neptis Foundation, 2000.

[32] Anne-Marie Séguin and Annick Germain, "The Social Sustainability of Montreal," in Polese and Stren, *Social Sustainability of* Cities, pp. 52-53.

functions that, by their nature, will increase inequities and inconsistencies. As a result of a new service realignment in the second half of 1996 (discussed in Chapter 6), Ontario has taken over a substantial portion of education costs but given its municipalities increased or total responsibility for such services as social assistance, public health, social housing, land ambulances, and public transit.

There are also several examples of intermunicipal sharing of costs – quite apart from the sharing that occurs within the reformed municipal structures that have been established. To illustrate:

> After transferring responsibility for a number of social programs to the municipal level in the late 1990s, the Ontario government acknowledged the externalities associated with local delivery of such services by mandating a scheme under which social assistance and social housing costs are equalized across all municipalities in the Greater Toronto Area.

> A regional transit coordinating agency was established in 1989 to bring together representatives of the Montreal Urban Community transit system, the south shore system, and the system of the city of Laval. By setting up such an agency, the province combined financial responsibility for subway operating deficits and for previous municipal long term transit debt among all municipalities served by the three systems.[33]

> Translink (the Greater Vancouver Transportation Authority) was set up in 1998 to plan and finance a regional transportation system that supports the regional growth strategy of this area.[34] Translink is governed by a board of directors comprising mostly local representatives appointed by and from the Greater Vancouver Regional District, and it is authorized to raise revenues through various means including taxes, levies, toll charges, and user fees. It also receives three cents per litre of the fuel taxes collected by the province.

To sum up, if improving equity is a major objective, it can be achieved through a wide range of policies and programs that are best provided by senior levels of government. The fact that a number of

[33] Andrew Sancton, "Metropolitan Government in Montreal," in Sharpe, *The Government of World Cities*, pp. 138-139.

[34] Information on this agency is available at its web site www.translink.bc.ca, accessed July 29, 2003.

these programs have been provided in Canada presumably helps to explain why equity issues have not been as pronounced here as in the United States. But government restraint over the past decade has undermined some of these programs, with the result that equity may become more of a concern despite all the restructuring there has been.

Controlling Sprawl

Amalgamating municipalities in an effort to control urban sprawl means having to restructure on a continuing basis, constantly expanding boundaries outward in an attempt to catch up with the ongoing population overspill. It can also lead to the creation of municipalities that are too large in relation to their other important roles.

Rather than expanding local governments until they cease to be local, provincial governments could – and should – provide more leadership with respect to sprawl, since they obviously have the broader jurisdiction needed and the authority and resources to be effective. Indeed, at least in the case of the four largest urban agglomerations in Canada, it is arguable that only the provincial level is in a position to provide the overall planning and control necessary to manage growth effectively. An example would be provincial efforts to limit further growth in already built up areas coupled with policies and incentives to attract and stimulate growth in less developed areas. This was the basis of Ontario's regional development initiatives of the 1960s and its Toronto Centred Region Plan of the early 1970s. The logic underlying this provincial involvement was a recognition that "the province was not dealing with a metropolis and a set of lesser centres that could be allowed to develop autonomously, but with a highly integrated urban complex which spread right across the southern portion of the province."[35]

While these provincial actions had little impact in altering the unfolding development patterns, the need for growth management in the Greater Toronto Area has increased even as the provincial role has declined. Stein argues that the provincial government failed to invest in roads, sewers, and water mains in the right places, demonstrating a "failure of nerve" that contributed to the worsening urban sprawl.[36]

---

[35] Warren Magnusson, "Metropolitan Reform in the Capitalist City," *Canadian Journal of Political Science*, September 1981, p. 565.

[36] David Lewis Stein, "The Region at 25," *Toronto Star*, January 1, 1999.

Stein is even more critical since the election of the Conservatives in 1995, claiming that they have taken the province out of planning cities (by allowing regions to amend official plans on their own), have cut financial support for cities, and have downloaded provincial costs on them.[37] The short-lived Greater Toronto Services Board lacked the authority to undertake broad-based planning, and there is little indication that the Smart Growth Panels that have been most recently established will have anything but an advisory role.

In a generally positive analysis of the Toronto area, Savitch and Kantor also raise concerns about recent developments on the planning front. They describe a "cooperative confluence of power," a "triple alliance" involving the province, Metropolitan Toronto, and its six lower tier municipalities, that successfully oversaw planning and development in the area up until the late 1990s.[38] But they note that recently the province has begun to undercut provincial planning, has softened restrictions, and has allowed localities more discretion on development – with the predictable result that "development has begun to slip past smaller suburbs into a formless sprawl...."[39]

A more constructive provincial response has appeared recently, in connection with the Oak Ridges Moraine, as outlined below.

Box 5.1 Protecting the Oak Ridges Moraine

The Oak Ridges Moraine is a unique area stretching for 160 kilometres east from the Niagara escarpment across the top of the Greater Toronto Area and into neighbouring Durham Region. It acts as a rain barrel feeding 65 rivers and streams that flow into Lake Ontario and also directly provides water to over 250 000 people. Environmentalists have been increasingly concerned about the threat that urban sprawl poses for the moraine, and a series of battles were fought, culminating in a year-long Ontario Municipal Board hearing in 2000-2001 concerning 8000 new homes in the Richmond Hill area.

This piece-meal approach to protecting the moraine was obviously slow, expensive, and uncoordinated, and it was equally obvious that an area the size of the moraine could not be brought under the jurisdiction of one municipal government, even in amalgamation-prone Ontario. The provincial government responded with a six month freeze on development in the moraine, followed by legislation in December 2001 (The Oak Ridges Moraine Conservation Act) that provides regulatory power for the province to identify various categories of land within the moraine and to specify what type of development may occur where.

---

[37] *Ibid.*

[38] H. V. Savitch and Paul Kantor, *Cities in the International Marketplace*, Princeton, Princeton University Press, 2002, pp. 176-180.

[39] *Ibid.*, pp. 279-281.

The uncharitable have suggested that the province was moved to action by an approaching by-election in the area (which it lost), and not all environmentalists are especially happy with the new legislation or the fact that any protection for the moraine is covered by regulation and can be amended or removed the same way. But, however effective this initiative turns out to be, it illustrates a situation in which the province is certainly in a much better position than municipalities, restructured or not, to address this issue.

The Ontario government's unsuccessful efforts to control growth and sprawl in the Toronto area in the 1970s were followed by quite similar efforts and outcomes in the Montreal area a few years later. In 1978 the provincial government presented a preferred development option for the region of Montreal. But largely as a result of opposition from some suburban municipalities and also from some elements within the provincial government, little specific action was taken on the plans for controlling urban sprawl.[40]

A positive example of provincial leadership in regional planning and development is found in British Columbia with its 1995 Growth Strategies Act which, along with the Livable Region Strategic Plan of the Greater Vancouver Regional District, enabled municipalities across the Lower Mainland to take actions to control sprawl, limit automobile use, and protect environmentally sensitive lands. The new legislation requires municipalities to plan regionally, authorizes the province to intervene where local governments fail to act cooperatively, and provides for dispute resolution as a last resort.[41] According to Smith, this initiative demonstrates that provincial governments can contribute to urban solutions and that regional governance is a viable alternative to regional government.[42]

Fowler and Hartmann note that Surrey withdrew its commitment to the plan in 1997 and question whether the project is viable,

---

[40] For details on this initiative, see François Charbonneau, Pierre Hamel, and Michel Barcelo, "Urban Sprawl in the Montreal Area – Policies and Trends," in Frances Frisken (ed.), *The Changing Canadian Metropolis*, Vol. 2, Toronto, Canadian Urban Institute, 1994, pp. 459-495.

[41] Information on this strategy is available at www.mcaws.gov.bc.ca, accessed June 26, 2003.

[42] See Patrick Smith, "Restructuring Metropolitan Governance: Vancouver and BC Reforms," *Policy Options*, September 1996, pp. 7-11, on which this summary is based.

given that regional authorities lack effective mechanisms to ensure implementation of the plan and that the province has been unwilling to fund the public transit that would underpin the desired land use objectives.[43] More recently, however, the mayor of Surrey has become chair of Translink and the province has committed a share of fuel taxes, as noted above. Especially since the creation of Translink, a case can be made that there are a number of mechanisms to ensure implementation of planning objectives, with the region controlling transit, major roads, and air pollution abatement, and having access to a variety of revenue sources.

Leo emphasizes the importance of higher level involvement in local planning and points out that provinces routinely intrude into other aspects of municipal operations. What is needed, in his words, is "a provincially supervised public participation process to set goals, legislation mandating them, and, for a change, a little bit of provincial political will to practice what they preach instead of letting local municipalities carry the freight."[44]

Eliminating Clash and Conflict

Proponents of amalgamation often point to intermunicipal disagreements and turf wars as reasons why boundary changes are needed. Municipalities are too parochial, it is claimed. They won't cooperate sufficiently. They won't pursue the joint ventures that might bring about savings. Their wrangling makes it difficult for joint boards to function. Combining these fractious municipalities into one governing unit resolves these problems. It facilitates urban planning and economic development. But does amalgamation eliminate wrangling and, more to the point, should it?

Presumably the different points of view expressed by municipalities prior to their amalgamation reflected underlying values and concerns within their local populations. These differences don't magically disappear just because there is an amalgamation. In fact, when amalgamations bring together quite diverse areas – such as when urban and rural areas are combined in Ontario's Chatham-Kent or

---

[43] Edmund Fowler and David Siegel (eds.), *Urban Policy Issues*, 2nd Edition, Toronto, Oxford University Press, 2002, p. 163.

[44] Christopher Leo, Urban Development: Planning Aspirations and Political Realities," in Fowler and Siegel, *ibid.*, p. 233.

Nova Scotia's Halifax – it may be that the differences will be heightened or exacerbated. If the amalgamation process is "softened" by introducing a ward system of election based on the former municipal boundaries, then one can expect this electoral system to perpetuate and reinforce the differing views and values that have been thrown together. The same is true when community councils or committees are established with boundaries that encompass the municipalities that have been amalgamated.[45] These bodies will attempt to ensure that the particular interests and concerns of their area are not overlooked by the new, enlarged municipality – and fulfilling this role is presumably why they were established in the first place. Even without a ward system or community councils, the diverse views found within an enlarged municipality will continue to demand attention – as they should in a democratic system. It must be appreciated, then, that amalgamation doesn't eliminate differences and clashes; it brings them inside a single council chamber.

Box 5.2 All For One and One For All?

Consider the council of the new city of Montreal, elected in November 2001. Former mayor Pierre Bourque had fought hard for the amalgamation that created the new city and suburban voters responded by defeating Bourque and electing Gerald Tremblay and a majority of his Montreal Island Citizens Union Party. Proponents of amalgamation had claimed that it would end decades of conflict and bickering between the suburbs and the city. Instead, this split has simply been carried over into the new council, with the suburban representatives currently holding the upper hand. Prospects for a harmonious term of office are not promising.

It is also important to recognize that amalgamation is likely to alter the balance of power on the local scene. For example, by merging middle class suburbs with inner city areas, amalgamation may push local politics to the right.[46] It is likely that this kind of consideration was on the mind of the Conservative government in Ontario when it imposed the amalgamation that created the new city of Toronto. The expectation was that representatives elected to city council from the more conservative suburban areas would be able to curb the more free spending inclinations (at least from the province's perspective) of councillors from the old city. This observation is also made by Savitch

---

[45] As discussed in Chapter 9, such bodies were established in such amalgamated cities as Winnipeg, Toronto, Montreal, and Halifax, although in this last instance boundaries were deliberately not based on the old municipal boundaries.

[46] Keating, "Size, Efficiency and Democracy," p. 122.

and Kantor, who note that the province also believed that once social programs were downloaded to the city, councillors would have an added incentive to be more frugal.[47]

To Compete in a Global World

Amalgamation is advocated to reduce harmful intermunicipal competition and "beggar-thy-neighbour" policies designed to attract industry, and also to create an enlarged municipality more capable of holding its own in the increasingly competitive global market place. It may be recalled that reducing intermunicipal competition for business was cited in the amalgamation that created Halifax, and the amalgamations in Montreal, Toronto, and Ottawa were also promoted as creating bigger cities that could handle themselves better on the world stage.

As long as municipalities must continue to rely on the property tax as their main source of revenue, it is inevitable that they will devote considerable effort to attracting growth and development and thus expanding their tax base. This point has been taken to its limits, one might say, by the writings of Paul Peterson, who claims that the policies adopted by a city will be constrained and shaped by how the policies affect the overriding objective of promoting economic growth.[48] More specifically, he argues that cities will favour developmental policies designed to strengthen the local economy and to attract more growth. They will not pursue redistributive policies that involve income transfers from higher to lower income segments of the population, lest these adversely affect their objective of enhancing existing business and attracting further development.

One doesn't have to accept Peterson's position completely[49] to appreciate that a preoccupation with growth and the excessive competition that often accompanies it can certainly be self-defeating. But this problem can be addressed in ways other than amalgamation. The most obvious alternative would be a tax-sharing scheme under which some portion of the yield from new growth brought to an area

---

[47] Savitch and Kantor, *Cities in the International Marketplace*, p. 182.

[48] Paul Peterson, *City Limits*, Chicago, University of Chicago Press, 1981.

[49] Among those who question aspects of Peterson's arguments, see Mark Scheider, *The Competitive City*, Pittsburgh, University of Pittsburgh Press, 1989 and Clarence N. Stone and Heyward T. Sanders (eds.), *The Politics of Urban Development*, Lawrence, University Press of Kansas, 1987.

would be shared between the various municipalities in return for joint marketing and promotion efforts. Depending on the formula for distribution, such schemes can also be effective in reducing inequities within a regional area. One of the best known tax sharing schemes is that found in Minneapolis-St Paul, which has operated for over 30 years. Another is EDGE, the Economic Development/Government Equity program of Montgomery County, Ohio, set up in 1992. Twenty-eight municipalities participate, including the city of Dayton, and the areas that attract new business make contributions to a fund that finances infrastructure investments for local communities.[50]

The argument that amalgamation is required because of globalization is very much open to dispute. It appears to be derived from the fact that globalization has made cities and city-regions increasingly important – and on that point there is no argument. "City-regions have come to be recognized as key nodes of the global economy; as places where capital, workers, institutions and infrastructure (soft and hard) come together to provide the foundations for successful economic activity."[51] While national boundaries (and their governments) may have become less important in the new global economy with its various international trade agreements and organizations, major urban centres have come to the forefront because their very concentration of population and economic activity enhance efficiency and innovation.[52]

But does it follow that this increased economic importance of cities and city-regions requires amalgamations that create municipalities large enough to embrace them? To the extent that broader, regional strategies and actions are needed, are there alternative mechanisms for achieving them? It is instructive to recall the findings of Richard Florida, summarized in Chapter 3, that in today's knowledge-

---

[50] The EDGE program is discussed in Rush, *Inside Game, Outside Game*, Chapter 10, and Orfield, *Metropolitics*, examines the tax sharing plan and other regional initiatives in the Minneapolis-St Paul area.

[51] Meric S. Gertler, "City-Regions in the Global Economy: Choices Facing Toronto," *Policy Options*, September 1996, p. 12.

[52] Peter Dreir, John Mollenkopf, and Todd Swanstrom, *Place Matters: Metropolitics for the Twenty-First Century*, Lawrence, University Press of Kansas, 2001, p. 25. See also Allen J. Scott, John Agnew, Edward W. Soja, and Michael Storper, *Global City-Regions*, in Allen J. Scott (ed.), *Global City-Regions*, Oxford, Oxford University Press, 2002.

based economy businesses are attracted to areas that have a talent pool, which, in turn, means that places that can attract talented people will enjoy economic success.[53] Vibrant neighbourhoods, ample recreational facilities, an atmosphere that welcomes and nurtures diversity and creativity – all of these contribute to the rich quality of life that is the key to success. Building healthy and vibrant communities is less about formal government structures and more about building relationships. The required emphasis on governance rather than government is described by Thomas as follows:[54]

> It involves sharing power, the creation of formal and informal networks of interaction, more open and responsive flows of information and intelligence in all directions, decision-making on multiple levels and across multiple sectors and dynamic changes. This more complicated and kaleidoscopic approach to agenda setting recognizes that governments do not have a monopoly on the knowledge, skills and capacity to achieve economic and social improvement.

The argument that amalgamation is needed to contend with global competition falters in the face of the fact that many of the most dynamic and competitive regions in North America (such as the Boston and Dallas areas and Seattle-King County) are among the most fragmented. To illustrate:

> ➢ Pittsburgh has enjoyed an economic renaissance recently with more than 120 separate elected municipal governments in the central city and Allegheny county.[55]
> ➢ It wasn't a unified municipal structure that spearheaded the economic success of Silicon Valley, California; rather it was a private sector initiative that brought together key stakeholders (including municipal government) in the San Jose region to develop a vision and discuss means of attracting and main-

---

[53] Florida's publications include *The Economic Geography of Talent*, Pittsburgh, Carnegie Mellon University, 2001, *The Rise of the Creative Class*, New York, Basic Books, 2002, and *Technology and Tolerance: The Importance of Diversity to High-Technology Growth*, Washington, The Brookings Institution, June 2001.

[54] Paul Thomas, *Globalization, Competitive Regionalism and Municipal Tax Sharing*, July 2002, accessed January 17, 2003 from www.gov.mb.ca/ia/capreg.

[55] Sancton, *Merger Mania*, pp. 77-78. Further examples are found in Andrew Sancton, "Globalization Does Not Require Amalgamation," *Policy Options*, Montreal, Institute for Research on Public Policy, November 1999, pp. 54-58.

taining computer-associated manufacturing. Collaboration and networking have been the distinguishing features of governance in this area, highlighted by such initiatives as Joint Venture: Silicon Valley, a public private partnership that addressed key regional issues such as education and that brought together a group of business, government, and community leaders to develop a vision for 2010. This project, in turn, led to the Silicon Valley Civic Network, that is promoting public discussion of the 2010 vision and goals.[56]

If the municipalities within an urban area are amalgamated, the unified structure will doubtless make it easier to promote and market that area. But amalgamation is not a prerequisite to economic growth, as the preceding examples illustrate. Even if there is an amalgamation, much will still depend on the degree of collaboration that can be achieved between the enlarged municipality, the local business community, and the wide variety of agencies and organizations that collectively contribute to the well-being of the area. Ultimately, this broader collaboration is arguably more important than the particular municipal structure that is in place. If it is not forthcoming at all, amalgamation may be considered a "better than nothing" option. But if other avenues are being followed successfully, then it is unclear why amalgamation would be required or necessarily advantageous.

Less Government/Less Bureaucracy

This argument for amalgamation reflects the view that people are over-governed and desire less government, less "red tape," and fewer politicians. It is consistent with the anti-government bias that is central to the right-wing revolution that swept across North America in the past several decades. The reduced role of government and government regulations is also very consistent with the demands of the business community and the perceived requirements of the new global economy.

Nowhere has this rationale been more in evidence than in the restructuring initiatives pursued by the Conservative government in Ontario in the second half of the 1990s. They premised their restructuring on the notions that local politicians and staff are "the problem,"

---

[56] Douglas Henton, "Lessons from Silicon Valley: Governance in a Global City-Region," in Scott, *Global City-Regions*, pp. 396-397.

that there are too many of them, that they are wasteful in their practices, that their operations are inefficient, that they tax too readily, and that they spend irresponsibly.[57]

The answer, according to the Conservatives, is to provide less government. Every amalgamation in Ontario prompted a press release from the Ministry of Municipal Affairs that tracked how many fewer municipalities and municipal politicians there were as a result. By the time the restructuring initiative was abandoned (at least temporarily) in early 2001, the number of councillors had been reduced by almost 2000, representing a 40% reduction in local representation. This reduction was presented by the province as a self-evident gain to society, but why is it so desirable to have fewer elected local politicians in a democracy? What are the implications of enlarging municipalities to the point where serving on council ceases to be a part time activity available to all, and becomes the preserve of the full time professional politician? One consequence of this change is that council salaries go up to handle increased workloads, often cancelling out virtually all of the savings that were supposed to result from reducing the number of politicians – not that councillors' salaries are in any way a significant factor in the overall costs of municipal government.

The provincially-promoted amalgamations did not really produce less government, of course; instead, they produced bigger government and, as discussed below, more bureaucratic government as well. One explanation for this obviously incorrect provincial message may be that what the Conservatives really meant (and wanted) was not less government in terms of size, but a reduction in the prominence and role of local governments. Less government for them might be equated with the enhanced role for the private sector reflected in the enthusiastic provincial promotion of alternative service delivery options (including privatization) and public private partnerships.

Another concern about the supposed virtues of less government is the very large populations that are now represented by relatively small councils. When restructuring proponents cite with approval the reduction in the number of local politicians that has been achieved, they are really talking about a reduction in local representation. Each councillor now represents a much larger number of

---

[57] T. J. Downey and R. J. Williams, "Provincial agendas, local responses: the 'common sense' restructuring of Ontario's municipal governments," *Canadian Public Administration*, Summer 1998, p. 234.

people, usually over a much larger area. The link between citizens and their *local* government is weakened as a result.

A Different Perspective On Less Bureaucracy

In addition to the doubts about less government, it is equally hard to understand the claim (again particularly from the Ontario government) that municipal amalgamation brings less bureaucracy. To the contrary, amalgamation creates larger municipalities that have more complex organizations, more layers of management, and more opportunities for red tape. Moreover, equating less bureaucracy with reduced duplication and reduced barriers and red tape for business is a very narrow way of looking at this subject. Recent writings on the features of what are termed post-bureaucratic organizations address fundamental changes relating to purpose, people, and performance.[58]

Box 5.3 Features of Post-Bureaucratic Organizations

➢ The external and internal environment is assessed continuously to determine challenges, threats, and opportunities and to communicate them with staff. Clear direction is established for the organization.

➢ The emphasis is placed on inspiring and gaining the commitment of staff to the goals and directions of the organization.

➢ A culture and climate is created where staff can work together collaboratively to achieve high levels of performance and personal satisfaction.

Post-bureaucratic organizations are people-centred, change-oriented, results-oriented, decentralized, revenue-driven, and competitive.[59] It is these features that make them less bureaucratic, and the presence or absence of these features has virtually nothing to do with amalgamation. It is sometimes suggested that creating a new municipality through amalgamation provides the opportunity to introduce such features. But the upheaval caused by amalgamation, and the lengthy process involved in bringing about its full implementation, can divert the time and energy of new municipalities and keep them from pursuing these innovations. This was the experience of the new city of Toronto. At least two-thirds of the very substantial savings predicted for Toronto (about $150 million to $250 million annually) was not

---

[58] See, for example, Kenneth Kernaghan, Brian Marson, and Sandford Borins, *The New Public Organization*, Toronto, Institute of Public Administration of Canada, 2000, on which this section is based.

[59] *Ibid.*, p. 270.

related to amalgamation but was to arise from "efficiency enhance-ments." As it happens, these savings did not materialize in the first few years, according to the Director of Toronto's Amalgamation Office, who claimed that achieving such savings was not a reasonable expecta-tion "in the short run."[60] Poel reports similar experiences in Halifax, where the theme in the first three years was not savings but "don't drop the ball." He emphasizes that a great deal of time and energy is needed to get a new organization up and running effectively.[61]

Old Versus New Regionalism

Much of what has happened and hasn't happened, with respect to municipal restructuring in Canada, can be related to contrasting views of urban and regional issues and the way to resolve them. Traditional or old regionalism was preoccupied with the need for boundary changes and with structural reforms through amalgamation and the establishment of new one tier or two tier municipal systems. Over the past couple of decades, however, new ways of addressing these issues have emerged and have become known as the new regionalism. One of the best-known expressions of this new approach is found in the writings of Myron Orfield cited earlier in this chapter. Another is Neil Peirce's *Citi-States*, which chronicles both the challenges facing major centres in the United States and the varied ways in which these are being tackled through the combined efforts of many players, of which municipal governments are but one, and not always the leading one.[62]

Key features of the new regionalism are summarized in the following table.[63]

---

[60] As quoted in Laura Eggerston, "Becoming One: Lessons Learned From Amal-gamation," *Forum*, Ottawa, Federation of Canadian Municipalities, November/ December 2000, p. 18.

[61] D. Poel and M. Dann, "The development of political leadership in the context of change," *International Journal of Public Administration*, forthcoming.

[62] Neil R. Peirce, *Citi-States: How Urban American Can Prosper in a Compet-itive World*, Washington, Seven Locks Press, 1993.

[63] Allan Wallis, "The New Regionalism: Inventing Governance Structures for the Early Twenty-First Century," a paper presented to the Elected Officials Symposium at the University of Alberta, June 21, 2000.

Box 5.4 Features of the New Regionalism

- Focusing on governance, not government, by establishing a vision and goals and setting policies to achieve them.
- Focusing on process instead of structure, through such means as strategic planning, resolving conflict, and building consensus.
- Accepting that boundaries are open and elastic and building cross-sectoral governing coalitions that vary with the issues being addressed.
- Emphasizing collaboration and voluntary agreement rather than hierarchy and top-down power.
- Building trust as a binding element in relations among regional interests.
- Moving away from a focus on power and how it is allocated among levels of government, and shifting to an emphasis on empowering neighbourhoods and communities and drawing them into regional decision making.

Where Do Canadian Reforms Fit?

In spite of the growing attention being paid to the ideas underlying the new regionalism, it is the old regionalism that predominates in local government reform and restructuring in Canada, including the most recent wave of reform during the 1990s. In Ontario and Quebec and, to a lesser extent in Nova Scotia and New Brunswick, the emphasis has been on structural reform, reflected in amalgamations and the creation of some quite large and diverse new municipalities. Hamel and Rousseau suggest that the Quebec government's approach in the Montreal area has been both more complex and rather contradictory. It followed the old regionalism in forcing the merger of municipalities to create the new city of Montreal. But the province is also acting consistently with the new regionalism in counting on the cooperation of municipalities and other local actors to work with the new Montreal Metropolitan Community in achieving governance for the larger metropolitan area.[64]

There are other Canadian initiatives that fit within the new regionalism. A number of examples are provided below, not as a definitive list but simply to illustrate the kinds of activities that can be placed under the new regionalism umbrella.

➤ The Alberta Capital Regional Alliance and its efforts to improve coordination and sharing of services across the region.
➤ The Capital Region Committee and Capital Region Panel in Winnipeg with such objectives as promoting regional planning,

---

[64] Hamel and Rousseau, "Revisiting Municipal Reforms in Quebec," p. 15.

collaborating to attract business opportunities from beyond the province, and encouraging the development of tax sharing models for the region.

➤ The initiative of the Pelly Trail Economic Development Committee in setting up a regional association covering the Town of Russell and four surrounding municipalities to promote a coordinated approach to economic development and to pursue a tax sharing plan for future commercial and industrial development.[65]

➤ The Ontario Competitive City Regions Partnership (OCCRP) formed in 1999 to promote linkages between business, government, education, and community leaders to generate innovative approaches to developing competitive city regions and action plans to galvanize community involvement.[66]

➤ The Toronto City Summit Alliance, comprising 45 leading citizens (among them, bank executives, university and college presidents, labour leaders, and politicians – including several former Premiers), which released a 2003 action plan for Toronto containing specific recommendations for all levels of government as well as business, labour, voluntary organizations, and citizens.[67]

➤ Community development efforts that mobilize diverse groups, such as the Partners for Jobs initiative in Ottawa that brings together the city government and business, labour, and anti-poverty groups to deliver customized training and employment related support to unemployed people.[68]

➤ The many joint boards found in Atlantic Canada (and discussed in Chapter 4) that have pursued intermunicipal service delivery and cooperative actions – with varying degrees of success.

---

[65] *Final Report of the Capital Region Review Panel*, 1999, Part 5 – Recommendations, available at www.gov.mb.ca/ia/capreg/reports, accessed May 20, 2003.

[66] More details about this initiative and its actions to date can be found at the OCCRP web site, www.occr-partnership.ca, accessed May 20, 2003.

[67] Details on this organization and its action plan are available at www.torontocitysummit.ca, accessed August 4, 2003.

[68] See City of Ottawa, *Partners for Jobs: Action Phase Progress Report*, 2000, accessed May 20, 2003 from the city's web site at www.city.ottawa.on.ca.

➢ Last, but far from least, the regional districts of British Columbia.

It is interesting to find the regional districts on a list of new regionalism initiatives when they were established before this term and way of thinking came into play. Much has been written about the largest of these bodies, the Greater Vancouver Regional District, and some may suggest that it more properly belongs under old regionalism. Perhaps it straddles both old and new regionalism, which is another reason that this model merits more attention than it has received[69] – especially from those who have been busy imposing old regionalism models on Central and Eastern Canada in recent years.

Concluding Comments

If amalgamation is the answer, what was the question? If saving money is the primary objective, there are many other responses that are at least as likely to be successful. In any event, getting bogged down in a debate over whether amalgamation saves money is pointless. There are too many variables to be able to isolate the impact of just amalgamation. There is no way to predict the changes that will arise and affect the operations of amalgamated municipalities – just as there is no way to know how events would have unfolded if municipalities had not been amalgamated. Statistics can be assembled to demonstrate almost any point of view that one wants to promote, but ultimately this debate simply diverts attention from more important issues.

One of those is certainly the concern about equity, but this problem is most effectively addressed by provincial and federal government programs and financial supports – the same programs and supports that have been eroded by more than a decade of deficit and debt reduction initiatives on the part of these governments.

As for problems associated with urban sprawl, it is arguable that these also may require more action on the part of the provincial level – at least in the four largest urban agglomerations in Canada. The

---

[69] See Andrew Sancton, "Canadian Cities and the New Regionalism," *Journal of Urban Affairs*, 2001, Volume 23, Number 5, pp. 543-555, for a discussion of the Greater Vancouver Regional District, Greater Toronto Services Board, and Montreal Metropolitan Community.

areas involved are so large that they cannot be brought within the boundaries of a "local" government. This is still the case in spite of the recent major amalgamations that created the new cities of Toronto and Montreal. These new municipalities have the same outer boundaries as the two tier systems of Metropolitan Toronto and the Montreal Urban Community that were eliminated during the amalgamation process. Neither city has jurisdiction over its wider urban area. Since the Quebec government was willing to impose the amalgamation in Montreal, Hamel and Rousseau wonder why it then settled for a much weaker body (the Montreal Metropolitan Community) for planning and coordination over the wider metropolitan area.[70] The same question is applicable, even more so, to the Ontario government, which created the new city of Toronto in the face of strong opposition, but has shown no such willingness to create structures that can address the broader problems of the Greater Toronto Area. The very fact that areas such as these are so vital to the economies of their provinces, and of Canada, makes one wonder why it should be left to the local level alone – however restructured – to address the problems caused by sprawl.

If the issue is the fragmented structure of local governments within urban areas, is this inevitably a problem, and one that requires amalgamation to resolve? Commenting on the much more fragmented structure found in the United States, Stephens and Wikstrom contend that although it may be assailed as "chaotic, confusing, crazy-quilt, or simply incomprehensible to the average citizen," it is "seemingly viable and far from broken." They go on to argue that "the bewildering structural array of general-purpose and special-purpose bodies governments splashed across the usual metropolis are largely responding to and meeting the varied service needs of the citizenry," although they acknowledge that the less fortunate may, to some extent, fall outside "this deft generalization."[71]

It is arguable that policy makers in Canada have been too narrowly focused on municipal amalgamation as the response to urban and metropolitan issues. There are, in fact, many mechanisms that can be used to address issues that cross municipal boundaries. In Walker's whimsically titled *Snow White and the 17 Dwarfs*, Snow White is metropolitan American and the 17 dwarfs are 17 approaches to

---

[70] Hamel and Rousseau, "Revisiting Municipal Reforms in Quebec," p. 14.

[71] Stephens and Wikstrom, *Metropolitan Government*, p. 169.

regional service delivery – ranging from informal cooperation and local service agreements through special purpose bodies and councils of government all the way to two tier restructuring and amalgamation.[72]

Some of these alternative approaches have certainly been used in Canada, as evidenced by the examples in Chapter 4. But it is widely held that such mechanisms as joint servicing agreements and joint boards are complex, confusing, and lacking in accountability and should be replaced by amalgamating the municipalities in question. Yet an analysis of intermunicipal agreements and amalgamations in Canada concludes that they should not be seen as alternatives to each other and that intermunicipal agreements will continue to be prominent even where amalgamation takes place. It cites the examples of York and Durham where "even within two-tier systems designed specifically to provide an upper-tier institutional framework for the provision of services that transcend any particular lower-tier municipality (municipalities that are themselves the result of significant amalgamations when the reorganized systems were created), there is still a dense network of inter-municipal agreements covering everything from animal control to public transit."[73] Nor have amalgamations eliminated the need for joint boards, even amalgamations on such a large scale as those in Toronto and Montreal, which continue to experiment with bodies such as the Greater Toronto Services Board, the Smart Growth Advisory Panels, and the Montreal Metropolitan Community in an attempt to find a means of addressing the wider issues of their urban areas.

As Chapter 4 made clear, many of the joint boards established over the years were hampered by internal wrangling and often failed to achieve their objectives. This experience leads some to conclude that municipalities are too parochial and must be forced to collaborate through amalgamation. But could it be that the successful example of the British Columbia regional districts works as well as it does precisely because municipalities know that they do not face the threat of forced amalgamation?[74] By contrast, when cooperative ventures and

---

[72] David B. Walker, "Snow White and The 17 Dwarfs: From Metro Cooperation to Governance," *National Civic Review*, January-February 1987, pp. 14-28.

[73] Andrew Sancton, Rebecca James, and Rick Ramsay, *Amalgamation vs. Inter-Municipal Cooperation: Financing Local and Infrastructure Issues*, Toronto, ICURR Press, 2000, p. 73.

[74] This point is also made by Sancton, "The New Regionalism," p. 553.

joint agreements are used against municipalities, as proof that they are interdependent and should become one, these tactics hardly encourage collaboration.

Municipal restructuring will doubtless continue, but it would be helpful if provincial policy makers who have zeroed in on amalgamation as an all-purpose solution to municipal problems demonstrated a greater appreciation of both the nature and causes of these problems and the varied ways in which they can be addressed.

Chapter 6
Intergovernmental Relations

Local governments must get beyond the limiting mindset that they are but constitutional orphans who must constantly plead for better treatment from the provincial (and federal) government. They need to recognize their growing importance, convey that reality more forcefully to their local communities, and build their strength upward from that local foundation.

Introduction

Intergovernmental relations involving local governments usually focus on relations with the provincial government. This is understandable, since local governments lack any recognition in the constitution of Canada and are simply one of the powers given to the provinces to exercise as they see fit. Over the years, there have been many complaints about the nature of the local-provincial relationship, as well as some moderately encouraging developments more recently. While these matters will be addressed first, relations between local governments and the federal government are also important – in spite of the constitution – and these have also been going through problems and changes. Broadening our perspective even further, local governments are also involved in international relationships of growing significance, as result of globalization and international agreements and organizations associated with it. However, as discussed in the concluding section, local governments must not let themselves be defined by, and limited to, these formal, hierarchical relationships.

The Provincial-Local Relationship

The evolution of provincial-local relations in Canada has involved, for the most part, a pattern of increasing provincial supervision, influence, and control. Departments of municipal affairs were established by the beginning of the 20th century in a number of provinces "to give leadership and guidance in municipal development and to provide for the continuous study of the problems of municipalities."[1] The Depression of the 1930s and attendant municipal defaulting on financial obligations led in several provinces to the establishment (or strengthening) of municipal departments and municipal boards exercising a variety of supervisory powers in relation to local government.

The period following the Second World War brought a further increase in provincial supervision and control, largely because of growing service demands on local government arising from the extensive urbanization of the time. As the revenues from the real property tax became less and less adequate to finance the growing expenditures of municipal government, the provinces increased their financial assistance. Most of this increased assistance, however, was in the form of conditional grants. By attaching conditions, provinces were attempting to ensure that certain services were provided to at least a minimum standard regardless of the varying financial capacities of their individual municipalities. But as municipalities participated in more of these shared cost programs, their local expenditures increasingly reflected provincial priorities.

In some instances, provincial intervention was even more direct, with the provincial government taking over all or partial responsibility for functions traditionally exercised by the local level on the grounds, often quite valid, that the function had outgrown local government – or at least its limited boundaries – and now had much wider implications. Especially during the first half of the 20th century, this pattern of responsibilities shifting upward to more senior levels occurred with respect to such matters as roads, assessment, the administration of justice, education, public health, and social services. A related development in some of the provinces saw the establishment or enlargement of a number of intermunicipal special purpose bodies that were ostensibly part of the local government structure and yet came under increasing provincial influence and control. Here again there was a valid concern on the part of the province about minimum standards in such areas as health and education, but the end result was a further weakening of municipal government in relation to the provincial level. As one analyst saw it:[2]

---

[1] K. G. Crawford, *Canadian Municipal Government*, Toronto, University of Toronto Press, 1954, p. 345. Chapter 17 of this text provides a good description of the historical evolution of provincial-local relations.

[2] Vernon Lang, *The Social State Emerges in Ontario*, Toronto, Ontario Economic Council, 1974, p. 61.

> The succession of efforts to enlarge local administrative structures in education, public health, welfare, and toward regional municipalities has simply reduced the number of units confronting the provincial administrator at any one time.... The taxpayer's dollar has been the fulcrum of power for the bureaucrat to use in organizing things, ostensibly for the citizen's benefit but inevitably for the bureaucrat's benefit as well.

By the 1960s, then, local governments had been subjected to three decades of developments that undermined their operating independence and brought them increasingly into the orbit of the senior levels of government.

Box 6.1 Three Decisive Decades

1. As a result of the Depression of the 1930s, municipalities experienced increased provincial surveillance over their financial activities and they lost their historical place in the social services field to the provincial and federal governments.
2. During the 1940s, massive centralization occurred because of the war effort. As part of the tax-rental and then tax-sharing agreements brought on by the wartime emergency, municipal governments were squeezed out of such fields as income tax and sales tax, and confined to their historical dependence upon the real property tax as their main source of revenues.
3. By the 1950s, the greatly increased demands of the post-war period resulted in further provincial and federal encroachment on the operations of local government.

Even where municipalities retained some jurisdiction over traditional functions, they found themselves increasingly entangled with the senior levels of government. To a considerable extent this intertwining of activities is inevitable, and reflects the interdependence of the programs and policies of all three levels of government. As O'Brien points out,[3] the various functions are interrelated in ways that would require intergovernmental activity even if they were all parcelled out in separate pieces to one level only – which they aren't and can't be (and arguably shouldn't be, as discussed later in this chapter).

> The line between health and welfare is not always easy to find. Welfare and social housing are part of one policy. Housing density depends on transit or the automobile. The latter affects the environment and depends on energy policy. Add the need for planning and financing and there is no escaping the fact that governance in our society requires a lot of communication among governments at various levels.

---

[3] Allan O'Brien, "A Look at the Provincial-Municipal Relationship," in Donald C. MacDonald (ed.), *Government and Politics of Ontario*, Toronto, Van Nostrand Reinhold, 1980, p. 167.

Disentangling or Downloading?

Notwithstanding the inevitability of overlap, the past few decades have seen a number of provincial initiatives to reallocate and disentangle responsibilities. While the New Brunswick changes go back almost 40 years and the first Quebec initiative was 25 years ago, the 1990s saw major initiatives in Ontario and Quebec. The added incentive during this past decade was the increased fiscal restraint facing provinces, partly as a result of cuts in federal transfers to them. Reducing the duplication and overlap in provincial and municipal service delivery was seen as a way of cutting costs. It was also felt that the entanglement of service responsibilities obscured lines of responsibility and reduced political accountability, thereby removing or weakening the pressure on governments to strive for more efficient service delivery.[4]

The approaches taken in the various provinces, the underlying objectives, and the results achieved have all varied widely, as will be seen from the descriptions that follow. It will also be apparent that a number of the more recent initiatives seem to be more concerned with downloading than disentangling and that some result in arrangements that are at least as entangled as before.

The New Brunswick Experience

The earliest initiative, and one of the most substantial, began with the Byrne Commission of 1963 (discussed in Chapter 4) and led to the 1967 Program for Equal Opportunity. On the basis of the Commission's identification of services appropriate for the provincial and local levels, the New Brunswick government took over responsibility for the administration of justice, welfare, and public health, and financial responsibility for the provision of education. Property assessment and property tax collection also became provincial responsibilities. The primary objective of achieving greater equity in services was achieved, but the extent of the provincial takeover of formerly local responsibilities, and the fact that the province replaced municipalities in providing services in rural New Brunswick, caused many to worry that the improvement had been achieved at the price of municipal government.

---

[4] Igor Vojnovic, "The fiscal distribution of the provincial-municipal service exchange in Nova Scotia," *Canadian Public Administration*, Winter 1999, pp. 512-513.

The Quebec Experience

The Quebec government undertook a significant realignment of responsibilities and financing in 1980. School board revenues from property taxes were substantially reduced and their revenues from provincial transfers were increased. To offset its increased costs for education, the province also significantly reduced its transfer payments to municipalities, thereby increasing municipal reliance on the property tax.[5] As a result, the share of school board expenditures financed by provincial transfers increased from 60% to 93% between 1969 and 1989. Even more dramatic, with these changes Quebec municipalities were meeting 96% of the cost of local services through their own fees, charges, and local taxes,[6] a degree of fiscal autonomy not approached in any other province.

Two further changes were introduced at the beginning of the 1990s, prompted by the provincial government's concern about its growing expenditure burden and its perception that the revenue-raising potential of the property tax had not yet been fully tapped.[7] In 1990 the province transferred to Quebec school boards the expense of maintaining school facilities while authorizing the boards to levy a property tax (to be collected by municipalities) covering up to 10% of their expenditures.[8] The result was to reduce the share of provincial financing of school board operations to about 88%.[9] The following year the Quebec government introduced changes that shifted to municipalities greater responsibility and financing obligations for public transit, roads, and policing. Both of these changes were seen, at least in part, as an attempt by the province to shift back to the property tax the burden for financing some of the expenditures that had been assumed by the 1980 reforms – a move strongly opposed by the Quebec Union of Municipalities.[10]

---

[5] F. Vaillancourt, "Financing Local Governments in Quebec: New Arrangements for the 1990s," in *Canadian Tax Journal*, 1992, Vol. 40, No. 5, pp. 1123-1139.

[6] Canadian Urban Institute, *Disentangling Local Government Responsibilities – International Comparisons*, Toronto, January 1993, p. 27.

[7] This view is frankly expressed by Claude Ryan, Minister of Municipal Affairs, in a December 14, 1990 statement, *The Sharing of Responsibilities Between The Government and Municipalities: Some Needed Adjustments*.

[8] *Ibid.*

[9] Vaillancourt, "Financing Local Governments in Quebec," p. 1137.

[10] Katherine A. Graham, Susan D. Phillips, and Allan M. Maslove, *Urban Governance in Canada*, Toronto, Harcourt, Brace & Company, Canada, 1998, p. 72.

The Nova Scotia Experience

The disentanglement process in Nova Scotia arose out of a provincial initiative that was originally focused on reducing the number of municipalities in the province. The *Task Force on Local Government* reported in April 1992, and called for a major restructuring of municipal government in the five most urbanized areas of the province, as discussed in Chapter 4. It also cited the position of the Union of Nova Scotia Municipalities that:[11]

> Property services should be supported by property taxes and delivered by municipal government. People services are the responsibility of the provincial government and should be financed by general provincial revenues. Both orders of government should continue efforts to reallocate the delivery and financing of services recognizing this basic principle.

The report also reflected the position of the municipal association in calling for any reallocation of services to be revenue-neutral, meaning that neither the provincial nor the local level would be better or worse off financially as a result of the changes.

More specifically, the task force proposed that rural municipalities would have to start providing their own policing and roads (as urban municipalities had been doing) and that the province would take over the municipal share of the administration and financing of general welfare assistance.[12] In one of several parallels with the Ontario experience (described below), these disentanglement proposals caused greater concern among rural municipalities than urban. The urban municipalities have larger social assistance obligations (which the province would assume) and they were already paying their own way with regard to policing and roads.

The Liberal government elected in 1993 adopted the principle of service exchange proposed in the 1992 task force report. The province would provide a five year period of transition payments and, during this time, municipalities would "be relieved of responsibility for social welfare services and contributions to the cost of correctional services."[13] To offset this shift and to maintain the fiscal neutrality of

---

[11] Report to the Government of Nova Scotia, *Task Force on Local Government*, April 1992, p. 11.

[12] Allan O'Brien, *Municipal Consolidation in Canada and Its Alternatives*, Toronto, ICURR Press, May 1993, p. 18.

[13] Kell Antoft and Jack Novack, *Grassroots Democracy: Local Government in the Maritimes*, Halifax, Dalhousie University, 1998, p. 11.

the swap, rural municipalities would take over the costs of policing and residential streets (services already being paid for by urban municipalities). But as these changes were being implemented, the province became increasingly preoccupied with deficit reduction. As a result, it capped the amount available for equalization payments to financially weak municipalities, causing particular hardship to a number of coastal towns formerly dependent on the ground fishery.[14]

More generally, an analysis by Vojnovic finds that while the service swap in Nova Scotia was intended, in part, to assist financially distressed municipalities, it resulted in an increased financial burden for some of the fiscally weakest municipalities. In his view:[15]

> The overwhelming emphasis on maintaining a revenue-neutral exchange between the province and the municipalities, and ensuring a government structure where one level of government provides a single public service or governance function, redirected the attention of the province and the municipalities away from the basic distributional aspects of the reform.

Poel points out that the services swap was not as straight-forward and clear-cut as originally intended.[16] The municipal and provincial levels continued to exercise a degree of shared responsibility with respect to bridges, some social services, and correctional services. In addition, the development of provincial solid waste resource regions across the province involves a combination of provincial policies and performance targets and municipal responsibility for operations – providing another example of the difficulty of distinguishing between general and local services.

In April 1998, the province and the Union of Nova Scotia Municipalities signed a memorandum of understanding under which the municipal contribution to social service costs was phased out between 1998-1999 and 2002-2003. A comprehensive review of roles and responsibilities was initiated, the first phase of which involved the identification of issues affecting the provincial-local relationship. One of the concerns expressed by municipalities was that they should have more say with respect to services for which they have a financial re-sponsibility. For example, rural municipalities complained that service

---

[14] *Ibid.*, p. 12.

[15] Vojnovic, "The Service Exchange in Nova Scotia," p. 516.

[16] This discussion is based on Dale H. Poel, "Municipal Reform in Nova Scotia," in Joseph Garcea and Edward LeSage (eds.), *Municipal Reform in Canada: Dynamics, Dimensions, Determinants*, forthcoming publication.

standards, the level of police service, and RCMP budgets are set by the federal and provincial governments, but funded by municipalities. Similarly, it was argued that if municipalities are required to contribute to the cost of roads, they should have some say about roads standards, presently determined by the province.[17]

Ontario's Disentanglement Experience

Social services figured prominently in the reallocation of responsibilities in New Brunswick and Nova Scotia, and it was also social services that launched disentanglement in Ontario.[18] The *Report of the Provincial-Municipal Social Services Review* recommended in 1990 that Ontario follow the lead of most other provinces and take complete responsibility for the cost of social assistance. The province agreed with this shift in principle but was not prepared to absorb the approximately $800 million in extra costs that this would entail. A follow up study examined the entire division of powers between the provincial and local level and recommended that: (1) Functions should be assigned clearly and unambiguously to one level to the extent possible, and (2) Financial relationships should be simplified so that the province would continue to provide conditional grants to municipalities only in areas where there is a legitimate provincial interest.

The 1991 report[19] resulting from this study prompted the newly elected NDP government to invite the Association of Municipalities of Ontario to participate in a joint examination of possible service reallocation with the objectives of creating better, simpler government; improving the efficiency and effectiveness of services to the public; clarifying which level of government is responsible for what services; and improving financial accountability and fiscal management.[20] A key guiding principle was that the exercise had to be

---

[17] These examples are from Richard Ramsay, *Report to the Union of Nova Scotia Municipalities and the Department of Housing and Municipal Affairs*, October 23, 1998, p. 8.

[18] The summary which follows is based on David Siegel, "Disentangling Provincial-Municipal Relations in Ontario," *Management*, Toronto, Institute of Public Administration, Fall 1992.

[19] *Report of the Advisory Committee to the Minister of Municipal Affairs on the Provincial-Municipal Relationship* (Hopcroft Report), Toronto, January 1991.

[20] Ian Connerty, "Disentanglement: Changing the Provincial-Municipal Balance," *Municipal Monitor*, Association of Municipal Managers, Clerks and Treasurers of Ontario, October 1992, p. 182.

fiscally neutral – echoing the guiding principle of revenue neutrality that was to guide Nova Scotia's deliberations. A draft agreement was reached in January 1993, under which the province would assume responsibility for general welfare assistance in return for the municipal level assuming greater responsibility in connection with roads, paying for property assessment services, and receiving reduced provincial grants (to achieve the fiscal neutrality objective). Small and rural municipalities were not comfortable with the proposed roads for welfare swap, given that roads constituted their primary function and expenditure. In any event, the tentative agreement fell apart when the province, in response to its growing deficit and debt problems, introduced a social contract and expenditure control program that included major cuts in transfer payments to the local level.

Disentanglement returned, albeit with some important changes in approach and emphasis, following the election of the Conservative government in June 1995. A *Who Does What* panel, chaired by former Toronto mayor David Crombie, was appointed on May 30, 1996, to begin a complete overhaul of who does what in the delivery and funding of many government services. The stated goal of the panel was "to ensure the very best service delivery by reducing waste, duplication and the overall cost of government at the provincial and local government levels."[21] The panel's recommendations culminated in a summary report in December 1996, which largely followed the services to property versus services to people distinction cited earlier in the Nova Scotia exercise. It called for increased municipal responsibility with respect to roads, transit, ferries, airports, water and sewer systems, and policing, and increased provincial responsibility for social services (notably social assistance and child care) and education.

The Ontario government's response, in January 1997, was a proposed realignment of responsibilities that ignored the recommendations of *Who Does What* in several key respects. In particular, the province proposed to download to municipalities increased responsibility for a number of social programs, including public housing, public health, homes for special care, long term care, and general welfare assistance. In return, the province would assume all of the education costs previously borne by residential property tax payers. The nature and speed of the government's response suggested that it had been pursuing its own internal agenda, while using the *Who Does What* panel almost as a front or a diversion. That agenda, it seemed,

---

[21] According to Ministry of Municipal Affairs and Housing, *News Release*, August 14, 1996.

was to gain full control of education decision making in Ontario.[22] Subsequent events (discussed below) support this interpretation.

In the face of widespread criticism and evidence that the proposed service swap was not fiscally neutral, the province accepted a number of modifications that arose from joint discussions with the Association of Municipalities of Ontario. Central to the new agreement is the fact that residential property tax payers continue to pay half of the education costs they had been financing (about $2.5 billion), but with the province now responsible for setting the education tax rate. With the money saved from not taking over all of the education financing from residential property tax payers, the province found itself able to retain a number of responsibilities relating to social programs (such as long term care and homes for special care) that were to be shifted to the local level. However, it still transferred additional responsibilities and/or costs relating to a number of social programs (including public housing, public health, land ambulances, and general welfare assistance), along with public transit, policing (in rural areas), and water and sewer systems (although after the Walkerton water tragedy[23] provincial financial support for these latter services was increased).

While these changes represented a number of concessions that the province had earlier indicated it was not prepared to contemplate, statements from the Premier and the Minister of Municipal Affairs suggested that they were quite satisfied with these changes, which still met their objectives. Interestingly, the Minister, in a statement to the Legislature on May 1, 1997, when he introduced these changes, explained that the first priority of the whole exercise had been "to reduce taxes by ending the spiralling costs of education in this province."

Effective January 1, 1999, the province agreed to share half of the municipal costs for public health and land ambulances, in part to ensure provincial standards in the delivery of these services. Since provincial grant support was adjusted to reflect this change, there was

---

[22] These observations, with which we concur, are made by, among others, Katherine A. Graham and Susan D. Phillips, "Who Does What in Ontario: The Process of Provincial-Municipal Disentanglement," *Canadian Public Administration*, Summer 1998, pp. 186-187.

[23] Seven people died in the small community of Walkerton in 2000, and many more became seriously ill, as a result of a contaminated water supply caused by a mixture of improper local operating procedures and inadequate provincial supervision and inspection. The report of the Walkerton water inquiry is available at www.attorneygeneral.jus.gov.on.ca/english/about/pubs/walkerton/, accessed July 27, 2003.

no net financial gain for municipalities. But the initiative may indicate some provincial sensitivity to the complaint that municipalities should not have to pay for services whose standards are set by the province. This is essentially the same complaint about violation of "pay for say" noted above with respect to Nova Scotia municipalities. Before leaving this section, we should note that the province has dropped the use of the "who does what" terminology – notwithstanding the contribution of the Crombie panel of the same name – and now insists upon referring to this whole exercise as a local services realignment or LSR.

Disentanglement Potential and Pitfalls

Those who propose the disentanglement of provincial and local responsibilities cite a number of advantages. These include simplified arrangements, less overlap and regulation from above, and increased local autonomy. It has also been suggested that the local level will be left with clearly assigned services and access to sufficient revenues to carry these out, which would enhance public accountability and lead to more citizen involvement in government. This is an impressive list of advantages, but the provinces have been less than precise or consistent in the approach used to achieve them, and especially on the basis on which powers would be divided between the provincial and local level.

The Rationale for Service Allocation

When municipal institutions were established, their limited role consisted mainly of providing services to property financed, quite logically, by a tax on property. The property tax came under increasing criticism as the 20th century advanced not only because it was no longer adequate to generate all of the revenues required but also because it was seen as no longer appropriate to finance the services to people that were becoming part of municipal operations. Those looking for a rationale for a new distribution of provincial and municipal responsibilities often seized upon this services to property versus services to people distinction for their purposes. They argued that services to people should be handled by the provincial level. They pointed out that services such as education provided benefits well beyond the boundaries of any one municipality and should be financed appropriately. They also noted that social services involve an income redistributive function tied to broad provincial (even national) standards and objectives, should not be open to local variation, and, as a result, were not appropriate for local administration.

These distinctions have been used, at least in part, in several studies related to disentanglement, including New Brunswick's Byrne Commission (1963), the Michener Commission in Manitoba (1964), the Graham Commission in Nova Scotia (1974), and Ontario's *Who Does What* panel (1996). For example, the Graham Commission contended that municipal responsibilities should be divided into two groups: "... local services, which are of primarily local benefit or which might best be provided by municipal government, and general services, which are of more general benefit to the province or which the province might best provide."[24] A similar distinction underlies the services swap in Nova Scotia.

Cameron[25] is critical of this approach, which suggests that municipal responsibilities don't extend beyond the provision of services, however defined, and therefore ignores the representative and political role of municipal government. Second, he finds the allocation of responsibilities arbitrary and likely to result in a municipal system that is responsible only "for that which is unimportant or inexpensive." Sancton is critical of disentanglement's underlying rationale that municipalities should concentrate on those responsibilities that are inherently local, an approach which he suggests inevitably means a narrower range of municipal functions. He describes the faulty assumption made by advocates of disentanglement as follows:[26]

> To base municipal government's existence on a mission to concern itself with inherently local issues is to insure its quick death. Does anyone really believe that there are *any* issues which are still inherently local?

Sancton points out that there are provincial rules and regulations in place for almost any municipal function that one can cite,[27] and notes as examples garbage disposal and sewers – once thought of as local matters. Indeed, he has demonstrated elsewhere that even metropolitan and regional governments have not been able to handle functions such as public transit, water supply, and garbage disposal, which have increasingly come under provincial jurisdiction.

---

[24] *Royal Commission on Education, Public Services, and Provincial-Municipal Relations, Report*, Halifax, Queen's Printer, 1974, Vol. II, p. 3: 22.

[25] David Cameron, "Provincial Responsibilities for Municipal Government," *Canadian Public Administration*, Summer 1980, pp. 222-235.

[26] Andrew Sancton, "Provincial-Municipal Disentanglement in Ontario: A Dissent," in *Municipal World*, July 1992, p. 23.

[27] Andrew Sancton, "Canada as a Highly Urbanized Nation," in *Canadian Public Administration*, Fall 1992, pp. 281-316.

If, as argued at the beginning of this text, municipalities are to act as a political mechanism through which a local community can express its collective objectives, then it is essential that municipalities be involved in as many activities as possible that are of interest and concern to the local community. This means expanding, not reducing, their sphere of influence. It means becoming (or staying) involved in functional areas in which the municipalities cannot expect to be autonomous. As Sancton wryly observes: "If municipal politicians are not interested in *all* government policies that affect their community, they can hardly complain if many in the community are not interested in municipal government."[28]

Even viewed only from the narrow perspective of services and their delivery, it can be argued that disentanglement efforts are misguided and are as likely to reduce efficiency as to increase it. In this regard, it is instructive to recall the discussion in Chapter 5 about the production of local government services.[29] It cited research that demonstrated how within any one function (such as policing) different activities possessed different characteristics and, as a result, economies of scale were best achieved by allocating these activities over varied areas of jurisdiction – some small and some large. While the discussion in Chapter 5 related to the benefits of flexible governing arrangements, there is also a lesson here with respect to disentanglement. When a responsibility is shared by more than one level of government, it should not automatically be assumed that this arrangement represents wasteful duplication. Yes, it may, but it might also represent a logical and beneficial division of responsibility that is much more likely to generate economies of scale and operating efficiency than would arise from consolidating total responsibility for the function in question at one level only.

Contrasting Service Reallocations

It is instructive to examine the markedly different approaches taken in New Brunswick and Ontario. Under the Program for Equal Opportunity, the New Brunswick government took over responsibility for the administration of justice, welfare, and public health, and financial responsibility for the provision of education. These were services to people, not to property, and they were viewed as general or universal services, not local ones, so the shift in responsibilities to the province

---

[28] Sancton, "Disentanglement Dissent," p. 24.

[29] *Supra*, p. 152.

was consistent with the criteria usually cited as a rationale for service reallocation. As noted above, however, these changes – coupled with other reforms that saw the province abolish rural counties and take over direct provision of some services to rural areas – led to criticisms that the Program for Equal Opportunity had diminished the role of municipal government in New Brunswick.

In contrast, the Ontario experience seems to represent the other extreme in service reallocation. Instead of the province retaining, or even assuming greater responsibility for, various social programs – as has been the pattern in other jurisdictions and was recommended in a series of previous Ontario studies including those of the *Who Does What* panel – the province downloaded to local governments more responsibility and costs with respect to a number of social programs (social assistance, social housing, and public health in particular). These actions were completely at odds with the criteria and rationale generally accepted as appropriate for service reallocation.

Nor can the nature and scope of the downloading in Ontario be explained or justified by the principle of subsidiarity that has gained prominence in recent years. That principle proclaims that responsibilities should rest at the lowest level *capable of providing them*. While the notion of subsidiarity can be traced back to the writings of Aristotle,[30] it has come to the forefront in connection with the debate about how responsibilities would be assigned within the European Union. The principle of subsidiarity has been cited in numerous studies, including the Golden Report on the GTA.[31] It is our contention, however, that the Ontario government has downloaded responsibilities that are beyond the capability of the municipal system. Moreover, to overcome this problem, the government also embarked on a very aggressive campaign to force amalgamations, with the intention of creating large enough units to be able to handle this download. In our view, these actions seriously distort what was intended by the concept of subsidiarity. As Courchene has pointed out, "there is a flip side to the principle of subsidiarity," which means that where externalities and spillovers exist, policy areas should be transferred upward to the jurisdictional level that can internalize these spillovers.[32]

---

[30] Alan Norton, *The Principle of Subsidiarity and its Implications for Local Government*, Birmingham, Institute of Local Government Studies, 1992, pp. 6-11.

[31] Report of the GTA Task Force, *Greater Toronto*, January 1996, p. 163.

[32] Thomas J. Courchene, *A State of Minds*, Montreal, Institute for Research on Public Policy, 2001, p. 26.

Because the Ontario government downloaded inappropriate responsibilities, ones that are of wider than local significance, it has been obliged to introduce or expand the standards that must be maintained with respect to many of these services. This is evident from the provincial requirements that now exist with respect to the provision of such services as public health, social housing, and water and sewage services. Ironically, the result is that provincial and local entanglement has been increased, not decreased.

It should be noted that not all Ontario municipalities object to the increased responsibilities that have been downloaded to them. Differences in rural and urban views are evident, just as they were at the time of the previous disentanglement exercise at the beginning of the 1990s. Small and rural municipalities, which are heavily represented in the Association of Municipalities of Ontario, generally support the services to property versus services to people distinction, and have been opposed to the downloading of social programs. However, the regional governments and a number of the large cities recognize the importance of social programs as a way of "connecting to diverse communities and promoting quality of life" and they also recognize that the quality of life in urban areas is "the key instrument of economic development in a global economy."[33] Accordingly, they are interested in the possibility of greater responsibility for social programs, *if* commensurate financial resources are also provided – a condition that they would argue has not been met.

The Fiscal Neutrality Fixation

The preoccupation with ensuring that any service reallocation was fiscally neutral seriously compromised the whole exercise. A true disentanglement exercise would determine what services were best handled by what level of government and would then shift them accordingly, *regardless of* the financial impact. There would be "winners" and "losers" as between levels of government, but since there is only one set of taxpayers in Canada (as governments are fond of repeating), then the overall impact would balance out. If provincial costs went up as a result of a service swap, then municipal costs would go down by a corresponding amount and the total provincial and municipal taxes paid should remain about the same.

Whatever superficial logic this theoretical argument has, it totally ignores political reality. It matters greatly to governments which level is perceived as spending more or less – especially in the

---

[33] Graham and Phillips, "Who Does What in Ontario," pp. 194 and 205.

current climate. As a result, the disentanglement exercises of the 1990s have had as an overriding objective the achievement of fiscal neutrality – a pledge that neither level of government will be better or worse off financially as a result of any service swap. The requirement of this objective is understandable to a point, but it effectively destroys the disentanglement exercise. One cannot shift functions to the level where they most logically belong; one must manipulate the final service swap in such a way as to balance the books.

The extent to which this financial requirement can distort disentanglement is painfully apparent in the Ontario experience. The province was determined to take over responsibility for education, to cut back on what it regarded as excessive spending by school boards. The same logic that made education an appropriate provincial responsibility also extended to the other social programs such as social assistance and social housing. But taking over all of these services would have meant an increase in provincial costs and a decrease in municipal costs. Instead, the combined forces of the fiscal neutrality pledge and the provincial government's own financial and tax-cutting priorities reduced the disentanglement exercise to "basic arithmetic." Since the province wanted education, it needed to download enough other services to offset that cost. This largely explains why social housing, which wasn't even part of the *Who Does What* panel's deliberations, got tossed into the mix.[34]

Ultimately, it may be that efforts at disentanglement are not only flawed in ways described above, but pointless or inappropriate. The needs of citizens may best be addressed by more than one level of government. For example, "acknowledging the legitimate local interest in human-service delivery, while retaining responsibility for income redistribution at the provincial level, would contribute to recognition of the diversity of circumstances and needs across communities and affirm a vital role for local governments in the social domain."[35] In addition, as argued above, having different aspects of a responsibility handled by more than one level of government may be the best way to achieve economies of scale rather than being wasteful duplication.

The Changing Provincial-Local Financial Relationship

Disentanglement, of a sort, is also occurring with respect to intergovernmental financial relations. It has been driven and shaped by the

---

[34] *Ibid.*, p. 187.

[35] Graham and Phillips, "Who Does What in Ontario," p. 205.

deficit and debt reduction measures that preoccupied the senior levels throughout the 1990s. In what has been characterized as an era of fend-for-yourself federalism, the federal government reduced its transfers to the provinces, while softening the blow by making them less conditional. The provinces responded in kind, with respect to their financial assistance to municipalities. The result, in Brodie's colourful language, has been a kind of "demolition derby – a scurry of fiscal off-loading onto newly designated 'shock absorbers.' "[36]

If this trend continues, municipal governments will find themselves (whether willingly or not) with greater financial independence. They are being required to find a growing portion of the funds they need from their own revenue sources, much as they had to do in the early years of their existence. As discussed in Chapter 7, transfer payments represented only 14% of municipal revenues in 2001, while the property tax had increased to 52% of the total as it expanded in an attempt to make up the shortfall. That chapter also discusses municipal concerns about provincial encroachment on the property tax field – to fund provincial responsibilities with respect to education and social programs.

The Changing Legal Relationship

Unlike provincial and federal governments, local governments were not given any guaranteed right to exist under Canada's constitution, but were simply identified as one of the responsibilities that provinces could exercise. In response, provincial governments passed legislation that provided for the kinds of municipalities that could be incorporated, their governing structures, functions, and financial resources. These statutes were traditionally very prescriptive in nature, detailing what municipalities could do – and often how they could do it – in what was often described as a "laundry list" approach. The courts usually took the position that if a provincial legislature had specified some items, then anything not specified was not intended. As a result, if municipalities could not find express legal authority for an action, they could not undertake it – or would face the risk of a court challenge (usually successful) if they proceeded in the absence of such express authority.

This very narrow scope for municipal action reflected "Dillon's Rule," as set down by Iowa Supreme Court Judge John F. Dillon in the 1860s, who equated municipalities with business

---

[36] Janine Brodie, "Imagining democratic urban citizenship," in Engin Isin (ed.), *Democracy, Citizenship and the Global City*, London, Routledge, 2000, p. 120.

corporations, both of them limited to the powers expressly granted
through their incorporation.

Box 6.2 Dillon's Rule[37]

A municipal corporation possesses and can exercise the following powers and no
others; first, those granted in express words; second, those necessarily implied or
necessarily incident to the power expressly granted; third, those absolutely essential to
the declared objects and purposes of the corporation – not simply convenient but
indispensable; and fourth, any fair doubt as to the existence of a power is resolved by
the courts against the corporation.

A contrasting approach is that of "home rule," which is
common in the western United States, and which essentially provides
that municipalities can do anything that is not explicitly prohibited by
state (or provincial) legislation, instead of only what the legislature
specifically authorizes.[38] While the contrasting approaches associated
with these two rules provide a useful spectrum along which to measure
efforts to reform municipal legislation in Canada, the contrast between
them should not be exaggerated. The reality, as depicted in the figure
below, is that between these two extremes lies a "mushy middle" in
which the scope for municipal action is greater than Dillon's Rule
would suggest and less than home rule would imply.[39] We will return
to this point toward the end of this chapter.

Figure 6.1 The Scope for Municipal Action

Municipal governments and their associations, notably the
Federation of Canadian Municipalities (FCM), have long lobbied for
some constitutional recognition that might provide them with at least

---

[37] John F. Dillon, from an 1868 decision in *Merriam vs. Moody's Executors*, as
quoted in Harold Wolman and Michael Goldsmith, *Urban Politics and Policy: A
Comparative Approach*, Oxford, Blackwell, 1992, p. 72.

[38] Robert L. Bish and Eric G. Clemens, *Local Government in British Columbia*,
3rd Edition, Richmond, University of British Columbia Municipalities, 1999,
p. 18.

[39] Patrick J. Smith and Kennedy Stewart, "Beavers and Cats Revisited, Creatures
& Tenants vs. Municipal Charter(s) and Home Rule, Has the Intergovernmental
Game Shifted?" paper prepared for the Municipal-Provincial-Federal Relations
Conference, Institute of Intergovernmental Relations, Queen's University, May
9-10, 2003, available at www.iigr.ca, accessed May 25, 2003.

a degree of protection from arbitrary provincial actions. However, these requests have fallen on deaf ears. Municipal governments were ignored in both the Meech Lake and Charlottetown constitutional accords and they were also left out of the 1982 Constitution Act that repatriated the constitution. Given the widespread feeling that the country has wasted too many years in divisive and ultimately futile attempts to bring about constitutional change, few now seem interested in pushing constitutional recognition for municipalities. In any event, both L'Heureux[40] and Cameron have argued that it would be more realistic and appropriate to protect municipal interests by way of provincial constitutions. In Cameron's words:

> Municipalities have no place in a federal constitution, at least not beyond the present references which consign them to provincial jurisdiction. Any further reference could only serve to remove decisions about the provincial-municipal division of power to extra-provincial constitutional processes. Any direct participation by municipalities in the federal-provincial constitutional process could only occur at the price of their becoming special interest groups. [41]

Since the beginning of the 1990s, municipal associations in a number of provinces have pushed for some form of provincial charter that would recognize the existence of a separate level of municipal government. The Union of British Columbia Municipalities (UBCM) called for a charter or bill of rights in 1991, followed by similar demands from the Union of Nova Scotia Municipalities (UNSM) in 1993 and the Association of Municipalities of Ontario (AMO) in 1994. The lobbying by the associations seemed to have an impact, since most provinces over the past decade have enacted new legislation that reflects – to varying degrees – the changes being sought.

A More Positive Legislative Framework?

The first breakthrough came with Alberta's Local Government Act of 1994 and the most recent initiative is also found in Western Canada, with British Columbia's community charter legislation that came into force on January 1, 2004. In the intervening decade, positive legislative changes were also enacted in most other provinces, notably

---

[40] Jacques L'Heureux, "Municipalities and the Division of Power," in Richard Simeon, Research Coordinator, *Intergovernmental Relations*, Vol. 63, Royal Commission on the Economic Union and Development Prospects for Canada, Toronto, University of Toronto Press, 1985.

[41] Cameron, "Provincial Responsibilities for Municipal Government," pp. 222-235.

Saskatchewan, Manitoba, Ontario, Nova Scotia, and Newfoundland. These changes usually incorporated some combination of the following key features:

i)   the provision of natural person powers;
ii)   authorization to act within broad spheres of jurisdiction;
iii) a commitment to advance consultation;
iv)   a requirement for municipal approval before certain actions (notably amalgamation) could proceed; and
v)   a commitment to provide resources commensurate with the municipal responsibilities being allocated.

While the last three points are self-explanatory, the significance of the first two features is explained in the following table.

Box 6.3 Key Concepts in New Municipal Legislation	
Natural person powers	Vesting municipalities with natural person powers gives them a general authority to do those things that a person can do – such as hiring and dismissing staff, contracting for services, purchasing land or buildings, or selling or otherwise disposing of assets. These are things that municipalities have always done, but they had to find express authority in statutes before taking any such actions. While granting natural person powers gives municipalities greater flexibility, no additional powers are conveyed with this designation. Rather, the natural person powers are used as a tool for implementing the responsibilities otherwise assigned to municipalities.
Spheres of Jurisdiction	Spheres of jurisdiction (or spheres of authority) authorize municipal action on the basis of broad and general categories. They provide an alternative to allocating powers to municipalities by itemizing specifically what they can do – as in the previously cited laundry list approach. The problem with such a list is that anything not mentioned, even inadvertently, is likely to be ruled beyond municipal jurisdiction on the grounds that if the provincial government had intended such a matter to be assigned, it would have been specified. Assigning broad spheres of jurisdiction is supposed to give municipalities greater flexibility and discretion. However, the scope of these spheres is constrained by limits that may be provided elsewhere in provincial legislation, and there are also some subjects that are not covered by the spheres and are addressed separately and in a more prescriptive fashion.

Alberta's Local Government Act was the first to give municipalities natural person powers and it also gave them general by-law making authority similar to spheres of jurisdiction. But many municipal powers still require provincial approvals and nothing in the Act requires the province to consult with municipalities. One analysis points out that within six months of the Act coming into force several hundred amendments were enacted.[42] The flow of amendments has continued in the years since, leading to some concern that their cumulative impact will be to undermine the freedom and flexibility originally intended for this legislation.[43]

Saskatchewan passed a new Cities Act in July 2002, modeled upon similar legislation in other provinces and giving municipalities natural person powers and two broad areas of authority to pass by-laws for the "peace, order and good government of the city" and for "the safety, health and welfare of the people and the protection of people and property."[44] The Act also gives cities the authority to levy additional property taxes to pay for a specific service or purpose. There are also some new public accountability provisions that balance the increased autonomy and flexibility for cities with requirements to involve and inform the public of decisions.

Manitoba passed a Municipal Government Act in October 1996, but it limits municipal discretion to a narrower range of permissive powers than the Alberta legislation and it does not give them natural person powers. However, one recent analysis points out that the new Act has eliminated many of the detailed instructions that used to severely constrain municipal operations. It also concludes that the new provisions encouraging contracting for services are intended to create a more competitive atmosphere in which market pressures will bring about greater collaboration and integration in service delivery (without the need for the municipal restructuring for which there has been strong public opposition in the province) and expresses some reservations about the implications of relying on this type of market model.[45]

---

[42] Kristen Gagnon and Donald Lidstone, *A Comparison of New and Proposed Municipal Acts of the Provinces*, paper presented at the 1998 annual conference of the Federation of Canadian Municipalities, p. 22.

[43] Edward LeSage, *Municipal Reform in Alberta: A Review of Statutory, Financial and Structural Changes Over the Past Decade*, paper presented at the Canadian Political Science Association annual meeting, Quebec City, May 28, 2001, p. 8. Much of this paper has been incorporated into the Alberta chapter of Garcea and LeSage, *Municipal Reforms in Canada*.

[44] Saskatchewan Ministry of Government Relations and Aboriginal Affairs, *The Cities Act – An Introduction*, available from www.municipal.gov.sk.ca, accessed March 15, 2003.

[45] Mark Piel and Christopher Leo, "Governing Manitoba's Communities: Legislative Reform in the 1990s and Beyond," in Garcea and LeSage, *Municipal Reforms in Canada*.

This new Municipal Act does not apply to the city of Winnipeg, which has had its own charter since its formation in 1972. That charter was amended in 1998, but mainly in connection with some internal restructuring relating to the council and senior administration. However, a new City of Winnipeg Charter Act was enacted in 2002 (effective January 2003), partly to incorporate or keep up with the changes that had appeared in the 1996 general municipal legislation. The new Act combines large numbers of previously detailed and scattered powers into 14 broad spheres of authority, and also gives Winnipeg natural person powers.[46] However, the analysis previously cited finds that natural person powers are limited to a brief reference at the beginning of the Act, which otherwise deals with the more traditional corporate powers, and it suggests that over time the concept of natural person powers may contain "more politics and public relations than legal substance."[47]

Ontario's new Municipal Act was passed in December 2001, and took effect on January 1, 2003. It authorizes municipalities to exercise natural person powers and governmental powers within 10 general spheres of jurisdiction. In what has been a fairly common pattern, the legislation combines the increased municipal powers with greater accountability and reporting requirements. The new Act endorses the principle of ongoing consultation with municipalities in relation to matters of mutual interest, and a memorandum of understanding has been signed by the province and the Association of Municipalities of Ontario (in December 2001) setting out these consultation arrangements.

Nova Scotia amended its Municipal Government Act in December 1998. The new legislation does not give municipalities natural person powers or broad spheres of jurisdiction, continuing instead the traditional approach of giving municipalities a list of specific powers. But it does provide somewhat more autonomy by reducing the number of provincial approvals relating to financing and by-laws. In addition, the Act provides that the provincial government must give municipalities 12 months notice of any initiatives that may affect municipal finance.[48]

The Government of Newfoundland and Labrador enacted a new Municipalities Act in May 1999 that has been described as "one of

---

[46] City of Winnipeg Charter Act (Bill 39), S.M. 2002, c. 39.

[47] Piel and Leo, "Governing Manitoba's Communities."

[48] Department of Housing and Municipal Affairs, "Municipal Legislation Gets Makeover." October 27, 1998.

the most modern of Municipal Acts in Canada, offering more opportunity for flexibility and autonomy within a framework of municipal
self-government."[49] It provides for the province to consult with the
mayor of a city before it enacts or amends legislation or makes
regulations or policies that affect the city. According to Lidstone,
"although the legislation eliminates may of the paternalistic, centralized controls under the current legislation, the greater autonomy,
flexibility and powers are combined with increased requirements for
accountability, transparency and public participation."[50]

Turning finally to British Columbia, there has been a series of
positive legislative changes. These began with Municipal Act revisions
in 1998, in an amending bill which incorporated by reference British
Columbia's protocol of recognition signed by the province and the
Union of British Columbia Municipalities (UBCM) two years earlier.
The Act was renamed the Local Government Act in June 2000, with
amendments that facilitated public private partnerships and provided
more flexible revenue raising authority for municipalities.

Most attention, however, has been focused on the new community charter legislation that recently appeared in British Columbia.
A Community Charter Council Act was passed in August 2001,
providing for the appointment of a Community Charter Council (of
provincial and local representatives) to oversee the preparation of
community charter legislation governing municipalities.[51] The
legislation (Bill 14) was passed in April 2003 and came into effect
January 2004. Its key features include:[52]

> ➢ recognition of municipalities as an "order of government"
>   within their jurisdiction;
> ➢ requirement of provincial consultation prior to changes in the
>   Act or to provincial grants to municipalities;
> ➢ provision for consultation agreements between the provincial
>   government and the UBCM on matters of mutual interest;

---

[49] Federation of Canadian Municipalities, *Early Warning: Will Canadian Cities Compete?*, May 2001, p. 7.

[50] Donald Lidstone, "A Comparison of New and Proposed Municipal Acts of the Provinces: Revenues, Financial Powers and Resources," prepared for the 2001 annual conference of the Federation of Canadian Municipalities, May 27, 2001.

[51] British Columbia Minister of State for Community Charter, *The Community Charter: A Discussion Paper*, October 2001.

[52] Ministry of Community, Aboriginal and Women's Services, *Highlights Community Charter*, www.mcaws.gov.bc.ca, accessed May 30, 2003.

> ➤ provision of a dispute resolution process, including binding arbitration where all parties to a dispute choose this method;
> ➤ provision that municipal amalgamations cannot proceed unless approved by a vote in the affected jurisdictions;
> ➤ provision of natural person powers;
> ➤ provision of power to provide any service that the council considers necessary or desirable;
> ➤ provision of autonomous or concurrent authority (with the province) to regulate, prohibit, or impose requirements in relation to 13 broad spheres of authority in which municipalities typically operate; and
> ➤ new accountability requirements including an annual municipal report and a public meeting to present this report.

The new community charter has been characterized as the most empowering local government statute in Canada. In a recent report card on municipal legislation, the British Columbia legislation ranks second only to the new Winnipeg Charter (phase two) and well ahead of the other legislation enacted across Canada over the past decade.[53] However, Smith and Stewart have a number of reservations about the community charter legislation.[54] They note, for example, that the legislation continues the province's authority to impose limits on municipal property tax increases in particular circumstances, and continues the commitment to "work toward the harmonization of provincial and municipal enactments, policies, and programs,"[55] and they wonder how this latter provision will work in those instances where a municipality wishes to pursue a unique approach.

Smith and Stewart are particularly critical of the legislation's failure to address municipal accountability, which, in their view, requires such responses as electoral financing reform and the removal of such barriers to electoral participation as at large elections in large municipalities including Vancouver. They don't find the call for annual reports and public meetings an adequate means of strengthening

---

[53] Donald Lidstone, "Municipal Acts of the Provinces and Territories: A Report Card," prepared for the June 1, 2003 "Future Role of Municipal Government" Forum held during the annual conference of the Federation of Canadian Municipalities.

[54] The discussion that follows is based on Smith and Stewart, "Beavers and Cats Revisited," pp. 18-19 and Kennedy Stewart and Patrick Smith, "Community Charter," *Vancouver Sun*, March 15, 2003.

[55] Bill 14, *The Community Charter*, "Principles of the Provincial-Municipal Relationship," Part 1, Sec 2.

accountability. Indeed, these mechanisms reflect a corporate model of accountability that does not seem particularly applicable to the municipal government sphere.[56] Carrel is very concerned about measures in the charter legislation that would structure local government on the corporate model and dismisses the new annual report requirement as a very inadequate tool for accountability. In his view, "to set up the annual report as the principal tool of accountability and citizen involvement is an open invitation to accepting justification, white wash and obfuscation as a substitute for accountability."[57]

Significance of the Legislative Reforms

The key features of the reforms, not found in all provinces, are the provisions for natural person powers, more general municipal authority within broad spheres of jurisdiction, and a commitment to advance consultation with municipalities. These changes are most welcome, although in several instances (notably British Columbia, Saskatchewan, and Ontario) they are accompanied by new requirements presented as enhancing the accountability of municipal governments. In the case of Ontario, at least, there are concerns that these requirements may increase the accountability of municipalities to the province rather than necessarily to their local electorates.

It is also clear that the new legislation is being used in some provinces to further ideological leanings of the provincial governing parties. As noted above, Piel and Leo describe the promotion of partnerships and the market model in Manitoba, and this theme is also reflected in the legislation in British Columbia and Ontario. A business or corporate emphasis is also evident in provisions for accountability in both the British Columbia and Ontario legislation, with efficiency and effectiveness measures and annual reports and meetings advocated more than provisions to strengthen local democracy.

While the new legislative initiatives are generally positive and a welcome step in the right direction, they don't protect municipalities from adverse actions being taken by their provincial governments. For example, the same year (1996) that British Columbia introduced its Recognition Protocol, the province also unilaterally eliminated

---

[56] Peter Kenward, *The British Columbia Community Charter – What Is Going On, and What Does It Mean For You?*, McCarthy Tétrault, October 2001, www.mccarthytetrault.ca, accessed November 15, 2001.

[57] André Carrel, "The Community Charter: Strengthening or Weakening the Citizen Voice at City Hall?" Langora College Continuing Studies, May 10, 2002.

municipal grant guarantees, reduced grants, transferred major highway responsibilities, and closed local courthouses – all without any real consultation with municipalities.[58] As noted earlier, Alberta and Ontario introduced their new Municipal Acts during times when they were also curtailing, or had curtailed, their provincial grant support.

Yet municipalities need expanded, not reduced, financial resources if they are to have the capacity to take action on behalf of their residents – whatever their legislation may allow. In that regard, consider LeSage's observation that Alberta municipalities have approached "with kid gloves" the natural person powers and spheres of jurisdiction allocated to them, with the result that, by anecdotal accounts, the general exercise of municipal affairs in Alberta is not much different than it was under the previous Act. The prevailing view is that smaller municipalities don't have the resources to take advantage of the legislation and that larger municipalities are being cautioned by their legal advisors about the legal risks to which they might expose themselves.[59] Andrew also notes that cuts in provincial grants compromised the potential of the new municipal legislation and states that " it is not at all clear that the legislation has made any difference to municipal behaviour in Alberta."[60]

The new Municipal Act in Ontario endorsed the principle of ongoing consultation with municipalities in matters of mutual interest, and a memorandum of understanding was signed by the province and the Association of Municipalities of Ontario (in December 2001) setting out these consultation arrangements. Yet the campaign platform released by the ruling Conservatives in mid-2003 contains a proposal that any future tax increases by Ontario municipalities will have to be approved in a local referendum.[61] There was no consultation with the Association of Municipalities of Ontario about this proposal, which would constitute an unprecedented intrusion into municipal decision making. This example reminds us that whatever new legislation may be introduced, the provincial-local relationship is still very much one of superior-subordinate, and municipalities still

---

[58] Lidstone, "A Comparison of New and Proposed Municipal Acts, 2001," p. 6.

[59] Edd LeSage, presentation at workshop, "New Community Charter in British Columbia," June 14, 2002, Local Government Institute, University of Victoria.

[60] Caroline Andrew, "Globalization and Local Action," in Timothy L. Thomas (ed.), *The Politics of the City*, Toronto, ITP Nelson, 1997, p. 143.

[61] See Policy Paper "A Fair Deal for Municipalities," which is part of *The Road Ahead*, the PC campaign platform for 2003, available at www.ontariopc.com, accessed June 10. 2003.

remain vulnerable to capricious actions taken by their provincial governments. This doesn't mean that an improved legislative framework is not worth pursuing, just that if achieved it will not alter the underlying imbalance in the distribution of power and authority.

It must also be remembered that the potential of these various initiatives to improve municipal legislation is somewhat dependent on the interpretations that will be given by the courts in the cases that will inevitably arise. One of the early examples of such a development is not overly reassuring. This is the Alberta Court of Appeal decision (noted in Chapter 1) quashing a Calgary by-law that limited the number of taxi licences.[62] The court found that while the old legislation had expressly conferred a power to limit the number of taxi licences, this power was not found in Alberta's landmark 1994 legislation, and Calgary's by-law, therefore, lacked specific authorization. This decision, currently under appeal, is clearly inconsistent with the notion that municipalities should be able to take action within broad spheres and not require specific authorization for every action. It should be of great concern to those jurisdictions (Saskatchewan, Manitoba, Ontario, Nunavut, and the Yukon) that utilize "spheres of jurisdiction."[63]

Pursuing Individual City Charters

Paralleling the demand for more permissive provincial legislation for local governments in general has been a growing demand that Canada's largest cities receive individual charters that would set out responsibilities appropriate to their size, resources, and importance. Having specific charters is not a new idea, of course, as indicated below.

Box 6.4 Charter Cities in Canada	
Saint John	Incorporated by royal charter in 1785. City has natural person powers. The Charter is exclusive of generally applicable municipal legislation unless there is a conflict with provincial statutes.
Vancouver	Charter dates from 1886 and is the exclusive authority except for a few provisions from generally applicable municipal legislation.
Montreal	Original charter dates from 1890s. New "city contract" entered into between province and new city of Montreal in June 2002 in support of the city charter.
Winnipeg	Charter dates from the amalgamation that created the city in 1972. Major revisions effective 2003 to provide greater autonomy, in line with changes in new Municipal Act of 1996.

[62] See *United Taxi Drivers' Fellowship of Southern Alberta v. Calgary (City of)*, 2002, ABCA, 131, accessed January 5, 2003 from www.albertacourts.ab.ca.

[63] Lidstone, "A Report Card," p. 43.

Conspicuous by their absence from this list of charter cities are Calgary, Edmonton, and Toronto (especially). Toronto, among others, argues that it is quite distinct from most other municipalities in Canada and needs special governing arrangements that can be best provided by having its own charter.[64] A model framework for a city charter was adopted by the Big City Mayors Caucus of the Federation of Canadian Municipalities on May 30, 2002.[65] A year later, the first official summit of the Creative Cities Coalition was held just prior to the Federation's annual conference and it is continuing the campaign to get provinces to adopt the standardized city charter.[66]

Treating different classes of municipality differently may seem arbitrary and could be seen as an implied criticism of those municipalities excluded from charter status. On the other hand, it can also be argued that such an approach could be beneficial for the small and rural municipal governments that make up the vast majority of Canada's municipalities. They often feel that policies are enacted to address concerns of the larger centres, without sufficient regard to how appropriate such policies may be for them and their much different needs and conditions. If the needs of the largest cities can be handled through separate charters for them, then it may be possible to develop general municipal legislation that is more suitable for the smaller and more rural municipalities to which it will apply. For this reason, some feel that "a charter for cities achieves a balance between a group of municipalities that needs more enabling power (cities) and those that are content with the status quo (smaller communities)."[67] If we can countenance asymmetrical federalism at the federal and provincial levels, it would not seem unreasonable for us to consider comparable arrangements between provinces and their widely varied municipal governments.

---

[64] For a series of articles relating to this issue, see Mary W. Rowe, *Toronto: Considering Self-Government*, Owen Sound, The Ginger Press, Inc., 2000.

[65] Available from the Federation web site at www.fcm.ca, accessed May 2, 2003.

[66] Details on that first conference, hosted by the city of Winnipeg, are at http://www.winnipeg.ca/interhom/mayors_office/creativecities/home.html, accessed June 12, 2003.

[67] Denis Wong, *Cities at the Crossroads: Addressing Intergovernmental Structures for Western Canada's Cities*, Canada West Foundation, August 2002, p. 9, available at www.cwf.ca, accessed April 14, 2003.

The Federal-Local Relationship

While local governments don't have any direct link with the federal government according to the constitution, nothing could be further from the truth. Federal programs and policies have long had a major impact on local government operations. As described in Chapter 3, there is no better example than the federal contribution, through financial assistance for housing, to low density sprawl and all of its associated municipal servicing problems. Decisions by the Department of Transport concerning rail services have had a critical impact on the economic vitality of communities, as have various industrial incentives and other programs offered by the federal government. Immigration policy is another federal responsibility that affects municipalities, dramatically so in the case of Canada's largest urban centres. But as Frisken notes, "federal immigration policy makes little attempt to ease the strains imposed on cities or city neighbourhoods by large influxes of new immigrants...."[68] Consider the case of Toronto, which received more than 30% of immigrants and refugee claimants during the 1990s, which pays out $30 million annually for refuge claimants alone (for social assistance, housing, and health services), and which has refuge claimants occupying 10% of the space in its emergency hostels on any given night. If the federal government wants an open door policy for refugee claimants, why should the cost of looking after them fall mainly on the residents of Toronto and other urban centres such as Montreal and Vancouver?[69]

These examples should suffice to demonstrate that a kind of federal-local relationship existed long before it was given any formal recognition during the 1970s. Indeed, one study found that by the late 1960s, "more than 117 distinct programs administered by 27 departments in Ottawa influenced metropolitan development plans."[70] In almost every case, however, the federal programs were introduced without regard to their impact on the local level. Municipalities had no opportunity for advance consultation and little hope of obtaining

---

[68] Frances Frisken, "Introduction," in Frances Frisken (ed.), *The Changing Canadian Metropolis*, Volume 1, Toronto, Canadian Urban Institute, 1994, p. 19.

[69] Statistics from Michael Valpy, "Constitution makes it easy to push Toronto around," *Toronto Star*, October 13, 1999.

[70] Elliot J. Feldman and Jerome Milch, "Coordination or Control? The Life and Death of the Ministry of Urban Affairs," in Lionel D. Feldman (ed.), *Politics and Government of Urban Canada*, Toronto, Methuen, 1981, p. 250.

adjustments after the fact. In many cases, the varied federal initiatives were not even coordinated with each other.

The Once (and Future?) MSUA

By the end of the 1960s, however, two major factors combined to produce strong pressure for a closer and more formalized federal-local relationship. First, there was a growing municipal interest in the possibility of increased federal funds being made available to deal with major service demands, especially in urban areas. Second, there was a growing federal appreciation that, because of the large number of Canadians living in urban areas, the ability of municipal governments to meet their needs was of more than local, or even provincial, interest. A federal task force on Housing and Urban Development was appointed in mid-1968 and its report recommended a greatly expanded federal role. After some delays, during which the head of the task force (Minister of Transport Paul Hellyer) resigned from the cabinet in protest, the government acted by establishing a Ministry of State for Urban Affairs (MSUA). As recommended by the task force, the new ministry was not to be a traditional operating department but was to concentrate on developing policy and on coordinating the projects of other departments. Also emphasized was the need to increase consultation and coordination among all three levels of government in dealing with the challenges of urbanization.

The new ministry began with ambitious objectives considering "the absence of any authority with which to control the legislative or spending proposals of other agencies."[71] One analysis observed that "it was created as a new David without a sling; the new ministry of state could fulfill its mission only with mutual trust and goodwill."[72] These commodities turned out to be in short supply and none of the approaches attempted by the ministry had much success. A closer look at these approaches seems timely, given that the federal government is currently considering a recommendation to appoint (again) a Minister with responsibility for urban Canada.

Initially, in an attempt to gain credibility, "MSUA offered to represent the interests of municipalities and provincial governments in discussions with other federal agencies."[73] But this role brought it into direct confrontation with other federal agencies and little was accomp-

---

[71] Cameron in *ibid.*, p. 245.

[72] Feldman and Milch, "Coordination or Control?," p. 254.

[73] *Ibid.*, p. 255.

lished. By 1972 MSUA had adopted a new strategy – it would promote coordination by arranging meetings among representatives of all three levels of government and the various federal ministries whose programs affected urban areas. This approach had already been advocated by the Canadian Federation of Mayors and Municipalities (now the Federation of Canadian Municipalities) and partly through the efforts of the Federation the first ever national tri-level conference was held in Toronto in November of 1972. The fact that the municipal level was represented in its own right was something of a breakthrough, but the extent to which the conference might be considered a success depends upon the expectations of those participating in it. A Joint Municipal Committee on Intergovernmental Affairs presented several well-researched papers but little progress was made because of the uncompromising attitude of the provinces, especially Ontario.[74]

A second national tri-level conference was held in Edmonton in October 1973. It was decided to undertake a study of public finance with particular reference to the adequacy of municipal revenue sources, a development seen optimistically as "the first important piece of firm evidence of the success of the tri-level process."[75] But delays in launching the Tri-Level Task Force on Public Finance led to the third tri-level conference being postponed – forever, as it turned out.

With the national tri-level conferences stalled by provincial intransigence, MSUA adopted another strategy. It attempted to move from persuasion to power – which it sought through the Canada Mortgage and Housing Corporation, which controlled major expenditures. Here again, however, successes were limited and by 1975 there was "a state of open warfare between MSUA and CMHC."[76] Within 18 months the MSUA personnel were cut by 40%.

It adopted yet another approach at this point. It made no effort to initiate meetings, but let it be known that it would organize them if requested. "MSUA thus evolved from an agency that had flirted with the imposition of policy to an urban consultant active only on invitation."[77] This final phase of MSUA activity was received more favourably, but this was largely because of its much more modest mission, not because of any real support. By the spring of 1979 it had fallen

---

[74] For an assessment of this first conference, see *Urban Focus*, Vol. 1, No. 2, "The Tri-Level Conference – The Morning After," Queen's University, Institute of Local Government and Intergovernmental Relations, January-February 1973.

[75] *Urban Focus*, Vol. 2, No. 1, November-December 1973.

[76] Feldman and Milch, "Coordination or Control?," pp. 257-258.

[77] *Ibid.*

victim to the politics of austerity. "Total savings would be less than $4 million (perhaps closer to $500 000), but the public would be impressed by a government prepared to abolish a whole ministry in the name of fiscal responsibility."[78] Lacking the clout that comes with specific program responsibilities, regarded with suspicion by federal bodies protecting their turf, and disliked by provincial governments also protecting their (municipal) turf, MSUA never really had a chance.

The death of MSUA did not in any way signify the end of tri-level relations in Canada. In fact, the federal influence may have been greater during the 1980s, as evidenced by major development projects in almost all of Canada's major metropolitan areas. Some of these projects (such as Harbourfront in Toronto and the Rideau Centre in Ottawa) were the result of election promises, while others reflected the regional influence of a member of the cabinet – such as the Winnipeg Core Area Initiative promoted by Lloyd Axworthy.[79] Whatever their impetus, these projects demonstrated the continuing significance of the federal presence in urban Canada.

However, with the demise of the MSUA, federal policies continued to appear without much regard to their urban impact, leading one analysis to conclude that "[f]ederal initiatives in the cities have been not only incoherent and irrational, often they have been inconsistent and unequal."[80] Yet there has never been a greater need for coherent urban policies. As one recent analysis points out, Canada faces the likelihood of "a permanent set of place-based winners and losers."[81] According to this analysis, the settlement pattern of those who immigrate to Canada is helping to create one set of places that exhibits social diversity and rapid growth, while other places are growing slowly, if at all, are socially homogenous, and have an aging population. As a result, Canada's complex policy challenge is how to manage growth and also plan for decline, while adapting to heterogeneity and an aging population.[82]

---

[78] *Ibid.*, p. 260.

[79] Caroline Andrew, "Federal Urban Activity: Intergovernmental Relations in an Age of Restraint," in Frisken, *The Changing Canadian Metropolis*, p. 430.

[80] Feldman and Milch, "Coordination or Control?," p. 263.

[81] Larry Bourne and Jim Simmons, "New Fault Lines? Recent Trends in the Canadian Urban System and their Implications for Planning and Public Policy," *Canadian Journal of Urban Research*, Volume 12, Issue 1, Summer 2003, p. 40.

[82] *Ibid.*, p. 32.

The 1980s and 1990s saw repeated calls for a tri-level approach to infrastructure financing. The election of the Liberals in 1993 led to a *Canada Infrastructure Works* program under which the federal level provided $2 billion over a two year period, matched by similar amounts from the provinces and municipalities. Over the past few years, however, a series of developments brought the financial challenges facing Canadian cities much more to the forefront and increased the pressure on the federal level to assume a more active role.

Box 6.3 Cities To the Forefront
In March 2001 the Federation of Canadian Municipalities released its second report on the quality of life in urban Canada, which found that poverty and income inequality had continued to expand in large urban communities since the first study in 1999.[83]
A May 2001 research paper from the Federation found that European and American governments were investing powers and financial resources in their cities at a much greater rate than is happening in Canada. [84]
May 2001 saw a historic meeting of the mayors of Vancouver, Calgary, Winnipeg, Toronto, and Montreal, a group that has become known as the C5. Discussions emphasized that far more revenues flow out of Canada's largest cities (in the form of taxes collected by the senior levels of government) than flow back into them. A prime example cited was the fact that "$4 billion in motor fuel taxes is going out of cities across Canada to the federal government, and less than 3.5% of that money is reinvested back in the cities that generated it in the first place."[85]
The Toronto Board of Trade picked up on this theme in its June 2002 report *Strong City: Strong Nation*, in which it contended that in 2000 there was a net outflow of $9 billion from Toronto to the provincial and federal governments – with the bulk of it ($7.6 billion) going to the federal level.
An April 2002 report from the TD Bank concluded that Canada's cities were at a disadvantage because of lack of access to revenue streams other than the property tax.[86]

In the midst of this flurry of reports and demands for action, the federal government established, in May 2001, a Prime Minister's Caucus Task Force on Urban Issues (chaired by Judy Sgro) to examine the challenges and opportunities facing Canada's urban regions. It issued an interim report in April 2002 and a final report in November

---

[83] Federation of Canadian Municipalities, *Quality of Life in Canadian Communities, 2001 Report*, Ottawa, March 27, 2001. This report is available at the Federation's web site at www.fcm.ca, accessed December 12, 2002.

[84] Federation of Canadian Municipalities, *Early Warning: Will Canadian Cities Compete?*, Ottawa, May 2001, accessed December 12, 2002 at www.fcm.ca.

[85] Remarks by Winnipeg mayor Glen Murray at the first C5 meeting on May 25-26, 2001, Winnipeg, as reported in *Ideas That Matter*, Volume 2, Number 1, Owen Sound, The Ginger Press, 2001.

[86] TD Economics Special Report, *A Choice Between Investing in Canada's Cities or Disinvesting in Canada's Future*, April 22, 2002.

2002.[87] The findings and recommendations provide a striking parallel with the Hellyer Task Force of 30 years earlier. The Sgro reports emphasized the growing urbanization of Canada and the importance to the national economy of vital urban regions. As major pillars of a new urban strategy for Canada, the reports called for long term funding for affordable housing, transit/transportation, and sustainable infrastructure. A key recommendation is the appointment of a cabinet minister with responsibility for developing Canada's urban strategy and implementing an action plan to ensure that the voices of urban regions are heard.

It is hard to disagree with the general sentiments of the Sgro Task Force, but it remains to be seen if the rhetoric will be matched by federal action, including a substantial financial commitment. Early indications are not especially encouraging, notably the fact that both the finance minister (John Manley) and the Prime Minister have rejected the idea of transferring federal tax resources (such as a portion of gas taxes) to aid the cities.[88] However, Paul Martin, who is almost certain to be the new Liberal leader (and Prime Minister) by the time this book appears, has promised to share gasoline taxes with the municipal level – in a manner not yet specified. As for the recommendations calling for new federal money for housing, transportation, and infrastructure, they will have to compete with other pressing financial demands on the federal government – notably health expenditures in the aftermath of the Romanow Report on the future of Canada's health care system. It is also unclear at this point how a new minister with responsibility for developing an urban strategy would avoid the infighting and fate that befell a very similar initiative in the form of the Minister of State for Urban Affairs.

While most attention has focused on the amount of federal financial assistance that may flow to cities as a result of the Sgro reports, a recent analysis by Wolfe provides a much broader (and more insightful) perspective.[89] She finds the Task Force too preoccupied with building cities to compete in the global economy, to the neglect of other important issues and considerations. There is no discussion,

---

[87] Both reports are available at www.liberal.parl.gc.ca/urb, accessed February 15, 2003.

[88] Graham Fraser, "PM won't aid cities with tax revenue," *Toronto Star*, June 12, 2002.

[89] Jeanne M. Wolfe, "A National Urban Policy for Canada? Prospects and Challenges," *Canadian Journal of Urban Research*, Volume 12, Issue 1, Summer 2003, pp. 1-21.

for example, of the extent to which the cities are being shaped by corporate agendas, the way big box stores "drain traditional business districts, and turn the city inside out."[90] Wolfe finds that the Task Force ignores the nature of civic life and how it is changing, and has little to say about poverty problems and the widening income gap between rich and poor. Nor do the Task Force reports address urban distributional problems, as reflected in the increasing concentration of population in a few major urban areas and slow population and economic growth in much of the rest of the country. Echoing the already noted views of Bourne and Simmons, Wolfe argues that "[b]urgeoning metropolitan areas, medium sized centres with a viable economy, and declining towns require very different policy responses."[91]

Whatever form it takes, federal involvement with the municipal level, and especially with Canada's major cities, has been extensive for some time and will continue to be. Bradford argues that the pivotal role of cities in determining the quality of national life demands close collaboration among all levels of government. In his view:[92]

> The issue is not simply one of helping municipalities cope with their responsibilities but, equally, one of ensuring that macro-level policy interventions of upper level governments are sufficiently informed by the locality's *contextual intelligence* to work effectively. [emphasis in the original]

While the federal government has to be sensitive to provincial jurisdiction over municipalities, this constitutional reality should not be used as an excuse for federal inaction. "Whether the federal government is to be involved or excluded from new governance patterns will depend on political choices, not constitutional formalities."[93] In support of this position, Jane Jacobs and Alan Broadbent gave the federal government a list of more than a dozen actions that it could take without "violating the federal-provincial balance" – suggestions that ranged from tax deductions of transit passes provided by corporations to employees, to full rebating of the GST for rental projects, to a per

---

[90] *Ibid.*, p. 11.

[91] *Ibid.,* p. 12.

[92] Neil Bradford, *Why Cities Matter: Policy Research Perspectives for Canada*, Ottawa, Canadian Policy Research Networks, Discussion Paper No. F\23, June 2002, available at www.cprn.org, accessed May 20, 2003.

[93] Jane Jenson and Rianne Mahon, *Bringing Cities to the Table: Child Care and Intergovernmental Relations*, Ottawa, Canadian Policy Research Networks, Discussion Paper No. F\26, 2002, p. 20, available at www.cprn.org, accessed May 20, 2003.

capita settlement payment that follows refugees and immigrants where they move in Canada, based on an index of costs in various cities.[94]

International Relations

In addition to relations with the provincial and federal governments, there is a growing appreciation that municipalities are also affected, directly and indirectly, by the globalization of the economy and the international organizations and agreements related to that process. What is less clear is whether the overall impact of these developments on municipalities will be positive or negative.

The negative or pessimistic view is that globalization has increased the power of private capital and that municipal governments have no choice but to implement the prevailing neoliberal, free market agenda.[95] Municipalities now have reduced bargaining power in dealing with developers and Leo comments that "mobile companies often call the tune in their dealings with local governments, and, in the process, they can cancel development plans, zoning rules, building code regulations, and even the taxes that are levied to support the city's services."[96]

There is also growing evidence of the extent to which municipalities (as well as provincial and federal governments) are constrained by such factors as the North American Free Trade Agreement (NAFTA) and the World Trade Organization (WTO). For example, the NAFTA created extensive rights for foreign firms to sue governments under a very broadly defined category of expropriation. In 2001 a British Columbia Supreme Court Justice reviewed the decision of a NAFTA Tribunal that had ruled that American toxic waste firm Metalclad had to be compensated for a number of actions taken by the federal, state, and local governments in Mexico. He stated that:

> In addition to the more conventional notion of expropriation
> involving a taking of property, the Tribunal held that expropriation
> under the NAFTA includes covert or incidental interference with
> the use of property that has the effect of depriving the owner, in

[94] Alan Broadbent, *The Place of Cities in Canada: Inside the Constitutional Box and Out*, Ottawa, Caledon Institute of Social Policy, June 2002, p. 4.

[95] For example, see Gary Teeple, *Globalization and the Decline of Social Reform*, Toronto, Garamond Press, 1995.

[96] Christopher Leo, "Planning Aspirations and Political Realities," in Edmund P. Fowler and David Siegel (eds.), *Urban Policy Issues*, Toronto, Oxford University Press, 2002, p. 223.

whole or in significant part, of the use or reasonably-to-be-expected economic benefit of the property. This definition is sufficiently broad to include a legitimate rezoning of property by a municipality or other zoning authority.[97]

According to Lidstone, "Metalclad is a wake-up call for municipalities throughout North America."[98] He also points out that the General Agreement on Trade in Services (GATS) expressly applies to services provided by or on behalf of municipalities, and requires the federal government to ensure that local authorities fulfill the obligations and commitments made by the federal government. From the way services are defined under the GATS, Lidstone concludes that public private partnerships, contracting out, design-build arrangements, and privatization would be subject to the GATS provisions.[99] In this regard, the Greater Vancouver Regional District dropped plans to construct a water filtration plant under a $400 million public private partnership plan because it could not receive satisfactory assurances about the possible risk of losing control of this plant in the future from trade challenges under the NAFTA and GATS provisions.[100] Another analysis also sounded a caution about the GATS, pointing out that it adversely affects the ability of municipal governments to supply and to regulate basic services such as water and sewage services, waste management, transportation services, public transit, road building, land use planning, and library services.[101]

Globalization has had quite an impact on the local level in an indirect way through the pressure that it has placed on senior levels of government to scale back and downsize their operations in support of the more competitive atmosphere demanded by the international

[97] Supreme Court of British Columbia, "Reasons for Judgment of the Honourable Mr. Justice Tysoe, *United States of Mexico v. Metalclad Corporation*, May 2, 2001, as quoted in Ellen Gould, *International Trade and Investment Agreements: A Primer for Local Governments*, Union of British Columbia Municipalities, June 2001.

[98] Lidstone, "A Comparison of New and Proposed Municipal Acts, 2001," p. 11.

[99] *Ibid.*

[100] See *GRVD Decides Against Design-Build-Operate Arrangements for Construction Drinking Water Filtration Facilities*, GVRD Press Release, June 29, 2001 and Murray Dobbin, "Municipalities Take on Ottawa's Trade Agenda," *National Post*, September 17, 2001.

[101] Michelle Swenarchuk, *From Global to Local: GATS Impacts on Canadian Municipalities*, Ottawa, Canadian Centre for Policy Alternatives, May 2002, p. v.

market place. One of the primary ways that they have made this adjustment, as discussed elsewhere in the book, is by shifting responsibilities and costs downward, where they have ultimately landed in the laps of local governments.

Local governments are also affected by the fact that globalization and international trade rules and regulations now make it almost impossible for senior governments to pursue the kinds of regional policies that used to be provided in support of have-not areas; such policies would almost certainly be challenged at the World Trade Organization as unfair trade practices.[102] The result is that local economies face increasingly stiff competition – from virtually anywhere in the world – and must respond without at least some of the provincial and federal government supports that used to exist.

Globalization has had a positive impact in making cities and city-regions increasingly important as key players in the world economy. But does it follow that the municipalities within these urban areas have also become more important? Not necessarily, one would think, given the municipal limitations that have been frequently cited. However, Courchene seems to have no doubts about the positive future for cities. As he sees it, "the issue is not so much *whether* they will be able to extricate themselves from their current "constitutionless" status as wards of their respective provinces, but rather *how* they will increase their autonomy and forge more formal linkages with both levels of government."[103] [emphasis in the original] For this to happen, cities need to stop thinking of themselves only in constitutional terms, as creatures of the province.

Concluding Comments

The examination of intergovernmental relations in this chapter began with the traditional hierarchical approach, tracing municipal relations upward – to the province, the federal level, and even the international sphere. While these relationships are essential to an understanding of municipal operations and their scope and constraints, they certainly do not tell the whole story. Viewing municipalities through only the

---

[102] Christopher Leo, with Susan Mulligan, "Rethinking Urban Governance in the 21st Century," paper presented at the Canadian Political Science Association conference, Halifax, May 2003, p. 9.

[103] Courchene, *A State of Minds*, p. 277.

constitutional lens presents a limited and, in some respects, distorted picture.

For example, it was noted earlier that Smith and Stewart have identified a mushy middle that may characterize more accurately where municipalities operate – or at least where they have the potential to operate – than the supposedly precise locations defined by Dillon's Rule and home rule. In support of their contention, they provide three examples of the capacity of local governments to act *"despite constitutional and statutory inferiority."*[104] [emphasis in the original] The first case describes how the city of Vancouver led the way in intergovernmental dealings in pursuit of a new approach to drug treatment that emphasizes harm-reduction. Vancouver's decision to hold a referendum on Canada's bid to hold the 2010 Winter Olympics in that city is the basis for the second case study. It reveals how the city used bargaining leverage that it enjoyed temporarily (while there was uncertainty about how much the newly elected mayor and council might oppose the Olympic bid) to gain some concessions from both the province and the federal government. The last example describes global activities by Vancouver such as twinning (with Odessa in the Soviet Union, in 1944) and declarations of peace, anti-war, and making the city a nuclear weapons free zone – all done without any formal authority, and sometimes in conflict with senior government authorities.[105] To some extent, Vancouver seems to embrace the oft-quoted Nike slogan "Just Do It."

Another way of looking at municipal relationships is provided by Leo and Mulligan, who suggest that instead of focusing on which functions are, or should be, assigned to particular levels of government (as was the approach of the disentanglement exercises described above), we need to recognize that more than one level of government is quite appropriately involved with different aspects of the same function. They see a role for the federal government in setting broad policy objectives, while lower levels of government work out how these objectives can best be met in different areas of the country. To illustrate this point, Leo and Mulligan describe national policies and programs relating to immigration, welfare, and affordable housing and show how these issues have their own particular features in Winnipeg and benefit from distinctive local applications.[106] They call for a new approach to governance in the 21st century based on "an acceptance of

---

[104] Smith and Stewart, "Beavers and Cats Revisited," pp. 19-25.

[105] *Ibid.*, p. 23.

[106] Leo, with Mulligan, "Rethinking Urban Governance," pp 11-16.

the declining power of the national state, the reduction in its role from interventionist programme-provider to supporter of programmes driven by the local and provincial level, and thereby the elevation of local governments and community groups to a more central role in the formulation of both economic and social policy."[107]

If more local governments are to take the initiative by moving toward the mushy middle or by fine-tuning the local application of senior government programs, they need to stop seeing their roles and potential through the perspective of only the constitutional lens. That cities need to become much more assertive is a theme which has been advanced by several others as well. Jane Jacobs delivered this message at the first meeting of the C5, and her words merit repeating at some length.[108]

> I think you have an ingrained mindset of dependency and that this is going to be the hardest thing for you to overcome....You must somehow gather your self-esteem not to be apologetic about yourselves. Certainly the country needs to be educated about how important the cities are. But if the cities themselves don't believe it or are apologetic about it, or are afraid to bring it up, even aggressively, the education of the country and the understanding of what really is necessary and what ails us, is never going to come about.

Andrew advances a similar argument after expressing a number of concerns about the approach that federal and provincial governments have been taking to the needs of the cities.[109] She finds that the federal government seems to lack an understanding of the role and importance of large cities in the global economy and that provincial governments have been either ineffective or even anti-urban. She calls for a broader perspective that focuses on urban governance rather than urban government, therefore providing the opportunity for municipalities to link with the many other organizations and interests that can strengthen the response to the challenges in our urban areas – an approach quite similar to that advocated by Leo and Mulligan above.

According to Andrew, the future of local governments depends more on their actions than on some constitutional breakthrough. In her words: "City governments will not become more effective actors through provincial or federal recognition or power-sharing arrangements; rather, they can become more effective through

---

[107] *Ibid.*, pp. 16-17.

[108] Quoted in *Ideas That Matter*, p. 20.

[109] Caroline Andrew, "The shame of (ignoring) the cities," *Journal of Canadian Studies*, Winter 2001, pp. 100-110.

their creation of more inclusive urban governance regimes."[110] Her concluding observation, reminiscent of the above-noted advice of Jane Jacobs, is: "We should not ignore our cities, but this will happen only when they demonstrate to us and to the other levels of government that we cannot ignore them."[111]

---

[110] *Ibid.*, p. 109.

[111] *Ibid.*, p. 110.

Chapter 7
Local Government Finances

"A report on Canadian public finance, released today, foreshadows the decline and fall of municipal government as we know it in Canada within five years."

Introduction

According to the report cited above, if present trends continue "autonomous municipal government will not survive without huge increases in property taxes or unacceptable cutbacks in services city residents now demand, or both." This is certainly a viewpoint widely expressed today, but the report being quoted is actually 30 years old.[1] Municipalities are obviously still very much with us, but concerns about the financial problems they face have remained and intensified. What is the nature and cause of this financial crisis and how can it be resolved or eased? Attempting to answer these questions is the central purpose of this chapter.

What Is the Financial Crisis?

The conventional wisdom is that local government faces a serious and growing financial crisis because of a number of problems. One complaint is that the local level is short-changed within the Canadian system of public finance by not having access to sufficient sources of revenue in comparison with the provincial and federal levels. This is essentially the same argument made by the Tri-Level Task Force on Public Finance in Canada whose 1976 report prompted the response quoted at the beginning of this chapter. According to the Task Force,

---

[1] Canadian Federation of Mayors and Municipalities, *Puppets On a Shoestring*, Ottawa, April 28, 1976. Both quotes are from p. 1.

Canada's public finance system generated enough money to meet the needs of government in the aggregate, but did not distribute enough of this money to the local level, especially in light of the growing proportion of government expenditures being made by this level.

The unfair distribution of public revenues continues to be a source of complaint. Between 1995 and 2001, local government revenues increased by only 14% compared to increases of 38% and 30% at the federal and provincial levels, respectively.[2] Contributing to this local revenue shortfall is the closely related complaint that federal and provincial fiscal restraint objectives resulted in cuts in transfer payments over the past decade or so that "passed the buck" down to the local level. While municipalities increased property and related taxes substantially in 2002, their transfers from the provincial level were cut by $302 million, leaving them with an overall deficit of $41 million.[3]

In addition to these revenue considerations, concern has also been expressed about increasing local expenditures and expenditure needs. These are said to arise from a number of factors including (as discussed in Chapter 3) the rapid urbanization being experienced in Canada and the accompanying urban sprawl with its expensive servicing requirements. Such growth requires an investment in infrastructure (such as roads and bridges, water supply and sewage treatment facilities, solid waste disposal facilities, schools, libraries, and arenas) and, in addition, much of the existing infrastructure has deteriorated and now needs replacing – at a cost of many billions of dollars.

Caught between insufficient revenues and rising expenditure needs, municipalities find themselves in an increasing financial squeeze. Continued reliance on the real property tax as the primary source of municipal revenues is widely criticized as inappropriate as well as inadequate. The other revenues sources available to Canadian municipalities are regarded as quite limited and insufficient – especially when compared with the experience of municipal governments in the United States and many parts of Europe.

A closer look at the various sources of revenue for Canadian municipalities, and how they have been changing and evolving, will

---

[2] TD Economics, *A Choice Between Investing in Canada's Cities or Disinvesting in Canada's Future*, Special Report, April 22, 2002, p. 2.

[3] Statistics Canada, *The Daily*, June 18, 2003, p. 3, accessed June 21, 2003, from www.statcan.ca.

provide further insight into the nature and magnitude of the financial problems facing municipalities. On that basis, we can then consider possible solutions to these financial problems.

Transfers Payments to Local Government

As municipal expenditures increased in the 20th century, and the inadequacies of the real property tax became more pronounced, provincial governments began to introduce a variety of grants to local governments, mostly conditional in a nature. For example, the 1901 *Highway Improvement Act* in Ontario introduced the roads grant, the first conditional grant apart from education. The number and variety of these grants proliferated, especially following the Second World War, and reached over 100 in Ontario by the 1980s. In the meantime, a much smaller number of unconditional grants were also introduced. A third form of transfer is the payment in lieu of taxes, often referred to as a PIL or sometimes a PILOT. It is paid to municipalities with respect to provincial (and federal) properties because they are exempt from taxation. As a result, it is often grouped together with the real property tax or with miscellaneous local revenues (both discussed later in this chapter), but it is also valid to consider it (as we do here) as an unconditional transfer payment.

Rationale for Transfer Payments

Transfers from the provincial level are offered for a variety of economic and political reasons.[4] One of the strongest economic arguments is that of externalities – the fact that a service provided by one municipality generates benefits (or costs) that spill over into other jurisdictions. Conditional grants can be used to cover the value of that spillover. Without such grants, inequities are likely to arise in the provision of, and costing for, services, with some municipalities enjoying a "free ride" at the expense of others. Grants also can be provided to close a fiscal gap and ensure that municipalities have sufficient funds to cover their expenditures. These usually take the

---

[4] The discussion that follows is based on Harry Kitchen, *Municipal Revenue and Expenditure Issues in Canada*, Canadian Tax Paper No. 107, Toronto, Canadian Tax Foundation, 2002, pp. 159-163.

form of an unconditional per capita or per household grant. Unconditional grants are also provided for equalization purposes – to shore up
the financial base of municipalities in remote areas, or in areas with
low levels of assessment and tax capacity, for example, or to ensure the
provision of comparable services at comparable taxes by supplement-
ing municipalities with a weak assessment base.

The rationale for some grants is much more political than
economic in nature. Conditional grants may be provided simply to
induce municipalities to provide a service that the province regards as a
priority. Sometimes such grants are even provided as a way of making
local governments (and their citizens) aware of the benefit of a new
service, on the assumption that it will then be possible to withdraw the
grant and have the service continued at local expense. Of course, it is
precisely this instability with respect to transfer payments that municipalities find so troubling.

Whatever the rationale, there was a growing feeling in the
second half of the 20th century that the process had gone too far,
resulting in "a rapidly diminishing relationship between the taxes paid
to any one level of government and the services rendered by it."[5] The
main problem with such arrangements has been described as follows:[6]

> Through the development of a complex transfer system, each level
> of government can influence the nature and scope of the services
> provided, take a share in the political rewards, maintain the fiction of
> autonomy, and have a convenient excuse for avoiding any criticism
> for inadequate services. The only drawback is that the public never
> knows who is responsible for what or how much the services
> provided really cost

There are also federal transfers to the local level, in spite of the
provincial responsibility for this level of government. While these
transfers are quite small, one can make a case for federal grants to local
governments (and especially to cities).[7] One rationale is that federal
grants are appropriate, indeed desirable, when it is federal policies or

---

[5] Ontario Economic Council, *Government Reform in Ontario*, Toronto, 1969,
p. viii.

[6] *Ibid.*, p. 19.

[7] This discussion is based on Kitchen, *Municipal Issues*, pp. 183-184 and Enid
Slack, "Intergovernmental Fiscal Relations and Canadian Municipalities:
Current Situation and Prospects," Report to the Federation of Canadian Municipalities, May 8, 2002, p. 11, available at www.fcm.ca/newfcm/Java/slack.htm,
accessed June 12. 2003.

actions that give rise to municipal expenditures. The best example is federal immigration policy, under which the vast majority of immigrants settle in Canada's largest cities, giving rise to additional municipal expenditures that the federal government does not cover. Another example is when the federal government makes international commitments, such as the Kyoto protocol on the environment, which will require expenditures by local governments to implement.

Federal grants also can be justified with respect to matters of national interest, such as the problems of homelessness and lack of affordable housing. These problems are played out in the streets of our cities, but they are arguably a matter of national concern justifying much more federal financial assistance than has been forthcoming to date. Since these problems have largely arisen because of neglect by the federal and provincial levels, the prospect of transfer payments from them to address these problems seems unlikely.

A third rationale derives from the recognition that the infrastructure and services provided by cities confers benefits beyond the municipal boundaries. This is the externalities or spillover argument again, although infrastructure benefits are fairly local and most spillovers are likely to stay within a regional context. In addition, it is increasingly appreciated that cities generate the bulk of the economic activity and growth in Canada. As a result, the health of the cities is a matter of national interest, one justifying federal transfers. This is essentially the argument advanced at the beginning of the 1970s as one of the main reasons for the introduction of a Ministry of State for Urban Affairs and it is echoed in the November 2002 report of the Task Force on Urban Issues and its call for a federal Ministry and new federal funding for affordable housing, transit/transportation, and sustainable infrastructure.

The Transfer Record

As previously noted, transfer payments from the federal and (mostly) provincial levels had become quite prevalent by the period following the Second World War and accounted for over 50% of municipal and school board revenues by 1975. Municipalities and their associations expressed concerns about senior government priorities being imposed on the municipal level because of the fact that 90% of these transfers were conditional in nature. As David Siegel points out, "be careful what you wish for," because you may get it. He notes that municipalities are now much less hampered by conditions attached to transfer payments, "although at least some local governments wish that they had not been so successful in liberating themselves from provincial funding assistance."[8]

The dramatic change that has taken place is evident from the record of the past decade. Provincial and federal transfers declined from 45.7% of municipal government revenues in 1990, to 25.4% in 1994, to only 17.9% in 2000.[9] Since federal transfers represented less than 1% of municipal revenues throughout this period, this drama-tic decline was the result of cuts in provincial grants to municipalities. In some cases, the provinces attempted to soften the blow by making the reduced grants less conditional.

Alberta and Ontario typified this approach. Alberta termi-nated its Municipal Assistance Grant and replaced it with a new Unconditional Grants Program. Funds from four other conditional grants programs (relating to urban parks, public transit, policing, and family and community support services) were then transferred into the new unconditional program. But the budget for the unconditional program was then steadily reduced, from $169 million in 1994-1995 to $126 million the next year and to only $88 million in 1996-1997.[10] In strikingly similar fashion, the Conservative government in Ontario announced following its election in 1995 that three existing grant programs (the unconditional grant, roads grant, and northern roads assistance) were being converted into a single block grant – the Municipal Support Grant. This new grant was then reduced from what would have been a $1.4 billion transfer to $887 million in 1996 and $666 million in 1997, before disappearing as a separate grant in 1998.

Federal financial assistance has remained more stable during this period, but at a very modest level. As part of a job creation program promised during the 1993 election campaign, the Liberal government introduced the *Canada Infrastructure Works* program. Under this program, the federal government provided $2 billion in funding for approved projects, matched by the same amount of funding from provinces and municipalities, and directed toward

---

[8] David Siegel, "Urban Finance at the Turn of the Century: Be Careful What You Wish For," in Edmund P. Fowler and David Siegel (eds.), *Urban Policy Issues*, 2nd Edition, Toronto, Oxford University Press, 2002, p. 36.

[9] Statistics Canada information as compiled in Kitchen, *Municipal Issues*, p. 16.

[10] Figures from Alberta Municipal Affairs, *News Release*, February 24, 1994.

upgrading the quality of the physical infrastructure in local communities. In June 2000, the federal government established two "Green Municipal" Investment Funds with a combined value of $250 million to provide financial support to projects that help to improve the environmental efficiency and cost-effectiveness of municipal infrastructure and, in the December 2001 budget, another $2 billion for infrastructure funding was announced. How modest these federal investments are will become evident when international comparisons are made in a later section of this chapter.

Revenue and Tax Sharing Agreements

In their search for a more stable and continuing source of financial support, municipalities have often sought long term revenue sharing or tax sharing agreements. Ontario was the first to enter into such an arrangement, in 1973 – with its "Edmonton Commitment"[11] to increase its transfers to local governments at the rate of growth of total provincial revenues – but it was also one of the first to abandon revenue sharing, in 1977. In the second half of the 1970s, provinces such as Manitoba, Saskatchewan, and British Columbia introduced plans that guaranteed their municipalities specified levels of transfer payment, but these last two did not endure.

Manitoba continues to have a Provincial Municipal Tax Sharing (PMTS) program, under which municipalities receive payments comprising an amount equal to 2.2% of provincial personal income tax revenue and 1% of corporate income tax revenue.[12]

There are also currently tax sharing arrangements in British Columbia and Alberta, but they are of recent and uncertain status.[13] The British Columbia Revenue Sharing Act of 1978 was discontinued in 1994 and replaced with the Local Government Grants Act. In 1997,

---

[11] For those curious as to why an Ontario revenue-sharing commitment is named after the Alberta capital, this resulted from the fact that the commitment was made by the Ontario government during the second (and last) tri-level conference (in Edmonton) sponsored by the Ministry of State for Urban Affairs.

[12] Manitoba Government, "Unique Program Provides $82.5 million to Manitoba Municipalities," *News Release*, September 10, 2002.

[13] The summary that follows is partly from Canada West Foundation, *Big City Revenues: A Canada-U.S. Comparison of Municipal Tax Tools and Revenue Levers*, September 2002, p. 27.

provincial transfers were cut and only partially replaced with the sharing of provincial traffic fine revenue. The province assigns a share of its retail sales tax to municipalities. In addition, municipalities may request that the hotel room tax be levied at 10%, rather than 8%, with the additional yield being transferred to them. The Alberta government agreement deals with fuel tax sharing; it has been far from stable, and it is only with the province's two largest municipalities. In fact, as the examples below indicate, arrangements with individual municipalities are more common than general provincial-municipal agreements.[14]

Box 7.1 Revenue-Sharing Agreements

- ➤ The British Columbia government remits 11 cents of its fuel tax per litre to the Greater Vancouver Regional District, which applies this money to the capital and operating costs of transit services and major roads within its jurisdiction. The province also remits 2.5 cents of its fuel tax per litre to the transit system of the Capital region (Victoria and environs).
- ➤ Vancouver receives a portion of the provincially controlled gaming (casino) revenues under the Host City Agreement of 2000. It also receives a portion of a hotel tax collected in the city, under the Hotel Room Tax Act.
- ➤ Calgary and Edmonton receive 5 cents per litre of the Alberta fuel tax.[15]
- ➤ Saskatchewan, Manitoba, and Quebec have authorized their municipalities to levy amusement taxes.
- ➤ Municipalities in Manitoba are authorized to levy sales taxes on liquor, hotel accommodation, and restaurant meals, subject to the approval of the provincial cabinet and with collection provided by the province.
- ➤ Municipalities in Manitoba, Nova Scotia, and Quebec have the right to levy a land transfer tax on the value of transferred property.
- ➤ Montreal receives 1.5 cents per litre from the province for each litre of fuel sold in that city.
- ➤ Municipalities in Newfoundland and Labrador are authorized to impose a tax on coal, fuel and propane.

---

[14] The examples are drawn from a variety of sources including Kitchen, *Municipal Issues*, pp. 229-230; Kitchen, *Municipal Finance in a New Fiscal Environment*, Commentary No. 147, C. D. Howe Institute, November 2000, p. 20; Federation of Canadian Municipalities, *Early Warning: Will Canadian Cities Compete?*, Ottawa, May 2001, p. 7; Toronto Dominion Bank, *Investing or Disinvesting*, p. 9; and Canada West Foundation, *Cities at the Crossroads*, August 2002, pp. 3-4.

[15] In a development that demonstrates the precarious nature of municipal finances even with agreements such as these, the Alberta government unilaterally reduced this payment to 4.2 cents per litre in October 2001 and then to 1.2 cents per litre in its budget of March 2002, only to restore it back to 5 cents per litre shortly after – in the face of strenuous local opposition.

Even with these various arrangements, however, it is widely perceived that municipalities do not have access to the variety of tax sources and senior government transfers available to municipalities in the United States and elsewhere, leaving them overly dependent on the property tax in attempting to meet their growing expenditure needs.

The Impact of Declining Transfers

There seems little doubt that municipal governments are not getting their "fair" share of the revenues raised within the public sector in Canada. The backlog in infrastructure investment is also widely documented. For example, the Association of Consulting Engineers of Canada reported that the municipal infrastructure deficit was estimated to be $12 billion in 1984; 12 years later that figure had more than tripled to $44 billion.[16] It is now estimated to be growing at about $2 billion a year.[17] McMillan expresses caution about accepting at face value infrastructure estimates provided by local governments and contractors, especially when accompanied by requests that someone else should pay. Since he believes that infrastructure benefits are mainly local, he also suggests that any revenue capacity problem at the local level should be resolved by providing the necessary revenue base and making municipal decision makers answerable to local taxpayers (beneficiaries) for the expenditures that are made.[18]

As to the extent to which municipalities are caught in a financial squeeze, an analysis by McMillan is revealing in this regard. It begins by noting the previously cited drop in transfer payments to local governments. But it also finds that municipal expenditures as a percentage of Gross Domestic Product (GDP) were essentially the same in 2001 (4.4%) as in 1988 (4.54%).[19] An examination of municipal program expenditures as a percentage of combined provincial and local program expenditures over this period also reveals virtually no change

---

[16] Federation of Canadian Municipalities, *Will Canadian Cities Compete?*, p. 14.

[17] Toronto Dominion Bank, *Investing or Disinvesting*, p. 15.

[18] Communication from Melville McMillan, June 3, 2003.

[19] Melville L. McMillan, "Municipal Relations with the Federal and Provincial Governments: A Fiscal Perspective," a paper prepared for the Municipal-Provincial-Federal Relations Conference, Queen's University, May 9-10, 2003, (April 2003 Draft), p. 7.

(from 16.1% in 1988 to 16.3% in 2001).[20] Thus the municipal expenditure burden does not appear to have increased in spite of the many municipal complaints about increased costs, including provincial downloading of costs and responsibilities (especially in Ontario).

A different picture emerges when McMillan analyzes the revenue side of the equation. The reduction in transfer payments led to an increase in municipal own source revenues, from 76.9% of total revenues to 83% between 1988 and 2001.[21] Most of this increase occurred with property taxes, which increased from 32.2% of total revenue to 41.9% over this period.[22] The magnitude of this change is reflected in the fact that real property taxes during this period increased 26.8% as a percentage of the GDP, 30.6% as a percentage of personal income tax, and 33.9% as a percentage of personal disposable income.[23] McMillan concludes that it is here, on the revenue side, not the expenditure side, that the municipal fiscal squeeze has mainly been felt.[24] Moreover, he finds that the financial impact has been most pronounced in Ontario, largely as a result of the provincial downloading of various social programs to the municipal governments. As a result, real property taxes as a percentage of personal disposal income (PDI) rose in Ontario by 1.38% between 1988 and 2001, compared to an average 0.35% increase in the other provinces.[25]

McMillan is not optimistic that municipal fiscal pressures will be resolved by increased transfer payments, observing that "senior governments seem to be fickle friends when it comes to providing grants."[26] To the extent that this description is accurate, municipalities will have to continue (increasingly) to rely on their own revenue sources – to which we now turn our attention.

---

[20] *Ibid.*, p. 8.

[21] *Ibid.*

[22] *Ibid.*

[23] *Ibid.*, p. 9.

[24] *Ibid.*., pp. 9-10.

[25] *Ibid.*, p. 12.

[26] *Ibid.*, p. 21.

Real Property Tax

From the outset it was envisaged that the new municipal institutions being established in Canada would be financed by a tax on real property – defined essentially as land and buildings on land. In Upper Canada, for example, the first Assessment Act was passed in 1793, to provide a basis for the collection of property taxes to finance the expenditures of the townships that were then being established across the colony. Since the very limited services then being provided by municipalities (such as roads and fire protection) were services to property, it made sense to pay for them out of a tax on property – especially since property was the main form of wealth in those days. As Chapter 2 pointed out, so closely was the property tax associated with municipal government that the development of the system was delayed in several provinces by public antipathy toward the introduction of this tax. Over the years, there have been some variations to the basic tax on real property, as summarized below.

Box 7.2 Variations on Basic Property Tax

In the early years, the property tax often applied not only to real property but also to personal property (generally defined as all goods and chattels and property not included in the term real estate). Problems with the administration of the personal property tax led to its abolition as early as 1904 in Ontario, but it was still in existence in the mid-20th century in Prince Edward Island, Nova Scotia, New Brunswick, Manitoba and Alberta.[27]

At that time some form of municipal business tax (almost always levied upon the tenant of the property, not the owner) was also in effect in all provinces, although its use was optional in several of them. Over the past decade the trend has been to abolish the business tax in favour of higher tax rates on business (commercial and industrial properties). There is no longer a separate business tax in Prince Edward Island, New Brunswick, Ontario, the Northwest Territories, Nunavut or the Yukon. This tax is optional in British Columbia (and seldom used), Saskatchewan, Quebec and Alberta, and it is mandatory in Nova Scotia, Newfoundland and the City of Winnipeg.[28]

Ignoring these comings and goings of personal property taxes and business taxes, it is the basic tax on real property that originally was – and has become again – the mainstay of municipal revenues. A closer look at this tax and how it measures up is, therefore, in order.

---

[27] K. G. Crawford, *Canadian Municipal Government*, Toronto, University of Toronto Press, 1954, p. 214.

[28] Kitchen, *Municipal Issues*, p. 78.

Evaluation of the Real Property Tax

As its name suggests, the real property tax is not a tax on income but on property and its value. How that value is determined is specified in provincial statutes, which stipulate market value, current value, or real and true value – all terms that refer to the price that would be obtained in the open market with a willing buyer and a willing seller. In practice, however, properties have traditionally been assessed at far less than market value, although reforms in recent years are overcoming this problem.

Once assessment values are determined, the calculation of the property tax is, or can be, relatively straightforward. When a municipality determines its total expenditure requirements and subtracts the non-tax revenues available to it that year (essentially transfer payments from the provincial and federal levels and funds from miscellaneous local revenues like user fees), it arrives at the amount that it needs to raise from taxation. Dividing this amount by the total taxable assessment of the municipality produces the tax rate – the factor that, when applied against the available assessment, will generate the required revenue. Tax rates have most commonly been expressed in mills, with a mill being one-tenth of a cent. Another way of expressing the same relationship is to cite the tax in dollars per $1000 of assessment value. As a result of recent reforms to assessment and property taxation in Ontario, property taxes there are now expressed as a percentage rather than in mills.

The value of the assessment base is the key to the revenue generating capacity of a municipality. If the assessment doubles, the same amount of revenue can be raised with half the taxes – as in the simple example below.

Table 7.1 Assessment Is the Key	
Situation 1: $\dfrac{\text{Amount required} \quad \$1,000,000}{\text{Assessment} \quad \$200,000,000} = 0.005$	Situation 2: $\dfrac{\text{Amount required} \quad \$1,000,000}{\text{Assessment} \quad \$400,000,000} = 0.0025$

In practice, calculations can be considerably more complicated than the example above, since there may be requirements to weight different classes of property differently and to determine separate tax rates for different classes. For example, wherever rate differentials exist, residential and farm properties almost always enjoy rates lower than those attached to business properties.

As already noted, the property tax appeared to be both adequate and appropriate when it was first established. It is a tax easily administered within the relatively small areas encompassed by most municipalities. It is also easily enforced, since the tax base – property – cannot be concealed and can be sold by the municipality if taxes are not paid. In addition, there is at least some link between taxes paid and benefits received, which is one measure of a valid tax.

However, the enduring and pervasive nature of the property tax has certainly done nothing to alter the negative feelings toward it that were recorded from the days of the earliest settlers. Indeed, in the words of Bird and Slack: "No tax in Canada has been more vilified than the property tax." As they explain:

> It has been called inherently regressive, inelastic, and an inadequate generator of municipal revenues. It has been labelled "unfair" because it is unrelated to ability to pay, "unrealistic" because it is unrelated to benefits, and "unsuitable" because it supports services unrelated to property.[29]

However, they go on to note that "the residential property tax on the whole appears to be about as fair and efficient a tax as can be administered at the local level," and that its defects are largely correctable, in part through more frequent reassessment of property values.[30]

Indeed, a number of the problems attributed to the property tax have really been problems relating to the assessment of properties. Properties were traditionally underassessed, often markedly so, with Ontario being particularly delinquent in this regard. It was not unusual in Ontario to refer, even as recently as a decade ago, to a "typical" house assessed at $10 000. There was no consistency in the degree of underassessment of properties either, which resulted in widespread inequities when the municipal tax rate was applied to the assessments. Over the years, provincial governments have become increasingly involved in the assessment process, in an attempt to achieve consistency. Assessment is a local responsibility only in Alberta and Quebec and in the cities of St. John's, Winnipeg, Regina, and Saskatoon.[31]

---

[29] Richard M. Bird and N. Enid Slack, *Urban Public Finance in Canada*, 2nd Edition, John Wiley & Sons, 1993, p. 100.

[30] *Ibid.*, p. 101.

[31] Kitchen, *Municipal Issues*, p. 66.

Provincial governments have introduced also a variety of payments to ease the tax burden on those with lower income levels, in an effort to offset the regressive nature of the property tax. Such programs are found in virtually every province today, and range from grants to exemptions to tax credits to deferrals. In most provinces, as well, municipalities are given discretion to reduce property taxes for those in need of relief. These various forms of tax relief are provided almost exclusively with respect to residential and farm properties.[32]

Tax relief programs are in part a response to the visibility of the property tax. It is not deducted at source, in the quietly efficient manner of an income tax, but is collected directly from citizens in a few large, lump sum payments,[33] on the basis of tax rates set in highly publicized municipal council meetings. In one respect, this visibility is desirable in that it enhances municipal accountability. On the other hand, the highly visible nature of the property tax makes councillors very reluctant to increase it, even when the result can be to postpone necessary expenditures that only become greater over time.

Councillors are understandably attracted by opportunities to increase the assessment base in their municipality, and thus be able to generate more revenues without increasing taxes. This can lead to an acceptance of growth and development that is not always best for the municipality, a shortsighted approach sometimes referred to as "dollar planning." Ironically, it can also lead to financial problems rather than a financial windfall, since growth sometimes overloads existing services and infrastructure and triggers new expenditures that can more than offset the revenues gained from the enlarged assessment base.

While critiques of the property tax often focus on its inadequacy in meeting municipal revenue needs, economists are more concerned about the inefficiency of the property tax as it currently operates.[34] As a benefits tax, the property tax would be efficient as long

---

[32] *Ibid.*, p. 73.

[33] Although more and more municipalities are increasing the number of instalment payments that they use, some even introducing a monthly payment plan. In addition, those paying mortgages often have their property taxes included.

[34] See Kitchen, *Municipal Issues*, Chapter 5; Bird and Slack, *Urban Public Finance*, Chapter 5; Kitchen, *New Fiscal Environment*, pp. 7-12; and Paul A. R. Hobson, "Efficiency, Equity and Accountability Issues in Local Taxation," in Paul A. R. Hobson and France St-Hilaire (eds.), *Urban Governance and Finance*, Montreal, Institute of Research on Public Policy, 1997, pp. 113-132.

as it is used to fund services that benefit the local community. As long
as those who benefit from local public services are paying for them,
the property tax can be considered fair and municipalities are clearly
accountable to the local taxpayers for the cost of the services provided.[35] But a number of factors distort these relationships.

> ➤ As already noted, underassessing properties to varying degrees
> creates inequities and unfairness, although this problem has
> been at least partly addressed by provincial assumption of the
> assessment function in most jurisdictions.

> ➤ When a constant tax rate is applied to these varying assess-
> ments, it results in differences in the effective property tax rate
> within and across properties within a community. Since this
> differential tax treatment of properties does not reflect differ-
> ences in the cost of providing municipal services to them, it
> creates a number of distortions and inefficiencies.[36]

> ➤ Further distortions arise from the fact that every province has
> authorized the imposition of higher taxes on commercial and
> industrial properties, even though studies have shown that it is
> residential properties that receive proportionately more bene-
> fits from local government services.[37] The result is an unfair
> burden of taxes on businesses, one that can make them less
> competitive at a time when they are exposed to much greater
> international competition as a result of globalization.

> ➤ Yet another distortion can be seen as contributing to the urban
> sprawl that has become such a concern in Canada and else-
> where. Since it costs much more to provide services to
> scattered, low density development, an efficient property tax
> would reflect these higher costs and, in turn, serve to discour-
> age further sprawl. But if property taxes are higher in the
> urban core, as is often the case, they create an incentive to
> move to the suburbs and thus contribute to further sprawl.[38] In
> the words of Slack: "Higher property taxes provide an

---

[35] Kitchen, *Municipal Issues*, p. 102.

[36] Kitchen, *New Fiscal Environment*, p. 9.

[37] *Ibid.*, pp. 9-10.

[38] Kitchen, *Municipal Issues*, p. 113.

incentive for less-dense projects and lower densities mean that the city is likely to expand in a way that is socially inefficient.[39]

Provincial Invasion of the Property Tax Field

The ability of municipalities to finance an increasing portion of their expenditures from their own revenue sources is threatened by the fact that the real property tax is less and less their own to use as they wish. Since the beginnings of municipal government in Canada, this tax has been portrayed as the mainstay of municipal finances. Yet municipalities have been gradually losing control over the use of the property tax.

Much of the provincial incursion has occurred with respect to education financing. At one time, education costs were mainly funded from the property tax. Gradually, provincial financial assistance grew, along with increasing provincial control and supervision of educational matters. Provincial governments also amalgamated school boards, in a move paralleling and exceeding in scope the amalgamation of municipalities described in earlier chapters. Prompted by the desire to reduce costs and to improve access and equity, provinces began – as early as the 1930s in Alberta – to consolidate school boards and school areas.[40]

This process continued and intensified in the 1990s, as indicated by the following examples.

> ➤ New Brunswick reduced the number of school boards from 42 to 18 in 1992 and then eliminated the remaining boards in 1996, replacing them with provincial superintendents advised by 18 district councils. However, it reversed this policy at the end of 2000, providing for the election of 14 district education councils that will oversee the operations of schools in the province. While they control their own budgets, the councils can't raise taxes and are funded by the province.[41]

---

[39] Enid Slack, *Municipal Finance and the Pattern of Urban Growth*, Commentary No. 160, C. D. Howe Institute, February 2002, p. 8.

[40] For a summary of consolidation activities up to the mid-1990s, see Robert Carney and Frank Peters, "Governing Education: The Myth of Local Control," in James Lightbody (ed.), *Canadian Metropolitics: Governing Our Cities*, Toronto, Copp Clark Ltd., pp. 248-251.

[41] Kelly Toughill, "School reform 'flop' tossed out in N.B.," *Toronto Star*, November 30. 2000.

> Alberta reduced the number of school boards from 181 to 57 in a two-stage process that began in 1994. At the same time, the province assumed almost complete responsibility for the financing of education. It sets the education tax requisition, which it has been reducing in recent years, but municipalities remain responsible for levying and collecting school taxes.[42]

> Twenty-two boards were amalgamated into six regional boards in Nova Scotia, along with one province-wide board for Acadian and Francophone education.[43]

> Effective January 1, 1998, Ontario cut the number of school boards in half, to 66. It also took over responsibility for half of the education costs previously borne by residential property taxpayers, and sets the education tax rates for both residential and business properties. Like Alberta, Ontario has been reducing the education tax rates in recent years.

> On July 1, 1998, the Quebec government replaced 159 religious boards with 72 linguistic boards.

While there are many issues that could be raised with respect to the educational reforms, of particular concern in this context is the extent to which provincial governments have invaded the property tax field to fund at least a portion of the educational costs – an incursion found in British Columbia, Alberta, Manitoba, Ontario (most recently), New Brunswick, and Prince Edward Island.[44] Currently, only Manitoba and Saskatchewan retain traditional property tax

---

[42] Edward LeSage, *Municipal Reform in Alberta: A Review of Statutory, Financial and Structural Changes Over the Past Decade*, paper presented at the Canadian Political Science Association annual meeting, Quebec City, May 28, 2001, pp. 11-12. Much of this paper has been incorporated into the Alberta chapter of Joseph Garcea and Edward LeSage (eds.), *Municipal Reform in Canada: Dynamics, Dimensions, Determinants*, forthcoming publication.

[43] The preceding examples are all from Ontario Ministry of Education and Training, Backgrounder, *Education Reform and Finance in Other Provinces, 1997*.

[44] Andrew Sancton, "The Municipal Role in the Governance of Cities," in Trudi Bunting and Pierre Filion (eds.), *Canadian Cities in Transition*, 2nd Edition, Toronto, Oxford University Press, 2000, p. 431. See also Karim Treff and David B. Perry, *Finances of the Nation 2001*, Toronto, Canadian Tax Foundation, 2001, p. 10-4, for a summary of the arrangements for public school financing, by province and territory.

supported school boards.[45] McMillan points out that the school
property tax made sense when a local contribution to schooling was
required and the only sufficient local tax base was property, but that it
is not well related to school benefits or ability to pay. He suggests that
the elimination of provincial property taxes for education (at least on
residential properties) would free up some tax room that might then be
available to meet other municipal expenditure needs.[46]

This provincial incursion has not been confined to the field of
education. Beginning with the Program of Equal Opportunity in New
Brunswick in the mid-1960s, provinces have been appropriating a
portion of the property tax field and directing it to the financing of
specified provincial services. As a result, the provincial role in the
property tax field is much larger than the role of state governments in
the United States. "Not only is the tax now basically provincial in
New Brunswick, Prince Edward Island, and, for education, in British
Columbia, but the local tax rates are at least partly determined by
provincial grant levels...."[47] In New Brunswick and Prince Edward
Island the province acts as the collection agency for both its own
property tax levies and those for municipal governments.

The distentanglement exercises of the 1990s added to this
pattern of encroachment. For example, when Nova Scotia took on
administrative responsibility for a number of "people services" in the
1995-1996 program of service exchange, it still required municipalities
to include a provincial education levy in their tax bills and to contribute to the social and correctional services programs that became
provincial responsibilities.[48] As a result, a substantial portion of the
municipal tax base is devoted to supporting provincial programs.
Similarly, under Ontario's realignment of services following the *Who
Does What* exercise, the province assumed responsibility for half of the
education costs previously paid by residential property tax payers. But,
as noted above, the province also took over responsibility for setting
the residential property tax rate to finance the other half of those costs,
and for setting the property tax rate paid by business properties.

---

[45] Kitchen, *Municipal Issues*, p. 28.

[46] McMillan, "Municipal Relations," p. 17.

[47] Bird and Slack, *Urban Public Finance*, p. 92.

[48] Kell Antoft and Jack Novack, *GrassRoots Democracy: Local Government in
the Maritimes*, Halifax, Dalhousie University, 1998, p. 95.

More recently, the Ontario government has shown a willingness to encroach on municipal decision making with respect to property taxes. While the property tax reforms introduced toward the end of the 1990s were supposed to give municipalities greater discretion to set tax policy, the province was not satisfied with the extent to which municipalities employed their tax tools to reduce the tax burden on business properties. As a result, the province imposed a cap on tax increases on business properties – at first for a three year period and then, under the Continuing Protection of Property Taxpayers Act 2000, on an ongoing basis. The gravity of this provincial action was well expressed by the Executive Director of the province's largest staff association in commenting on the initial three year capping.[49]

> Make no mistake, this is a devastating decision for municipal government in Ontario. For decades, municipal associations have been lobbying for access to more revenue sources to supplement property taxes and reflect the scope of municipal responsibilities. This decision places the Provincial Government firmly in control of property taxes in Ontario.

While the property tax is not as bad as its critics often claim, neither it is as good as it could be. In particular, inequities in tax burden (as between multi-residential and single family properties and between business and residential properties) still need to be addressed more effectively and the level of taxation should be more closely aligned with the cost of delivering services. These and other suggestions will be examined more fully in a later section that considers possible solutions to the financial crisis facing local governments.

Other Local Revenues

While local government revenues largely derive from property taxes, they also include "grants in lieu of taxes, sales of goods and services, rentals, concessions and franchises, licences and permits, remittances from own enterprises, interest, interest and penalties on taxes, fines and other miscellaneous local revenues."[50] Historically, these other

---

[49] Ken Cousineau, "Editorial," *Municipal Monitor*, December/January 1998/ 1999, Association of Municipal Managers, Clerks and Treasurers of Ontario.

[50] Bird and Slack, *Urban Public Finance*, p. 63.

local revenues have been very limited, but they have been called upon increasingly in recent years as the main alternative for municipalities facing falling transfer payments and public resistance to property tax increases. User charges or fees, in particular, have become more prominent, almost doubling from 6.5% of municipal government revenues in 1965 to 12.2% in 1980, and then almost doubling again, to 21.3% by 2000.[51] As we will see, user fees have been both promoted as a panacea for municipal revenue needs and criticized for their failure to bring about a more efficient allocation of resources.

User Fees

In simplest terms, a user fee is a charge levied upon an individual for the use of a specific public service. User fees work best when the service involved is a private good (a private sector-type service) that benefits the individuals who use it and that can be kept from those who don't pay for it. Examples would be water, sanitary sewers, solid waste management, and airport – all of which can be fully or substantially funded by user fees. In contrast, police and fire services are more in the nature of pure public goods, readily available to the whole community and not easily divisible into separate lots for purchase. Such public goods are more appropriately funded from the property tax.

A variety of revenue earning enterprises at the local level employ user fees to finance at least a part of their operations. Examples include recreational and cultural facilities such as arenas, libraries, pools, golf courses and community centres, and public utilities providing such services as water supply, sanitary sewage collection and disposal, electricity, public transportation, airports, public housing, and municipal parking. Many of these services and facilities are administered by local boards and commissions – such as arena boards and public utility commissions – and rely heavily on user fees as they are increasingly called upon to bring their operations closer to break-even.

Less Than Meets the Eye: Ontario Experience With User Fees

User fees that are properly designed and priced can be used to ration output to those willing to pay, and to signal how much people are

---

[51] Kitchen, *Municipal Issues*, p. 16, Table 2-2.

willing to pay for what. Instead, however, they are often relied upon as a source of much needed additional municipal revenues. There is no better example of this approach, and its shortcomings, than the Ontario experience of recent years.

The province's omnibus Savings and Restructuring Act of January 1996 supposedly expanded greatly the municipal authority to raise revenues from user fees. It authorized municipalities and local boards (except school boards and hospital boards) to impose these fees on any class of persons for services or activities provided, for costs payable by a municipality or board for services or activities provided, or for use of its property. Since the legislative changes initially provided that by-laws could provide for user fees that were in the nature of a direct tax for the purpose of raising revenue, a number of municipalities took the position that they could levy such charges as gasoline or sales taxes or a poll tax. The Minister of Municipal Affairs and Housing denied any such possibility and then specifically ruled it out through amendments to the legislation before its final passage.

Significantly, this provision that user fees and charges are in the nature of a direct tax for raising revenues was removed entirely from the new Municipal Act that took effect in January 2003 – the one portrayed as greatly increasing municipal powers and discretion. Other limitations have been introduced under provisions that the Minister may prescribe activities or services for which municipalities may not impose a user fee (which has been done), and may impose conditions and limits on the powers of a municipality under this section, including limits on the fees that can be charged.

In addition, there are indications that the courts will constrain municipal efforts to exploit this revenue source. The first challenge of Ontario's legislation, known as the Harvey Township case,[52] involved municipal imposition of a flat $50 user charge for every occupied trailer site in a trailer park in the township. The court held that fees or charges under this legislation cannot be unreasonably high, must relate to the provision of a service, and cannot be used to replace or supplement what had traditionally been provided as a service to residents funded through general municipal revenues. In another case, *Urban Outdoor Trans Ad v. Scarborough (City)*,[53] the Ontario Court of Appeal

---

[52] *Ontario Private Campground Association v. Harvey Township (1997)*, 39 M.P.L.R. (2d) 1.

[53] Accessed May 1, 2003 at www.ontariocourts.on.ca.

ruled that a user fee is not a tax but a fee and, as such, must bear a reasonable relation to the cost of providing the service. Finally, the Supreme Court of Canada also ruled on user fees under Ontario's Savings and Restructuring Act in connection with a case involving provincial probate fees.[54] It repeated the general principle that there must be a direct correlation between the cost of the service benefiting the payer and the actual fee. According to the Supreme Court, a more general approach, in which user fees are used to defray the costs of a general government program, would be considered a tax and rejected.

The Case for User Fees

Economists point out that user fees promote efficiency in the consumption of goods and services – if the price equals the marginal cost of providing the service.[55] In practice, however, the user fee either bears no relation to the cost of providing the service or, at best, is based on average cost, which is easier to calculate.[56] As a result, such user fees often result in unplanned consequences and do nothing to promote conservation of resources. For example, Kitchen cites the still common practice of charging a flat rate for water, regardless of the quantity consumed. Far from encouraging conservation, such a practice effectively provides a subsidy for wealthier individuals with larger lawns and gardens to water. He goes on to offer the following observations and suggestions:[57]

➢ The underpricing of water and sewage results in investments in water and sewage treatment facilities that are larger than would exist under a more efficient pricing policy.

➢ While user charges are used for many parks and recreational facilities, they cover only a small portion of operating costs. In

---

[54] *Eurig (Re) [1998]*, S.C. R. 565.

[55] See, for example, Slack, *Urban Public Finance*, and Kitchen, *New Fiscal Environment*.

[56] For those interested in such distinctions, the efficiency measures now being provided by many municipalities across Canada are based on average costing, in that the total volume of the service (tonnes of garbage for example) is divided by the total cost of the service to arrive at a unit price (per tonne). Marginal cost pricing, by contrast, would establish a user fee per unit of output equal to the extra cost of providing the last unit (last tonne of garbage collected).

[57] These points are based on Kitchen, *New Fiscal Environment*, pp. 14-18.

addition, the lack of a peak-load pricing policy, which would even out demand over days and weeks, had resulted in an over-investment in recreational facilities.

> A user charge that covered the full costs of solid waste collection and disposal would prompt a more efficient use of local resources and provide an incentive for individuals to reduce the amount of garbage that they generate. Realistically, however, a somewhat lower fee is prudent to avoid negative spillover in the form of individuals avoiding the fee by dumping their garbage in rural areas or along roadways.

> While public transit fees (fares) cover only 50% to 75% of operating costs, higher transit fees would only be efficient and fair if automobile users paid a charge that reflected their social cost – which they certainly do not.[58]

> Having fire services funded from general municipal revenues does not take into account the variables that fire insurance companies consider when setting their rates. If there is no differentiation in the price of fire services, there is no incentive for owners of risky properties to take steps to minimize their need for fire protection (through such actions as using fire-resistant building materials and installing sprinkler systems).

While there is considerable logic in the arguments advanced by Kitchen and other economists, expanding user fees in this manner is not without problems. Shifting the financing of municipal services from the property tax to user fees is likely to appeal to middle and upper income citizens. They would have no difficulty in paying such fees, and would presumably welcome the arrangement by which they only pay if they use the service. This option may lead them to obtain some services from the private sector instead, with recreational facilities being one example where such alternatives exist in the form of private fitness facilities. But the more they use private alternatives, the more they are likely to resent paying property taxes to underwrite the cost of municipal services (such as recreational facilities) that they are

---

[58] One study goes farther and suggests user fees in the area of non-public transportation by making use of new technologies to collect tolls. It argues that charging the full cost of travel for highways and roads in the downtown core of large cities like Toronto would benefit both society and the municipal bottom line. Toronto Dominion Bank, *The Greater Toronto Area (GTA): Canada's Primary Economic Locomotive In Need of Repairs*, May 22, 2002, p. 26.

not using. Yet lower income families certainly cannot afford to finance these facilities solely through user fees. Indeed, such fees may make municipal services less accessible for them.

While Kitchen acknowledges that lower user fees for services like recreation permit individuals to use facilities comparable to those they cannot afford in the private sector, he contends that "this type of subsidization is neither efficient nor fair because municipalities ought not to be concerned with major questions of income redistribution."[59] That may be true, but there seems little reason to expect provincial governments to accept increased responsibility for income distribution policies and programs at a time when they have downloaded some programs of this type (notably social services and social housing in Ontario) to the local level. Unless municipalities are prepared to introduce some form of income relief policies at their level, any substantial increase in user fees, at least for some services, is likely to have an adverse impact on lower income individuals and families.

Development Charges

Another local revenue source of note is that of development charges, also known as development cost charges, development cost levies, off site levies, and assessment levies. These charges are levied by local governments in British Columbia, Alberta, Saskatchewan, Ontario, and the Yukon and Northwest Territories to cover the growth-related capital costs associated with new development (or, in some cases, re-development).[60] Traditionally, such charges have been used to finance the building of water supply systems, sewage treatment plants, trunk mains and roads, but the services covered are somewhat broader in provinces such as Ontario.

In areas experiencing growth, development charges are obviously an important source of revenue and a way of ensuring that servicing costs relating to new development are paid for by the developer (and, ultimately, by the occupants of the new buildings) rather than by all property taxpayers. But these charges are, or can be, more than an alternative source of revenue; they can be a useful tool in encouraging efficient use of land and infrastructure. To do so,

---

[59] *Ibid.*, p. 16.

[60] Slack, *Municipal Finance*, p. 14. In Ontario, school boards can also levy such charges.

however, the charges have to be structured to reflect the true cost of providing public services.[61] These costs are usually higher for low density neighbourhoods and for developments located farther away from existing services. Accordingly, development charges should be higher for developing land on the outer edges of a community, which would discourage urban sprawl. Uniform development charges across a municipality, as is often found, subsidizes inefficient uses of land and can contribute to urban sprawl.

Unfortunately, development charges are not usually employed to reinforce planning goals. A recent analysis finds that development charges in Ontario "are geared almost exclusively to their revenue-raising role and are disconnected from planning goals."[62] It suggests that this usage reflects the underlying political reality that local politicians are more concerned with reducing the impact of growth on their own taxpayers than on maximizing benefits for society as a whole. It further suggests that while provincial politicians are in a better position to reconcile the revenue and planning issues involved, they are also primarily interested in how much revenue development charges can generate – to help municipalities finance the provincial responsibilities and costs being downloaded to them.[63]

Responding to the Financial Crisis

On the surface, the response seems obvious. Local governments need more money – both in local tax sources of their own and in improved transfers from the provincial and federal level. It is conventional wisdom that Canadian local governments do not enjoy nearly the financial capacity and support experienced by their counterparts in other jurisdictions. The overview below confirms this pattern, while also suggesting that far away fields are not necessarily greener in every respect.

---

[61] This discussion is based on Slack, *Municipal Finance*, pp. 16-17.

[62] Ray Tomalty and Andrejs Skaburskis, "Development Charges and City Planning Objectives: The Ontario Disconnect," *Canadian Journal of Urban Research*, Volume 12, Issue 1, Summer 2003, p. 158.

[63] *Ibid.*

Are Far Away Fields Greener?

Municipalities in the United States and Europe receive financial support from their state and national governments at a much higher level than Canadian municipalities. For example, the Liveable Communities for the 21st Century initiative in the United States established a wide range of programs that include substantial financial support for transportation, the environment, and housing. Of particular note is the six year Transportation Equity Act for the 21st Century (TEA-21), initiated in 1999, which has allocated over $100 billion for urban transportation.

By contrast, the Canadian government's current infrastructure program allocates $2 billion ($1.2 billion U.S.) for all types of infrastructure – water and wastewater systems, transportation, housing, and the rest.[64] With only three provinces (British Columbia, Alberta, and Quebec) still providing financial support for public transit in 2001, an analysis by the Federation of Canadian Municipalities found that "The combined effort of these provinces amounts to only 5% of the cost of operating transit and of its capital needs. By contrast, combined state and federal funds in the U.S. account for 25% of operating costs and 54% of capital spending on public transportation."[65] Ontario did resume funding of public transit in late 2001, but at 33% of the costs compared to the 75% that it used to fund – still leaving the picture for Canadian municipalities well behind that of those in the United States.

Turning to own source revenues, Canadian municipalities are much more heavily dependent upon the real property tax than their counterparts elsewhere. Census data from 1996 shows that property taxes accounted for 49.5% of municipal revenues in Canada compared to only 21% in the United States. Conversely, other taxes generated only 1% of revenues for municipalities in Canada compared to 13.5% in the United States. American municipalities also gained 32.6% of their revenues from user fees compared to only 20.2% for Canadian municipalities.[66]

While property taxes account for more than 90% of all local tax revenues in Canada, that was the case in only 4 of the other 27

---

[64] Federation of Canadian Municipalities, *Will Canadian Cities Compete?*, p. v.

[65] *Ibid.*, p. 14.

[66] *Ibid.*, p. ii.

countries in the OECD. In contrast, 9 OECD countries obtained less than 10% of their tax revenues from the property tax. Instead, in countries like Denmark, Finland, Luxembourg, Norway, and Sweden, income taxes (corporate and personal) account for more than 90% of local tax revenues.[67]

All cities in Arizona receive a 25% share of state sales tax. Phoenix alone receives 33% of the total amount provided to municipalities because of its population. This combined with a separate local sales tax generates 45% of the revenue of the City of Phoenix. A local income tax is the principal tax source for cities in Sweden. German cities have a constitutionally protected share of 15% of personal income taxes. In Denmark, cities also have access to a local personal income tax. Each municipality sets its own rate and the tax is deducted at source. It is collected by the central government and then rebated. Municipalities also receive 20% of the central government's corporate income tax revenue. Cities in Japan have access to over 17 different types of taxes.[68]

Municipalities in the United States and elsewhere also have access to a number of financial tools not generally available to Canadian municipalities. These include:[69]

Box 7.3 Financial Tools For Municipalities

➤ Fiscal authority to engage in public-private partnerships through mechanisms such as municipal permission to hold a mortgage;

➤ opportunities to leverage private sector investments through direct tax incentives (tax exempt municipal bonds in the United States and national fiscal policy in France);

➤ tax-increment financing under which a city can designate an area for improvement and then earmark any future growth in property tax revenues to pay for initial and ongoing economic development spending, and can fund initial costs by floating debt backed by the anticipated new tax revenues;

➤ access to permanent lending programs for infrastructure, such as state-run infrastructure banks for transportation and clean water/drinking water revolving funds widely available in the United States.

While the financial situation is much brighter for municipalities in other jurisdictions in some respects, a closer look at the

---

[67] Kitchen, *Municipal Issues*, pp. 37 and 39.

[68] Canada West Foundation, *Framing a Fiscal Fix-Up*, January 2002, p. 20.

[69] Federation of Canadian Municipalities, *Will Canadian Cities Compete?*, p. 23 and Toronto Dominion Bank, *Investing or Disinvesting*, pp. 11-12.

American experience suggests a more qualified assessment. For example, there are problems associated with some of the financial tools available in the United States. While issuing tax exempt bonds to finance a project provides a municipality with a lower cost of financing, this benefit is at the expense of the state and federal taxes that are foregone. Thus, this type of bond benefits one sector of the population (those within a particular municipality), but imposes the cost on another sector (the general population, which bears the burden through lower state and federal tax revenues – effectively allowing a city to compel non-residents to finance its infrastructure.[70] These shortcomings are pertinent, given that the Ontario government announced, in its 2002 budget, that it is authorizing its municipalities to issue tax exempt "opportunity bonds."

The supposedly bright financial picture for American cities (as compared to Canadian) has dimmed considerably of late, as a result of unforeseen developments, changed federal priorities, and reduced state revenues.[71] Homeland security has understandably become a top priority in the aftermath of the September 11th terrorist attacks, but only a fraction of municipal spending on new security measures has so far been covered by promised federal transfers. American states face a collective deficit of $60 billion or more, largely because of weak tax collections and it is anticipated that American cities will bear the brunt of the cuts that will be required to address this fiscal crisis.

Even the much more varied local revenue sources available to American municipalities are not without their problems. At least 46 of 50 states have some kind of tax and expenditure limits (TELs) on their local governments.[72] The best known, and most severe, of these TELs is Proposition 13, in California, which dates from 1978. Not surpris-

---

[70] This example is based on *ibid.*, p. 13.

[71] These changed circumstances are described in a number of reports from the Brookings Institution including an article by Bruce Katz, "American Cities: Federal Neglect Imperils Their Rise," *Baltimore Sun*, January 9, 2003, on which the following discussion is based.

[72] According to a 1995 study of the Advisory Commission on Intergovernmental Relations, *Tax and Expenditure Limits on Local Governments*, as quoted in a paper by Robert L. Bish, "Local Government Finance Issues in the United States," June 2002. The Bish paper, which provides the basis for much of the discussion in this section, is available at the web site of the University of Victoria at http://web.uvic.ca/lgi/working.htm, accessed June 3, 2003.

ingly, one effect of the TELs has been to reduce local government reliance on the property tax and to increase reliance on state aid and on other local revenue sources such as income taxes, business taxes, and sales taxes. The strict limits on the property tax are problematic in that they remove the discretion for municipal councils to vary tax rates as part of the process of balancing costs and benefits in local budgeting processes. This discretion is needed for flexibility and for accountability to local taxpayers, who pay much closer attention when local councils set tax rates than when services are funded by "other people's money."[73] The alternative is an increasingly centralized financial regime, as has already happened to education financing in the United States and in such Canadian provinces as Alberta and Ontario.

The fact that American municipalities have access to other local tax sources is also a mixed blessing. While these sources provided a healthy yield during the prolonged expansion in the economy during the 1990s, revenues from sales and income taxes fall sharply during a decline in the economy and this has recently caused some serious financial problems in cities dependent upon these sources.[74] The rapid increase in shopping via the Internet is also raising concerns about future sales tax yields.

One analysis of the financial status of Canadian and American municipalities concludes that cities on each side of the border face a series of trade-offs. In its words:[75]

> Is it better for a city to be overly reliant on property taxes, but at the same time free from restrictions on the tax rate, the revenue generated, and the use of revenues? Or is it more desirable to have access to a small local general sales tax and more selective sales taxes that provide better revenue-generating capacity during the good times, but where the tax rates are capped, revenues are earmarked, and any slowdown in the economy threatens the tax base?

New Revenue Sources

Over the years, a variety of tax sources have been suggested by and for Canadian municipalities, including the poll (or head) tax, income tax,

---

[73] *Ibid.*, p. 13.

[74] *Ibid.*, p. 5.

[75] Canada West Foundation, *Big City Revenue Sources*, p. 31.

sales tax, and fuel tax. Some of these taxes, of course, were once used by municipalities in this country. For example, they used to have access to the income tax field and were levying these taxes (along with provincial governments) long before the federal level entered the field – as a "temporary" measure – in 1917. "By the end of the 1930s, some form of municipal income tax was accepted in every province in Canada."[76] But when the provinces entered into wartime tax rental agreements with the federal government in 1941, they surrendered their right and the right of their municipalities to levy income taxes – and no municipality has been authorized to levy an income tax since.

A similar pattern unfolded with respect to the poll tax, which used to be authorized for municipalities in every province. It was used primarily by municipalities in Atlantic Canada and then gradually abandoned, beginning in the 1950s and ending, in the 1990s, with its termination in Newfoundland and Saskatchewan. In contrast, experience with a municipal sales tax is confined to municipalities in the province of Quebec, between 1935 (when it was introduced by the City of Montreal) and 1964.[77]

Of all the potential alternatives, Kitchen believes that a municipal fuel tax would make considerable economic and political sense, especially in large urbanized areas that are suffering from severe traffic congestion.[78] He also states that a general municipal sales tax and, more specifically, a hotel and motel occupancy tax could be justified, on a basic level, as a benefits-based approach to municipal taxation.[79] Kitchen points out that giving municipalities additional tax sources would permit a broader distribution of the tax burden among those who benefit from municipal services, whether they are residents, commuters or visitors, and would make the municipal tax structure more flexible and adaptable to local conditions.[80]

---

[76] Kitchen, *Municipal Issues*, p. 224.

[77] *Ibid.*, p. 226.

[78] But the impact of this tax can be very uneven. For example, a "gasoline alley" of service stations (usually interspersed with fast food restaurants) adjacent to major transportation routes could provide a revenue bonanza for the surrounding municipality, while exporting the fuel tax to a large number of non-residents. Communication from Melville McMillan, June 3, 2003.

[79] Kitchen, *New Fiscal Environment*, p. 21.

[80] Kitchen, *Municipal Issues*, p. 337.

A key issue is the basis on which municipalities would be given access to any tax fields already occupied by the provincial and federal government. Giving municipalities the authority to set their own tax rates provides the greatest discretion and the greatest local accountability. But any significant variation in the level of sales tax or fuel tax, for example, from one municipality to the next is likely to prompt consumers to cross municipal boundaries in search of a better deal. The fact is that the small size of most municipalities makes it too easy to avoid some of the alternative tax sources under consideration.

For a locally determined tax relating to vehicles, McMillan suggests a municipal vehicle registration charge, which could be collected as part of the provincial registration system to minimize administration and compliance costs. Since vehicle registration is linked to residence, such a tax could not be easily avoided. He also offers tolls on road use as another possibility, particularly for controlling congestion in urban area – as with the toll that has been introduced in central London (England).[81]

In some respects, the simplest approach is to have municipalities piggy-back on to existing federal or provincial tax programs and receive a pre-determined share of the yield collected by them. This approach also provides an opportunity to avoid an increase in the overall tax burden that could otherwise result from municipalities gaining access to these fields. For example, one study suggests that to avoid double taxation the federal government and provinces could agree to cut their gasoline excise taxes by two cents per litre each, with municipalities given the authority to levy up to four cents each.[82] But giving municipalities a previously agreed upon portion of the tax yield of the provincial or federal level is essentially providing them with an unconditional grant, not an additional taxing power to be used at their discretion. Other drawbacks with this arrangement, according to McMillan, are municipal vulnerability to potential arbitrary changes by the 'sharing' government and a weak tax-benefit linkage.[83]

Another option might be a municipal personal income tax, particularly for large, metropolitan municipalities. This tax reflects

---

[81] McMillan, "Municipal Relations," pp. 22-23.

[82] Toronto Dominion Bank, *Primary Economic Locomotive*, pp. 29-30. This study estimates that such a new tax arrangement would generate between $160 million to $240 million for cities in the Greater Toronto Area alone.

[83] McMillan, "Municipal Relations," p. 22.

ability to pay better than the property tax and so the two in combination may result in a better matching of benefits and costs at the local level.[84]

In addition to possible new tax sources, additional municipal revenues would have to come from expanded local non-tax sources or from increased transfer payments from the provincial and federal levels. Among non-tax revenue sources, user charges appear to have the greatest potential and are also favoured by economists because of the strong link that they provide between benefits and costs. The potential for expanded user charges has been illustrated earlier in this chapter.

As for transfer payments, probably the strongest case for increasing them is with respect to the social programs that are found at the local level, especially in Ontario. It is almost universally accepted that income redistribution programs are not an appropriate responsibility for local government, and especially not for funding from the property tax on which municipalities must rely so heavily. The best solution to this problem would be to transfer such responsibilities to the provincial and/or federal levels, where they arguably belong. Unless and until that happens, however, there is a strong case for increased transfer payments in support of such programs.

The other area in which there is widespread support for increased transfers is with respect to municipal infrastructure. While the overwhelming majority of transfer payments have come from the provincial level, there is an emerging consensus that the backlog in infrastructure investment facing our cities can only be addressed through action by the federal government and that, in any event, the importance of the cities to the economic health of Canada more than justify such a federal involvement. A Federal Task Force on Urban Issues has singled out affordable housing, transit/transportation, and sustainable infrastructure as the three pillars of a new urban strategy and called for investment in these areas to reduce pressures on municipalities for large capital expenditures.[85]

However, the ensuing 2003 federal budget was disappointing for those who had hoped that the Task Force report signalled the beginning of a major new federal financial commitment. While the

---

[84] *Ibid.*, pp. 23-24.

[85] Final Report, Prime Minister's Caucus Task Force on Urban Issues (Chair, Judy Sgro), *Canada's Urban Strategy: A Blueprint for Action*, November 2002, p. 10.

budget did commit more funds to such municipal concerns as home-lessness and affordable housing, it pledged only $100 million a year (over the next 10 years) for municipal infrastructure. To keep things in perspective, however, McMillan points out that one should not expect significant fiscal relief from the federal level because the current transfers are so small than even if they increased by 2.5 times their 2001 level that increase would only cover 1% of municipal expenditures.[86]

While the focus has been on additional municipal revenue, the financial pressures facing municipalities could also be eased if provincial governments took over the funding of programs that are arguably more properly their responsibility. A prime example, already cited, is Ontario, where "a return to provincial responsi-bility for funding all socials service, social housing, and land ambulance expenditures, in keeping with the practice in the rest of Canada, would not only assist the municipal sector but also make sound economic sense – all income-distributional services should be the responsibility of the two senior levels of govern-ment."[87]

In a similar vein, Vander Ploeg argues that if the property tax is to continue as the main source of municipal revenues, "then cities should not have to engage in activities that redistribute income, whether they be affordable housing, homeless shelters, or programs for the disadvantaged." In his view, "a comprehensive disentanglement exercise focused tightly on core civic competen-cies would leave redistributional programs to senior govern-ments."[88] Another example is the number of provinces that tax real property to finance schooling costs that they have assumed. Such costs should be financed, more appropriately, out of the varied revenue sources available to the provinces, thereby freeing up a significant portion of the property tax for more legitimate municipal use.

---

[86] McMillan, "Municipal Relations," p. 20.

[87] Kitchen, *Municipal Issues*, p. 336.

[88] Casey Vander Ploeg, "Same old Fiscal song out of Tune with the Times," *Calgary Herald*, April 29, 2002.

Concluding Comments

Whatever benefits Canadian municipalities might gain from new revenue sources and financial assistance from the senior levels of government, such financial support is far from certain. For this reason, municipalities need to take actions on their own, and there is much that they can do – in some cases only indirectly relating to finances. To illustrate, we offer the following suggestions.

Municipalities should ensure that they are making the best, and wisest, use of the revenue sources that they already have. Chief among these is the property tax, which will continue as the main source of municipal revenue. To the extent that they have the discretion to do so, municipalities need to align property taxes with the cost of delivering services and to remove inequities that currently exist in the distribution of tax burden between property classes. In many cites, as noted earlier in this chapter, commercial properties are overtaxed relative to residential properties, downtown properties relative to suburban properties, and rental housing relative to owner occupied housing.[89] These distortions drive businesses and people out of the downtown core, contributing to urban sprawl and its associated costs, and they also discourage the construction of rental units and contribute to the problem of homelessness.

As also discussed above, municipalities need to employ user fees and development charges in ways that limit urban sprawl rather than encouraging it and that, in the case of user fees, promote conservation and more efficient use of resources.

In addition to more enlightened financial policies, municipalities need to pursue planning policies that will promote urban density not sprawl. In the Greater Toronto Area, for example, "changes in land-use planning strategies and the more flexible application of zoning by-laws have helped to spur a boom in condominium development along public transit nodes."[90]

While revenues, or lack thereof, have understandably attracted attention and energy, municipalities also need to make

[89] Toronto Dominion Bank, *Primary Economic Locomotive*, p. 2.

[90] *Ibid.*, p. 26.

every effort to ensure that their expenditures are appropriate and represent best value. This means more long term planning and priority setting by councils, so that the scarce resources of the municipality can be directed toward the achievement of a limited number of major goals and objectives rather than being used to perpetuate past spending patterns without any discernible priorities. It may call for municipalities to refocus and to get back to their "core programs," just as many private companies are pulling back from overly ambitious expansion plans and rediscovering the value of "sticking to the knitting."[91] It may mean having to eliminate some programs, or find someone else to deliver them, and reducing the level of service in others. Taking the trouble to survey local citizens may identify areas that are not regarded by the public as high priorities and where some curtailment is acceptable.

Ensuring best value for expenditures does not mean holding the line on taxes (although that may be one result). Too many municipalities react to financial pressures by cutting expenditures (often "across the board") until they achieve a zero increase in taxes. But this approach leads to cuts that are ill-considered, usually made in haste, and often without an appreciation of their long term impact on municipal operations. That impact is often felt in reduced quality of service.

In contrast, a growing number of municipalities have taken a different approach that harnesses the creative energy and ideas of all employees in seeking new and more efficient ways of delivering programs. Much of the focus is on streamlining procedures and removing "red tape" to improve service to local citizens. Such changes can also reduce costs and improve productivity, with the result that municipalities can reduce expenditures (and hold the line on taxes) while maintaining, or even increasing, the level of service provided. This outcome is particularly likely if programs are in place for measuring, reinforcing and rewarding gains in productivity – programs that approximate the bonus pay or pay for performance long found in the private sector.

---

[91] The phrase used by Tom Peters and Robert H. Waterman, Jr., *In Search of Excellence*, New York, Warner Books, 1982, p. 15 and pp. 292-305, to describe companies that stuck with the businesses they knew and avoided venturing into different areas of operation.

These latter suggestions obviously relate to the way municipalities are governed and to the central relationship between councillors and staff, matters that are the focus of the next chapter.

Chapter 8
Governing the Municipality

The various municipal governing models used over the years, and the philosophies underlying them, have for the most part focused on efficiency and coordination in the delivery of services to the relative neglect of the representative and political aspects that are (or should be) equally a concern of municipal government.

Introduction

An examination of how municipalities are governed logically starts with their internal governing machinery, and particularly the way councils and staff are organized and interrelate. A number of different governing structures have been found in Canada's municipalities over the years, each with particular strengths or shortcomings. Institutional structure is important "because it is the vehicle through which the basic purposes and values a society wishes to pursue through local government are carried out. It is thus presumed that institutions matter – that political and policy outcomes will differ as institutional structure differs."[1]

A number of variations on the basic municipal structure have been introduced over the years. These institutional reforms have usually been a response to changes in the prevailing values and roles associated with municipal government and, in turn, the new structures arising from the reforms have their own impacts on the local level and the distribution of power within it. As will become evident, much of that impact tended to affect adversely the representative and political nature of municipal government.

But municipal institutions have become less the focus in recent years, as attention has shifted to new governing arrangements that increasingly extend to organizations and operations outside the

[1] Harold Wolman, "Local Government Institutions and Democratic Governance," in David Judge, Gerry Stoker, and Harold Wolman, *Theories of Urban Politics*, London, Sage Publications, 1995, p. 135.

municipal structure. This broader focus reflects the growing appreciation of the distinction between government and *governance*, a distinction briefly introduced in Chapter 1 and referred to several times since.[2] Government refers to the formal institutions of the state, election arrangements, and decision making processes. Governance is a broader term that refers to the relationships between the formal institutions of government and civil society. Governance is more flexible (and less well-defined) and can embrace a wide variety of relationships. Local government, therefore, refers to democratically elected municipal councils and their departments of municipal staff. In contrast, local governance encompasses these governing structures as well as other public, private, and voluntary bodies that are harnessed to address community needs.

Some view the concept of local governance as little more than a device for shifting responsibilities from local governments to the private and voluntary sectors – a means of offloading expenditures or of providing an opening for private companies to pick up business. A more positive view is that local governance is not a replacement for local government but an additional mechanism for achieving broader cooperation and coordination at the local level. While the latter objective is possible and laudable, the former outcome is more likely and more in evidence to date.

The Machinery of Municipal Government

Before venturing into the larger and less distinct world of local governance, let's begin with the machinery of local government. More specifically, we will examine the machinery of *municipal* government – not including the structures that may be found amongst the wide variety of agencies, boards and commissions that form part of local government.

---

[2] The discussion of these terms that follows is an amalgam of definitions and comparisons provided by Robin Hambleton, Hank V. Savitch, and Murray Stewart (ed.), *Globalism and Local Democracy*, London, Palgrave Publishers Ltd., 2002, pp. 150-151; H. V. Savitch and Paul Kantor, *Cities in the International Marketplace*, Princeton, Princeton University Press, 2002, pp. 329-330; and Mario Polese and Richard Stren (eds.), *The Social Sustainability of Cities*, Toronto, University of Toronto Press, 2000, pp. 17-20.

On the surface, this approach sounds quite straightforward, and the basic structure of municipal government is certainly simpler than that found at the provincial and federal levels, with their separate executive and legislative branches. There aren't separate branches of government at the municipal level; responsibilities are concentrated in the elected council and are carried out by appointed staff who are mostly organized into a number of functionally specialized departments.

The Municipal Council

The powers assigned to a municipality are exercised on behalf of its residents and ratepayers by a council elected by them. Members of council are expected to represent the local community and act on its behalf. They also exercise a policy making role through which they determine services and service levels, approve budgets, enact rules and regulations, and generally shape the local community and the quality of life within it. A third role of councillors is managerial (for want of a better term) and it involves providing an oversight of municipal operations to ensure that policies are implemented as intended, funds are expended as authorized, and programs are delivered efficiently and effectively.

Provincial legislation usually includes provisions for the form of council and such details as the number of councillors and whether election is by general vote or by ward (a distinction discussed below). However, the new municipal legislation passed in most provinces over the past decade (and discussed in Chapter 6) often gives municipalities somewhat more discretion with respect to such matters. Municipal councils consist of a head (known as warden or chair in counties and other upper tier governments, as mayor in cities and towns, and as reeve, chair, or overseer in villages and townships) and a widely varying number of other councillors. While the total membership varies greatly, there has been a tendency to have small councils of from 5 to 15 members, largely on the grounds that a small group is less unwieldy and more efficient in making decisions. As discussed in Chapter 9, small councils can make it more difficult for municipalities to fulfill their representative role.

Perhaps the most distinctive feature of the council as a governing body is that it combines both executive and legislative responsibilities. As an executive body it initiates proposals for municipal action, makes a myriad of specific decisions – such as hiring a particular employee – and supervises the administration of the policies and programs of the municipality. As a legislative body, it makes by-laws which are the laws governing its citizens. At the senior levels of government, these functions are the responsibility of the two separate branches described above. The fact that these functions are combined in the council means, among other things, that the line between making policy and administering policy is often quite blurred at the local level.

Ward Versus General Vote

While directly elected heads of council are chosen by a general vote of the entire municipality, members of council may be elected on the basis of a ward system. In the latter case, the municipality is divided into several geographic areas with a number of members (usually an equal number) to be chosen from each of these areas. Candidates don't run over the whole municipality but only in "their" ward, and voters are limited to choosing from among the candidates in their particular ward. Whether election is by ward or general vote may be dictated by provincial statute; it may be at the discretion of the council; or it may be decided by council subject to the approval of the municipal electors.

Both methods of election have their proponents and their alleged advantages and disadvantages. Supporters of the ward system argue that under this approach the voters are much more likely to be familiar with the limited range of candidates from whom they must choose and the candidates will be more aware of the particular needs and interests of their constituents. It is also contended that ward elections ensure that all areas of the municipality will be represented on council, that they mean less expensive campaign costs, and that they bring a higher voting turnout, an assertion that appears to have some validity.

On the other hand, those supporting election by general vote claim that ward elections tend to perpetuate and even accentuate differences and divisions within the municipality. It is argued that a ward council is very parochial in outlook, with councillors worrying about their individual bailiwicks wherein they must seek reelection rather than being concerned about the good of the whole municipality. It is also contended that some representatives get elected on a ward basis who would not have been chosen if they were running over the entire municipality. Election by general vote is therefore felt to result in stronger, better-qualified candidates since they must have support throughout the municipality. Proponents of a general vote also assert that it results in a council more capable of taking a broad view of the overall needs of the municipality.

There are rebuttals and counter-arguments for most of these points. For example, ward elections do not ensure that every area of the municipality is represented on council since candidates do not have to live in the ward in which they run – although "outside" candidates are rarely successful unless they have some sort of attachment to the ward. To the allegation that representatives get elected on a ward basis who would not otherwise be chosen in at large elections, the response is that this outcome is precisely why ward elections are needed – to ensure a broader cross-section of elected representatives, including those who may lack the profile and deep pockets to be successful in an at large campaign. To take one more example, where is the proof that elections at large result in better quality candidates, and how is this quality measured? Is it on the basis of education, income and social class, or is a high quality candidate one who serves with dedication and integrity regardless of socio-economic background?

Whatever the respective merits of these two methods of election, it might be assumed that beyond a certain population size (which is difficult to specify precisely) election by ward becomes almost inevitable to ensure that the citizens will have some prospect of knowing the candidates and that the candidates will not be faced with the financial and time demands of canvassing an excessively large population. While this relationship between the population of a municipality and the method of election generally holds true, there are exceptions, with the most notable one being the system of elections at large in the city of Vancouver. Local voters have on more than one occasion given their support to the system of ward elections abandoned in 1936, but never with the 60% approval required to bring about the change. However, this issue is back on the agenda following the election of a council controlled by the Committee of Progressive Electors (COPE) in the 2002 municipal election. COPE is committed to the introduction of a ward system and there appears to be some solid evidence to support the introduction of wards, evidence that validates many of the arguments outlined above.[3]

As was very evident during the turn of the century reform era of 100 years ago (discussed in Chapter 2), the issue of ward elections versus elections at large revolves around the distribution of power within city government. Ward elections make it more likely that the diversity of interests within a municipality will have a voice on council. Indeed, it was precisely for this reason that the middle class business people who were central to the reform movement of a century ago pushed for the abolition of wards. In Western Canada, for example, wards were viewed with disfavour because they provided a means through which the growing labour movement and the large numbers of impoverished Europeans settling in major cities could gain a voice.[4] It remains true today that efforts to abolish ward systems of election, and to reduce the size of councils, have the effect of diminishing local representation.

The Head of Council

No discussion of municipal council would be complete without an examination of the position of head of council. This position has become important over the years in spite of its lack of formal powers. While heads of council in Canada are not limited to the largely ceremonial role of their British counterparts, neither are they comparable to the American "strong mayor" who has extensive authority in connection with the preparation of current and capital budgets, planning, hiring, and firing.

Consider Ontario's new Municipal Act, which took effect on January 1, 2003. According to this legislation, it is the role of the head of council to act as the chief executive officer, preside over council meetings, provide leadership to the council, represent the municipality at official functions, and carry out the duties of the head of council under this or any other Act. Not only are these duties quite vague and general, but the new Act actually omits three provisions that used to

---

[3] Kennedy Stewart, *Think Democracy: Options for Local Democratic Reform in Vancouver*, Vancouver, Institute of Governance Studies, Simon Fraser University, 2003, especially pp. 16-21 and 53-77.

[4] Jack Masson with Edward C. LeSage Jr., *Alberta's Local Governments: Politics and Democracy*, Edmonton, University of Alberta Press, 1994, p. 274.

be found in the legislation.[5] For reasons that were never explained, the Ontario government ignored the opportunity to strengthen the position at the time of the new Municipal Act.

The legislation goes a little farther in some provinces. For example, Manitoba, British Columbia, and Quebec provide a limited form of veto by authorizing the head of council to return any matter to the council for its reconsideration. The latter two provinces and Saskatchewan grant the head of council the power to suspend any officer or employee, subject to subsequent confirmation by council. The fact that the mayor of Winnipeg appoints the members of that city's executive committee adds to his or her power and influence. In no instances, however, do heads of council in Canada possess significant executive powers.

In spite of their lack of formal power, Canadian mayors have high local political visibility, in large part because of the tendency for the media in a community to contact the mayor for short summaries of municipal business or comments on current controversies.[6] Their ceremonial and symbolic functions are also important and can be the basis for popularity and reelection, and – if used effectively – for building links between the diverse elements of a local community. The mayor does not have any real authority over staffing and the administrative structure, but can exercise considerable influence by providing a link between senior managers and council. "With easier access to senior officials than other council members enjoy, and the ability to interpret council's wishes when they have not been clearly stated, the mayor can exert considerable influence within the municipal bureaucratic apparatus."[7]

Given these limits on their formal power, heads of council in Canada must rely heavily on their personality and persuasive skills in attempting to provide leadership. Except in those limited instances where organized political parties exist, a council is made up of a group

---

[5] These provisions were to be vigilant and active in causing the laws of the municipality to be executed and obeyed, to oversee the conduct of all subordinate officers, and to communicate to the council from time to time such measures as may tend to improve the municipality.

[6] Andrew Sancton, "Mayors As Political Leaders," in Maureen Mancuso, Richard Price, and Ronald Wagenberg (eds.), *Leaders and Leadership in Canada*, Toronto, Oxford University Press, 1994, pp. 179-180.

[7] *Ibid.*, p. 180.

of individuals with potentially different interests and concerns and no sense of cohesion or collective will. As a result, the challenge facing a mayor has been likened to "herding cats" in an article discussing the task facing Bob Chiarelli when he was elected in November 2000 as the first mayor of the new city of Ottawa. The new council was described as divided by geography, political beliefs, urban-rural concerns, ethnicity, and specific interests. A number of factions were in evidence: "left wing versus right wing, downtown councillors, rural councillors, the east-end group, the west-end group, the French lobby, the youth wing, and the old Nepean lobby.[8] Expecting any head of council to build a consensus and provide effective direction in circumstances such as these is quite a tall order.

Yet the record shows that mayors, even when facing opposition from council members, can accomplish a good deal "if they are competent, shrewd, and, most important, popular with the electorate."[9] A number of colourful and long-serving mayors certainly "put their stamp" on their cities, with names like Elsie Wayne of Saint John, Stephen Juba of Winnipeg, Jean Drapeau of Montreal, and Hazel McCallion of Mississauga coming readily to mind. McCallion's career provides an excellent example of how personality and temperament can forge an indelible public image.

Box 8.1 Hurricane Hazel[10]

As this book is being written, Hazel McCallion is poised to celebrate the 25th anniversary of her first election as mayor, with a victory in the November 2003 municipal election. Her public image was established early in her career by her response to an incident in November 1979, when a chemical-laden CPR train went off the tracks at a Mississauga crossing, forcing the evacuation of a large portion of the city. Early on in the week-long drama, McCallion injured a leg, but she remained on the scene throughout, hobbling around on a cane. The perception of her as tough and graceful under pressure was fixed forever, and she remains a formidable figure to this day, legendary for her seven day work week and apparently boundless energy. When she was back at work only a couple of days after being hit by a pick-up truck in February 2003, this incident only served to reinforce her image of invincibility.

---

[8] Ken Gray, "Mayor's job like herding cats," *Ottawa Citizen*, January 17, 2001.

[9] Allan Levine (ed.), *Your Worship: The Lives of Eight of Canada's Most Unforgettable Mayors*, Toronto, James Lorimer and Company, 1989, p. 2.

[10] The following description is largely based on Jim Coyle, "Hazel's world reigns supreme," *Toronto Star*, October 11, 2000; John Barber, "Hurricane Hazel going strong at 80," *Globe and Mail*, February 12, 2001; and Jim Coyle, "Mayor Hazel 1, pickup truck 0," *Toronto Star*, February 18, 2003.

The Administration

In addition to the elected council, the governing machinery of the municipality includes the appointed staff who are responsible for administering the programs and policies of council and for assisting council in making decisions by providing expert advice. There is, of course, a tremendous variation in the number and organization of staff, depending on the population of the municipality and the range of functions. At one extreme, and increasingly rare, is the municipal staff of one, perhaps part-time at that. This individual may act as clerk, treasurer, tax collector, by-law enforcement officer, dog catcher, and building inspector while performing a variety of other duties – and all without any formal job description whatsoever.

Box 8.2 Carrel the Crusader[11]

André Carrel wasn't the dog catcher, but he couldn't find one anywhere, so he was stuck with the responsibility for doing something when a pack of stray dogs became a serious problem during his first municipal job in Fort Simpson in the Northwest Territories. He got that job, as secretary-manager, in 1970, because the other applicant for the position couldn't type and he could. He could also fire a gun and that is how he addressed the dog problem after some small children were attacked. Carrel's next position was as city manager of Dawson City where he learned that a municipal manager who hoped to survive in a hostile political environment "needed to be one-quarter lawyer, one-quarter accountant, on-quarter engineer, and three-quarters son-of-a-bitch." He left Dawson City in 1981 to become the first full time executive director of the Association of Yukon Communities, headquartered in Whitehorse. From there he moved to the senior staff position in Rossland, British Columbia, where he played a key role in that municipality's innovations in direct municipal democracy, discussed in Chapter 9. While municipal staff are known to wax eloquent about the latest budgeting or managerial technique, Carrel is unusual in that his passion is the importance of municipal democracy and of the central role that must be played by local citizens, as outlined in his already cited book, *Citizens' Hall, Making Local Democracy Work*.

At the other extreme is the staff of thousands, grouped into twenty-odd functionally specialized departments, with job descriptions and operating manuals and an elaborate hierarchy. In this latter instance, the municipality obviously has much greater staff resources and expertise available. Bigger is not always better, however, and as with all larger organizations, the municipality often has difficulty drawing these resources together into a coordinated operation.

---

[11] Based on information provided in André Carrel, *Citizens' Hall, Making Local Democracy Work*, Toronto, Between the Lines, 2001, especially Chapter 2.

Traditionally, there has been a requirement for municipalities to appoint certain statutory officers, but new legislative requirements in several provinces have removed or reduced this requirement, ostensibly to provide municipalities with greater flexibility to develop staffing arrangements that best meet their needs. For example, 1998 amendments (Bill 31) in British Columbia eliminated the required titles of municipal clerk, regional district secretary, and treasurer, but did give formal recognition to the position of chief administrative officer. Ontario's new Municipal Act still requires the appointment of a clerk and treasurer, but states that neither of them needs to be an employee of the municipality – a provision that seems designed to facilitate the currently popular philosophy of contracting out municipal services.

A brief look at the roles of staff indicates that they are closely related to the roles of councillors cited earlier.[12] The most obvious role is to administer the policies and programs of the municipality. Those staff directly involved in the provision of services are the ones with whom the local public most often have contact. As a result, such staff also have a public relations role because most citizens form their opinion of their municipal government on the basis of the chance encounters that they have with municipal staff. In the course of this public contact, staff often find themselves acting as brokers or arbiters of conflicting local interests, seeking to find common ground. Senior staff have two very important roles – advising council on policy matters and managing and supervising the staff within their departments or sections.

It is clear from even this brief outline that both councillors and staff have extensive public contact, are involved in the making of policy, and are involved in policy implementation. The close link and potential conflict between the roles of councillors and staff is evident in the operations of the standing committee system, traditionally a very common structure that might even be considered part of the basic municipal government model.

The Standing Committee System

This system features the establishment of a number of ongoing committees, each focused on a major functional area of municipal

---

[12] The discussion that follows is partly based on C. Richard Tindal, *Municipal Administration Program*, Unit Two, Association of Municipal Managers, Clerks. and Treasurers of Ontario. 2002.

operations. The committees are normally responsible for overseeing the operations of one or more municipal departments within their functional area and for making recommendations and presenting reports as requested by council – although sometimes the committees exercise only this latter, policy-advisory role. They are composed of councillors, and may also include (infrequently) some citizen members. These committees are usually created entirely at council's discretion, and are not to be confused with the statutory committees and boards whose establishment is authorized or mandated by provincial statute. Examples of the latter would be committees of adjustment and land division committees which exercise planning responsibilities at the local level in Ontario. A typical committee system is depicted below.

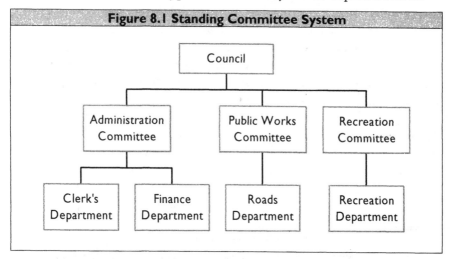

Figure 8.1 Standing Committee System

The use of a standing committee system is held to be advantageous because it speeds up work in council since the committee sifts through the details of an issue and presents a positive recommendation to council. It also allows councillors to specialize in the fields of administration under the jurisdiction of their standing committees rather than to attempt to be knowledgeable in all fields. It is also alleged that the informal atmosphere of a committee meeting encourages more "give and take" in debate, facilitates participation by municipal officials, and also provides a good opportunity for interested groups or individuals to be heard. In this latter connection, it is argued that the delay built in when matters are referred to committee gives public opinion a chance to develop and to be heard and guards against overly precipitous action.

However, there are also a significant number of alleged disadvantages of the standing committee system. While some delay in decision making may be beneficial, referrals from council to one or more committees and back to council can create a very slow process and the opportunity for buck-passing. If committee discussions are duplicated in council, much time is wasted and the value of the committee's specialized scrutiny is lost. There are often too many committees, with the result that a councillor's already limited time is seriously overburdened. An associated problem in many smaller municipalities is the tendency to establish standing committees when they are not necessary given the volume of work. Often such committees have no terms of reference, no regular schedule of meetings, and no systematic procedure of reporting to council. As a result, they are not an effective addition for managing the municipality.

Another criticism, and one of particular relevance for the ensuing discussion, is that standing committees tend to reinforce the departmentalization inherent in the municipal organization and thus contribute to a fragmented outlook. This is because members of a committee may put the interests of their particular department or departments first, an attitude which is hardly conducive to a coordinated approach or to a broad view of the municipality's needs. Often difficulties arise in this respect because the committee system has simply expanded with the increase in municipal departments. Yet the departments themselves may have grown without sufficient forethought and, if this structure is poorly organized for coordination, then what can one expect from a committee system similarly designed? Finally, it is argued that committee members tend to become overly preoccupied with matters of administrative detail and internal management of the departments under their jurisdiction. This is a common problem with councils generally but it is felt to be accentuated by the greater contact and familiarity with administration that the specialized scrutiny of committees permits.

Reconciling Politics and Professionalism

The council-staff relationship, and the operation of municipal government in general, is complicated by the difficulty of striking a balance between the concerns and emphasis of the politicians and the professionals. In theory, the latter serve at the behest of the former, lending their expertise to the development and implementation of policy decisions made by the politicians. Rather than political and professional perspectives blending in the service of the local community, however, they have often appeared to operate at cross-purposes. Increasingly, the claims of professionalism, and the associated emphasis on improvements in efficiency, have come even more strongly to the forefront – to the relative neglect of political considerations and the associated emphasis on serving the public interest and local democracy. A brief review will illustrate how this pattern evolved over time.

The notion of professionalism in the local public service arose in both North American and Britain as a result of concerns about whether local governments could handle the increased responsibilities that they were acquiring as a result of industrialization and urbanization. As early as the mid-19th century, British reformers worried about corruption and nepotism in local government and criticized the fact that "new public works projects and new regulatory powers created conditions conducive to corruption and the capture of municipal officers by local interests."[13] In response, they encouraged the development of a professional corps of staff who would be immune to inappropriate local pressures.

The push for professionalism in North America arose during the reform movement of 100 years ago. Like the earlier British reforms, the impetus was a reaction against corruption and inefficiency in local government operations. As discussed in Chapter 2, reformers sought to replace patronage appointments and the spoils system with a municipal public service appointed for their technical qualifications. The belief that sound administration could solve municipal problems was reinforced by a scientific management movement that also developed in the early 20th century and that promoted the benefits of general management principles.

Because much of the professionalization developed in response to the expansion of local responsibilities, it was specialized in nature and was focused on separate technical disciplines such as social work, planning, public health, and education. But the specialized knowledge that was a key feature of each of these professions also made their members insular, protective of their turf, and resistant to coordination,

---

[13] Martin Laffin and Ken Young, *Professionalism in Local Government*, Harlow, Longman, 1990, p. 13.

with the result that local governments were "in essence loose confederations of semi-autonomous empires."[14]

Central authorities in Britain and North America supported and encouraged professionalism in local government as a way of achieving minimum standards and consistency in the provision of services. They saw professionalism as a countervailing force to localism. It advanced the standardization favoured by central governments at the expense of local autonomy and diversity.[15] The impact on British local government following the Second World War is described by John Stewart in the following terms.[16]

> The politics of consensus was based on acceptance of the universalism of expertise and knowledge. Councillors of all parties had confidence in the services and in the advice given by officers on their development. Officers put their faith in established professional practice. Universal solutions based on expert knowledge were pursued for what were seen as common problems for all local authorities. There was little apparent need for local government or local choice.

The experience in Canada was similar, with the desire to maintain minimum standards in the provision of services leading not only to an emphasis on professionalism and consistency, but also to an increase in provincial supervision and control. Specialists at the local and provincial level often felt allied in a common cause in furtherance of their particular discipline. Both the fragmentation of local administration and the strong links between local and provincial professionals were reinforced over the years by provincial grants that ensured expenditures on specified functions and by the isolation of functions into separate special purpose bodies – such as school boards, planning boards, and health boards.

Inherent in the professionalism of municipal staff was the sense of a commitment to certain public service ideals, including the protection of the public interest. This concept has been associated with the historic office of British Town Clerk for well over a century.[17]

---

[14] T. Smith, *Town and Country Hall*, London, Acton Society Trust, 1966, p. 29.

[15] Laffin and Young, *Professionalism in Local Government*, p. 17.

[16] John Stewart, *The New Management of Local Government*, London, Allen & Unwin, 1986, p. 10.

[17] T. E. Headrick, *The Town Clerk in English Local Government*, London, George Allen & Unwin, 1962.

How it is interpreted today varies widely, but some senior staff believe that they have an obligation to argue against councillor views that they feel are misguided. Some staff have experienced "a sense of belonging to a public service which was both larger and more continuous than their immediate service with their current council suggested."[18] Taken to an extreme, the commitment to professionalism can be viewed as a kind of countervailing force that exists to limit or moderate political power in the interest of local democracy. From this perspective, "professional officers have a duty to moderate and constrain any abrupt policy changes thrown up by local politicians."[19]

Given their background and expertise, municipal staff may understandably feel that they have the best grasp of matters requiring policy action by council. It may seem to them that some of the policy ideas being championed by individual councillors are little more than an attempt to placate or please some specialized segment of the local populace. If they hold these views strongly enough, senior staff may resist the policy overtures of councillors and use a variety of tactics to thwart those that they find unworthy.[20] If that doesn't work, staff still have a great deal of influence because of their role in researching and recommending a specific course of action.

> ...the amount and kind of information, the method of presentation, the manner in which alternatives are identified and appraised, and the making of, or abstention from, recommendations – all provide opportunities for the bureaucracies to impress their own discretion and preferences....The object is constant; to guide the official's decision into the channels that the bureaucrats regard as wise and prudent.[21]

In fairness to staff, the policy direction provided by council is often far from clear. There may be a variety of different and even contradictory policy signals being provided by individual councillors, since the absence of a governing group within the council (with the exception of Vancouver and a number of Quebec municipalities) makes it difficult to develop a coordinated position. Sometimes the only way for councillors to achieve such a position is to compromise

---

[18] Laffin and Young, *Professionalism in Local Government*, p. 75.

[19] *Ibid.*, p. 77.

[20] Masson and LeSage, *Alberta's Local Governments*, p. 222.

[21] Wallace S. Sayre and Herbert Kaufman, *Governing New York City*, New York, W. W. Norton, 1965, pp. 420-421.

until the policy direction has become vague enough to avoid offending anyone. Even when members are not divided, they may still find it difficult to identify precisely what they want from staff. With respect to matters such as land use planning and economic development, staff may be told: "This is the sort of direction we want to move in. We would like you to negotiate with the relevant groups and do the best you can to move us in that direction."[22] When council essentially abdicates its policy making responsibility in this manner, staff are placed in an ambiguous and difficult position.[23] In addition, there are situations in which the policy intentions of council are, at best, misguided, or are without legal authority, and staff have a responsibility to object in these situations.

How far staff should go in providing policy advice is also open to debate. On the one hand, they are expected, as professionals, to provide an objective and dispassionate analysis of the facts – although Lindblom and others have pointed out that there is no such thing as a decision based solely on the facts because facts are assembled, analyzed, and presented by people, individuals with their own backgrounds, experiences, values, and judgments that inevitably colour what is presented.[24] On the other hand, councils often express displeasure at advice that they regard as unrealistic, "pie-in-the-sky," and not sufficiently sensitive to local political realities. Staff who provide advice that is technically sound but politically problematic are often criticized. Yet those who temper their advice to take into account political considerations may be criticized just as strongly by councillors who feel that all political considerations are their prerogative and preserve.

Siegel cautions that the more staff modify their advice in response to their perception of local political realities, the more their neutrality is compromised.[25] If their advice shows a sensitivity to the views of a majority of councillors, then they may antagonize the

[22] David Siegel, "Politics, politicians, and public servants in non-partisan local governments," Canadian Public Administration, Spring 1994, p. 9.

[23] T. J. Plunkett and G. M. Betts, The Management of Canadian Urban Government, Kingston, Queen's University, 1978, p. 161.

[24] Charles Lindblom, The Intelligence of Democracy, New York, The Free Press, 1965, pp. 138-143; and Richard S. Rosenblom and John R. Russell, New Tools for Urban Management, Boston, Harvard University Press, 1971, p. 229.

[25] The discussion in this section is based on Siegel, "Politics, politicians," pp. 26-28.

remaining councillors whose views were apparently not given as much weight. If they focus too much on providing advice that will be acceptable to council, they may recommend what they think council want to hear rather than what it should hear – which is not a desirable state of affairs. When staff know that their best technical and professional advice will not be politically acceptable to council, Siegel suggests the following course of action.[26]

> Public servants should recommend what they see as the best course of action for the municipality from their administrative perspective, regardless of its political consequences for any particular councillor or even for council as a whole. It is important for council to have the best possible objective and professional advice. If there are political factors to be injected into the decision-making process, it is council's job to introduce them.

The relationship between council and staff does not get any easier with respect to the implementation of policy. The staff have the primary role when it comes to enforcing by-laws, delivering programs, or administering services to the local community, but councillors also have a responsibility to provide a general oversight of these activities – to ensure that policies are being implemented as intended and with due regard for the tax dollar. As Crawford explains so well, different perspectives on the implementation of policy cause an inevitable tension between a council and its staff in connection with policy implementation.[27] He points out that members of council are constantly approached by individuals who feel they are unfairly dealt with under the general application of municipal policies and regulations. They attempt to persuade the councillors that their case merits special consideration.

> Because he is elected to represent the people and under the system of popular election his political life depends on keeping his people satisfied, and because the individual's claim is usually plausible, the representative tends to be more concerned with the exceptions than the rule. The permanent officials, who in most cases have been long in office and expect to continue there, are more conscious of the difficulties which result from making exceptions to general rules and, in the interest of equity to all, tend to resist requests for special treatment.

---

[26] *Ibid.*, p. 27.

[27] K. G. Crawford, *Canadian Municipal Government*, Toronto, University of Toronto Press, 1954, pp. 165-166.

Modifications to the Machinery

Over the years, a number of changes to the basic municipal government model have been introduced. These have mainly involved the introduction of executive committees to improve coordination and executive direction at the council level and coordinating officers to improve coordination and leadership at the staff level. The former have not been very effective, for the most part. The greater success with coordinating officer models has contributed to the service delivery and efficiency objectives of municipal government but somewhat at the expense of its political and representative role.

Executive Committees

Over the years the most persistent method of attempting to deal with the various problems of political leadership has been the establishment of executive committees of council. An early and prominent version of this structure was the board of control, introduced as part of the turn of the century reforms of 100 years ago. This model was quite widespread in Ontario during the first half of the 20th century. Other forms of executive committee were established, at least initially, in a number of large cities or metropolitan municipalities in an effort to duplicate a cabinet organization and a semblance of the parliamentary system.

Board of Control

As described in Chapter 2, the board of control first appeared in Canada in the city of Toronto in 1896. It was not really a board, but a statutory executive committee of council, assigned important responsibilities relating to such matters as budgets, contracts, and staffing. Its recommendations could only be overturned or altered by a two-thirds vote of council (of which the controllers were voting members). While it didn't make much of an impact in other provinces, the board of control became mandatory for cities over 100 000 in Ontario, although it could be dispensed with by a two-thirds vote of council if affirmed by the Ontario Municipal Board.

It was anticipated that the board of control would provide effective leadership and contribute to a more efficient management of the affairs of the municipality. But the board's similarity to a cabinet was superficial at best; instead of a body unified by the glue of party loyalty and discipline, the board was made up of individuals without necessarily any common purpose. With only four board members plus the mayor, the board became increasingly overburdened in attempting to oversee the administrative activities of the municipality and usually clashed with standing committees where they were retained. Most serious of all, however, was the friction between the board and the rest of council. The latter were particularly resentful of the two-thirds vote requirement for overturning board decisions. Gradually, municipalities took steps to abolish their boards of control, until this once so prominent structure remains only in the city of London, but with the two-thirds vote provision removed.

Other Forms of Executive Committee

A variety of other executive committees are found in Canadian municipalities. Some of these are similar to a board of control in having a statutory foundation, including those established in a number of the reformed local municipal structures. There are also non-statutory executive committees. By their nature they are much harder to categorize, especially since they do not always use the name "executive" committee. Their purpose is reflected in their make-up, however, which usually comprises the chairs of the major standing committees in the municipality plus the head of council, and in their mandate, which usually includes responsibility for the budget and for providing leadership and coordination. The accompanying figure illustrates this government structure.

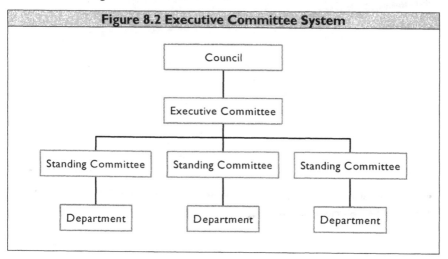

Figure 8.2 Executive Committee System

Council

Executive Committee

Standing Committee   Standing Committee   Standing Committee

Department   Department   Department

Montreal is likely the Canadian city with the longest experience with an executive committee, since there are references to such a body as early as the 1850s. By the 1960s, this committee had evolved into a powerful position because of the emergence of dominant political parties within Montreal's council. For example, during Jean Drapeau's long tenure as mayor (1960-1986), his choices for membership on the executive committee were ratified by a council controlled by his Civic Party, and the committee could initiate actions with every expectation that it would be supported by the council. The cities of Quebec, Hull, and Laval established executive committees in the 1960s, after studies that found that their government machinery exhibited weaknesses of excessive council involvement in administrative detail, lack of executive direction, and uncoordinated administration. As with the situation in Montreal, the existence of local political parties within the municipal councils of these three cities provided a basis for strong political leadership.

In contrast, the executive committee established by the Municipality of Metropolitan Toronto in 1954 was unable to provide strong leadership. It was composed of the chair of the metro council, the mayors of the six lower tier municipalities in the system, and seven other specified representatives from the lower tier councils. With that large a membership, serving by virtue of a prior position elsewhere in the municipal government structure, and without the unifying force of local political parties, the executive committee lacked cohesion or common focus, and also lacked a support base within the rest of council. Similar constraints continued to affect the executive committee set up in the new city of Toronto, which came into existence in 1998. Known as the Strategic Policies and Priorities Committee, this body (no longer in existence) was made up of the chairs of Toronto's five standing committees, the chairs of its six community councils, the deputy mayor, the budget chief, and the mayor of Toronto. It was almost as large as a cabinet, but lacked cohesiveness and common purpose and depended upon the willingness of members to cooperate and work together.

This is the dilemma facing executive committees. The board of control model was rejected because it was seen as too powerful, owing to the two-thirds vote provision. Executive committees backed by political parties can be quite powerful (just as they have always been at the provincial and federal levels where they operate as the cabinet) but, except in the province of Quebec, voters have shown a great reluctance to support the introduction of political parties at the local level. In the absence of either of these options, we are left with executive committees that must rely on good will and persuasion to develop a position and then to obtain council support for it.

Coordinating Officers

Experiences with coordinating officers have been more varied, and more successful, than efforts to establish executive committees of council. The most common form of this position is the chief administrative officer, but it also embraces other forms of coordinating officer.

Chief Administrative Officer System

Chief administrative officers (CAOs) are found in Canadian municipalities under a variety of names and with a variety of powers and responsibilities. Titles used include city administrator, city manager, commissioner, chief commissioner, and director general. Plunkett uses the term CAO to encompass all types of structure (including manager systems) that have a single appointed officer as head of the administration. On this basis, he found that by 1989 some 170 urban municipalities in Canada had adopted this structure.[28] Among the larger cities in this category are Vancouver, Edmonton, Calgary, Saskatoon, Regina, Winnipeg, Windsor, Hamilton, Toronto, Ottawa, Sudbury, Quebec City, Saint John, Halifax, and St. John's.[29]

     The earliest and most powerful form of CAO is that of the city manager or council manager system, which spread into this country from the United States in the early 1900s. The first Canadian city manager was appointed in Westmount in 1913 and the system is still found particularly in Quebec, where legislation has authorized municipal councils to appoint a manager since 1922. In contrast, not until a 1970 amendment did Ontario's Municipal Act give municipalities the authority to appoint any type of CAO. While the number of CAO positions has increased markedly since, most are not full-fledged managers but rather weaker forms of coordinating officer or expanded clerk-treasurer, as described below.

---

[28] T. J. Plunkett, *City Management in Canada: The Role of the Chief Administrative Officer*, Toronto, Institute of Public Administration of Canada, 1992, p. 21.

[29] *Ibid.*, p. 25.

The Council Manager System

As it developed in the United States, this system is predicated on a complete separation of the policy and administrative activities of the municipality. It involves the appointment of a professional administrator – the manager – to whom is delegated complete responsibility for administering the programs of the municipality, including the coordination and supervision of all staff. The council, usually small in number, is elected at large and directs its attention to its representative role and the formulation of overall policies for the municipality. In the "pure" council manager systems found in the United States, there are not usually any standing committees and therefore not any regular council contact with the administration except through the manager. The relatively simple, compact structure is depicted in the following figure.

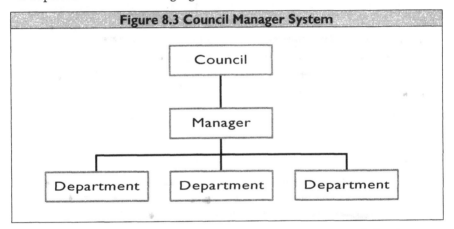

Figure 8.3 Council Manager System

Proponents of the council manager system contend that it provides for greatly improved coordination of administrative activities, frees the councillors from unnecessary detail, and allows them to concentrate on their primary role of policy making. While there is considerable potential for improved coordination in the organization of the manager system, its greatest weakness is the premise on which it is based – that it is possible to separate policy and administration in municipal government. To the contrary, it is very difficult to identify in advance whether a particular issue is a routine administrative matter or has political implications. Even if this distinction could be made, it is not desirable to rigidly separate the two activities. In practice, much policy arises out of ongoing administration and the council's complete separation from the administrative activities of the municipality leaves it "making policy in a vacuum."

Moreover, while the system provides for a more effective administrative structure, it does not provide for strong political leadership. Indeed, because of the focus on the manager, he or she is often a more conspicuous public figure than the members of council including the mayor. In addition to producing friction and jealousies that frequently result in the dismissal of managers, this situation also leads to managers becoming publicly identified with particular viewpoints and policies. If, as a result, they become embroiled in political controversies, their role as administrative leaders is impaired and they will likely be replaced. One book dryly observes that a manager's departure from work is often the result of illness or fatigue: "The council was sick and tired of him."[30]

The Manager System in Canada

As adapted to Canada, the council manager system has undergone certain modifications that minimize some of the problems noted above and, at the same time, minimize somewhat its strength and coordinating potential. Not surprisingly, these modifications reflect both the different governing principles of Canada and the United States, and the differing conditions that prevailed at the time of the system's introduction.

In most Canadian cities in the early years of the 20th century the need for such an administrative reform seemed less pressing or necessary than in American cities. Corruption and the worst excesses of local party politics were much less evident in Canadian cities, and appointments based on merit were much more prevalent. Moreover, administrative coordination was being achieved informally by utilizing the potential of certain key municipal positions, notably that of clerk and treasurer. Especially where the positions were combined in people with leadership skills, their overall knowledge of the municipality's operations and the influence inherent in their responsibilities for preparing agendas, background reports, minutes, by-laws, budgets, and financial reports, often made them unofficial chief administrative officers. Some municipalities confirmed the coordinating potential of

---

[30] Wayne Anderson, Chester A. Newland, and Richard J. Stillman, *The Effective Local Government Manager*, Washington, International City Management Association, 1983, p. 68.

these positions by formally designating the clerk or treasurer as something more – resulting in such positions as clerk-comptroller, clerk-treasurer-administrator, and clerk-coordinator.

Even where the council manager system was adopted, the Canadian version usually incorporated certain features designed to maintain the significance and prestige of the elected council.[31] First, the Canadian council manager system does not attempt to enforce a complete separation between administration and policy. The council usually has a direct relationship with at least its main department heads as well as the manager. This is normally accomplished "by the attendance of the department heads at a meeting of a limited number of standing committees of council when matters affecting their particular areas of jurisdiction are under review."[32] Second, the responsibility for the appointment of staff is exercised by council, not the manager, although often council exercises this responsibility only after receiving recommendations from the manager.

With such modifications, Young feels that the Canadian version managed to avoid the fundamental problem of council's complete separation from administration. He explains that council in a Canadian manager system continues to concern itself with administration but "does so from a much broader viewpoint." The advice and recommendations of staff are coordinated by the manager, and "it is this opportunity and ability to place such recommendations within the broader perspective of the city's needs as a whole which represents his greatest value to the council in his capacity as policy advisor."[33]

The Commissioner System

This system involves the appointment of a few commissioners, who are charged with supervising and coordinating the various departments under their jurisdiction. They may also meet together as a board of commissioners under the direction of a chief commissioner, to provide overall coordination of municipal operations.

---

[31] See Dennis A. Young, "Canadian Local Government Development: Some Aspects of the Commissioner and City Manager Forms of Administration," in Lionel D. Feldman and Michael D. Goldrick (eds.), *Politics and Government of Urban Canada*, Toronto, Methuen, 1976, pp. 276-278.

[32] *Ibid.*, p. 277.

[33] *Ibid.*, p. 278.

The commissioner system is similar to a council manager system except in two important respects. Policy and administration are not as completely separated under the commissioner system, particularly when the mayor sometimes sits as a member of the board of commissioners – although the wisdom and effectiveness of this combination has been a matter of some debate. The second difference is that having more than one commissioner permits a degree of specialization not possible under the manager system where one person must supervise the entire administrative structure no matter how large and complex. Typically, one commissioner is responsible for hard services, another for soft services, and a third (if provided) for finance and planning, as illustrated in the following figure.

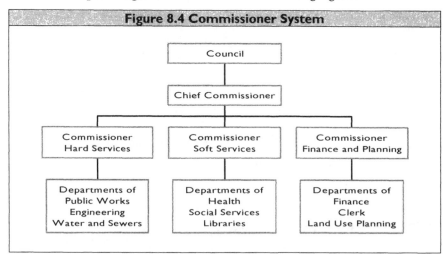

Figure 8.4 Commissioner System

The commissioner system was found mostly in Western Canada, but has gradually been replaced by manager or CAO positions over the past couple of decades. Some cities, such as Red Deer, Prince Albert, and Estevan, have appointed a single commissioner, in what amounts to a misnamed manager system.[34] Others, such as Edmonton and Winnipeg have abolished their commissioner systems (in 1984 and 1998 respectively) and replaced them with CAO systems. Ironically, as the commissioner system disappears in Western Canada, it is turning up in Ontario – albeit in modified form. The Ontario initiative involves the appointment of commissioners (also sometimes called directors) as senior staff in charge of groups of related departments.

---

[34] Plunkett, *Role of Chief Administrative Officer*, p. 53.

These senior staff may meet regularly with the CAO (and head of council) as a management committee, rather like the board of commissioners previously found in Western Canada.

This new model has appeared particularly in new municipalities created as a result of Ontario's widespread amalgamations. It incorporates a distinction between internal, support services and services delivered to the public (or what used to be termed staff and line departments) and usually features four groups of related departments along the lines indicated in the table below. Note the similarity with the commissioner groupings.

Table 8.1 New Coordinating Model in Ontario			
Hard Services	Soft Services	Planning & Development	Corporate Services
Public works	Parks & recreation	Long range and	Clerk
Transportation	Culture & heritage	strategic planning	Treasurer
Engineering	Libraries	Planning approvals	Legal services
Water/waste water	Seniors homes	Economic	Human resources
Fleet & facilities	Emergency services	development	Computer services

Canadian CAOs Today

Plunkett sees the growth of the CAO system in Canada as the result of the growth in municipal departments with the urbanization following the Second World War and the recognition that the issues confronting municipal governments required more analysis and synthesis than could be provided through such a fragmented departmental structure. He explains that most municipalities can now appoint a CAO under the general municipal legislation of their province.

The success of any particular CAO will depend, in large part, on how well the individual is able to work with the diverse mix of department heads in the municipality. Some of these managers may have strongly opposed the introduction of a "senior coordinating officer," while others may have unsuccessfully sought the position themselves. In either case, they are unlikely to welcome a new CAO or to support the position. If standing committees have been retained, department heads may attempt to use these as a buffer or a means of blocking CAO initiatives.

Plunkett suggests that relationships between CAOs and department heads tend to fall into three categories:

1. *Passive:* CAOs who simply forward, without comment, reports received from department heads.

2. *Active*: CAOs who include with departmental reports an accompanying memo setting out their comments.
3. *Dominant*: CAOs who hold back reports from departments until these conform to their general policy viewpoint.[35]

The second category is probably the most common and certainly the most desirable. It ensures that both the technical knowledge of the specialist department head and the broader perspective of the CAO are sent forward, and it gives council the benefit of the most complete range of information on which to make a decision.

Another problematic relationship that can arise is between the CAO and the head of council, given the way the latter position is defined in provincial legislation. The potential for a clash exists if a mayor has a strong personality and a determination to provide "hands-on" leadership consistent with his or her statutory authority to oversee subordinate officers and (under the legislation in some provinces) to act as chief executive officer). While a CAO faced with such a conflict could appeal to the council, which is ultimately responsible for the management of the municipality, such a course of action is by no means certain of success – especially since councillors are all too inclined to view CAOs with suspicion and to fear that they will become too dominant. Prudent CAOs usually make every effort to avoid an overt power struggle.

No matter how effectively a CAO system may work, it provides administrative, not political, leadership. Indeed, this system may even act as a constraint on political leadership and on the local political process in general. It is widely held, for example, that council-manager systems, "which emphasize the expert professionally trained manager as the effective executive," pay less attention to citizen demands and concerns than do mayor-council systems under which such demands are expressed more directly through the political process.[36]

Effectiveness of the Modified Machinery

While generalizations are difficult, it is probably fair to say that reforms at the administrative level have been more successful than those at the political level. In particular, the establishment of a chief

---

[35] *Ibid.*, pp. 28-29.

[36] Harold Wolman and Michael Goldsmith, *Urban Politics and Policy: A Comparative Approach*, Oxford, Blackwell, 1992, p. 76.

administrative officer system has the potential to effect improved coordination and integration of municipal programs and activities. This system may help to develop an expanded research and analytical capability and the provision of more comprehensive policy advice and recommendations to council, but much depends on whether complementary changes are introduced in the management and decision making process of the municipality.[37] Designating a CAO also provides a specific focus of accountability and responsibility for the administrative performance of the municipality.

Perhaps surprisingly, reforms at the political level have largely ignored the strengthening of the position of head of council. Instead, the focus has been on the establishment of various forms of executive committee system, with quite limited success. Most of these committees have lacked political cohesion and have not had any means, except persuasion, to ensure that their initiatives receive the necessary support of council. The effectiveness of these committees has been dependent upon their method of selection and whether or not they are reinforced in their position and activities by the existence of organized political parties on council. In most cases, they are not, and the committees have lacked any power base as a result. On the other hand, bodies such as Ontario's board of control and the executive committees in Quebec backed by a bloc of party votes have been regarded as too strong and dominant. Striking a balance in these matters has been a challenge.

Are Political Parties the Answer?

Those seeking a strong executive within municipal government often call for the introduction of organized political parties, a topic of great controversy. What is it about parties that would create a strong executive and why are parties opposed so strongly?

Basically, parties perform the same task locally as they do at the senior levels; they organize the council into a governing group and an opposition group. The creation of a governing party is significant because it provides the basis for concerted action. If heads of council are chosen by council, they would presumably be leading members of the majority party or majority group on council, and thus would have

---

[37] These complementary changes relate to such matters as strategic planning, long term financial planning, and a top-down, priority-driven budget exercise. These process changes are at least as important as structural changes in bringing about improvements in municipal operations.

a power base to support their leadership. If they in turn choose their executive committee from the ruling group, then the committee has cohesiveness because of the common party affiliation and is somewhat analogous to a federal or provincial cabinet.

Political parties provide the potential for not only strong leadership but also more effective scrutiny of the municipality's activities through an organized opposition or alternative governing group. As a result there is a group within council pledged to scrutinize and criticize municipal activities, an important role which is normally left to everybody – and nobody. The mayor and executive committee members need to retain the confidence of council since they owe their positions to council, not the electorate.

In addition, with political parties the operations of council become more understandable and accountable to the public. Since councillors run as a group on the basis of specific programs, there is a greater likelihood that citizens will vote on the basis of substantive issues and policies instead of on the usual basis of selection among personalities. It is also argued that an election campaign organized around opposing parties and alternative approaches generates greater public interest and a higher voting turnout. In part this is because parties can be expected to play their usual roles of aggregating interests, mobilizing public support, and trying to draw more citizens into the political arena. More importantly, at the end of a term the public can attach responsibility for performance to the governing party since this group had the means to effect change. It is not possible for a ruling party to evade responsibility for action or inaction as individual councillors can and do.

How well things work will depend, of course, on the nature of the political parties involved. Proponents of party politics in local government assume a balanced situation with two or more parties which would alternate in power. If one party dominates council for a lengthy period, there is likely to be insensitivity to public opinion and other abuses, traits exhibited by the provincial and federal govern- ments in the same situation. Another issue is whether there would be local parties, focused on local issues, or just branches of national parties. In the latter case, the concern is that local issues would be neglected and that local election results might reflect the popularity or unpopularity of "parent" parties. On the other hand, purely local parties are often short-lived coalitions of local interests that display little cohesion or concerted action once elected. They may be more properly described as factions that reappear under a variety of names at election time and attempt to ensure the election of certain types of candidates, but do not exercise disciplined party voting within council.[38] Such factions clearly don't provide the basis for a strong governing group or opposition.

Critics of political parties at the local level question the validity of a number of their alleged advantages.[39] For example, evidence from the senior levels of government hardly supports the claim that parties provide clear platforms and alternatives for the voter, or stick to their platforms after elected! Nor is it apparent that parties at the senior levels provide strong leadership – at least according to the complaints often heard from both those within the system and from the public. Accountability at the municipal level arises from the small scale of operations and ready accessibility of the decision makers (in most municipalities) and does not need parties to ensure it. In fact, in can be argued that parties make councillors less accountable to the voters, because they are expected to vote with their party on issues. As for the likelihood of increased voter turnout with parties, how beneficial this would be depends on the reason for the turnout. If municipal electors had gone to the polls in record numbers in municipal elections in the early 1990s to defeat Conservative candidates because of their dislike of Brian Mulroney and the GST, this would hardly be striking a blow for local democracy.[40]

There are, of course, a number of other arguments against the introduction of organized political parties at the local level. Chief among these is the assertion that parties introduce division where none exists or should exist. "There is no political way to build a road," claim proponents of this viewpoint which reflects the lingering notion that local government activities are administrative, not political, in nature. Yet if the actual construction of a road is a matter of engineering, not politics, the decision on where to locate a particular road is certainly political. The decision on whether the traffic problem in question should be solved through building a road or providing an alternative

---

[38] Harold Kaplan, "Electoral Politics in the Metro Area," in Jack K. Masson and James Anderson (eds.), *Emerging Party Politics in Urban Canada*, Toronto, McClelland and Stewart, 1972, p. 147.

[39] See, for example, David Siegel, "City Hall Doesn't Need Parties," *Policy Options*, June 1987, pp. 26-27, on which the following points are based.

[40] *Ibid.*, p. 27.

form of public transit is also clearly political. The decision on whether the scarce financial resources of the municipality should be used on transportation or some other pressing need is again political. Indeed, if the municipal council is concerned with establishing priorities in relation to conflicting public needs and demands, its role must be political.

Since political decisions are an essential element of municipal operations then, they are not carried into the local arena by parties. But parties may help to make the unavoidable political decisions more systematic and accountable to the public. At the same time, it must be acknowledged that parties tend to exaggerate differences and also to criticize excessively for purely partisan purposes. These traits have often been evident in the actions of the parties operating at the senior levels of government.

Another major objection to parties is the feeling that they bring corruption and unsavoury practices into local government. This feeling was undoubtedly strongly influenced by the excesses of party politics and the spoils system in the United States in the period leading up to the turn of the century reform era of 100 years ago. Nor were such practices entirely absent from Canadian local government, as illustrated by discussions in Chapter 2. However, it should be re-membered that it is people who are potentially corruptible, not that specialized subgroup known as politicians. If there are opportunities for dishonesty and abuse, some people may succumb to the tempta-tion, but they will presumably do so whether they are individual councillors or members of an organized political party.

Ultimately, it doesn't really matter how soundly based are the arguments for or against political parties in municipal government. In practice, there is a strong public antipathy towards any such move. As the next chapter illustrates, efforts by the national parties to contest local elections have usually been rebuffed. Yet voters have often elected coalitions of like-minded candidates masquerading as non-parties and committed to the defeat of organized parties.

Governance Machinery and Processes

As indicated at the outset of this chapter, the governing of the municipality involves more than the internal governing structures examined above. A number of developments have shifted the focus to the broader notion of governance, which includes the formal governing machinery already described but also extends to other public, private, and voluntary bodies that are increasingly involved in the provision of services. Within this governance framework, the municipal council and staff still play key roles, but different ones in important respects.

These changes were prompted by growing criticisms of government at all levels because of mounting deficit and debt problems during this period and global pressures to reduce regulations and tax levels. According to these critics:[41]

> ➤ Governments had become too large and intrusive, largely because of the machinations of self-serving bureaucrats and politicians (a view rooted in public choice theory and popularized by the *Yes, Minister* television series);
> ➤ Governments, as monopolies, were inefficient in delivering services and not sufficiently sensitive to the wishes of those receiving the services; and
> ➤ Internal controls intended to prevent abuses had become so widespread that they reduced or blurred accountability while stifling initiative. In making sure that public servants couldn't do anything bad, these controls also kept them from being able to do anything good.

A new ideology, variously referred to as neoliberalism or neoconservatism, called for a much reduced role for government and a corresponding increase in activity by the private sector. Further impetus for new approaches came from a number of best selling and much hyped books[42] that preached the need to reinvent government and to banish bureaucracy. The various new approaches being advocated from these and other sources became grouped together into what has become known as the new public management (NPM), the key features of which are summarized below.

---

[41] Mohamed Chirah and Arthur Daniels (eds.), *New Public Management and Public Administration in Canada*, Toronto, Institute of Public Administration of Canada, 1997, pp. 15-18.

[42] Leading examples of this genre are David Osborne and Ted Gaebler, *Reinventing Government*, New York, Penguin Books, 1993; and David Osborne and Peter Plastrik, *Banishing Bureaucracy*, New York, Penguin Books, 1998.

> **Box 8.3 Features of the New Public Management**
>
> - Distinguishing more clearly between the policy and service delivery roles of government, along the lines of the steering versus rowing distinction made popular in the previously cited *Reinventing Government*.
>
> - Increasing the autonomy and discretion of public managers so that they can operate with more of the freedom and flexibility associated with private sector operations. This was to be accomplished mainly by shifting service delivery responsibilities from the traditional departmental structure to separate operating agencies.
>
> - Establishing performance standards and an increased customer focus as the primary method of ensuring accountability.
>
> - Measuring and rewarding organizations and individuals on the basis of how well they meet standards and targets.
>
> - Using performance contracts to reinforce accountability and to introduce a competitive atmosphere in which public servants must continually measure up to retain and renew contracts.
>
> - Considering alternative service delivery options – including the not-for-profit and private sectors – to offer services traditionally provided directly by government.

NPM at the Local Level

A number of the features of the NPM have been quite prominent at the local level in Canada for some time, in some cases even before they were combined under this terminology.

One manifestation has been an increase in cooperation and co-production between municipalities and various local bodies. Many community associations, for example, have become increasingly involved in "running sports, education and fitness programs; undertaking community environmental and aesthetic activities (parks maintenance, recycling); organizing social events (block parties and picnics); assisting in safety and security programs (block parents); and providing, independently or by contract with the municipality, charity, goodwill, and social services."[43] The voluntary sector, which used to play a very substantial role in the delivery of public services before the rise of the welfare state, is again being called upon to step up and take on more responsibility as governments retrench.

---

[43] Katherine A. Graham, Susan D. Phillips, and Allan M. Maslove, *Urban Governance in Canada*, Toronto, Harcourt Brace & Company, 1998, p. 128.

The business sector has become more directly involved in the provision of municipal services because of the attention now being directed to joint ventures and partnerships. The contracting out of services such as garbage collection and parks maintenance and the introduction of public private partnerships for the construction and operation of water supply and sewage treatment plants illustrate this pattern. Opinions are divided on whether these joint ventures for capital purposes are really any cheaper. After all, municipalities large enough to be engaged in financing major capital projects can usually borrow money at least as cheaply as private companies and the total cost of municipal operations does not have to include the profit margin required by private operations. Since private companies can't tax to generate the revenues that they need, it is obvious that a shift to privately owned capital facilities will be accompanied by a marked increase in user fees to finance such ventures. This raises the question of whether this arrangement is at least partly designed to allow governments to avoid the appearance of raising taxes on a tax-weary public, and whether user fees are ultimately the fairest way to pay for the operation of facilities from which a broader segment of the public than those paying the fees will benefit.[44] Another concern is the confidentiality that private companies require when part of such joint ventures, as compared to the relatively transparent nature of municipally-owned operations. Even greater concern arises when services are privatized, and Brodie charges that privatization is "incompatible with democratization and citizenship rights."[45]

Measuring What For Whom?

Much of the NPM emphasis at the local level has been reflected in new practices and procedures that emphasize measurement, comparison, competition, and entrepreneurship. Municipalities make increasing use of such private sector concepts as performance measurement, benchmarking, and the search for best practices, as summarized below.

---

[44] Heather R. Douglas, "The Capital Investment Plan Act, 1993 and the Community Economic Development Act, 1993: New Opportunities for Public and Private Sector Partners in Capital Project Financing," in *Structuring and Financing Public-Private Partnerships*, Toronto, Insight Press, 1993, p. 103.

[45] Janine Brodie, "Imagining democratic urban citizenship," in Engin Isin (ed.), *Democracy, Citizenship and the Global City*, London, Routledge, 2000, p. 122.

Box 8.4 Measuring Municipalities	
Performance Measurement	The primary measures that are receiving attention in government operations are the three Es – economy, efficiency, and effectiveness, with the last two being the main focus at the local level. *Economy* involves obtaining goods and services at the best cost. *Efficiency* is obtaining the best relationship between the input of resources and the output of goods or services. *Effectiveness* measures the quality of the goods being provided and the impact on the population being served.
Benchmarking	Pinpointing the superior performances, wherever found in public or private organizations, that establish the standard by which delivery of a particular good or service should be judged.
Best Practices	Determining the particular approaches and techniques used by the benchmarked organization, so that these can be applied to improve one's own operations.

There is no question that the use of such measures and practices can be beneficial in some respects. Having solid data on the cost of providing defined levels of output allows a municipality to build budgets on a realistic foundation. Budgets built in this manner provide an improved insight into the real causes of any over spending or under spending that may occur. They also indicate the results that are expected from the expenditures that are made. Performance measures can be used internally to set improved targets, year by year. These measures can provide a better basis for the annual budget discussions between councillors and staff, allowing council to exercise true policy control by establishing what services will be provided at what level, while leaving staff more freedom to use their experience and expertise – provided that they meet the standards specified within the budget allocation. Performance measures can also be used as the basis for new incentive and reward systems that can unleash creativity and improved productivity in municipal employees. If the costs of providing defined levels of output have been established, then employees who can meet (or exceed) the defined level for less money than budgeted can receive some portion of the resulting savings – in what is essentially a pay for performance scheme of the sort long found in the private sector.

The increasingly competitive atmosphere that develops from the use and comparison of performance measures is supposed to stimulate increased productivity in municipal operations. There is no doubt that competition can be very positive, if properly managed. Whether we are talking about the public or private sector, "when there's competition, you get better results, more cost-consciousness, and superior service delivery."[46] This reality is demonstrated by an interesting study of the solid waste experiences of two municipalities in the Greater Vancouver area.[47] One had periodic competition because of a contract with a private firm and the other had a permanent public monopoly under which city crews collected all solid waste. During the study period of the 1980s, crew productivity increased sharply for *both* municipalities. According to the study authors, the key factor in explaining this pattern was the regional competitive pressure on solid waste producers in the Greater Vancouver area. They explained that public producers were often exposed to unsolicited bids and to cost comparisons among municipalities in the region.

Two other well documented examples of the positive impact of competition are those of Phoenix and Indianapolis. In the first instance,[48] the public works department of Phoenix lost out on several bids for garbage collection activities in various areas of the city, only to win a contract in its sixth year of competition. Morale soared as a result of this breakthrough. Management held a dinner for all staff and handed out new hats with the city logo and the words "Sanitation #1." Employees knew that they had won the contract because they were the best and had demonstrated that fact in open competition. After 10 years, the department had won back contracts for garbage collection in all areas of the city. But employees can never rest on their laurels, because there are always contracts coming up for renewal. They must continue to demonstrate that they are the best.

When a pro-privatization mayor was elected in Indianapolis in the early 1990s – over the strong opposition of a very concerned union movement – the first few months of the new administration were understandably strained.[49] However, the two sides gradually reached agreement on a new approach of managed competition instead of privatization, under which public sector employees and their managers

---

[46] Auditor James Flanagan, as quoted in Osborne and Gaebler, *Reinventing Government*, p. 79.

[47] James McDavid and Gregory Schick, "Privatization versus union-management cooperation: the effects of competition on service efficiency in municipalities," *Canadian Public Administration*, Fall 1987, pp. 472-488.

[48] The description of Phoenix is based on Osborne and Gaebler, *Reinventing Government*, pp. 76-78.

[49] The description that follows is based on Peter Holle, "Enlightened Unionism," *Cordillera Institute Journal*, 1997, Issue 3, pp. 19-20.

compete with private firms for the right to provide a given service. To be competitive in this new operating environment, the union developed broader job descriptions that made staff more flexible and cross-trained and upgraded employees, which led to savings from a reduction in supervisory personnel no longer needed. Bids submitted with union involvement were successful 80% of the time, and the new atmosphere in the city contributed to a decline in grievances from about 300 a year to about 20 a year. As the union leader sums up the situation, "we win 4 out of 5 contracts that the union bids. When we do the work we do it for 25% less than it was done in the past because of competition and because you start asking people to bring their brains to work instead of parking them at the door."[50]

In spite of positive experiences such as the ones cited, the competitive pressures now found at the local level can be threatening to employees and harmful for morale – because of a concern that poor productivity may lead to contracting out while productivity gains may be used as a basis for reducing municipal staff. Price argues that the new public management is a direct threat to the municipal work force and to the power and resources of municipal departments. He points to the instability and insecurity in municipal employment with the constant competition and the threat of contracting out and downsizing.[51] If measurement and competition are to provide a stimulus to increased productivity, there will have to be a climate of trust and confidence between council and staff, one that is often missing.

There are also problems and difficulties in applying measurement to government. As Keating points out, it is commonly found that increasing the number of police officers leads to a higher rate of reported crime, "not because police officers cause crime, but because they discover more of it."[52] Using performance measures to make external comparisons can also be quite misleading. Such comparisons can actually be "apples to oranges" because of differences in the way costs are allocated by competing organizations or other distinctions that render such comparisons invalid. In addition, external comparisons tend to focus on efficiency measures in the search for cheaper

[50] Quoted in *ibid.*, p. 20.

[51] T. Price, "Council-Administration Relations in City Government," in James Lightbody (ed.), *Canadian Metropolitics*, Toronto, Copp Clark Ltd., p. 208.

[52] Michael Keating, "Size, Efficiency and Democracy: Consolidation, Fragmentation and Public Choice," in Judge et al., *Theories of Urban Politics*, p. 121.

alternative delivery options, even though considerations of quality (effectiveness measures) are equally important.

Another potential problem with performance measures is that they could be used by a provincial government to impose standards upon municipalities. Under Ontario's new Municipal Act, for example, a municipality must:

> ➢ establish objectives and standards with respect to any matter designated by the Minister related to the efficiency and effectiveness of the municipality's operations,
> ➢ provide the Minister with any information specified, and such information is subject to review or audit in the manner and form designated by the Minister,
> ➢ provide at least annual public notice of improvements in the efficiency and effectiveness of the delivery of services and any barriers thereto, and
> ➢ comply with any service standards prescribed by the cabinet or face financial penalties.

It is easy to see how these statutory provisions could be used to dictate provincial standards for municipal operations.

An emphasis on business-like measurements is also found in some of the provisions of the new community charter legislation in British Columbia. As noted in Chapter 6, critics do not find the call for annual reports and an annual public meeting to be adequate means of making municipalities accountable, and reject these as an inappropriate corporate model of accountability.

New Business Governing Models

In addition to these potentially significant process changes, NPM at the local level has also manifested itself in some new business models of governing and in an unfortunate outburst of business jargon that has infected municipal discourse. The first step in developing the business models involves identifying the core businesses of the municipality – essentially groupings of related municipal services or functions as is evident from Figure 8.5 below. Each core businesses is then divided into a number of business units that consolidate the functions and processes that relate to the delivery of particular products or services. Creating these separate cost/profit centres makes it easier to isolate all of the expenditures (and revenues) associated with a particular service, and to determine how close it comes to operating at break-even. This structure also makes it easier to examine all of the processes related to the provision of a particular service, with the objective of streamlining these processes to improve customer service and operating efficiency. The business units are expected to deliver defined service standards within budget limits, in accordance with their business plans. In many cases, these plans call for enhancing the revenues generated by the program or service being offered, so that it moves closer to break-even.

The example below is the enterprise model recommended by KPMG for the new city of Kingston in 1997 and subsequently adopted by the new municipality of Chatham-Kent, which also came into existence as a result of amalgamation that year.[53]

Figure 8.5 Chatham-Kent's Business Model[54]		
Strategic Core	Support business units	Service delivery business units
Strategic and Land use planning Budget and Performance management Economic development	Human resources Legal services Accounting Information services Engineering Fleet management	Community & client services Health and social services Public works Protection services (Fire) Police services Public utilities

The key elements of this new organization, as outlined in a November 1997 KPMG report to Chatham-Kent, were as follows:[55]

> The Strategic Core reports to Council and is responsible for corporate and strategic planning, policy development, the business planning and budget process, and arranging the "contracts" or business plans with internal and external service providers that will directly provide services. The Service Centres are the "one-stop" contact points for residents and other clients requiring service from the municipality. The Service Delivery function will be carried out by Business Units within the administration or external contractors that will be responsible to deliver services at the level of service and level of cost agreed to by Council. The Strategic Core will monitor their

---

[53] For a discussion of this model, see Thomas R. Hollick and David Siegel, *Evolution, Revolution, Amalgamation: Restructuring in Three Ontario Municipalities*, Local Government Case Studies No. 10, London, University of Western Ontario, 2001.

[54] Accessed April 16, 2002 at www.city.chatham-kent.on.ca.

[55] Brian V. Bourns, KPMG Management Consultants, *Organizational Design, Municipality of Chatham-Kent*, November 4, 1997, p. 6, as quoted in Hollick and Siegel, *Evolution, Revolution, Amalgamation*, p. 219.

performance. The Support Business Units will provide centralized
services to all the other business units and provide input to policy
and strategy development within the Strategic Core.

Whatever the merits of this business model, it is not that new
in several fundamental respects. We have always had two kinds of
government department: line and staff. Line departments are directly
involved in providing services to the public, whereas staff departments
function as "in house" support to the line departments. The various
staff departments of the past are now being designated as support
business units. The line departments are being grouped together into
service delivery and strategic core business units that are rather similar
to the planning, hard services, and soft services groupings that many
municipalities have used in the past in an attempt to link related
departments and activities.[56]

What is new, however, is that not only are the units designed
differently – in an attempt to overcome the silo problem inherent in
the old departmental structure based on functional specialization – but
they are expected to operate differently. There is a very strong
emphasis on performance and accountability inherent in these new
business models. The line departments or business units are expected
to deliver defined service standards within budget limits, in accordance
with their business plans. The staff departments/internal service
providers are also expected to demonstrate operating efficiency if they
wish to be "hired" by the line departments to provide their services.
Operations that don't measure up face the possibility of being replaced
by an alternative service delivery arrangement. Overall, then, the new
structure incorporates a distinctive new operating philosophy. The
rearrangement and repackaging of departments within the structure
provides a clearer focus for the application of measurement, comparison, and performance-based accountability.

It is suggested that municipalities that wish to embrace this
particular approach should concentrate more on these underlying
changes in process and operating philosophy and be less preoccupied
with couching everything in business terminology, no matter how
fashionable that may currently be with some provincial governments.
It is permissible to go on calling departments, departments, even after
they are regrouped into more effective combinations. The new public

---

[56] Note the general similarity between the Chatham-Kent enterprise model and
the coordinating model illustrated in Table 8.1 on page 282 of this chapter.

information centre can be called just that; it doesn't have to be known as one-stop shopping or one-window shopping. Employees can be challenged to strive for continuous improvement in performance (and rewarded accordingly), without there being a business plan, just as standards can be set, resources allocated, and results measured and monitored. What is actually being done is far more important than what it is called, especially when so much of the new terminology confuses more than it enlightens.

Concluding Comments

The various governing models used by municipalities over the years, and the governing philosophies underlying them have, for the most part, reflected a concern for efficiency and coordination in the delivery of services to the relative neglect of the representative and political aspects that are (or should be) equally a concern of municipal government. Because of the limited success of efforts to create effective executive committees, the most prevalent reform of coordinating machinery has been the chief administrative officer system. No matter how well this system works, however, it does nothing to strengthen political leadership and, to the contrary, may even detract from this objective by creating a bureaucratic system and by undermining the power and public status of the council.

Even more worrying are the developments in recent years that attempt to recast municipalities as businesses (or at least combinations of business units) and local citizens as consumers or clients. As one analysis describes the situation, "[u]nder various neo-liberal regimes of central government, local government structures and institutions in the global city have been radically transformed from democratic and representative into increasingly professionalized, marketized, entrepreneurial and managerial forms."[57] In the process, the importance of municipal government appears to have declined, with it now being increasingly portrayed as but one of many local service providers, public and private. In light of these developments, the subject of the next chapter – the methods by which citizens participate in municipal government – takes on added importance.

---

[57] Evelyn S. Ruppert, "Who governs the global city?" in Isin, *Democracy, Citizenship and the Global City*, p. 275.

Chapter 9
The Municipality and the Public

If we are to counteract the market model that would reduce municipal governments to but one of many possible service delivery agents, and local citizens to individual consumers, we must strengthen the political and representative role of municipalities and the avenues for citizen participation.

Introduction

The importance of the political, representative role of municipal government has been emphasized since the first chapter of this book, along with the concern that this role has been largely neglected because municipalities have been preoccupied with their administrative or service delivery role. As we near the close of this book, this issue is reexamined, especially in light of some of the developments that have been described in the intervening chapters.

We start by considering a number of aspects of representative government as it is exercised at the local level. A number of mechanisms for public participation in local government are then examined, including citizen groups, neighbourhood councils, local political parties, and tools of direct democracy.

The Nature of Representative Government

The principle of representative government is a central feature of democracies. It reflects an arrangement whereby eligible members of the population at large elect a small number of people to represent them and make decisions on their behalf. Presumably they elect individuals who care about the same issues that they do and share the same values – although specific or in depth information of this sort is not usually in evidence during an election campaign.

Size Does Matter

The functioning of representative government at the local level in Canada is affected by longstanding bias in favour of small councils of from 5 to 15 members. Some significantly larger councils have been established in recent decades, as a result of municipal amalgamations, but then have been reduced in size again. For example, the new city of Winnipeg started out with a council of 51 members in 1971, but the numbers were reduced twice to the current membership of 15. The new city of Toronto began with 58 members in 1998 but the council was reduced to 45 members after only one term. The new city of Montreal (established in 2002) tops the scales at the moment with a council of 73 members plus the mayor.

The smaller the council, the more likely that it will not represent adequately the diversity of its population, and that likelihood obviously increases the larger and more diverse the population. Yet many of Canada's largest municipalities have relatively small councils. Edmonton, for example, has had 12 councillors since the beginning of the 20th century, even as it has grown from a small town to a city of 650 000. Winnipeg has twice as many members of the provincial legislature as it has councillors – those representatives from the level of government that is supposedly closest to the people.[1] To cite one more example, the city of Mississauga has a council of 10 for a population of 600 000. It is in Ontario that the provincial government has been particularly keen to reduce the size of municipal councils in the name of efficiency, without any apparent regard for the representative role that these councils are supposed to play.

The Municipal Franchise

As noted in earlier chapters, municipal governments began with a very restricted franchise that favoured property owners. The franchise is now quite broad, however, and essentially gives the right to vote to Canadian citizens, 18 years and older, who meet limited residency requirements as specified in provincial legislation and who are not otherwise disqualified for limited grounds specified in the same legislation. In general, property owners within a municipality, whether

---

[1] These two examples are from Jonathon Barker and Christopher Leo, "Introduction," in André Carrel, *Citizens' Hall: Making Local Democracy Work*, Toronto, Between the Lines, 2001, p. 3.

residents or not, also have a vote, as do the spouses and same-sex partners of the same. However, a disappointingly low proportion of voters take advantage of their democratic opportunities every municipal election year. While the approximately two-thirds voting turnout in federal and provincial elections is not great, and is declining of late, there is even more reason to be concerned about the 40% or lower voting turnout at the municipal level.

Factors Affecting Voting Turnout

A number of factors are commonly cited as influencing the municipal vote. Studies lend some support to the notion that the turnout is higher in smaller municipalities than in larger ones,[2] which would suggest that the recent round of municipal amalgamations will do little to help the situation. The same type of relationship between population and turnout helps to explain why voting in populous municipalities tends to be higher with a ward system than with elections at large. Socio-economic factors such as the educational level of the electorate and the proportion of homeowners versus tenants also have an influence.[3] Not surprisingly, voting turnout is also affected by the extent of competition for the seats available. Acclamations for the head of council position usually result in a reduced turnout, while a close race for that position can have a very positive impact on turnout. A higher voting turnout is also common when there are "questions" on the ballot in the form of plebiscites or referendums (discussed later in this chapter). Indeed, there is an old saying that the most effective way to increase voter interest is to add a liquor licensing question to the ballot.

It is widely held that a major negative influence on voting turnout is the complicated nature of the municipal election process. At the provincial and federal levels, voters are accustomed to selecting one name from three or four or so, all of them normally associated with a political party. In contrast, the municipal voter must make choices

---

[2] This is the finding, for example, of an Ontario study reported in Joseph Kushner, David Siegel, and Hannah Stanwick, "Ontario Municipal Elections: Voting Trends and Determinants of Electoral Success in a Canadian Province," *Canadian Journal of Political Science*, September 1997.

[3] R. Vaison and P. Aucoin, "Class and Voting in Recent Halifax Mayoralty Elections," in L. D. Feldman and M. D. Goldrick (eds.), *Politics and Government of Urban Canada*, Toronto, Methuen, 1976, pp. 200-219.

within several different categories (or from multiple ballots) from among much longer lists of names, none of them further identified with any kind of party label. The voter, for example, might be required to choose 10 or more candidates for council from a list of 20 or more (if there isn't any ward system in the municipality), a half dozen members of the school board from a dozen or more names, a candidate for mayor from a choice of six or more, and – in some jurisdictions – candidates for utilities commissions, parks boards, or other local elected bodies. Exercising one's franchise in these circumstances requires considerable dedication.

Voting turnout may also be low because the act of voting has little meaning for many citizens. Some municipalities have retained historic boundaries that bear little relation to the living patterns of today. Citizens are unlikely to take an active interest in the activities of their municipality if their normal circle of movement for work, shopping, and recreation embraces quite different (and usually larger) areas. Lack of participation may also arise because of the patterns of urban development that have occurred, as discussed in Chapter 3. In addition, municipal decision making may not seem relevant because many of the issues of concern aren't handled by municipal councils but by separate boards. This is true in most jurisdictions for such matters as education and public health. The limited scope of municipal activities may contribute to the low voting turnout. If municipalities do little more than provide the physical services to support growth and development, as has been the case at least until the recent downloading in some provinces, what is there about this administrative role that will generate citizen interest and involvement? Is the voting turnout so low because the electorate "perceives whether intuitively or through overt knowledge that the social, economic and even environmental problems which beset the city lie beyond the city council's power to solve?"[4]

Whatever the merits of these points, municipalities often fail to help their own cause. Consider the issues and themes raised by candidates during election campaigns. Are voters given competing "visions" about the future of their municipality? Are they made part of an effort to define local interests and concerns, to identify the priorities that the community wants to address together? Is there even a hint in most

---

[4] Earl A. Levin, "Municipal Democracy and Citizen Participation," in Nancy Klos (ed.), *The State of Unicity – 25 Years Later*, Winnipeg, Institute of Urban Studies, 1998, p. 50.

municipal election campaigns that a fundamental democratic exercise is under way? The answer to all these questions is: no. By far the most common message offered to voters in municipal elections is "vote for me and I won't increase your taxes." While this is a popular thing to say, except to those voters who have stopped believing such promises, it is simplistic and probably also unrealistic. It says nothing about how and where tax dollars should be spent, or about what difficult choices must be made *if* tax increases are to be curtailed. A municipal election campaign provides an excellent opportunity to educate local citizens about the tough choices and exciting opportunities that face the municipality. If some of that excitement could be communicated to the voters, they might gain an understanding of the importance and significance of casting their ballots. Instead, the election campaign is reduced to a parade of candidates attempting to convince us of how frugal they would be if put in charge of our tax dollars.

It is acknowledged that promising no increase in taxes may work as a strategy for the election of individual candidates. But, the issue here is a much broader one – the general lack of voter interest and voting turnout in municipal elections. If the only point is to get individuals elected, then let them promise whatever the voters want to hear. But if the point is to develop an appreciation for the political role of municipal government and the vital issues which a municipal council can help its citizens to face and manage, then the campaign needs to be conducted quite differently.

Voting Results: Who Gets Elected?

Until recently, municipal council positions have been considered a part time responsibility, the preserve of the "gifted amateur"[5] rather than the professional politician. Given the strong influence which business has always wielded over municipal operations, it is not surprising to discover that the most common backgrounds of urban councillors are in business, the public service, education, and community organizations.[6] The percentage of women on municipal council, at least in

---

[5] Andrew Sancton and Paul Woolner, "Full-time municipal councillors: a strategic challenge for Canadian urban government," *Canadian Public Administration*, Winter 1990, p. 385.

[6] Katherine Graham, Susan D. Phillips, and Allan M. Maslove, *Urban Governance in Canada*, Toronto, Harcourt Brace & Company, Canada, 1998, p. 99.

major Canadian cities, is significantly higher than their representation
in provincial and federal governing bodies. Among the reasons which
have been given for this situation are that family responsibilities
preclude women from taking on the travelling involved in federal and
provincial service and that municipal issues are closer to the home and
of more interest to women.[7] Trimble challenges both of these explanations, claiming that they are based on incorrect and unflattering
assumptions about the nature of city politics and about women's
participation in the political process.[8] Moreover, even if homemakers
were interested in social issues, these receive very little attention in
small municipalities, where the focus tends to be on roads, snow
removal, and other hard service issues.

In contrast to the inroads being made by women on council,
visible minorities remain very poorly represented. Even in cities with
an ethnically diverse population, such as Vancouver or Montreal, there
have been few minority candidates.[9] With the growing cultural diversity of Canada's cities, there will be increased demands that electoral
politics be made more attractive and accessible to minority
communities.

The Councillor: Trustee or Delegate?

How much those elected should consult with the public during their
term of office is a matter of debate and controversy. Those who view
the councillor as a trustee believe that successful candidates should
exercise their own judgment as to the best course of action with
respect to the various issues that arise, while recognizing that the
public will pass judgment on their performance at the next election.
This leaves the public with a very passive role, although one consistent
with the caretaker or custodial role of municipal government
associated with the turn of the century reform movement of 100 years
ago – a role in which it was council's task to provide a modest range of
services while holding the line on taxes, carrying out a primarily
administrative role that didn't require public participation.

[7] Chantal Maillé, "Gender Concerns in City Life," in Timothy L. Thomas (ed.),
The Politics of the City, Toronto, ITP Nelson, 1997, p. 109.

[8] Linda Trimble, "Politics Where We Live: Women and Cities," in James
Lightbody (ed.), *Canadian Metropolitics*, Toronto, Copp Clark Ltd., 1995, p. 93.

[9] Graham et al., *Urban Governance in Canada*, p. 102.

The alternative view is that the councillor is chosen as a delegate, to govern in accordance with the wishes of the electorate and to act as a mirror faithfully reflecting their views. It is unclear how the councillor is to identify the views that are to be reflected so faithfully, how a diversity of viewpoints is to be handled, or how to avoid being overly influenced by the vocal minority.

Public Participation

Between these extremes of trustee and delegate lies a substantial middle ground of possible interaction between councillors and the public. The interaction may be initiated by either party and it may take a wide variety of forms. Stewart describes two dozen examples of what he terms "extra-electoral participation mechanisms," ranging from distributing municipal newsletters to using focus groups and advisory bodies, to self-funded neighbourhood associations.[10] Other techniques are summarized in the table below.

Box 9.1 Methods of Public Consultation
➢ Some municipalities take city hall to the public, by using a municipal information booth that is staffed by councillors and taken to shopping centres or other focal points in the community on a rotating basis.
➢ Stockholm set up a "scribbling wall", a large, prominently located, brightly lit billboard on which citizens are encouraged to express their views about public issues. People responded with great enthusiasm.[11]
➢ Some municipalities provide an opportunity at the start of council meetings for public remarks on agenda items – a kind of local question period.
➢ Many municipalities welcome new residents with a detailed information package. St Paul, Minnesota entitles its booklet "Owner's Manual," to underscore that it is the local citizens for whom the municipality exists.[12]
➢ Municipalities increasingly conduct annual surveys to determine the importance and the quality of the services being provided.
➢ Municipalities are making their web sites increasingly informative and interactive to facilitate public participation.

[10] Kennedy Stewart, *Think Democracy: Options for Local Democratic Reform in Vancouver*, Vancouver, Simon Fraser University, 2003, pp. 41-50.

[11] Michael Smither, "Encouraging Community Involvement," *Municipal World*, February 1997, p. 5.

[12] David Osborne and Ted Gaebler, *Reinventing Government*, New York, Penguin Books, 1993, p. 74.

In several important areas, municipalities have been developing processes that promote public participation in decision making. This is a significant shift in emphasis, one that goes well beyond the notion that public participation takes place at election time or should be confined to commenting on specific municipal actions or proposed actions. For example, land use planning has traditionally been regarded as the preserve of the expert, but a number of municipalities have revamped their approach to build in extensive public consultation. There is no better example than the process followed by the Greater Vancouver Regional District for updating its 1975 Livable Region Plan. Municipal budgeting has also been seen as a technical exercise, best carried out without any public involvement. Yet Burlington, Ontario responded to public complaints about tax levels by appointing a citizens' committee to review its budget and budgeting system.[13]

Participation Through Local Groups

Participation through groups is by no means new, and Chapter 2 described a number of groups that spearheaded the turn of the century reform movement of 100 years ago. Also of long standing are various residents' and ratepayers' associations established to protect the interests of the property owner. Over the years, they often broadened their membership and focus. Groups representing the business community and the middle class have also been prominent in a number of cities for more than half a century, often promoting the election of like-minded councillors and attempting to prevent the election of candidates representing labour or socialist viewpoints.

The 1960s and 1970s saw a great increase in local groups, as a result of the growing opposition to the pattern of growth and development that had been taking place in the post-war period. Concern about the quality of life and the preservation of established neighbourhoods deepened as rapid development seemed to threaten the fabric of the city. Attempts to respond to transportation needs by building more expressways (rather than by expanding public transit) met with increasing opposition, as did urban renewal projects that were often characterized as bulldozing neighbourhoods. The traditional reliance on technical expertise to find the answers was no longer acceptable and

---

[13] Both of these experiences are examined in Katherine Graham and Susan Phillips, *Citizen Engagement*, Toronto, Institute of Public Administration of Canada, 1998, a good source of information on this topic.

an aroused public contended that the views and concerns of those who would be directly affected by local decisions were just as important and valid. There were also demands that decision makers show a greater awareness of social and environmental considerations.

One analysis describes the changes during this period as "the politicizing of urban life" and refers to professional and skilled workers of the information economy forming a broad new social category referred to as the "new middle class."[14] If there was one common feature of most of these groups over the years, it was their attitude toward growth and development. Just as many of the earlier groups, especially those representing the business community, were pro-growth, so many of the later groups, representing neighbourhoods, were concerned with stability and the preservation of existing life-styles. According to Magnusson, a new reform politics developed, one that questioned long-held views about "sacrificing the neighbourhood to the larger community, observing the proprieties of bureaucratic procedure, respecting the judgments of professional planners, and accepting the leadership of elected officials...."[15]

It was largely members of this new middle class who rented or purchased housing in working class neighbourhoods in the centre of cities, in a process that became known as gentrification. These "gentrifiers" frequently joined forces with incumbent residents and their community organizations and with others such as environmental, feminist, peace, and gay and lesbian groups, to oppose urban renewal projects and other developments that were seen as a threat to the neighbourhood. But gentrification also brought increased property values in these areas, pushing housing costs out of reach for lower income residents.[16]

Higgins identified three elements in the citizen movement that began in the 1960s.[17]

---

[14] Paul Villeneuve and Anne-Marie Séguin, "Power and Decision-Making in the City: Political Perspectives," in Trudi Bunting and Pierre Filion, *Canadian Cities in Transition*, 2nd Edition, Toronto, Oxford University Press, p. 554.

[15] Warren Magnusson and Andrew Sancton (eds.), *City Politics in Canada*, Toronto, University of Toronto Press, 1983, pp. 33-34.

[16] Villeneuve and Séguin, "Political Perspectives," p. 556.

[17] Donald Higgins, "Progressive City Politics and the Citizen Movement: A Status Report," *City Magazine Annual 1981*, Vol. V, No. 1, Toronto, James Lorimer & Company, 1981, pp. 84-85.

Box 9.2 Elements in the Citizen Movement

1. Community groups – both reactive and narrowly focused ones, formed to oppose some development that was seen as adversely affecting their neighbourhood, and other groups that agitated for city-wide measures such as more public housing, child care, and public transit;

2. More reform candidates running for councils, and actually getting elected, thereby bringing to councils greater diversity, a younger average age, and a greater commitment to consultation; and

3. The alternative press, as reflected in such publications as *City Magazine*, *Our Generation*, and *This Magazine*.

However, Higgins also suggested that it was inappropriate to use the term "movement" to describe the political activities that were taking place because they were "...far from being uniform in direction, pace of evolution, strategy, tactics, kinds of personalities involved, content and so on...."[18] A few brief examples of the group activity of this period are outlined below, followed by an analysis of the effectiveness of this activity.

Urban Renewal and Expressway Battles

The Strathcona Property Owners' and Tenants' Association was established in 1968 to oppose Vancouver's urban renewal initiatives. They were typical of the time in that they involved the displacement of large numbers of families. When the federal government announced the following year that it would not provide funds for the urban renewal project in Strathcona unless the residents were involved in the planning process, the result was a working committee comprising government officials and members of the Association, "one of the first instances in Canada of citizens sharing this kind of decision-making with government."[19] As launched in 1972, the rehabilitation plan emphasized repairs and renovations rather than expropriation and became a model for other such programs.

Another well documented example of opposition to urban renewal occurred in the Treffan Court area of Toronto and resulted, as in Vancouver, in a new approach in which the affected citizens became

---

[18] *Ibid.*, p. 86.

[19] Donald Gutstein, "Vancouver," in Magnusson and Sancton, *City Politics in Canada*, p. 201.

involved in the development of the urban renewal plans.[20] In addition, ratepayers' and residents' groups were established or revived in response to the threat to middle and upper class neighbourhoods posed by the extent of high rise commercial redevelopment and apartment construction underway in the city. "In 1968, a Confederation of Residents' and Ratepayers' Associations (CORRA) was established as a coordinating agency; it not only linked the middle-class organizations with one another, but brought them into contact with community groups being formed in poorer neighbourhoods."[21]

A proposed Spadina Expressway for Toronto led to the creation of the Stop Spadina, Save Our City, Coordinating Committee (SSSOCCC).[22] Vancouver's various expressway schemes also prompted strong public opposition that led to their rejection on several occasions. Prolonged debate following the June 1967 release of the Vancouver Transportation Study culminated in a November meeting that was attended by 500 citizens and that heard briefs from 30 organizations and individuals.[23] As discussed in a later section, new political parties were also formed to challenge the approach being taken to develop the city. A similar pattern unfolded in Montreal, largely in response to the policies and actions of mayor Jean Drapeau. Opposition grew not only from radicals who deplored his failure to provide sufficient housing and social and recreational services in the poorer sections of the city but also from middle class groups concerned with stopping high rise development, saving the city's older buildings and neighbourhoods, and forcing a more democratic, open system of government.[24] These opposition forces came together in 1974 to form the Montreal Citizens' Movement, a political party that ultimately captured the city council.

---

[20] Graham Fraser, *Fighting Back*, Toronto, Hakkert, 1972.

[21] Warren Magnusson, "Toronto," in Magnusson and Sancton, *City Politics in Canada*, p. 115.

[22] The work of this committee and the expressway battle are outlined in Donald J. H. Higgins, *Local and Urban Politics in Canada*, Toronto, Gage, 1986, pp. 282-287.

[23] Christopher Leo, *The Politics of Urban Development: Canadian Urban Expressway Disputes*, Monographs on Canadian Urban Government, No. 3, Toronto, Institute of Public Administration of Canada, 1977, p. 46.

[24] Andrew Sancton, "Montreal," in Magnusson and Sancton, *City Politics in Canada*, p. 73.

Effectiveness of the Citizen Movement

By the 1980s, the citizen activism that had emerged two decades earlier had largely dissipated. There are, of course, still local groups agitating on behalf of various environmental and social issues. A good example is STORM, a coalition of 25 citizens' groups and individuals formed in 1989 out of concern for the economic integrity of the Oak Ridges Moraine in the Greater Toronto Area (profiled in Chapter 5).[25] Another example of a quite different kind was C4LD (Citizens for Local Democracy), which was formed to oppose the amalgamations that created the new city of Toronto and mounted a very high profile, but ultimately unsuccessful campaign.[26] But the general consensus is that the citizen activism of the 1960s has not been sustained. Several reasons have been offered for this situation.

Several observers have been critical of the citizens' groups of this period and the way that they operated. According to Sancton, these groups shared no common view about the role that municipal government should play in creating the ideal urban environment. While some were genuinely committed to various forms of neigh-bourhood self-government, most were concerned only with the particular issue at hand and were interested in their municipal government only to the extent that it had any decision making power with respect to that issue. Nobody in the new urban reform movement, Sancton contends, argued for truly multi-functional municipal governments subject to reduced provincial supervision. "In fact, many new urban reformers seemed profoundly suspicious of any political institutions, including municipal governments and local political parties, with the potential to overrule the expressed preferences of local neighbourhoods and their leaders."[27]

Sewell goes so far as to suggest that neighbourhood groups, that were the building blocks for reform efforts in the 1960s and 1970s, will be the stumbling block for any new reform movement. He

---

[25] Details on STORM and its activities are available at www.stormco.org, accessed March 10, 2003.

[26] For an analysis of C4LD and its lack of success, see Engin Isin, "Governing cities without government," in Engin Isin (ed.), *Democracy, Citizenship and the Global City*, London, Routledge, 2000, pp. 159-162.

[27] Andrew Sancton, "The Municipal Role in the Governance of Cities," in Bunting and Filion, *Canadian Cities in Transition*, pp. 433-434.

describes the earlier reform period as one in which neighbourhood groups fought to preserve the city built before World War Two – a city whose neighbourhoods contained a range of incomes and family sizes, a mix of uses and building forms. Residents wanted to preserve that diversity against the destructive impact of urban renewal, expressways, and private redevelopment. Then came Don Mills, Canada's first corporate suburb, and a new definition of neighbourhood based on exclusivity. This was the message presented in the carefully designed homes, the enforced colour coordination, the looping, curvy street design, and the modern house form.[28] According to Sewell, the land mass of most Canadian cities is now predominantly filled with the progeny of Don Mills. "Exclusivity has become the dominant characteristic of the urban area and the Not in My Backyard (NIMBY) lullaby is frequently sung to consistent applause."[29]

Frisken points out that citizen activism may be strongly biased against city government initiatives that are sensitive to social needs.[30] It may be aimed at preventing the provision of housing for low-income families, keeping public transit out of residential areas, or otherwise discouraging any municipal initiative that disturbs the status quo. Filion describes efforts by neighbourhood associations to resist affordable housing initiatives in Mississauga, Vaughan, Richmond Hill, Etobicoke, and Pickering, and he concludes that "neighbourhood influence is associated with a tight focus on the immediate interests of residents and a narrow consideration of a decision's consequences, most negative externalities being likely to materialize elsewhere."[31]

Participation Through Neighbourhood Councils

Another avenue for citizen participation is found in the residents' committees and neighbourhood councils that have been set up in a

---

[28] John Sewell, *Prospects for Reform*, Research Paper 180, Toronto, Centre for Urban and Community Studies, University of Toronto, January 1991.

[29] *Ibid.* Sewell has since elaborated his views about urban design in *The Shape of the City*, Toronto, University of Toronto Press, 1993.

[30] Frances Frisken, "Introduction," in Frances Frisken (ed.), *The Changing Canadian Metropolis*, Vol. 1, Toronto, Canadian Urban Institute, 1994, p. 30.

[31] Pierre Filion, "Government Levels, Neighbourhood Influences and Urban Policy," in Henri Lustiger-Thaler (ed.), *Political Arrangements: Power and the City*, Montreal, Black Rose Books, 1992, pp. 176 and 180.

number of (usually) larger municipalities, to provide a formal structure for public involvement. The model chosen by Quebec City, beginning in 1993, was distinctive in that it involved the establishment of councils composed equally of men and women, elected by the population of each neighbourhood, with city councillors from these neighbourhoods then added as non-voting members. The primary function of these councils is to facilitate the coordination of the population at the neighbourhood level on regulatory matters or on the nature and quality of city services.[32]

In a number of the largest municipalities created through amalgamation, an attempt has been made to provide additional local representation through the establishment of community councils or committees or other forms of sublocal entity.[33] The 13 community committees established when Winnipeg Unicity was created in 1972 are probably the best known (and documented) example of this type of body. They were originally seen as providing a forum for public involvement and a vehicle for political decentralization. Each committee was to be responsible for preparing its own budget for services with a local orientation that were assigned to it. Resident advisory groups (RAGs) were elected to advise and assist each committee. While these committees were initially seen as somehow taking the place of the former lower tier municipalities, they were not law making bodies, had no taxing powers, and were really little more than "subcommittees of the city council."[34] Enthusiasm for the resident advisory groups waned when their limited role became apparent, and the committees received little support from an increasingly centralized civic administration.[35] As noted in Chapter 4, the number of community committees and RAGs was gradually reduced over the years. The

---

[32] This description is based on Louise Quesnel, *Public Consultation: A Tool for Democracy*, Toronto, ICURR Publications, August 2000, pp. 15-16.

[33] This is the term used by Louise Quesnel, "Large Cities: An Opportunity for Innovation in Sublocal Entities?" paper presented at the Urban Affairs Association Annual Meeting, Boston, March 22, 2002.

[34] Donald J. H. Higgins, *Urban Canada: Its Government and Politics*, Toronto, Macmillan, 1977, p. 150.

[35] Lloyd Axworthy, "The Best Laid Plans Oft Go Astray: The Case of Winnipeg," in M. O. Dickerson, S. Drabek, and J. T. Woods (eds.), *Problems of Change in Urban Government*, Waterloo, Wilfrid Laurier Press, 1980, pp. 116-117.

RAGs were abolished in 1992, by which time there were only six committees left, with minimal duties and influence.

Montreal's experience with a similar type of consulting body was also disappointing. While in opposition, the Montreal Citizen's Movement party had made much of the importance of neighbourhood councils with decision making power that would be part of a decentralized city government. Following its election in 1986, however, what the MCM set up were nine district (not neighbourhood) advisory (not decision making) councils. All power remained centralized in the city council and its executive committee and there was growing disillusionment with the weakness of the district advisory committees (DACs).[36]

Notwithstanding this experience, a variation of this model has been introduced in the recently amalgamated city of Montreal (and four other amalgamated municipalities in Quebec). Community councils have been established in 27 boroughs or "arrondissement" in Montreal, mostly based on the boundaries of the municipalities that were amalgamated. As discussed in Chapter 4, the borough councils have administrative and consultative responsibilities, but no separate taxing power, and little independence from the city administration.

When the Halifax Regional Municipality was created through amalgamation in 1996, five community councils were established, each made up of the city councillors elected from districts located within their boundaries. These boundaries were drawn not to follow the old municipal boundaries.[37] A sixth council was established in 1996. If authorized by city council, these community councils can exercise certain land use planning powers, they monitor and make recommendations concerning the provision of services, and they submit proposed operating and capital budgets annually with respect to services and projects for their areas. Vojnovic views these councils quite positively, stating that they promote "a healthy local democracy by enabling residents to determine the characteristics of the service packages provided in their districts."[38] But making recommendations and proposing budgets does not mean actual decision making power.

---

[36] Timothy L Thomas, *A City With a Difference*, Montreal, Véhicule Press, 1997, pp. 108-109.

[37] This discussion is based on Quesnel, "Sublocal Entities," p. 3.

[38] Igor Vojnovic, "Municipal Consolidation, Regional Planning and Fiscal Accountability: The Recent Experience in Two Maritime Provinces," *Canadian Journal of Regional Science*, Special Issue, Spring 2000, p. 67.

Quesnel is more cautious about these community councils, pointing out that more needs to be known about how much, and in what ways, local residents are involved in the process.[39]

In the case of Toronto, six community councils were established, initially on the basis of the boundaries of the municipalities that had been amalgamated. Because these municipalities varied greatly in size, the result was community councils with memberships ranging from 4 to 16 (not counting the mayor, who is an ex officio member of all these councils). Six new communities were delineated in 2000, with boundaries more in harmony with those used for ward elections to city council and with reduced population disparities.[40] The community councils make recommendations to city council on local planning and development matters and also hold public meetings with respect to these matters – but their role is strictly advisory. Since every matter has to be ratified by city council, there is no real accountability at the community council level. Moreover, a great deal of time at city council is spent on these local issues, to the neglect of the larger city wide issues that should be the focus.[41]

Overall, it is not clear that these types of sublocal entity provide an adequate replacement for the local representation that is lost when amalgamations occur. In fact, their existence poses something of a dilemma. The rationale that originally prompts an amalgamation suggests that broad, municipal wide considerations should now prevail. Yet if these community committees or councils are established, particularly on the basis of the boundaries of the former municipalities, the expectation is that they are there to protect and promote more localized interests and concerns. If they do this well, do they undermine the ability of the new municipality to develop a broad, unifying focus? If the community committees and councils function as local decision making bodies, one may well ask why amalgamation was pursued at all – if the old municipalities are now to be replaced with a weaker form of quasi-municipality. It is suggested that other means must also be employed to ensure that the representative role of municipal government receives sufficient attention within restructured systems.

---

[39] Quesnel, "Sublocal Entities," p. 4.

[40] *Ibid.*, p. 6.

[41] According to Toronto councillor Joe Mihevc, Speaking Notes for the GTA Forum, "Visions for Structuring Toronto's Council," November 19, 2002, available from www.yorku.ca/gtaforum/notes.html, accessed May 12, 2003.

Participation Through Political Parties

Another vehicle for citizen participation in government is through political parties. There has long been, however, strong resistance to overt political party activity at the local level. The word overt is stressed, since many local councillors are widely known to be associated with one of the provincial or national party organizations. This type of link is apparently quite acceptable to the voters, but a more negative reaction could be expected if the same individuals were to run locally with a more specific party affiliation.

As will be evident from the examples that follow, those political parties that have enjoyed success at the local level are almost all purely local parties, not local branches of provincial or national political parties. The only senior level political party to make a concerted effort to elect candidates locally has been the NDP (and its predecessor, the CCF) but its successes have been quite limited. A number of the local parties have really been more a loose coalition of like-minded candidates than a formal political party. Indeed, in a few cities, these coalitions claim to exist in order to prevent the election of political parties – even though they attempt to achieve this objective by running slates of candidates and behaving very much like a party. Many of these local parties and local coalitions have lacked cohesion and have not endured.

Local Parties in Quebec

There has been some limited local political party activity outside of Quebec, and Vancouver continues to have political parties represented on its city council, but otherwise our current experience with this form of local political expression is confined to the province of Quebec. The development of municipal parties was encouraged by provincial legislation passed in 1978 that allowed parties to raise and spend money at any time, as long as they followed provincial regulations – which gave them an advantage over independent candidates, who had to limit their fund raising and spending to the official campaign period. Originally applicable only to municipalities with at least 20 000 residents, this legislation was subsequently broadened to include all municipalities with a population of at least 5000. There are more than 130 registered political parties in Quebec and more than one-third of the municipalities covered by the fund raising legislation previously cited have at least one political party.[42]

Party Activity in Montreal

The city of Montreal has experienced well documented local political party activity over the past 50 years, beginning with the Civic Action League which ran candidates in the 1954 election.[43] The League and its offshoot, the Committee for Pubic Morality, had forced a judicial inquiry into allegations of corruption in city government. One of the investigators for the inquiry was a young lawyer named Jean Drapeau. He became the League's successful candidate for mayor in 1954. When Drapeau was defeated in 1957, he formed a new political party – the Civic Party – and attracted to it most of the city councillors who had run for the Civic Action League. It was as head of his very disciplined new party that he returned to power as mayor in 1960, a position that he was to hold until his retirement prior to the 1986 election.

The continued success of the Civic Party led to an increase in citizen participation in local affairs in Montreal – not through the party, but as a reaction against the autocratic governing style of Drapeau, who concentred power in his office and in the executive committee that he appointed and controlled. Potentially strong opposition to Drapeau first surfaced in 1970 in the form of the Front d'action politique (FRAP), which was a grouping of trade unions and left wing nationalist organizations.[44] Whatever prospects this organization had were dashed by the FLQ kidnapping crisis of October 1970 and Drapeau's success in linking FRAP with the outlawed terrorist group and in capitalizing on the public's desire for stability and security.

By 1974 the growing opposition forces, including former FRAP supporters, had come together to form the Montreal Citizens' Movement (MCM), which made a surprising showing in the elections that November. Drapeau received only 55.1% of the popular vote – almost a rebuff in relation to his past results – and his Civic Party was reduced to 36 seats on council, with the MCM winning 18 and a group

---

[42] The preceding discussion is based on William Brown, "Party time," *Forum*, May/June 2001, Ottawa, Federation of Canadian Municipalities, p. 27.

[43] Sancton, in Magnusson and Sancton, *City Politics in Canada*, pp. 69-78, provides the basis for much of the discussion of developments in Montreal.

[44] *Ibid.*, p. 73.

called Democracy Montreal winning 1 seat. Internal divisions badly weakened the MCM over the next few years, however, and its new more socialist policy orientation also alienated the newly elected provincial government of the Parti Québécois, which, in any event, was not anxious to tangle with Drapeau and was quite prepared to stay out of city politics if the mayor would keep his influential voice out of the sovereignty-association debate. A new party, the Municipal Action Group (largely formed from the former moderate element within the MCM) emerged in time for the 1978 election, but Drapeau was easily reelected and his Civic Party won 52 of the 54 seats on council.[45]

Not until 1986 would the MCM gain power in Montreal, but its years in opposition had a positive impact on how the city operated and the kinds of decisions it made. With respect to the latter, it has been written that "the MCM, along with vocal community groups, can also share credit for improving the face of Montreal over the past decade: housing renovations have replaced rampant demolitions that scarred central city neighbourhoods in the 1970s. Beautification programs have transformed nondescript areas into well-lit back lanes and mini-parks. Bicycle paths and pedestrian malls line city streets where cars once dominated."[46]

According to Milner, the resurrection of the MCM in the early 1980s was largely due to its new leader, Jean Doré. While Drapeau was returned in 1982 and his Civic Party captured 39 of the 57 council seats, popular support was down – almost 18% less with respect to Drapeau. The 1986 election (which followed Drapeau's retirement) saw a massive victory for the MCM, with only one Civic Party councillor and two independents elected to council. In Milner's view, the Doré-led MCM "appeared reasonable and approachable, especially when contrasted with Drapeau's Gaullist style; its hammering at everyday bread and butter issues corresponded more closely to the emerging public mood than Drapeau's seeming preoccupation with grand projects."[47]

---

[45] Ibid., p. 76.

[46] Ingrid Peritz, "MCM Losing Radical Tinge After 10 Years at City Hall," Montreal Gazette, October 13, 1984, quoted in Tim Thomas, "When "They" is "We:" Movements, Municipal Parties, and Participatory Politics," in Lightbody, Canadian Metropolitics, p. 124.

[47] Henry Milner, "The Montreal Citizens' Movement: Then and Now," Quebec Studies, No. 6, 1988, p. 5.

In contrast to the autocratic, secretive style long followed by Drapeau, the new administration was characterized by a cautious and consensual approach. Consultation was the watchword. According to Hamel,[48] the new administration used three complementary mechanisms to implement its consultation objectives.

1. The establishment of five standing committees to study matters, hold public meetings, and make recommendations to council;

2. The creation of district advisory committees (DACS) for nine planning areas into which the city was divided. These committees were comprised of the councillors representing the electoral wards within each district. They held statutory monthly meetings to discuss public services and especially planning issues, to receive views and requests from citizens, and to make recommendations to council; and

3. The establishment of the Bureau de consultation de Montréal (BCM), an independent municipal organization that called upon senior staff to conduct public hearings on particular projects, and then to forward recommendations to the executive committee of city council.

In spite of these positive initiatives, it wasn't long before the grassroots nature of the MCM began to weaken. Developers and business people were not long in courting the new administration and party activists soon found little scope for their activities. Their best leaders had become city councillors or political advisors. Actions taken by the MCM in office increasingly alienated its traditional supporters.[49] During the Overdale controversy, the MCM sided with developers and investors against tenants and community groups of the Overdale housing complex, which was demolished to make way for luxury condos. It managed to upset both environmentalists and pacifists by allowing the Matrox company to cut down the last stand of black maples on the island of Montreal to expand its parking lot,

---

[48] Pierre Hamel, "Urban Issues and New Public Policy Challenges: The Example of Public Consultation Policy in Montreal," in Caroline Andrew, Katherine A. Graham, and Susan D. Phillips (eds.), *Urban Affairs, Back on the Policy Agenda*, Kingston, McGill-Queen's University Press, 2002, pp. 228-229.

[49] Timothy L. Thomas, "Political Representation and Community Politics," in Thomas, *The Politics of the City*, p. 214.

just after the company had signed a military contract with the United States government. Moreover, when some of the MCM members began to voice their concern over the actions being taken, rules were tightened up to enforce caucus confidentiality – the sort of muzzling action expected of old-line parties, not the MCM.

Four MCM councillors defected before the first term was up. They complained of overwhelming pressure to follow the party line and the silencing of debate within the party. The MCM dissidents set up their own party, the Democratic Coalition of Montreal (DCM), which they claimed was closer to the original ideals of the MCM.[50] The MCM held on to power in 1990, but in the 1994 election it was reduced to six seats and Doré was defeated for the mayoralty. Pierre Bourque was elected mayor, and the Vision Montreal party that he headed captured 38 other seats on city council.

Bourque's first term of office was marked by considerable controversy. Numerous charges of violation of municipal party financing rules were laid against the Vision Montreal party, and several convictions resulted. Some 15 councillors defected from the party, and in early 1997 Bourque faced a caucus revolt when he attempted to dismiss two members of the executive committee – an action subsequently ruled beyond his powers by the courts. There was also much criticism of Bourque's efforts to dismantle the public consultation machinery established by Doré and his return to the autocratic governing style that had been associated with Drapeau. The independent Bureau (BCM) was abolished, the DACS were replaced with 16 district councils that had a more limited mandate, and the responsibilities of the city's five standing committees were redistributed between two new committees.[51] In spite of these developments, Bourque and the Vision Party captured the same number of seats in the 1998 election. Doré did run again for mayor, but finished a humiliating fourth.

There was no "third time lucky" for Bourque, however. He was defeated in 2001 in the first election of the newly amalgamated city of Montreal – rejected, in large part, by suburban voters opposed to the amalgamation and angry with Bourque for championing the merger so strongly. Victorious was Gérald Tremblay, who had merged his original United Island of Montreal party with the MCM to form

---

[50] Karen Herland, *People, Potholes and City Politics*, Montreal, Black Rose Books, 1992, p. 14.

[51] Hamel, "Public Consultation Policy in Montreal," p. 233.

the Montreal Island Citizens Union. While Tremblay supported the amalgamation, his platform called for decentralization and a promise to delegate responsibilities to the boroughs being set up in the new city[52] and he was clearly seen as the lesser of two evils. Keeping his new party together will be a major challenge for Tremblay, even without the amalgamation issue. His Montreal Island Citizens Union has been described as "one very big tent: under it are people from the centre-right to the centre-left, suburbanites and city people, merger fans and de-merger advocates, and anglophones, francophones and allophones. It is the most heterogeneous Montreal party in memory, and by far."[53]

Local Parties Outside Quebec

The challenge of keeping local political parties together for any period of time is evident from the following summary of experiences in municipalities outside of Quebec. We begin with Toronto and then examine the experiences of two Western Canadian cities, Winnipeg and Vancouver. An attempt is then made to summarize some insights from this survey of political activity.

Toronto

Public resistance to efforts by national and provincial political parties to move into the municipal sphere was demonstrated by the 1969 municipal election results in Toronto. The Liberal party, fresh from its 1968 national election victory under Pierre Trudeau, was interested in establishing a stronger base in Toronto, partly as a necessary prerequisite to the overthrow of the long entrenched Progressive Conservative provincial government. The decision to enter a slate of candidates for municipal office was hotly debated, however, and the internal split in the party on this issue resulted in a less than wholehearted effort in the ensuing election.[54] Whatever the reasons, the election results were not encouraging for the national parties. The Liberal party's candidate for

---

[52] "Mega win for Tremblay," Editorial, *Montreal Gazette*, November 5, 2001.

[53] Henry Aubin, "Suburbs win big," *Montreal Gazette*, November 5, 2001.

[54] For an examination of this election campaign by one of the key participants, see Stephen Clarkson, *City Lib*, Toronto, Hakkert, 1972. See also the exchange of views between Clarkson and J. L. Granatstein in Jack K. Masson and James Anderson (eds.), *Emerging Party Politics in Urban Canada*, Toronto, McClelland and Stewart, 1972, pp. 60-67.

mayor, Stephen Clarkson, finished third with fewer than half as many votes as the victorious William Dennison. Significantly, Dennison had refused to run as an NDP candidate even though he was closely associated with that party. Only three candidates of the NDP and two of the Liberal candidates were elected to council.[55]

The 1969 election was also significant in demonstrating the influence of the citizens' movement of that era. It helped to elect a minority of reform candidates to council, and they were quite effective in defining their issues and concerns. The next election, in 1972, saw a dramatic breakthrough, with the election of a majority of reformers to council and a self-proclaimed member of the reform group – in the person of David Crombie – to the mayor's position.

Once elected, however, Crombie operated as a moderate and, in fact, voted against the reform councillors on many of the major issues facing council.[56] While he was genuinely concerned about the threat to neighbourhoods posed by the excessively pro-growth mentality of previous councils, Crombie was no less committed to private property and private enterprise. Rather, he wanted to find a way of providing continued development without the disruption and dislocation that had accompanied it in the recent past.[57] The Crombie-led council was not radical enough for some and the reform majority soon splintered (as discussed below). But it did establish for the first time a concept that is now taken for granted as common sense – that major development decisions are a legitimate matter of public concern, to be made only after extensive consultation and debate.

The reform group that had appeared to capture control of council in 1972 soon split into moderates and more militant reformers, with the latter becoming increasingly critical of Crombie's moderate policies. Ironically, while reform councillors continued to be elected throughout the 1970s, one of them, Michael Goldrick, persuasively argues that the election of 1972 was not the beginning but "the zenith of the reform movement." As he explains, the moderates were satisfied that the reform movement would ensure that neighbourhoods were protected, the automobile would be treated with common sense, and

[55] Donald J. H. Higgins, *Urban Canada: Its Government and Politics*, Toronto, Macmillan, 1977, p. 239.

[56] Jon Caufield, *The Tiny Perfect Mayor*, Toronto, James Lorimer and Company, 1974.

[57] Magnusson, in Magnusson and Sancton, *City Politics in Canada*, p. 119.

the style of development would be modified – all objectives of the middle class. But for the hard line reformers elected from working-class wards, the real objective was to redistribute wealth and power.

> They wanted real, not token, decision-making power shifted to neighbourhoods, not only the style of development controlled but its pace, location and ownership subject to public decision; they challenged private property rights exercised by financial institutions and development corporations and attacked the fortresses of civil service power. [58]

After the 1974 election, six of the more radical reformers established the "reform caucus," a disciplined group that attempted to develop alternative policies to those proposed by the moderates and the "old guard." While it was successful in expressing the interests of working class people, the reform caucus suffered from a negative, obstructionist image in the eyes of the media and from internal differences, partly based on personality conflicts. A key figure was John Sewell, undoubtedly the most conspicuous and widely identified member of the reform group, and a community activist who had been earlier associated with a number of the citizen confrontations with city hall.[59] Sewell was a very independent-minded politician and, while he had made some unsuccessful attempts to build a reform party around himself, when he ran for mayor in 1978 it was as an independent.[60] After one very controversial term, especially in relation to Sewell's defence of various inner city minorities and his demands for police re-form, he was defeated by Arthur Eggleton, a Liberal with strong ties to the business community. Eggleton was elected throughout the 1980s.

In the meantime, however, reform councillors continued to be voted on council, although increasingly identified with the NDP. By 1980 they had 9 of the 23 seats on council, with all but one of the victorious candidates having run with official party endorsement.[61] But the economic decline in the early 1980s prompted councils to adopt an increasingly pro-growth stance during this decade. An inevitable back-lash occurred in the 1988 election, which saw the voters defeat two

[58] Michael Goldrick, "The Anatomy of Urban Reform in Toronto," *City Magazine*, May-June 1978, p. 36.

[59] For his personal reflections on these experiences, see John Sewell, *Up Against City Hall*, Toronto, James Lewis and Samuel, 1972.

[60] Magnusson, in Magnusson and Sancton, *City Politics in Canada*, p. 123.

[61] *Ibid.*, p. 122.

pro-development aldermen, vote in a majority of designated reform candidates, and choose reform candidates to fill six of the eight city positions on the Metropolitan Toronto council.[62] More specifically, nine of the 17 members of the Toronto city council were considered to be members of the reform group, of which six were NDP members. One of the nine was acclaimed to office, but all others were endorsed by Reform Toronto, a citizens' coalition that was opposed to the pro-development old guard at city hall.

Another economic decline at the beginning of the 1990s influenced the election results in 1991, which saw a former chief commissioner of police and former councillor, June Rowlands, elected mayor over Jack Layton of the NDP (now the leader of this party on the national level). The deteriorating economic conditions clearly favoured the conservative, pro-development, and "law and order" plat-form of Rowlands, while Layton also had to contend with growing voter uncertainty about their wisdom in electing an NDP provincial government the previous year. But there was little change in the make-up of council itself; all incumbents who ran were reelected, along with three new councillors. The council remained split with six NDP mem-bers, two moderate or swing councillors, and eight right wingers.[63] The six NDP councillors were reelected in 1994, and an NDP candi-date, Barbara Hall, was elected mayor over June Rowlands. But the city had still not recovered from the severe recession of the early 1990s, leaving the council little room for manoeuvre.

By the next election, in 1997, Metropolitan Toronto and all of its constituent municipalities had been amalgamated to create a new city of Toronto. With the much larger city council needed to represent the 2.5 million people in this greatly enlarged municipality, the limited focus provided by political parties became more diffuse – even as, arguably, the need for the kind of cohesion that parties can provide became that much more pressing. In that 1997 election, Barbara Hall was defeated by North York's long time mayor, Mel Lastman, who is "nominally conservative"[64] and pro-business in orientation. As for the

---

[62] Michael Valpy, "Voters Demonstrate Power of Ballot Box," *Globe and Mail*, November 16, 1988.

[63] This at least was the assessment by Kent Gerecke shortly after the election, in "City Beat," *City Magazine*, Winter '91/'92, p. 5.

[64] This apt description was used by Colin Vaughan, "Bright spots on council hard to find." *Toronto Star*. November 9. 1998.

56 members of the new council, they had as many differences as there are flavours of canned soup. A dozen or so members roughly fit the label of NDPers, and there were another 6 to 10 councillors who voted with them, depending on the issue. There was also another group of perhaps 20 to 25 councillors who coalesced around Lastman.[65]

Instead of traditional left wing and right wing clashes, the new council tended to split more along geographic lines, notably with respect to such matters as property tax reform, transportation, and programs for the homeless. While some welcomed the apparent reduction of ideological clashes, the new council lacked a clear identity or any clear sense of purpose. It was characterized as "a debating society with 56 contesting opinions."[66]

The election in 2000 was for a slightly smaller council (44 members, plus the mayor), but the result was similar in terms of a diverse make-up of members. According to James, Toronto's council has at least five distinct groups: "the hard right wingers, neo-conservatives really; the mushy middle, center right councillors who usually carry the vote; the NDPers unabashed lefties; left wingers who don't want to be tarred as NDPers; and the lost souls whose votes are likely for sale in return for political favours or power."[67]

Winnipeg

Local political activity in Winnipeg received a great stimulus in 1919, when the General Strike of that year polarized the city. A Civic Election Committee was formed by downtown businesses to endorse, and raise funds for, anti-labour candidates. Until the end of the 1980s, this organization, later known as the Metropolitan Election Committee, the Greater Winnipeg Election Committee, and, finally, the Independent Citizen Election Committee (ICEC), continued to elect a majority of the members of council against the efforts of the Independent Labour Party, the CCF, and, most recently, the NDP. While essentially a pro-business local political party, the ICEC insisted that it was not a party at all and that support for its candidates would

---

[65] See Bruce Demara, "New united council a 'soup' of 57 varieties," *Toronto Star*, May 16,1998, on which this discussion is based.

[66] Colin Vaughan, "Time for council to shape up," *Toronto Star*, June 8, 1998.

[67] Royson James, "Factionalism in full bloom at budget time," *Toronto Star*, April 30, 2001.

prevent parties – especially socialist parties – from bringing their politics and policies into the municipal council chamber. As a result, the ICEC was able to avoid accepting the responsibility for leadership in spite of its dominant numerical position within Winnipeg council over the decades.

As discussed in Chapter 4, a radically new form of municipal government was introduced in Winnipeg in 1972. In the view of Thomas, the new Unicity structure was an attempt to weaken the alliance between public officials and land-based business by promoting citizen involvement and placing "other political actors representing neighbourhoods, broader communities, ethno-cultural groups, non-profits and advocacy groups on a more equal footing with the business interests."[68] The anticipated increase in citizen participation did not fully materialize, however, in part because the centre right candidates of the ICEC dominated the new Unicity council and entrenched a pro-development regime in Winnipeg, one with little sympathy for the consultative mechanisms that had been created.[69]

By the 1980 election, however, ICEC's veneer of nonpartisanship had worn quite thin, and the NDP scored a breakthrough by capturing 7 seats on the Unicity council, with another 9 going to independent candidates and the remaining 12 to ICEC candidates. Shortly before the 1983 election, the ICEC announced that it was disbanding. One analyst interpreted this step as a clever ploy rather than a sign of collapse. It removed from the scene a name associated with the past council's record, it put off the need for a consensus among the traditional ICEC candidates until after the election, and it avoided the need to provide an alternative to the NDP program.[70]

Whatever the motives underlying the dissolution of the ICEC, the election results were quite disappointing for the NDP. They lost one of their seven seats, and nearly lost two others. The local party was undoubtedly hurt by the controversial attempt by the NDP provincial government of Howard Pawley to entrench French as an official language in Manitoba, especially after this became a local referendum issue. In addition, however, the local party was hurt by its

---

[68] Paul Thomas, "Diagnosing the Health of Civic Democracy: 25 Years of Citizen Involvement With City Hall," in Klos, *The State of Unicity*, p. 47.

[69] Greg Selinger, "Urban Governance for the Twenty-First Century: What the Unicity Experience Tells Us," in Klos, *The State of Unicity*, p. 89.

[70] David Hall, "Twisted Tale of Intentions," *City Magazine*, April 1984, p. 14.

own internal divisions between "old guard" members and newer, more progressive members.

The NDP presence on council was reduced even further, to just two members, in the 1986 municipal election. The other 27 members elected were all independents, although the majority of them represented the now-disbanded ICEC. Indeed, one assessment identified 20 of these 27 "independents" as actively involved with the Progressive Conservative or Liberal parties,[71] continuing the domination of the ICEC type of candidate. According to one observer,[72] the provincial NDP again contributed to the poor showing of the local NDP, this time much more directly. He claimed that the provincial party created confusion for the local party by overruling its decisions, deciding for the local party that it would not run a candidate for mayor, and redirecting key party workers to the elections in Saskatchewan and British Columbia, thereby weakening the local campaign.

In 1989 a reform coalition composed of New Democrats and Liberals was formed under the hopeful name of WIN (Winnipeg into the Nineties).[73] It succeeded in electing members to one-third of the seats on council, establishing for the first time a cohesive reform block on Winnipeg city council. The response to this "threat" by the Conservative provincial government elected in 1990 was to abolish the right of political parties to make contributions to candidates running for city council, while authorizing donations from corporations and unions, actions which have been described as leading to the corporatization of civic government.[74]

In the 1992 election, WIN candidates retained their minority position, holding 5 seats on a council reduced from 21 to 15. But one commentator contends that Winnipeg's long-standing schism disappeared in 1992 when the city council was slashed to 15 and civic politics became a full-time job. "The demands on councillors in the new environment pretty well drove off the last of the bright lights on

---

[71] This is the assessment of Jeff Lowe, "Winnipeg: User-Unfriendly," *City Magazine*, Spring 1988, p. 9.

[72] Kent Gerecke, "Winnipeg Hits Bottom," *City Magazine*, Winter 1986/87, p. 35.

[73] Barton Reid, "City Beat," *City Magazine*, Winter '92/'93, p. 5.

[74] Selinger, "What the Unicity Experience Tells Us," p. 95.

the right and left, who no longer could pursue civic politics as a hobby."[75] WIN had disappeared by the time of the 1998 election. Former WIN member, Glen Murray, was elected mayor as an independent candidate, a position that he continues to hold. All member of council also sit as independents.[76]

Vancouver

As with Winnipeg, it was the threat of political gains by the left that led to the establishment of a pro-business party in Vancouver. The year was 1936, and three CCF candidates[77] were elected in the city's first at large municipal election. In response, business interests founded the Non-Partisan Association, its very name designed to conceal its real status as a local political party. By the 1960s, concern about the pace and location of developments, and especially about urban renewal and expressway projects, brought increased opposition to the NPA and led in 1968 to the formation of two new political parties to challenge its vision of the city

The first of these new parties was TEAM (The Electors Action Movement), a diverse coalition of reformers, especially anti-expressway forces, more conservative business interests, community workers, and academics. The second party, the Committee of Progressive Electors (COPE), was formed by the Vancouver and District Labour Council, with the objective of bringing together labour, ratepayer groups, the NDP, and other interested groups to establish a base to enter municipal politics.

An important breakthrough appeared to occur in 1972 with the defeat of the NPA and the election of a municipal council controlled by TEAM. It made some noteworthy changes including restructuring the bureaucracy, replacing the commissioner system with a single city manager with reduced executive powers, and making some moves to open up city hall to public involvement.[78] Leo concedes that TEAM was a liberal, establishment party, focused on middle-class issues, with only a limited concern for matters like "affordable

---

[75] G. Flood, "Civic Fight Sputters," *Winnipeg Free Press*, September 21, 1997.

[76] Brown, "Party time," p. 27.

[77] The CCF, forerunner of the NDP, was the Cooperative Commonwealth Federation.

[78] Gutstein, in Magnusson and Sancton, *City Politics in Canada*, pp. 206-209.

housing, inner-city education, homelessness, racism, and women's issues."[79] But he contends that TEAM made a valuable contribution by shifting attention from a conservative, development-oriented approach to city planning to one that addressed issues of "livability."[80] Whatever its accomplishments, within four years TEAM was badly divided and in the 1978 election the NPA reemerged as the major party on council.

Control of Vancouver council by the NPA faced new challenges in 1980 when Mike Harcourt, a New Democrat, won the mayoralty and COPE elected three councillors. But the left was still in a minority on council and discussions were often bitter, with members of the NPA, TEAM, and COPE increasingly polarized. In addition to this constraint on the mayor's activity, the Social Credit provincial government continued to protect business interests and obviously had concerns about the election of an NDP mayor.

Harcourt was returned as mayor in 1982, along with four COPE councillors and two independent NDP councillors. Gutstein refers to this election result as the "first successful challenge to business dominance at the local level in the city's 96 year history."[81] However, there were some difficulties in maintaining a progressive voting bloc on council, and continuing problems with interference from the Social Credit provincial government. Indeed, one book during this period expressed concern that local autonomy was being threatened by the neo-conservative forces in power provincially and their view that local authorities should not be allowed to follow policies contrary to the market-oriented revival being promoted provincially.[82] A similar pattern, even more pronounced, was also evident in British local government during this period, as Margaret Thatcher imposed her view of the appropriate scope of government activity on resistant labour-controlled municipal councils. This same pattern would also become apparent in Ontario in the second half of the 1990s, with the provincial Conservative party attempting to rein in what it regarded as

---

[79] Christopher Leo, "The Urban Economy and the Power of the Local State," in Frisken, *The Changing Canadian Metropolis*, Vol. 2, p. 690.

[80] *Ibid.*, pp. 690-691.

[81] Donald Gutstein, "Vancouver: Progressive Majority Impotent," *City Magazine*, Winnipeg, Spring 1983, p. 12.

[82] Warren Magnusson, William K. Carroll, Charles Doyle, Monika Langer, and R. B. J. Walker, (eds.), *The New Reality: The Politics of Restraint in British Columbia*. Vancouver. NewStar Books. 1984.

excessive spending by school boards and municipalities. As discussed earlier, the Ontario government forced major amalgamations on both, took over the setting of the educational tax rate, and imposed ceilings on municipal property tax increases.

On the surface, the 1984 election results were quite similar to those of 1982. Harcourt was reelected mayor, along with five progressive members – four of them from COPE. Opposing them were three members from the NPA and two from TEAM. According to Gutstein,[83] the polarization of the city was complete with this election. As he saw it, Vancouver is really two cities: a working class east side city and a middle class west side city – which elect two entirely different councils.

The 1986 election results were quite dramatic, bringing Vancouver's developers back into power at its city hall. The NPA captured 9 of the 11 seats on council – including its mayoral candidate, developer Gordon Campbell (now Premier of the province) – and 8 of 9 seats on the school board. According to Gutstein,[84] Campbell was successful in attracting the moderate voters in spite of his right wing, pro-development record, especially when the alternative was Harry Rankin of COPE, a long time socialist councillor who was seen by many as quite radical.

Campbell easily won reelection in 1988 and 1990, although COPE managed to increase its representation on council from three to five. The 1993 election was a near sweep for the NPA, with COPE winning only one seat. In an ironic twist of fate, the right wing city council found itself having to contend with an NDP provincial government led by Mike Harcourt – much as Harcourt, when head of a left-leaning council a decade earlier, had to contend with interference from the Social Credit provincial government.

Domination by the NPA continued throughout the rest of the 1990s, with the party winning all the seats on the council and school board in 1996 and 1999. Just when it seemed that COPE was finished, it came roaring back in the 2002 election, electing 8 out of 10 city councillors, 7 of 9 school trustees, and 5 of 7 members of the parks board. Also successful was its candidate for mayor, Larry Campbell, former RCMP officer and city coroner (who inspired the CBC

---

[83] Donald Gutstein, "Civic Election Wars," *City Magazine*, Summer 1985, p. 12.

[84] Donald Gutstein, "Vancouver Voters Swing Right," *City Magazine*, Winter 1986-87, p. 30. The brief outline that follows is based on the Gutstein article.

television show *Da Vinci's Inquest*). To at least some extent, COPE's victory was seen as a rejection of the cost-cutting actions that had been taken by the right wing Liberal government, headed by former Vancouver mayor Gordon Campbell, elected provincially in May of 2001. Once again, contrasting ideologies set the stage for potential strife between the city and the province.

Effectiveness of Local Parties

Efforts to establish local political parties that would gain power and implement progressive agendas that feature extensive public consultation have had very limited success in Canada. For one thing, we cannot assume that the local parties that gain power will necessarily be supportive of increased public consultation and involvement in decision making. That was not the case, for example, of the Civic Party in Montreal during Jean Drapeau's long tenure, nor was it particularly apparent in the actions of the Vision Party under Pierre Bourque in the 1990s.

Second, even when reform parties do gain power, they tend to moderate their position and objectives once in office. As Lorimer has stated, "the thrust for democratic reforms has been blunted by citizen-oriented politicians once in office. They are inclined to take their own election as an indication that the present political system can work reasonably well...."[85] This pattern was noted with respect to the experience of Toronto's city council after the election of reformers in 1972 and with the MCM's move toward the centre in Montreal. Milner's assessment of what happened to the MCM bears repeating:

> The syndrome is a classic one: the reformist movement takes power and effectively moves toward the centre of the spectrum, attempting to rule in the name of the electorate as a whole, not merely the party activists, who find their activities largely confined to vindicating such limited actions, raising money and recruiting new members. And with no opposition left in City Hall, the external enemy is gone: there's no one, out there, to fight.[86]

Third, the experiences outlined above demonstrate that outside factors can severely restrict the actions that progressive local parties may wish to take. Particularly noticeable has been the impact of

---

[85] James Lorimer, "Introduction: The Post-developer Era for Canada's Cities Begins," *City Magazine Annual 1981*, Vol. V, No. 1, p. 9.

[86] Milner, "Montreal Citizens' Movement," p. 8.

prevailing economic conditions. Boom times tend to bring out the excesses of unbridled growth and propel reform groups to power. But if those groups then find themselves governing during an economic slump, they have little choice but to temper the anti-growth posture that may have spurred their election. Such features as extended local consultations and strong environmental policies become something of a luxury when generating local jobs and shoring up the local assessment base claim centre stage. Thus it was, for example, that a provision in Toronto's Cityplan 1991 that new development *must conform* to environmental standards became – during that recessionary period – a proposal to *encourage* development to meet environmental objectives.[87]

Another example of an external constraint is the political party in power at the provincial level. While it was, ironically, a provincial NDP government that caused problems for local NDP candidates in Winnipeg in two instances cited above, conflict is more likely to arise when the party in power provincially has a different ideological bent than members of local councils. This pattern was noted above with respect to Toronto, Vancouver, and Winnipeg.

Direct Democracy Participation

Even more direct – although not necessarily more beneficial – ways of participating in the affairs of government are possible through such tools as the referendum and the recall. These features of what is usually termed direct democracy have received renewed attention over the past couple of decades, partly because of the national success of the Reform (now Alliance) political party. For greater precision, Quesnel distinguishes four tools of direct democracy, as outlined below.[88]

Table 9.1 Tools of Direct Democracy	
Recall	A vote by citizens to determine if an elected representative will be removed from office before the next scheduled election.
Initiative	The right of citizens to propose a project or action, which a municipality must act upon or submit to a vote (referendum).
Petition	Used to gather signatures in support of some local position.
Referendum	Vote by the electors on a given question.

---

[87] Edmund P. Fowler, "Decision Time for Cityplan '91," *City Magazine*, Winter '93, pp. 10-11.

[88] Quesnel, *Public Consultation*, p. 26.

She also distinguishes three categories of referendum: (1) those mandated by provincial legislation, (2) those held at the discretion of the municipality, and (3) those requested by local citizens via the process of initiative and petition.[89]

There are strongly divided opinions on how referendums affect public involvement and democracy. Among the arguments advanced in favour of referendums are the following:[90]

> Decisions are more legitimate because they reflect the will of the people.
> Decisions are more democratic because they provide a direct link between citizens and their government.
> During the period leading up to the vote, the municipality and the public engage in a thorough, informed debate on the issue.
> The process gets citizens more involved in their community and enhances their citizenship.

In countries such as Switzerland and the United States, where direct democracy is a common feature, however, voter turnout is disappointingly low. It has averaged only 35% for referendums and initiatives in Switzerland in recent years.[91] American studies indicate that referendums have little drawing power in getting voters out when held in conjunction with elections and even lower voting turnout when they are held separately. There are also concerns that the efforts required to get enough signatures to place a question on the ballot leads to domination by large special interest groups with the resources for the task. Indeed, there are businesses that specialize in gathering signatures, which are often obtained in exchange for payment, and a 1988 decision of the Supreme Court of the United States recognized the principle of what has been termed "cash and carry democracy."[92] These practices seem rather far removed from the notion that referendums somehow transfer power to ordinary citizens.

---

[89] *Ibid.*, p. 27.

[90] *Ibid.*, pp. 29-30.

[91] Mark Charlton, "The Limits of Direct Democracy," in Mark Charlton and Paul Barker (eds.), *Crosscurrents: Contemporary Political Issues*, 3rd Edition, Toronto, Nelson, 1998, p. 416.

[92] Quesnel, *Public Consultation*, pp. 56-57.

It is further held that complex issues cannot be reduced to a simple yes or no vote and that shortsighted and ill-considered decisions will result. The famous or infamous Proposition 13 is often cited in this regard. Passed in California in 1968, it capped property taxes and required a two-thirds local referendum to raise taxes. However welcome these measures seemed initially, they led to severe fiscal and servicing difficulties. This is because the result of Proposition 13 was to give control to one-third of the population plus one, no matter how great the public need.

Another argument against the referendum is that it does not promote consensus building.[93] If the object of democracy is persuasion rather than submission, the referendum is an unsuitable tool because it does not unite citizens behind a common project; instead, the minority must submit to the will of the majority without any follow up discussion.

Many Canadian provinces authorize councils to consult the public directly through referendums, and Quesnel provides a good summary of the varied legislative provisions relating to such consultations, which deal mainly with issues of zoning and municipal borrowing and bond issues.[94] She also examines the referendum experience of three Canadian cities and finds that referendum proposals have been approved by the public in a majority of cases – 70% of the proposals in Vancouver, 65.5% in Toronto, and 61.3% in Winnipeg.[95]

The specific requirements relating to referendums, however, can present quite a challenge to their use. For example, Alberta legislation appears to give the public significant power by providing that council by-laws authorizing long term debt must be published in the local newspaper and that such by-laws must be submitted to the public for approval if a petition is filed within the specified time demanding such a step.[96] But this legislation requires that at least 10% of the population sign such a position (up from the 5% minimum that used to apply) and that all signatures be collected within 60 days. The

---

[93] *Ibid.*, p. 31.

[94] *Ibid.*, pp. 33-49.

[95] *Ibid.*, p. 71.

[96] Jack Masson and Edward C. LeSage Jr., *Alberta's Local Governments, Politics and Democracy*, Edmonton, University of Alberta Press, 1994, p. 302.

difficulties that these requirements present in large urban areas is evident from the fact that in Edmonton or Calgary sponsors of a petition would need to collect 65 000 valid signatures, an average of more than 1000 a day within the two month time limit.[97] In this regard, it is interesting to note that the much-heralded new community charter legislation in British Columbia has raised from 5% to 10% of those on the voters roll the number of signatures required for a petition in that province that would compel a council to submit a decision, usually a capital spending decision, to a referendum.[98]

To take one more example, Ontario passed legislation in April 2000 extending the use of municipal referendums. Under this legislation, municipalities are authorized to submit a referendum question to their local electorate, the results of such a referendum are binding if there is a voting turnout of 50% of eligible voters and if 50% plus one of those voting answer yes to the question, and councils are required to act in a timely manner with respect to any such yes vote. If the voters reject the referendum question, then council cannot put that question to a vote again until after the next municipal election. Among the concerns about this legislation are the following:

> The province must approve any questions that are to be asked in a referendum and has excluded any questions on subjects that are prescribed as matters of provincial interest. One such excluded subject is gambling casinos, which is obviously a matter of the greatest local interest.

> Councils are not allowed to spend any money to support their position on a question.

> There is no way for citizens to petition or otherwise initiate a referendum; the use of this tool is solely at the discretion of council.

> Requiring a voting turnout of 50% of eligible voters makes it likely that very few referendums will receive sufficient public participation to be valid.

André Carrel believes that "the referendum can play an important and legitimate role in a democracy *if* it is a tool in the hands

---

[97] Graham et al., *Urban Governance in Canada*, p. 116.

[98] Robert L. Bish, "The Draft Community Charter: Comments," a paper prepared for the Workshop on the Community Charter, University of Victoria, June 14, 2002, p. 3.

of citizens, not a toy of the governing elite."[99] But holding an occasional referendum will accomplish little in the absence of other changes. The real value of the referendum is when it is provided as part of a series of changes that demonstrate a commitment to openness, consultation, and public participation on the part of the council and staff of a municipality. In Carrel's colourful words, "a referendum thrown to an angry and frustrated citizenry, like a bone to a hungry dog, is not a democratic act."[100] Carrel doesn't view referendum outcomes as a victory by citizens over council or of council over its citizens. Instead, he suggests that "the decisions are realignments of the fence within which council roams freely."[101]

Carrel speaks from experience, having been the administrator of Rossland, a small city in British Columbia which, since 1990 has pursued an exciting exercise of direct democracy.

Box 9.3 Direct Democracy in Rossland

Concerned about the growing rift between citizens and their governments in the aftermath of the collapse of the Meech Lake Accord, the councillors of Rossland and their city administrator searched for new approaches that would allow members of the community to exercise more control over their own affairs. The result was a paper entitled "A Constitution for Local Government," which gave local citizens three avenues to participate more directly in the city government. First, there would have to be a referendum for any change to be made to the new constitution by-law of Rossland. Second, either council or the citizens (providing that 20% of them signed a petition) could subject a council decision to public confirmation by initiating a referendum within 30 days after the third reading of a by-law. Third, members of the community (again with 20% backing) could initiate a referendum to force council to act on an issue.

The most important aspect of the Rossland approach is not the number of referendums (only a baker's dozen over the first decade) or their outcome, but the changed atmosphere in the community. Instead of just complaining about council action or inaction, more people began discussing policy issues. Because they had been given some say in municipal decisions, they felt a greater responsibility to be informed and to exercise their new power thoughtfully. They were also gaining a sense of ownership of city policy.

---

[99] André Carrel, "Government: Its Legitimacy, Efficacy and Relationship to Citizens," presentation to Capilano College, January 1998, p. 7.

[100] André Carrel, "Municipal Government Leadership," presentation to Capilano College, March 14, 1997, p. 6.

[101] Carrel, *Citizens' Hall*, p. 46. This highly readable book is something of a combined autobiography, philosophical treatise, and passionate defence of local democracy.

As one component of a wide range of initiatives focused on increasing public consultation and involvement in municipal government, a judicious and limited use of referendums may have a role. But unless those wider initiatives are in place, it is likely that many – if not most – of those who vote in a referendum may do so without having engaged in prior discussion and debate that would inform their decision. In the absence of such debate, individuals will understandably evaluate a referendum issue in terms of its impact on them personally. That impact is most visibly measured in the effect on property taxes, so projects are judged primarily on their fiscal effects. This means that instead of being evaluated on the basis of the common good or the greatest good for all, the matters of public policy addressed in the referendum questions are considered in light of the greatest individual good. The result is that referendums become "an instrument by which the disadvantaged are excluded and the privileges of the affluent are protected."[102]

Participation as a Consumer

In recent years yet another form of public participation has come to the fore, in the notion of the local citizen as customer or client, interacting with the municipality as supplier of goods and services. This emphasis has arisen in connection with a number of changes that have been advocated for government under the heading of the new public management (NPM), the key features of which were outlined in the previous chapter. As a result of these changes, civic involvement is now seen in terms of consumer processes, and strengthening the rights of citizens is equated with opening up public services to market forces.[103] According to this view, given some choice among alternative service providers and provided with more information about standards of service and opportunities for complaint and redress, citizens can become active consumers instead of passive recipients of services.

---

[102] Quesnel, *Public Consultation*, p. 56.

[103] Vivien Lowndes, "Citizenship and Urban Politics," in David Judge, Gerry Stoker, and Harold Wolman, *Theories of Urban Politics*, London, Sage Publications, 1995, pp. 174-176.

There is nothing wrong with municipalities attempting to improve service delivery; indeed, there is much to recommend in such an endeavour. Part of the way in which municipalities represent and act on behalf of their citizens is by providing them with quality services at a reasonable cost. It is not customer service, or its improvement, that is the problem. It is the tendency to depict local citizens as *nothing more than* customers and municipalities as *nothing more than* vehicles for service delivery that is the cause for concern.

Municipalities are not businesses. They don't have just occasional and specific contacts with customers; they have ongoing and complex relationships with citizens. "Citizens, unlike customers, have common purposes and rights, and among these are the right to be treated equitably."[104] Businesses, by contrast, practise target marketing, differentiate, discriminate, and take whatever actions are appropriate to increase market share or cut costs. If municipalities pursue business strategies, this approach opens up the possibility of inequities between individuals, " which runs counter to the equal and universalistic entitlements and obligations associated with citizenship."[105] As Seidle points out, such terms as customer or client do not capture the nature and complexity of the interaction that occurs when a government official services someone who is, among other things, "a taxpayer, a recipient of certain monetary benefits from the state, a voter and possibly a member of a political party and/or one or more voluntary organizations with an interest in public policy, and who carries expectations that extend beyond a particular contact with a particular public servant at a particular time."[106]

In the world of citizen as consumer, it is not the democratic aspects of government that are evaluated, but how municipalities apply such private sector concepts as performance measurement, benchmarking, and best practices – also discussed in the previous chapter. That chapter noted both uses and abuses of performance measures, and

---

[104] Ole Ingstrup, *Public Service Renewal: From Means to Ends*, Ottawa, Canadian Centre for Management Development, 1995, p. 4.

[105] Jon Pierre, "The Marketization of the State," in Guy Peters and Donald Savoie (eds.), *Governance in a Changing Environment*, Kingston, McGill-Queen's University Press, 1995, p. 57.

[106] F. Leslie Seidle, *Rethinking the Delivery of Public Services to Citizens*, Montreal, Institute for Research on Public Policy, 1995, p. 9.

one cause for concern is certainly their potentially adverse impact on the political role of municipal government.

Cochrane suggests that the preoccupation with measurement in recent years reflects an attempt to establish some sort of objective or rational means of determining how (and which) services should be provided locally, thus removing local service delivery from political controversy and, even more importantly, reducing local pressures to increase levels of spending. As a result, "stress has been placed on finding ways of standardising types of service to ensure that comparisons can be made in terms that focus on relative efficiency levels, rather than on differences in political approach."[107] In the process, financial or technical accountability replaces democratic (political or electoral) accountability. Cochrane concludes that notions of accountability through accounting or through the conversion of the citizen into consumer are ultimately unsatisfactory "precisely because they attempt to depoliticise what are inevitably processes of political choice."[108]

It is also important to remember that not all relationships between citizens and municipal government are about service delivery. Citizens are, or can be, active participants in the process of government, not just consumers of services. "The consumer analogy takes the politics out of citizenship and local government."[109] Serious difficulties result. "If citizenship is reduced to consumerism and governance to shopkeeping, how are issues of collective choice to be resolved."[110] A narrow focus on how well services are delivered to customers overlooks the fact that "the rationale of public services is not the satisfaction of individual demands, but meeting needs collectively within a framework of public policy."[111]

In a democracy, according to Carrel, "citizens must be recognized (and treated) as the *owners* of their government, not as its

---

[107] Allan Cochrane, "From Theories to Practices: Looking for Local Democracy in Britain," in Desmond King and Gerry Stoker (eds.), *Rethinking Local Democracy*, Houndmills, Macmillan Press, 1996, p. 198.

[108] *Ibid.*, p. 200.

[109] Lowndes, "Citizenship and Urban Politics," p. 175.

[110] *Ibid.*

[111] Dilys M. Hill, *Citizens and Cities*, Hemel Hempstead, Harvester Wheatsheaf, 1994, p. 228.

customers."[112] [emphasis in the original] As owners, citizens have responsibilities that are too often neglected. "A municipality's most serious liabilities are people who convince themselves that they are too busy to take an active interest in their municipality's affairs, who would rather complain that they are being victimized by government, and who look for scapegoats to be dumped in the next election."[113] Citizens, in the view of Carrel, "are the heart and soul of a democracy. If citizens do not actively participate in the shaping of public policy, democracy cannot function."[114]

Concluding Comments

Even the incomplete survey of mechanisms in this chapter reveals extensive variations in public participation. These variations stem from such factors as:

➢ The extent to which councillors see their role as trustees or delegates, which in turn influences the extent to which they attempt to consult with the local public between elections;
➢ The extent to which citizens groups are active in the community;
➢ The use of neighbourhood councils and committees;
➢ The existence of local political parties, the extent of their presence on council, and their posture on public participation;
➢ The availability and use of such direct democracy tools as the referendum, initiative, and recall; and
➢ The nature of the consultative features that may be employed by municipalities seeking to improve their customer and consumer focus.

These alternatives are not presented as an "either-or" situation. Generally speaking, the more avenues for public consultation and participation, the better. However, that best participation is likely to arise from processes that promote informed and continuing discussion between citizens and their government prior to a decision being made.

---

[112] Carrel, *Citizens Hall,* p. 32.

[113] *Ibid.,* p. 65.

[114] *Ibid.,* p. 100.

"The development of institutionalized processes whereby government can learn from citizens and citizens can learn from government opens up the process of public decision making to a wider range of ideas, interests, and influences than is available through the conventional system of political representation."[115]

Municipal councillors and staff today are overwhelmed with changes and challenges. Faced with such pressures, there may be a reluctance to encourage public participation because of the fear that it will bring delays, probably opposition to changes, and much time and effort consumed in dealing with this opposition. It may also be that municipal personnel will neglect public consultation more through oversight than deliberate decision, being so preoccupied with every day challenges that they forget to look outward to their communities.

This is no time to "circle the wagons," with councillors and staff huddled together, clutching their benchmarking reports to their chests for comfort. This is a time to open the circle and invite inside those directly affected by the difficult decisions that have to be made – the local citizens. They have a right to be involved and they can be a valuable asset and a powerful ally.

---

[115] David Prior, John Stewart, and Kieron Walsh, *Citizenship: Rights, Community and Participation*, London, Pitman Publishing, 1995, p. 137.

Chapter 10
Municipal Policy Making

Municipal governments appear to be at a crossroads with respect to their policy making role. While a number of constraints and complications affect this role, municipalities today also find themselves with an opportunity to take more initiative in policy making. If they rise to this challenge, they can better serve their local citizens while also enhancing their own stature and importance.

Introduction

The preceding chapters have raised a wide variety of policy issues relating to the operations of municipal governments in Canada. How municipalities respond to these issues, the local policy decisions that they make, collectively and cumulatively, can have a major impact on the nature of a local community and the quality of life for those living within it. As a recent text on this subject explains, policies are important "because they define how local governments interact with their citizens" and because they provide "the 'face' of local government."[1]

Municipal policy decisions have traditionally focused on which services are to be provided and to what level or standard. But a growing policy consideration today is whether a needed service should be delivered directly by the municipality or by an alternative service provider. Besides issues of servicing, there are also important local policy decisions of a regulatory nature. These have to do with such matters as the establishment of permitted land uses within a municipality, the licensing of local businesses, and the enactment of rules governing local behaviour – such as anti-noise by-laws and anti-smoking by-laws. Much attention is directed to policy issues facing

---

[1] Edmund P. Fowler and David Siegel, "Introduction: Urban Public Policy at the Turn of the Century," in Edmund P. Fowler and David Siegel (eds.), *Urban Policy Issues*, 2nd Edition, 2002, Toronto, Oxford University Press, p. 1.

large and urban municipalities, including urban transportation, housing and homelessness, and population diversity. But small and rural municipalities also have important policy decisions to make in relation to such issues as protecting the quality of groundwater supplies, dealing with the influx of "factory farms," and delivering protective services (including how to operate a combined force of volunteer and full time fire fighters).

In an attempt to shed light on policy making at the local level, we will begin by identifying some of the main variables and constraints that influence and limit the policy making role of municipalities. The examination of policy issues that follows illustrates a further complicating factor, which is the extent to which these issues are interrelated.

Constraints on Policy Making

The most obvious limits on municipal policy making are found within the municipality itself and relate to such matters as lack of jurisdiction or lack of adequate resources. But these matters, in turn, are related to external factors, notably the municipal subordination to the provincial level within the Canadian federal system. Even beyond the structure of governments and their interrelationships are numerous socio-economic constraints found in the surrounding environment. Each of these sets of influences, depicted in a general way in the figure below, will be examined in turn. As will also be discussed, however, policy making is almost never as straightforward and sequential as the tidy line of arrows below would suggest.

Figure 10.1 Influences on Policy Making

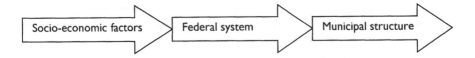

Socio-economic factors   Federal system   Municipal structure

Socio-Economic Constraints

This category embraces a number of factors including changes in the population, economic forces, interest groups, and the prevailing values or ideology.

Demographics

To the extent that government policies are developed in response to the wants and needs of society, the policy focus obviously changes – or should change – when society does. This point is best illustrated by the impact of demographics and the pattern of boom, bust, and echo made famous by David Foot.[2] As an increasing proportion of Canadian society becomes senior citizens, there are profound implications for everything from pensions and health care to elementary and secondary schooling. The effect of changing demographics on municipal governments is illustrated by the following three examples:[3]

➤ A decline in the demand for public transit was experienced by the 1980s, as baby boomers got married, moved to the suburbs, started a family, and became increasingly dependent on the automobile.

➤ As the boomers reach their sixties, however, they are likely to prefer smaller homes, closer to shopping and transportation, raising questions about the future demand for monster homes in the suburbs.

➤ An older population is also less involved in the recreational programs and activities that have traditionally received municipal attention and more interested in the arts and culture.

Economic Influences

Economic factors have a major influence on municipal policy making. The health of the local economy and of the municipal tax base imposes a basic constraint in terms of the capacity of the municipality to generate financial resources. Growth or decline in the broader regional, provincial, and even national economy obviously provides a positive or restrictive climate for local initiatives. When the economy is booming, attention is often focused on the need to manage and control such growth, to avoid undesirable impacts on the community, and to protect the environment. Such concerns tend to take a back seat, however, during times of economic decline. For example, the City of

---

[2] David K. Foot, with Daniel Stoffman, *Boom, Bust & Echo*, Toronto, Macfarlane Walter & Ross, 1996.

[3] David K. Foot, "Urban Demographics in Canada," in Fowler and Siegel, *Urban Policy Issues*, pp. 30-33.

Toronto's resolve to restrict the height and density of its downtown buildings weakened in the face of the economic slowdown that began in the mid-1970s and had become a severe recession by the early 1980s.[4] Another recession a decade later once again prompted the city to soften its approach, this time with respect to Cityplan 1991. A proposal, for example, that new development *must conform* to environmental standards became a proposal *to encourage* development to meet environmental objectives.[5]

International developments related to the globalization of economic activity also affect municipal governments – in varied ways and with an ultimate impact that has not yet been determined. There is no doubt that these international developments have curtailed the activities of the federal and provincial governments, and prompted their cuts in social spending and transfer payments, the result of which has been to shift more responsibility and expenditure burden to municipal governments. It is also evident that the very mobile corporations of the new economic order have reduced the bargaining leverage of municipalities.[6] On the other hand, Andrew and Morrison note that some analysts see globalization as leading to a revitalized role for local economies, one stimulated by infrastructure expenditures which can be made at the local level and can be used to "enhance the locational advantages of that particular community."[7]

Interest Groups

Interest groups also form part of the socio-economic environment, and some of these can exert considerable influence over policy making. To take but a few examples:

> ➢ Local residents and ratepayers groups have enjoyed some success in pressuring councils to hold the line on taxes, often at

---

[4] Frances Frisken, *City Policy-Making in Theory and Practice: The Case of Toronto's Downtown Plan*, London, University of Western Ontario, Local Government Case Studies, No. 3, 1988, p. 99.

[5] Edmund P. Fowler, "Decision Time for Cityplan '91" *City Magazine*, Winter '93, pp. 10-11.

[6] Christopher Leo, "Urban Development: Planning Aspirations and Political Realities," in Fowler and Siegel, *Urban Policy Issues*, p. 222.

[7] Caroline Andrew and Jeff Morrision, "Infrastructure," in *ibid.*, p. 239.

the expense of actions that should have been taken to upgrade infrastructure over the years.

➤ Environmental groups continue to draw attention to the adverse impact of much growth and economic activity and have made some progress in injecting notions of smart growth and sustainable development into policy discussions.

➤ Business groups such as the Canadian Home Builders Association and the Urban Development Institute, as well as more localized bodies such as chambers of commerce, promote the virtues of growth and development.

➤ The increasing diversity of society, especially in our larger cities, is reflected in the rise of groups representing ethnic, racial, and cultural communities and gay and lesbian rights, among other concerns.

➤ Advocacy groups for the poor and the homeless have also become more prominent.

Municipalities are more than neutral arbiters responding to the myriad of groups pressuring them for a response, but the policies that they adopt are likely to be influenced by the particular configuration of interest groups operating within their area.

Prevailing Ideology

Yet another environmental factor is represented by the extent to which policy making is supported or constrained by the prevailing values and ideology. The neoconservative or neoliberal philosophy that has prevailed over the past couple of decades has imposed constraints on policy making at all levels of government. While the policy making role of municipal government has long been rather neglected because of the tendency to view municipalities as little more than vehicles for service delivery, the current market model of municipal government is even more restrictive. It ignores the concept of the municipality as an instrument through which a community can identify and address its collective concerns. It also ignores the notion that governments, including municipal governments, exist to provide public goods for the betterment of society. Instead, the emphasis of the market model is on downsizing, on shifting operations as much as possible to the private and voluntary sector, and on increasing the revenue to expenditure ratio of whatever functions remain. The municipality is judged by how well it manages the bottom line, not by how well it serves the needs of its community.

The impact of the market model can be illustrated with reference to the field of recreation.[8] With this model, recreation becomes an end in itself, and is evaluated on the basis of such measures as the number of participants and/or the revenues that each program generates. But evaluating recreation essentially on the return on investment defines it simply "as a commodity to be purchased and consumed rather than something that leads to a higher human or social goal."[9] Clearly the philosophy reflected in the market model dictates quite different municipal recreational policies than would arise from a broader perspective that sees recreation as a method of personal and social development, a vehicle for helping people to improve their quality of life.[10]

The market model is also affecting recreation more indirectly, in a classic example of the unintended consequences of policy decisions. A recent report indicates that community sports and recreation groups are disappearing across Ontario as a result of escalating user charges for using municipal and school facilities, increased competition for space, a growing shortage of rinks, gyms, pools, and playing fields, and the loss of volunteers driven away by the growing stress and workload.[11] A primary cause of this crisis is the supposedly solid business decisions made by municipalities and school boards to increase user fees to operate on more of a break-even basis and to generate much needed revenue without a property tax increase. But what will the costs be of having to replace volunteers with paid staff? Given the links between recreational activities, fitness, and reduced vandalism and youth crime, what will be the health, social, and criminal justice costs of the loss of community recreational activities? A business plan embracing these broader considerations would quickly demonstrate that the increased user charges may be anything but a financial gain for local governments or society.

---

[8] This example is based on Bryan J. A. Smale and Donald G. Reid, "Public Policy on Recreation and Leisure in Urban Canada," in *ibid.*, pp. 189-190.

[9] *Ibid.*, p. 189.

[10] *Ibid.*, p. 190.

[11] James Wallace, "Across Ontario, community groups struggle to survive as costs soar," *Kingston Whig Standard*, August 9, 2003.

Legal and Jurisdictional Constraints

Notwithstanding the improved municipal legislation enacted by most provinces over the past decade, municipal governments are still, in Stephen Clarkson's blunt phrasing, "the lowest form of political life in Canada."[12] Many of the policy issues that concern them – such as sprawl, pollution, homelessness, urban infrastructure, and preservation of farmland – can only be addressed, at least in a comprehensive way, by concerted action on the part of the provincial and/or federal levels of government as well. But a comprehensive policy response to these issues has certainly not been forthcoming from these governments.

Federal Neglect

As discussed earlier in this text, the federal government has pursued many policies that affect the local level, but often with little apparent awareness of this impact. In more recent years, it has adopted policies that attempt to address problems *in* cities, but these separate initiatives do not constitute an urban policy. Nor do the federal initiatives show sufficient appreciation of the growing importance of cities in the new international economic order. For example, an analysis of the infrastructure program introduced by the federal government in 1993 reveals that it was seen by them primarily as a method of job creation, was designed to minimize friction with the provinces, was preoccupied with *who* pays rather than *what* should be built, and gave priority to traditional basic elements of infrastructure – roads and bridges, and water and sewage systems.[13] As a result, the infrastructure expenditures did little to improve the capacity of cities to compete in the new knowledge-based economy by developing a rich and diverse environment that attracts talented people, as discussed in Chapter 3.

Provincial Paternalism

Provincial governments have also adversely affected municipal policy making in a number of ways. For much of the past century, they have supervised and controlled municipal decisions to such an extent that municipalities often lacked the autonomy to act. Even when they had

---

[12] Stephen Clarkson, *Uncle Sam and Us, Globalization, Neoconservatism, and the Canadian State*, Toronto, University of Toronto Press, 2002, p. 103.

[13] Andrews and Morrison, "Infrastructure," pp. 237-250.

some local scope for action, municipalities often lacked the confidence to proceed. After being treated like children by paternalistic provincial administrations, they have found it difficult to stand on their own feet when the opportunity arises.

The scope for local decision making has been broadened by recent legislative changes in some provinces that give municipalities natural person powers and broad spheres of authority in which to operate. But it remains to be seen if they will have access to sufficient resources to make full use of any expanded jurisdiction. Since "the devil is in the details," it is also too soon to tell how much operating freedom the new legislation actually brings, and whether court decisions will support expanded municipal discretion. As noted elsewhere in this text, recent court rulings have been inconsistent in this regard.

Provincial (and federal) influences on municipal actions may be motivated by a variety of considerations. Frisken suggests that what she aptly terms "parent government" intervention in local affairs "may represent a simple assertion of formal authority, an effort to protect or strengthen the local economy, a concern with keeping down the costs of local services, an interest in effecting a redistribution of the costs and benefits of public and private economic activity more equally among municipalities or among individual citizens, or an attempt to appease politically-influential local interests."[14] It follows that the nature and extent of senior government influence over local policy making activities is not uniform but may vary depending on the particular municipality, the local circumstances, and the objectives being pursued by the senior level(s).

The Municipal Structure

There are also a number of constraints on policy making within the municipal structure itself. To begin with, a number of significant local matters are not directly under municipal council but are instead assigned to separate boards and commissions[15] that operate across the

---

[14] Frisken, *Toronto's Downtown Plan*, p. 17.

[15] Separate boards and agencies are extensively used in Western Canada for the provision of health, social services, and education on a regional basis, as summarized in Evan Jones and Susan McFarlane, *Regional Approaches to Services in the West: Health, Social Services and Education*, Canada West Foundation, February 2002, available at the Foundation's web site www.cwf.ca, accessed April 18, 2003.

municipality or a combination of municipalities. These arrangements are found in most provinces with respect to such functions as education, public health, some social programs, water management and conservation, and utilities. The governing boards of these bodies consist of appointed (most commonly) or elected officials and they are often quite dependent upon the provincial governments for policy direction, resources, and even approval of local decision making. As a result, such important policy fields as policing and transit are largely beyond the jurisdiction of municipal councils.[16] The consolidation of school boards in most provinces, and the centralization of decision making at the provincial level, has left very little scope for educational policy making at the local level.[17]

A different kind of fragmentation is found within the municipal structure itself, to the extent that there may be a number of separate municipalities existing within one urban area. While common intermunicipal problems may call for coordinated action, individual municipalities are understandably motivated to do what best serves the needs of their residents and ratepayers. In the short run at least, this preoccupation may lead them to focus quite narrowly on their own particular situation – leading them to compete vigorously with their neighbours for economic development, or to try to avoid paying toward regional facilities from which they may benefit, or to avoid contributing to the cost of social programs borne by the central city.

Within any one municipality, effective policy making is hampered by the lack of strong leadership and executive direction and the lack of cohesion and accountability within the council itself. As has often been stated, in municipal government everyone is responsible for everything, which also means that no one is really responsible for anything. This statement must be qualified to the extent that a municipality has a chief administrative officer and/or executive committee of council or where a strong mayor emerges in spite of the lack of formal powers attached to that office. In those circumstances, there may be a focus for improved policy advice and policy direction.

---

[16] For a good discussion of the many local boards and commissions that operate in Canada, see Dale Richmond and David Siegel (eds.), *Agencies, Boards and Commissions in Canadian Local Government*, Monograph No. 15, Toronto, Institute of Public Administration of Canada, 1994.

[17] Peter Woolstencroft, "Education Policies: Challenges and Controversies," in Fowler and Siegel, *Urban Policy Issues*, pp. 276-297.

Political Realities of Municipal Policy Making

Additional constraints on municipal policy making exist in the form of a number of political realities that are to some extent inherent in the points previously made. A good example is provided by Leo's observation that "it is not the official plan but developers' proposals that drive the actual process of development."[18] The fact that councillors often receive from developers and others associated with the property development industry a substantial portion of the funds that they require to conduct their election campaigns certainly does nothing to reduce the influence of developers. Nor is this influence evident with respect to only large companies in major urban centres, as Leo makes clear with his case study of the rural municipality of Springfield, Manitoba.[19]

Box 10.1 (Spring)Field of Dreams

The municipal plan for this township emphasized preserving agriculture and natural resources and preventing the proliferation of residential development. Yet the zoning provisions of this plan provided for much of the future residential development to occur in the larger of the two prime agricultural areas of the municipality. The rationale given was that because some individuals in the past had benefited financially from subdividing their rural land for residential development, it would not be fair to restrict others from having this opportunity. In this case, the reality was that "political pressures from constituents in a community small enough to allow almost anyone to have a personal relationship with her or his representative on council prevented the municipality from adhering to the principles stated in the plan."[20] It is these political realities that thwart efforts to pursue appropriate planning policies.

The limited geographic area embraced by any one municipality limits what it can do to provide a policy response to the issues and challenges it may face. We know, for example, that different pricing policies with respect to taxes and development charges could help to limit sprawl, but there is little that a municipality in the urban core can accomplish in this regard if some the surrounding municipalities are actively wooing new growth and development to them – a point discussed in more detail below. Similarly, efforts by one municipality to pursue policies that address social and environmental problems may prompt

---

[18] Leo, "Urban Development: Planning Aspirations and Political Realities," in Fowler and Siegel, *Urban Policy Issues*, p. 221.

[19] *Ibid.*, pp. 229-230.

[20] *Ibid.*, p. 230.

residents and businesses that are mobile to relocate to another jurisdiction that eschews such policies in favour of lower taxes and fewer
limits on business operations. This, of course, is essentially the
Peterson argument, introduced in Chapter 1, that municipal
governments have very little scope to pursue redistributive policies.[21]

Illustrating Municipal Policy Making

After discussing so many variables and constraints, the following
example of a not untypical municipal issue provides an opportunity to
review and apply these factors, as well as other considerations introduced in earlier chapters.

Box 10.2 Explaining a Municipal Policy Decision

A rapidly urbanizing township adjacent to a medium-sized city continues to experience
strong growth pressures. There is little undeveloped land left within the city. The other
nearby municipalities are small and rural, and lack the infrastructure necessary to
support any large scale development. The urbanizing township has an abundance of
serviced land and its council has been actively pursuing new growth for several years,
believing that the increased assessment is the key to financial survival. A prominent local
developer applies for a zoning amendment to allow a higher density mixed-use project.
This application is referred to the township's Planning Advisory Committee, consisting
mainly of citizen appointees – most with ties to the business community. The application
is supported by the Committee. There is some lobbying from a couple of local citizens'
groups opposed to the rezoning – one being a hastily formed coalition of neighbours
living adjacent to the proposed project. Another group expressing opposition is a rural-
based coalition of long-time residents who feel that the township is neglecting its rural
and farm interests in its obsession with growth and development. However, the rezoning is subsequently approved by council and upheld on appeal to the provincial
tribunal responsible for such matters.

On the surface, this is a straightforward exercise of decision
making power by the appropriately authorized bodies. Under provincial legislation, municipal councils have the authority to amend their
zoning by-laws. They can establish planning advisory committees to
provide assistance in the planning process. Objections to a rezoning
usually result in a hearing by a provincial tribunal, which then makes
the final decision.

But what explanations might be provided for the policy decision that was made by the municipality in this instance? Traditionally,
the first explanation would look for answers in the formal machinery
of municipal government. What we have here is a typically fragmented

---

[21] Paul Peterson, *City Limits*, Chicago, University of Chicago Press, 1981.

structure, with several different municipalities operating within one urban area (the city and its surrounding hinterland), each pursuing its own agenda. Thus, the pro-growth township is able to attract the bulk of the new development in the area, whether or not that might be the best location for development if viewed from a broader perspective.

Further fragmentation can be found within the structure of the township itself. While it is only advisory in nature, the planning committee does divide consideration of planning issues between council and this separate body. Moreover, the fact that the advisory committee consists mainly of citizen appointees increases the likelihood that it will have a different point of view than that of the council. The internal governing structure of the township may also be fragmented, depending on the specifics of its organization. Since it has been growing rapidly, it has almost certainly been adding new staff and departments in a rather ad hoc fashion. There may be a series of standing committees, each focusing on the activities of their department(s) and perpetuating or even reinforcing these specialized viewpoints. If there isn't any chief administrative officer, then the various department heads are officially equals. They will respond to development proposals such as the one outlined above largely on the basis of how such proposals might affect their departments. But what about the impact on the overall municipality? Where is that perspective found?

A second explanation for the planning decision outlined above is that it reflects the self-interest of the politicians and bureaucrats involved. From this point of view, politicians seek to be elected and then to maintain themselves in power, while staff seek to expand their empires and therefore their own importance. This public choice perspective (outlined in Chapter 1, and familiar to those who have seen the *Yes, Minister,* television series), suggests that politicians would support the rezoning application because they see the resulting development and increased assessment as enhancing or at least maintaining their political support base. To the township staff, continued growth means an almost certain increase in their operations, responsibilities, staff complements, and budgets – in short, expanded empires which would, in turn, enhance their stature.

The specific reaction of politicians and bureaucrats to an issue of this sort would also be influenced by such factors as the perceived capacity of the media to influence public opinion and the ability of interest groups to mobilize supporters. Given the outcome of the scenario outlined above, it can be concluded that the media did not "run" with this issue for any length of time, and that the citizens' groups lined up against the rezoning were not considered to carry much weight.

The significance and influence of the local groups within this municipality is at the heart of the third explanation of the planning decision. It sees decisions as the result of the interaction of groups, all seeking to influence policy outcomes. This pluralist perspective (also introduced in Chapter 1) views the government as an essentially passive force and government decisions as the outcome of a competition between organized groups that seek to protect or promote the interests of their members. Given the planning decision that resulted above, we must assume that, in addition to the citizens' groups opposed to the rezoning, there were other influential groups at work. These might include ratepayer groups and fair tax coalitions pressuring the township council to hold the line on taxes. To most councillors, this goal can only be achieved by increasing assessment and, therefore, by supporting the rezoning. They would certainly include business groups such as a local chamber of commerce, construction association, and homebuilders' association. Pluralists would presumably explain the planning decision above by conceding the stronger influence (and superior lobbying resources and tactics) usually exhibited by business groups.

One might also explain the planning decision above as an indication of the pervasiveness of capitalist values within Canadian society. The virtues of private enterprise and pursuit of profit are seldom questioned. The upswing of conservatism since the 1970s has reinforced the positive view of the operation of the market. The role of local government is seen as providing the physical services needed to support growth and development. Government decisions are seen as the outcome of the lines of cleavage in Canadian society that, in turn, result from the way wealth is distributed. Thus, the economic power of the property development industry prevails.

In the case of the planning decision above, the prevalence on the planning advisory committee of citizens with ties to the business community is of note. There might also be a similar pattern of close linkages between many of the councillors and the business community, perhaps reinforced by financial support from the development industry for the election campaigns of these councillors.

The Complexity of Policy Making

In addition to the constraints discussed above, there are a number of factors that complicate municipal policy making. The ones that we will examine in this section are the nature of the policy making process, the fact that policies get misidentified or misdiagnosed, the problem that policies often have unintended consequences, and the fact that so many policy issues are interconnected and interdependent.

A Far From Tidy Process

The first complication is that the policy making process in practice is quite different from the logical series of interrelated steps suggested by the rational-comprehensive or classical model of policy making. That model begins with the correct identification of the issue or problem, proceeds through a comprehensive analysis of alternatives, and culminates in the selection and implementation of the "correct" policy decision. This process may depict how many people feel that policy should be made, but it does not describe very accurately what happens in practice.

Probably the best known contrast to the rational model is found in the views of Charles Lindblom, who describes instead a policy making process of incrementalism or what he colourfully terms the "science of muddling through."[22] He argues that our problem-solving capacity is too limited to encompass all of the options and potential outcomes that might arise, that there is usually insufficient information to assess accurately all options, and that comprehensive analysis is both too time-consuming and too expensive – all points that certainly seem to apply to most municipalities in Canada, with their very limited research and analytical capacity.

Recognizing these realities, Lindblom claims, decision makers look for simpler approaches to problem solving. Instead of attempting to identify every possible course of action, they consider only those few alternatives that represent small or incremental changes from existing policies. Once again, this approach sounds consistent with municipal experience, given that the first question that is often asked about an issue is: "Did this ever come up before, and how did we

---

[22] Charles E. Lindblom, "The Science of 'Muddling Through,' " *Public Administration Review*, 19, Spring 1959, pp. 79-88.

handle it then?" Adjustments at the margin are more common in municipal decision making than are radical new policy directions – and this is true of more than just the annual municipal budget process.

Yates also rebuts the rational model of policy making, with the aid of metaphors based on three games that were prominent in the penny arcades of yesteryear. He compares the process of identifying the problems that require attention to being in a shooting gallery where targets keep popping up and passing by – forcing the player to decide which target (problem) to address, with the knowledge that choosing that target means letting others pass by without response. He goes on to suggest that the policy making characteristics of the problems that arise can vary just as randomly as the apples, oranges, and cherries that appear in various combinations in a slot machine. Those policy making variables include "the nature of the problem, the issue context, the stage of decision , the configuration of participants, the institutional setting, and the government function involved."[23] As a result, Yates contends that policy makers who follow a standard approach, or who rely upon one or two standard responses to policy issues, are likely to be off the mark much of the time. Finally, he compares the process of policy implementation to the operations of a pinball machine. "Given the central policy maker's weak control over his own administration, street-level bureaucrats, and higher-level governments, decisions once taken are likely bounce around from decision point to decision point."[24]

In the real world of policy making, those responsible cannot select their problems and analyze them with detachment and thoroughness. This is especially true when they face a constant barrage of new or changing problems and service demands, which has certainly been the case for municipalities in recent years. It is not possible to stop the world, freeze a particular problem, and then dissect it in clinical fashion. Moreover, policy makers regularly deal with problems which are not clearly understood or that generate conflicting political pressures. Rather than undertaking thorough research and analysis, the more likely response is to grope for a plausible remedy and hope that it works better than previous responses – essentially emulating the incremental approach already discussed.

---

[23] Douglas Yates, *The Ungovernable City*, Cambridge, M.I.T. Press, 1977 pp. 91-92.

[24] *Ibid.*, p. 93.

In light of the above, the rational model described above –
with its tidy, sequential process and specific start and end – becomes
instead a continuous process "in which a particular problem receives
brief, often frantic attention; some kind of decision is made, which
bounces around in the implementation phase; and then the problem
pops up again in a new or slightly altered form."[25] Examples of such a
pattern are fairly common.

> When property standards are strictly enforced, an unintended
>   result is often housing abandonment or higher rents, leading to
>   housing shortages for low income residents.
> In an attempt to prevent strip development along rural roads,
>   planning policies have traditionally encouraged infilling within
>   existing hamlets – but in many cases the increased population
>   in these hamlets led to well pollution and triggered the need
>   for very expensive piped water and sewage treatment systems.
> Garbage "bag tag" policies can be effective in encouraging
>   recycling and in covering some of the costs of garbage
>   collection, but they can also lead to an increase in garbage
>   dumped along back roads or burned in back yard barrels.

Complications can also arise at a very early stage because of the
way the policy issue is defined, or sometimes misidentified. The
standard policy response to problems of urban transportation provides
a classic example of this situation, as discussed next.[26]

More Movement Or Less?

Our policy responses with respect to urban transportation have
proceeded from the assumption that the objective is to move more
people to more places more quickly. So we spend ever-increasing
amounts of money and devote about half of our urban land to cars, in
what seems to be a losing battle to reduce urban gridlock. This policy
thrust is reinforced by the many participants in the "movement
business" – such as those involved in selling gas and oil, manufacturing
and selling cars, repairing cars, insuring cars, selling tires and other

---

[25] *Ibid.*

[26] Discussion of this issue is based on Edmund P. Fowler and Jack Layton,
"Transportation Policy in Canadian Cities," in Fowler and Siegel, *Urban Policy
Issues*, pp. 108-138.

auto parts, and building roads.[27] Those in the property development industry also promote the expansion of transportation routes, since these routes provide access to vacant fields that can be developed for financial gain. But there are also losses, financial and social, as a result of our approach to urban transportation – in the form of air pollution, health costs, the loss of prime agricultural land, and the negative social impact on communities that feature major highways, heavy traffic flows, and constant commuting. Transportation policies devoted to increasing movement have focused on the construction of more roads to carry more cars, thereby worsening these adverse conditions.

Policy responses that can reduce the reliance on car travel include the following:[28]

> Limiting car use and movement through such means as traffic calming features (speed bumps, planter boxes in the middle of intersections, four way stops, and very low speed limits), closing roads in sections of the city centre, setting parking fees that reflect the actual cost of parking, and charging a toll on clogged, inner city roads.

> Expanding the use of public transit, which, of course, is difficult while we continue to allow sprawling, low density development. Instead of curtailing transit service in a usually futile attempt to reduce the transit deficit, we need to point out the far greater extent to which taxpayers subsidize roads. We need to look at greatly expanded transit service, such as is found in Brazil where articulated buses in Curitiba carry up to 270 passengers and come by once a minute during rush hour, prompting even many who own cars (28% of bus users) to travel by bus.[29]

> Encouraging greater bicycle use, by such measures as the provision of bicycle lanes and even free bike programs.

Ultimately, however, the most effective way to address our transportation problems would be to shift the focus away from methods of *increasing* movement – whether by car or otherwise – and to concentrate instead of ways of *reducing* movement. If movement

---

[27] *Ibid.*, p. 116.

[28] *Ibid.*, pp. 129-133.

[29] *Ibid.*, p. 132.

can be reduced (mainly through more compact development that incorporates mixed uses), many of the problems cited above can also be alleviated. But any such dramatic reversal of the approach to transportation policy would have to begin with a recognition of the link between transportation and land use and the policy decisions that influence the pattern of land use – to which we turn our attention in the next section.

Sprawl and All

Complicating municipal policy making is the fact that so many policy issues are interconnected and interdependent, as will be illustrated first through a review of the issue of urban sprawl. As Chapter 3 made clear, urban sprawl and all of its attendant problems present a major challenge for our urban areas and for the local governments that operate within and across them. No government would set out deliberately to create urban sprawl – although Rusk presents a chilling fable about how a shadowy group set out 50 years ago to conquer America from within, by destroying its great cities through promotion of a new American Dream built around life in the suburbs. He then points out that no such imaginary group could have done a better job at this task than the federal government's own policies have done.[30]

To at least some extent, this same charge could be levied in Canada. The housing policies of the federal government, and especially the financial support for single family homes provided by the Canada Mortgage and Housing Corporation, encouraged low density residential development. Housing construction was a central component of the substantial government spending that Keynesian economics (the prevailing ideology in the post-war period) advocated as a key to economic growth. These policies responded to the housing preferences of young married couples and pleased those in the development industry and their allies within government. Provincial governments also supported this pattern of growth, in part through providing substantial transfer payments, particularly for road construction.

The municipal level must also accept its share of responsibility for the sprawl that occurred. Suburban municipalities were happy to accept the population overspill from central cities, gaining increased

---

[30] David Rusk, *Inside Game, Outside Game*, Washington, Brookings Institution Press, 1999, pp. 82-86.

tax assessment without having to provide city services, and using their resulting lower tax rates as a lure to attract further growth into their areas. Any municipalities that might have been prepared to slow growth and limit sprawl faced the reality that if they didn't accommodate the growth pressures they would just find an outlet in a neighbouring municipality. Unless all were prepared to work together with a coordinated policy to manage growth, this objective could not be achieved. As long as a few of them made it clear that they were "open for business," all of them had to be receptive or face a loss of assessment and tax revenues. In fairness, it is not reasonable to expect municipalities to act any differently in this situation. It is for this reason that Leo argues for a stronger provincial role in planning and development in urban areas.[31]

If a variety of governmental actions and inactions give rise to the urban sprawl, it in turn unleashes a variety of other major problems – ranging from economic decline in the inner city to traffic gridlock and air pollution, to increased costs for servicing less dense development, to loss of agricultural land, pollution of groundwater, and social isolation. The figure below attempts to illustrate the variables inherent in this policy issue, although the arrows in a straight line depict a much tidier and more sequential process than really exists.

Figure 10.2 The Policy Dimensions of Sprawl

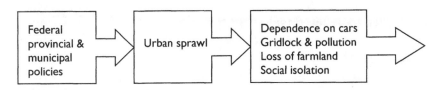

As a result of these complexities, it is almost impossible for any one municipality to mount an effective policy response to urban sprawl. Particularly in the very large urban areas such as the Greater Toronto Area (GTA), it is arguable that only the provincial government has the jurisdiction and resources to attempt to address this issue. The extensive municipal restructuring throughout the GTA did nothing to improve the situation, nor did the short-lived experiment with the Greater Toronto Services Board, which wrestled with the

---

[31] Leo, "Urban Development: Planning Aspirations and Political Realities," in pp. 232-233.

problems of urban transportation without having any control over the underlying land use patterns that were unfolding.

Pursuing Healthy Communities

Our second example to illustrate the complexity of municipal policy making is interesting in a variety of ways. Once again, all three levels of government are involved in this policy field, but the nature and extent of their involvement has changed significantly over the years. The interdependence of government initiatives is also illustrated, perhaps even more so in this example.

Local governments were in the forefront of the original public health movement that began almost 200 years ago.[32] That movement was largely concerned with the prevention of contagious diseases and epidemics. The focus was not on treating sickness but keeping people healthy by preventing sickness. Achieving this objective required action by local governments with respect to sanitation, sewage, and the treatment of drinking water. As discussed in Chapter 2, the newly incorporated city of Toronto established a board of health in 1834 and in Toronto and elsewhere the public works department grew out of the public health movement, as did urban planning, parks, housing, and social service functions.

Health was one of the responsibilities assigned to the provincial level in the British North America Act (Constitution Act) of 1867, but an even more important factor that directed attention away from the local role in this field was the development of the so-called medical model of health care. As the 20th century unfolded, powerful diagnostic and therapeutic tools such as x-rays, antibiotics, and effective anaesthesia appeared in medicine. Clinical supremacy took over from the public health movement and better health became equated – in the minds of the public and their political leaders – with doctors and hospitals. Expenditures and emphasis on prevention programs declined as the provincial governments (and, increasingly, the federal government through transfer payments) became involved in supporting the newer tools of health care.

There has been a growing appreciation, however, that Canada's health care system has essentially developed into a sickness

---

[32] The discussion in this section is substantially based on Trevor Hancock, "From Public Health to the Healthy City," in Fowler and Siegel, *Urban Policy Issues*, pp. 253-275.

care system, one in which only about 5% of the health budget is actually devoted to prevention.[33] According to the 1986 Ottawa Charter on Health Promotion, the prerequisites for health include peace, shelter, education, food, income, a stable ecosystem, social justice, and equity. The Premier's Council on Health, Well-Being, and Social Justice in Ontario came to a similar conclusion, finding that human health and longevity are linked to national wealth, household income, employment status, social support networks, level of education, early childhood development, and the quality of our natural and built environment. Yet it is program areas such as social assistance, affordable housing, and environmental protection – prerequisites for healthy living – that have been adversely affected by the cutbacks and downsizing pursued by the federal and provincial governments over the past couple of decades in response to global pressures. Here again, we find a striking example of the unintended consequences of policy decisions.

The recognition that we must approach health care from a broader perspective that embraces social, economic, and environmental considerations is reflected in a healthy cities or healthy communities initiative spearheaded by the World Health Organization. Within a decade of its inception in 1986, the healthy communities movement had spread to several thousand cities, towns, and villages in Europe, North America, Latin America, Asia, Africa, and Australasia.[34] Within Canada, Mississauga's mayor, Hazel McCallion, has been working with the World Health Organization's Centre for Health Development (in Kobe, Japan), and has launched the Mississauga model as a tripartite initiative of the city, the Centre, and the University of Toronto at Mississauga.[35] Activities include surveying water quality in local rivers, examining the ways in which the municipality contributes to global warming, studying how the municipality can help with the battle against obesity, and assessing health and stress in the workplace.

---

[33] This section is based on C. Richard Tindal, *A Citizen's Guide To Government*, 2nd Edition, Whitby, McGraw-Hill Ryerson Limited, 2000, p. 304.

[34] Hancock, "From Public Health to the Healthy City," p. 267.

[35] This example is based on Tom Urbaniak, "Rhetoric and Restraint: Municipal-Federal Relations in Canada's Largest Edge City," a paper prepared for the Municipal-Provincial-Federal Relations Conference, Institute of Intergovernmental Relations, Queen's University, May 9-10, 2003, pp. 34-35.

As the focus returns to the central role that the local level plays in maintaining health (as opposed to treating sickness), we are reminded that almost all policy areas addressed by municipalities have a direct impact on the creation of healthier communities. This interdependence of policies has been cited earlier as a major factor in the complexity of the municipal policy making efforts. The notion that in government everything connects is nowhere more evident than in the health field. To illustrate:[36]

> Whether a municipality pursues economic growth without regard to the adverse impacts that may result or focuses on achieving growth that is environmentally and socially sustainable is obviously pertinent.

> What pattern of development is encouraged, permitted, or restricted by the land use policies of the municipality, and to what extent do these policies allow low density sprawl which not only increases servicing costs but also our reliance on the automobile with all of its attendant health costs?

> The provision of clean drinking water and the maintenance of effective sewage treatment and waste disposal systems were primary objectives of the original public health movement of 150 years ago. These services remain essential to the health of our communities, as has been demonstrated so dramatically in recent years in places such as Walkerton, Ontario and North Battleford, Saskatchewan.

> The provision of adequate shelter is a basic determinant of good health, and the local role in this regard increased over the past decade in the face of reduced federal and provincial support for affordable housing.

> Transportation is a significant factor in health. "The automobile is associated with accidental injury and death, air pollution, the stress of commuting, a sedentary lifestyle, and a segregated-use urban sprawl that destroys a sense of community."[37] Through such actions as land use policies that limit sprawl, expanded public transit, and the promotion of a more pedestrian-friendly and bike-friendly urban design, municipalities can take steps that create a more healthy community.

---

[36] From Hancock, "From Public Health to the Healthy City," pp. 268-269.

[37] *Ibid.*, p. 269.

> ➢ The health of a community depends upon the human relations services available (such as education, health care, social services, recreation and culture) and the adequacy of the social safety net. While it is mainly in Ontario that municipalities have any substantial role in providing social services, the other responsibilities cited are exercised by municipalities or local boards and commissions.

> ➢ Police, fire, and emergency services have an obvious impact on the health and safety of the community.

It is clear from these examples, summarized in Figure 10.3 below, that the policy decisions made by municipalities are potentially of great significance to the lives – and health – of their local citizens. It is also evident, however, that coordinated municipal policy initiatives are complicated by the extent to which policy issues are interconnected and also intertwined with policy decisions taken by separate local boards and by the provincial and federal governments. In the specific instance of health, Hancock notes that reforms of the health care system in almost every province have shifted responsibilities to separate regional health authorities, and expresses concerns that these arrangements sever the direct link that should exist between municipal government services and the health of the public.[38]

Figure 10.3 The Policy Dimensions of Healthy Communities

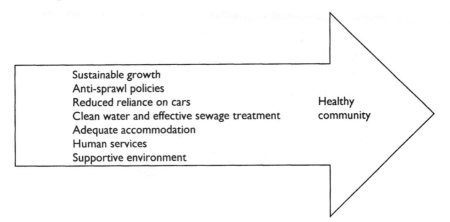

Sustainable growth
Anti-sprawl policies
Reduced reliance on cars
Clean water and effective sewage treatment
Adequate accommodation
Human services
Supportive environment

Healthy community

---

[38] *Ibid.*, p. 261.

Intergovernmental Policy Making

As briefly noted in Chapter 6, Leo and Mulligan respond to the
intergovernmental complexities of policy making by suggesting an
approach in which lower levels of government are given more
flexibility to determine how senior government policies and programs
can best be applied in particular localities. To illustrate their point,
they examine national policies and programs relating to immigration,
welfare, and affordable housing, and show how these issues have their
own particular features in Winnipeg and benefit from distinctive local
applications.[39] More specifically:

> ➤ Immigration policy is preoccupied with the problems (or
> perceived problems) associated with the very heavy influx of
> immigrants into a few major urban centres in Canada, and
> especially into Toronto, Montreal, and Vancouver. But a city
> such as Winnipeg is not going to be inundated with large
> numbers of any population. Rather than being a problem, an
> influx of immigrants would occupy some of Winnipeg's large
> stock of affordable housing, stimulate job creation, generate
> tax revenues, and help to enliven the inner city. In this connec-
> tion, Leo and Mulligan describe the positive experience of a
> provincial-federal agreement under which provinces can
> nominate immigrants in specific job categories. In their view,
> this initiative is one way of providing significant local input
> into national policy and significant variation in the local appli-
> cation of such policy.[40]

> ➤ In the case of housing, they point to the widespread variations
> in the availability and cost of housing across Canada as the
> reason why one national housing policy makes very little
> sense. Instead, they argue, federal and provincial housing and
> homeless funds need to be administered in a way that is
> responsive to local conditions. As an example of such an
> approach, they cite the Winnipeg Housing and Homelessness
> Initiative (WHHI), which provides a "single window" point of

---

[39] Christopher Leo, with Susan Mulligan, "Rethinking Urban Governance in the
21st Century," paper presented at the Canadian Political Science Association
conference, Halifax, May 2003.

[40] *Ibid.*, pp. 11-13.

contact in downtown Winnipeg, staffed by officials of participating agencies from all three levels of government.
➢ Their third example comes from the field of welfare. Leo and Mulligan describe how in 1994 and 1995 the city of Winnipeg put over 100 people on welfare to work, thereby saving the federal and provincial government some welfare expenses and converting these savings into the repair of some of the city's aging infrastructure. They note, however, that this initiative required complex negotiations among the three levels of government and only lasted for two years. What is needed, they suggest, is for the federal government to continue providing support for social assistance while allowing different work and training programs in different communities, in response to local conditions.

There is much to recommend in the approach outlined by Leo and Mulligan, although they acknowledge that the necessary sharing and cooperation will not easily be achieved, given that "bureaucratic and political interests at all levels of government run to possessiveness and aggrandizement."[41] The need for greater cooperation among levels of government was also emphasized in a project on social sustainability carried out by Canadian Policy Research Networks (CPRN). Because of the scale and complexity of urban issues and the linkages among them, participants called for such things as more cooperation among governments, an end to turf wars among the levels of government, having all players at the same table, and otherwise finding ways to bring together all levels of government (and other key players as well) to address urban policy issues such as housing, urban poverty, immigration, and the Aboriginal influx to urban areas.[42]

---

[41] *Ibid.*, p. 16.

[42] F. Leslie Seidle, *The Federal Role in Canada's Cities: Overview of Issues and Proposed Actions*, Ottawa, Canadian Policy Research Networks Inc., December 2002, pp. 15-16. This paper is available at the CPRN web site at www.cprn.org, accessed May 12, 2003.

Concluding Comments

As noted in Chapter 8, a primary role of municipal council is to enact policies on the basis of expert advice provided by staff and (one hopes) after taking into consideration local views, concerns, and input. In practice, as this chapter has attempted to demonstrate, the policy making process is considerably more complex and is subject to a number of influences and constraints. The latter include:

> Factors in the socio-economic environment such as demographics, economic influences, and interest groups;
> The prevailing political ideology;
> Legal and jurisdictional constraints;
> The structure of municipal government; and
> The political realities of the environment within which policy decisions are made.

Taking into account all of these constraints, together with the complexity of municipal policy making and the extent to which so many policy issues are interconnected and intertwined with provincial and federal jurisdictions, there might appear to be very little scope for municipal policy initiatives. On the other hand, it can be argued that circumstances today present municipalities with an opportunity to take more initiative in policy making. Those holding to this view cite such developments as the following:

> Without overstating the point, something of a vacuum has been created at the centre by the scaling back of federal and provincial government activities. This retrenchment has occurred because of the fiscal restraint pursued by the provincial and federal levels, arising from a sharp swing to the right in the prevailing political philosophy – in favour of downsizing and privatizing operations – and from restrictions imposed by transnational corporations and international trade agreements in this era of globalization.
> Many provincial transfer payments are gone, which means that the conditions that used to be attached to most of the payments, and which used to distort local decision making, are also gone.

➤ Amalgamation initiatives in Central and Eastern Canada (whether well-founded or not) have created a number of significantly larger municipalities that may be more prepared to challenge the restrictions imposed upon them by their provincial governments.

It would appear that municipal governments are at something of a crossroads when it comes to policy making. One path, along which they are being pushed by at least some provincial governments, leads to a diminished policy role centred on the selection of the cheapest alternatives for the delivery of local services. The other path leads to an enhanced policy role, one in which municipalities and their local citizens decide together how they want to define their community and provide for it. This path proceeds from an acceptance of the inherently political nature of municipal government – and the resulting importance of a policy process centred in, and responsive to, the local community.

Chapter 11
Municipalities in the 21ˢᵗ Century

How well municipalities fare in this new century will depend, as always, on how successfully they maintain a balance between their two primary roles: representative/political and administrative/service delivery. The tension between these two roles is reflected in two contrasting images of municipal government – as a democratic institution that responds to community concerns and as but one of many players in a competitive market place in which individual interests prevail.

Introduction

C hapter 1 concluded that municipal governments are at a cross-roads, facing "the best of times" and the "worst of times." The intervening chapters have described many of the opportunities and challenges that contribute to this mixed assessment of municipal prospects. This final chapter builds upon this background to offer a basic five point program for municipal success in the 21ˢᵗ century.

  i)   Revive the political role of municipal government;
  ii)   Be strategic and selective;
  iii)   Develop more community responsibility;
  iv)   Operate in a business-like manner, but remain focused on being a democratic government; and
  v)   Stop being a constitutional orphan and seek adoption by the local community.

Reviving the Political Role

The term "reviving" is used because municipalities were originally established with a political role that was at least as important as the service delivery role. If the settlers in Central Canada in the 1840s had only been interested in receiving services, there would have been no reason for them to push for elected municipal governments. They were already receiving local services from the Courts of Quarter Sessions. What they wanted, clearly, was something more – a say in those servicing decisions, a vehicle through which they could express collective concerns about their communities. No matter how many or what services are provided by municipalities, their primary importance is as an expression of local choice. As Clarke and Stewart explain it, there would be no point, other than administrative convenience, in local governments providing services in which there was no significant local choice.[1]

A series of developments, described in earlier chapters, undermined the political role of municipal government, to the point where it receives far too little attention today. The first significant influence to be noted is the turn of the century reform movement of 100 years ago, from which came the notion – still widely held – that politics has no place in municipal government and only serves to interfere with the technical decisions that must be made by staff experts facing complex servicing issues. The irony, of course, is that the reform movement did not really succeed in eradicating politics from municipal decision making, nor was that really the objective of many reformers. What the reforms of that era did was ensure that the political power of business interests and the middle class continued to prevail.

By the mid-20th century, municipalities had become closely intertwined with the operations of the provincial and federal governments and were increasingly seen as vehicles for servicing land in support of the economic growth objectives of these governments. Bradford, as noted in Chapter 3, refers to this period as "cities in the shadow of Keynesian space,"[2] in deference to the economic policies then being followed by the federal government. With the growing complexity of service demands arising from the rapid urbanization following World War Two, the importance of technical expertise as the basis for municipal decisions continued to hold sway. There appeared to be widespread support for municipal efforts to promote and accommodate rapid economic growth and municipal activities

---

[1] Michael Clarke and John Stewart, *The Choices for Local Government*, Harlow, Longman, 1991, p. 2.

[2] Neil Bradford, *Why Cities Matter: Policy Research Perspectives for Canada*, CPRN Discussion Paper No. F\23, Canadian Policy Research Networks, June 2002, p. 16. This document was accessed February 20, 2003 at www.cprn.org.

seemed more administrative than political in nature. Here again, as at the end of the 19th century, the reality was rather different. "Power was in the hands of politicians, bureaucrats, and developers, all of whom were involved in the transformation and expansion of cities – hence the focus was on efficiency and only limited debate occurred over policy orientations."[3]

Debate did intensify by the 1960s, as citizens and local groups increasingly mobilized to protest against the consequences of the pattern of economic growth and development underway. Urban renewal and expressway battles provided evidence of an increasingly politicized urban life. But many of the groups that sprang up during this period were very narrowly focused and cries of NIMBY (Not In My Back Yard) were frequently heard. By the 1980s, the citizens' movement had lost much of its momentum.

By this time as well, the political role of municipal government was increasingly constrained by changing economic and ideological forces. Deficit and debt reduction became the preoccupation of the provincial and federal governments, in part to ensure Canadian competitiveness in the global economy. Municipalities found themselves facing an increasing revenue squeeze. They also faced an even greater threat in the form of provincially imposed or encouraged amalgamation initiatives in several provinces in the 1990s. A number of very big municipalities have resulted from these initiatives, and they face their own challenges in representing the interests of large and often diverse populations. Whatever their size, municipalities today are being urged to operate more like a business as the best way of meeting the challenges that they face. In some respects we have come full circle and are back in another turn of the century reform era in which the political role of municipal government is ignored in favour of its service delivery role.

If municipalities are to play an important role in the 21st century, they must reassert themselves as municipal *governments*, centred on elected bodies that make *political* decisions. The municipal council must be recognized as a political mechanism for expressing and responding to the collective concerns of members of the community.

---

[3] Paul Villeneuve and Anne-Marie Séguin, "Power and Decision-Making in the City: Political Perspectives," in Trudi Bunting and Pierre Filion, *Canadian Cities in Transition*, 2nd Edition, Toronto, Oxford University Press, 2000, p. 554.

Among the important implications of this conception of municipal government are the following points:[4]

> If the municipality is an extension of the community, its identity and its purpose derive from that community, not from the particular services it provides.

> The municipality has a legitimate right to take actions that are needed by that community. The right derives from the nature of the municipality as an extension of the community, and does not depend on what specific powers have been assigned to it.

> The municipality's primary role is concern for the problems and issues faced by its community. The interests and values of the community are expressed and resolved through the municipality. It is "a political institution for the authoritative determination of community values."[5]

This conception of municipal government rejects the current wisdom that measurement and the market place should determine the kind of society we have. George Soros, a billionaire financier, argues that every society needs shared values to hold it together and that market values can never serve this purpose. This is because they reflect only what one market participant is willing to pay another in free exchange. In his words: "Markets reduce everything, including human beings (labour) and nature (land) to commodities. We can have a market economy but we cannot have a market society."[6] In addition to markets, Soros claims, society needs institutions to serve such social goals as political freedom and social justice.

Are municipalities that kind of institution? How often are concerns about social justice voiced during municipal budget debates? Such concerns should frame the budget debate, rather than the perennial preoccupation with zero tax increases. Granted, it is difficult for municipalities to pursue social justice – especially in today's global economy – because policies of redistribution may trigger out-migration

---

[4] These points are largely based on John Stewart, "A Future for Local Authorities as Community Government," in John Stewart and Gerry Stoker (eds.), *The Future of Local Government*, London, Macmillan, 1989, Chapter 12.

[5] *Ibid.*, p. 241.

[6] George Soros, "Toward a Global Open Society," *Atlantic Monthly*, January 1998, p. 24.

by business and the well-to-do, or so claims Peterson as discussed earlier in this book.[7] But it is not difficult to broaden the budget process into something more than an exercise designed to hold the line on taxes. That is not the only community value! It is true that if you ask citizens if they would prefer not to have a tax increase, they will almost certainly answer: yes. But if they were asked if they would be prepared to pay $50 more a year to maintain certain services or service standards, they might again answer: yes – except that they are almost never asked such a question. In our view the typical municipal budget process, which starts with the objective of zero tax increases, achieved through a long process of cutting and pruning, is both backwards and devoid of a political dimension derived from community values. It should start by identifying those services that the community needs and wants and is willing to fund. Such an approach could transform the budget process into a real exercise in setting community priorities.

Being Strategic and Selective

Central to the political role of municipal government are decisions about the services to be provided, to what level, by whom. In making such decisions, municipalities must avoid being trapped in the service delivery box. This problem often arises from the fact that municipalities have grown in a haphazard fashion over the years, and have operated on a model of self-sufficiency that equates responsibility for a service with direct provision of that service. As a result, municipalities have become ever busier with the day to day demands of service delivery. They feel constant upward pressure on scarce resources – financial and personnel – and are often unable to respond to perceived local needs because of these limited resources. Municipalities locked into this pattern can become so immersed in the details of delivering services that they lose sight of why they are doing so, or whether there is a better alternative. They become so busy rowing, in the words of Gaebler and Osborne, that they ignore their even more important responsibility for steering.[8] That steering role involves making political

---

[7] Paul Peterson, *City Limits*, Chicago, University of Chicago Press, 1981.

[8] David Osborne and Ted Gaebler, *Reinventing Government*, New York, Penguin Books, 1993.

and policy decisions about the future direction of the municipality. It is also consistent with the notion of governance cited frequently in this text, because steering organizations attempt to work with other governments and the private and volunteer sector in the achievement of community goals.

It is argued that steering organizations are able to define an issue or problem comprehensively because they are not limited to the resources that they can allocate to the matter. Having defined the issue broadly, steering organizations can then "shop around" for the resources needed to deal with it. They may regulate, license, or otherwise monitor some activity, they may enter into a variety of partnership arrangements – the options are almost endless.[9] A rather similar perspective is found in the concept of the "enabling authority," described in writings about British local government.[10] Since the municipality is defined by the needs and problems facing its community, it obviously cannot and should not always act on its own; it has to work with others. An enabling municipality is one "which takes a broad responsibility for the social and economic issues confronting its area and uses all the means at its disposal to meet the needs of those living in the area."[11]

The importance of steering has also come to the fore because the servicing-financing crunch facing municipalities demands that they give more attention to planning and prioritizing. It wasn't that long ago that governments operated on the basis of "doing more with more," simply raising additional revenues when they wanted to pursue new initiatives – although this rather expansive (and expensive) attitude was always exhibited more by provincial and federal governments than by municipalities. Next came an emphasis on more efficient governments, capable of "doing more with less." Most recently, the focus has been on governments "doing less with less," as they downsize in response to fiscal pressures and supposed global dictates.

---

[9] Osborne and Gaebler identify 36 alternatives to standard service delivery. See *ibid.*, p. 31 and pp. 332-348.

[10] This term is used by a number of British authors, including John Stewart in Stewart and Stoker, *The Future of Local Government*, and in Clarke and Stewart, *The Choices for Local Government*, Chapter 2, on which this discussion is partly based.

[11] Gerry Stoker, "Creating a Local Government for a Post-Fordist Society," in Stewart and Stoker, *The Future of Local Government*, p. 167.

We don't subscribe to a minimalist view of government, believing that a strong public sector is vital to society, and is even essential to support a healthy private sector. But it is clear that governments, including municipal governments, cannot attempt to be all things to all people. It is also clear that municipalities cannot continue with a budget process that amounts to "death by a thousand cuts." The end result is a skeleton operation in which services are provided more poorly and facilities are inadequately maintained. Instead, municipalities need to review their mandates and to define the priorities that will dictate the allocation of their scarce resources. It may be that the community would prefer to see fewer services provided better. Or it may be that the community would accept paying more to avoid losing certain services. It is time to find out the answers to such questions.

Over the past couple of decades, many municipalities have used strategic planning exercises as a way of canvassing local citizens (and other stakeholders) with respect to the challenges that they face and the priorities that they ought to adopt. These exercises can be a very effective means of involving the public, setting priorities, and reallocating scarce municipal resources accordingly. In very brief and oversimplified terms, strategic planning involves the following steps.

- ➤ The mandate of the municipality is reviewed to determine what it must do, may do, and isn't doing that it could do.
- ➤ A mission statement is developed, setting out in succinct but memorable language, what makes the municipality distinctive, unique, and worthy of preservation.
- ➤ The strengths and weaknesses of the municipality are evaluated in relation to the opportunities and threats that face it (the so-called SWOT analysis), usually on the basis of extensive consultations with stakeholders.
- ➤ From the many issues facing the municipality, the strategic ones are identified, those that must be addressed.
- ➤ Goals and objectives are developed in relation to the strategic issues, action plans are spelled out, and responsibilities and resources are allocated – to ensure implementation of the strategic priorities that have been identified by the process.

Strategic planning can give a municipality a heightened awareness of its external environment and a systematic method of selecting which of the many challenges on the horizon will be addressed with scarce municipal resources. It can also be an excellent means of involving the public in municipal decision making. If it incorporates an ongoing process of debate and dialogue with local citizens, the result can be not only clearer priorities but also greater public understanding of the issues facing council and greater council awareness of what is important to the public. The result is a much more solid foundation for fulfilling the political role of municipal government.

Developing Community Responsibility

Greater involvement of the public through exercises such as strategic planning can help to promote a greater sense of community responsibility for local issues and their resolution. All too often citizens respond to a problem by complaining "why doesn't the government do something about this," even as they decry the size of government and the heavy tax burden they bear. Adding to this paradoxical behaviour is the fact that more responsible actions on the part of citizens might avoid some of the problems that then lead to expensive responses from government. People used to undertake self help and community initiated ventures almost as a matter of course. But as the scope of government activity expanded over the past century, these tendencies disappeared. The notion somehow developed that once the government gets involved with some subject, then it is the government's problem, not ours. Governments have contributed to this unfortunate development by appearing to exclude the public, by acting as if only professionals and experts could have the answers.

Gradually this trend is being reversed. Progressive governments are working with communities to reduce the likelihood of problems arising in the first place. After a century of the medical model of health care, which consumes vast resources to treat people after they become sick, the "healthy cities" movement has revived efforts by municipalities and public health agencies to promote healthy communities and healthy life styles as primary methods of avoiding sickness and associated treatment costs. The same emphasis on prevention is evident in the shift to community policing, the opening of "storefront operations," and the provision of youth-related recreational facilities in an effort to reduce crime. Progressive fire departments recognize that their primary task is not to fight fires but to prevent them from happening, and they have devoted increasing resources to public education activities. Members of the community have often led the way with respect to environmental matters, pushing their municipalities to adopt recycling and blue box programs and to promote the three Rs (reduce, reuse, and recycle).

To take one more example, many municipalities have recognized their financial limits and the importance of community involvement by setting up mechanisms which encourage local groups, organizations, or businesses to accept responsibility for providing or maintaining particular facilities or services. A common example is an arrangement under which the municipality provides the site and the boards, but a neighbourhood group accepts responsibility for maintaining an outdoor rink in its area. Schemes to "adopt a park" or "adopt a flower bed" are also widespread. A plaque at the site identifies the organization taking on this role.

There is a danger, of course, that these latter arrangements can become little more than a scheme to shift public responsibilities and costs on to private shoulders. If that is the only objective of the exercise, it is unlikely to succeed for long. Equally foolish is the situation in which governments call for greater efforts from volunteers and community associations at the very time that they have been cutting grant support to such associations in the name of fiscal restraint! Adequate government resources and true partnership arrangements are needed "to enable communities in their efforts to rehabilitate housing, create employment, get rid of drug dealers, pimps and slum landlords, foster strong community schools, recover rivers for community use, and improve public health."[12]

Almost lost in all the recent talk about governments pursuing public-private partnerships is the importance of a new partnership between governments and their citizens, one that can generate the volunteer and community efforts that are so needed today. It is scarcely an exaggeration to say that governments spent the first three decades following World War Two building a welfare state that largely pushed aside volunteer organizations and the last two decades dismantling these social programs while underfunded charities struggled

---

[12] Greg Selinger, "Urban Governance for the Twenty-First Century," in Nancy Klos (ed.), *The State of Unicity – 25 Years Later*, Winnipeg, Institute of Urban Studies, 1998, p. 99.

to pick up the pieces.[13] Municipalities today increasingly recognize the value of volunteers and the fact that they can be involved in many areas other than the traditional field of recreation. With municipal resources so strained and limited, it only makes sense to draw upon community resources and expertise wherever possible. A case in point is Burlington's initiative in appointing a citizens' committee to review its budget process, as described in Chapter 9. Whitby, Ontario is known as a community of volunteers, whose activities extend to neighbourhood safety programs (operated in conjunction with schools, police, service clubs, the media, and local businesses) and programs in seniors centres.[14] In the words of a former community worker and municipal councillor from Western Canada, "civic bureaucratic expertise combined with community initiative can lead to a more dynamic, engaged civic culture and to stronger local democracy."[15]

As this quote suggests, what makes an effective government-community partnership so valuable is not the reduction in government workload but the increased feeling of community responsibility and ownership. The "adopt a park" program cited earlier does help to defray municipal program costs, but its main benefit is enhanced community involvement and a greater sense of ownership. This is reflected in reduced vandalism and general abuse of park facilities that are adopted in this manner. If members of the community have volunteered their time and energy to maintain a park, they view it quite differently; it is "their" park, not just a municipal park. They are not going to damage or neglect "their" park; nor are they likely to tolerate others being similarly inconsiderate. It was always their park, of course, since it was provided through tax dollars, but they didn't see it that way before.

Using Resources Wisely

Whatever planning and priority setting exercises may be carried out and however much community responsibility and collective

---

[13] This is the perspective of Carol Goar, "Don't mistake price tags for values," *Toronto Star*, February 13, 1999.

[14] C. Richard Tindal, *Governance Report, Town of Whitby*, January 2001, p. 18.

[15] Selinger, "What the Unicity Experience Tells Us," p. 99.

ownership can be engendered, municipalities still face the challenge of providing a wide variety of services and programs to their citizens with severely constrained financial resources. As a result, they need to take steps to ensure that they are using their limited resources as wisely as possible. As will be clear from the very brief examples that follow, these steps involve the use of tools and techniques from the business world – even though we have repeatedly rejected the notion that municipal governments should run like a business. There is no inconsistency here. In seeking to use their resources wisely, municipalities should employ any tools that can *assist* them in their decisions. It is not the business tools *per se*, to which we have objected, but situations in which business tools and market forces dictate decisions instead of simply providing background information on which political decisions are made by councils.

What, By Whom, and How Much?

Municipalities need to keep in mind that the provision of a service and the production or supplying of that service are two quite different things. The decision by a council (and its citizens) that a service is needed and will be provided does not necessarily mean that municipal staff will be hired or assigned to deliver that service directly. The first decision is a political and policy one – that this municipal servicing need will be addressed. A second decision is then required, concerning the best way to address this need, and options include the following:

Box 11.1 Alternative Service Delivery Options

➤ A municipality can directly deliver the service itself, using its own staff, in what might be considered the traditional approach.

➤ A municipality could contract with another municipality for the service.

➤ A number of municipalities could arrange for the delivery of a service or services on their behalf, often under the aegis of a joint services board.

➤ A municipality could contract with the non-profit, voluntary, or private sector through a wide variety of arrangements.

➤ A municipality could divest itself of any responsibility for a particular service, leaving it to the private sector or others to fill the need, or not. This represents the other extreme from the traditional approach first listed.

There is no "one best way" with respect to this matter. The point is simply that a municipality should not assume that it will directly provide all services just because that has been the predominant pattern in the past. It should explore the potential of a different role in which it acts as a service arranger or as the enabling authority discussed earlier. Any such exploration should be cautious and comprehensive, however, and municipalities should be aware of the fact that alternative service delivery options are often promoted as a euphemism for downsizing and privatizing. That is certainly not our objective in proposing consideration of such options. We find nothing inherently superior in private administration. In our view, municipalities will likely continue to provide directly most of the services required by their citizens. If an alternative supplier appears to be an attractive option, a municipality should be sure to consider such things as the following:

> How central is the service in question to the core mission and mandate of the municipality? Is it a service that should be kept under direct municipal control?

> Is there sufficient information on how costs are classified and apportioned by the alternative supplier and the municipality to be confident that the comparison is really "apples to apples?"

> In addition to cost and efficiency, has equal attention been given to the question of quality and effectiveness? What is the alternative supplier's track record in this regard?

> Will the alternative supplier be taking over full responsibility for the service in question (as opposed to, for example, being responsible for provision within a portion of the municipality's geographic area) and, if so, what happens to existing municipal staff who have been handling this service?

> If the municipality is no longer involved in providing this service, will it still have sufficient internal expertise to monitor the way it is being provided and to ensure that the service contract is being fulfilled?

> Have you done a "yellow pages test" to determine if there are several alternative suppliers of this particular service, in case the first one is no longer the preferred choice when the original contract comes up for renewal?

As discussed in Chapter 8, municipalities are making increasing use of performance measurement, benchmarking, and best practices, to improve their operations. These developments are welcome and the resulting information can enhance municipal decision making. But those pursuing an ideological agenda to downsize the public sector and to enhance private sector operations can distort performance measure to advance their cause. For virtually every municipal service, it is probably possible to find a quote from somewhere that promises cheaper delivery. But performance measures should not be used as a means of searching out the cheapest alternative. They are not intended for that purpose, or for the accountability "report card" mandated in Ontario – but as a way of helping managers improve program implementation. Rather than asking "is anyone doing this cheaper?" the question should be "is staff performance showing desired improvement, year by year?" Steady progress of this sort is more effective than the "quick fix" of what may be an ill considered privatization venture.

Building Strength From Below

It is perhaps surprising that we have reached this point in the chapter without the usual calls for constitutional recognition of municipal government, more empowering provincial legislation, or increased financial assistance from the provincial and federal levels. All of these matters are important, and have been discussed in earlier chapters, but they are also beyond the control of municipalities. As a result, if they become a central focus, municipalities are left in a very passive role, waiting for largesse from the "senior" government benefactors.

As Jane Jacobs and Caroline Andrew argue in Chapter 6, municipal governments must get beyond their mindset of dependency and become more assertive. Patrick Smith and Kennedy Stewart demonstrate in that chapter that constitutional and statutory inferiority need not be a complete barrier for creative and aggressive municipalities that take advantage of any bargaining leverage that they may temporarily enjoy. Chris Leo and Susan Mulligan, in the same chapter and in Chapter 10, envisage an enhanced role for municipalities in fine-tuning the local application of federal and provincial policies and programs.

Instead of being preoccupied with their place in the hierarchy of governments in Canada, municipalities need to look outward to the other local actors that they can bring together into more inclusive governing regimes. They also need to forge close links with their local citizens and make them an integral part of such regimes. By so doing, municipalities can build their strength upward from the local communities that they represent. It will be a slow process, not easily achieved, but it is something that is within the power of municipalities to do. It is action that they can take on their own.

Striking a Balance

How municipalities fare in this new century will depend, as always, on how well they maintain a balance between two contrasting visions of what they are and how they should operate and a balance between the two contrasting primary roles that underlie these visions.

A Vending Machine or a Barn-Raising?

For the purposes of this discussion, these two visions will be characterized as the vending machine and the barn-raising.[16] The vending machine image reflects the municipality's role as service provider. This view has always been prominent and it has received even greater attention in recent years with the emphasis on municipalities being more business-like and taking care of the customer. People drop money (tax payments) in the municipal vending machine, and the machine dispenses services. Sometimes the machine doesn't work, or is out of the particular product that people want, and they grumble and kick the machine. In response, people may be offered different products and different prices. They may be given a 1-800 number to call; they may even be offered guarantees about product availability or quality. Ultimately, however, there is nothing to encourage a close allegiance between citizens and the municipal vending machine. It is just a service provider. All it wants is for people to deposit their money in exchange for the products. All the people want is the products that satisfy their particular needs. Instead of being citizens of a wider community who have an interest in the needs of others, they are individual consumers. The vending machine view is essentially an extension of public choice theory, focusing on individual choice through markets. It provides a marked contrast to traditional theories

---

[16] These contrasting images of municipal government are described in Frank Benest, "Serving customers or engaging citizens: What is the future of local government?" an article originally published as an insert in the *International City Management Association Journal*, November 1996. Some of the ideas in this article provided the inspiration for the discussion in this section.

of local democracy that focus on the capacity for collective choice through voting.[17]

The barn-raising image incorporates the notion of citizen and community responsibility. People have collective needs and concerns. Instead of saying "why doesn't the government do something?" when a problem arises, they are as likely to say "what are we going to do?" The "adopt a park" initiative, properly conducted, is consistent with the barn-raising model of municipal government. So is a strategic planning exercise that draws upon the views and values, hopes and fears, of countless members of the community as a foundation for its planning and priority setting. Technical staff can write a strategic plan, but only the citizens of a community can provide the vision that illuminates such a plan. Storefront operations, efforts to involve and empower local groups and associations, initiatives to promote partnerships amongst groups to tackle community issues – all of these actions reflect the barn-raising model. This model is consistent with the notion of the municipality as an extension of the community, the community governing itself.

The Representative or Administrative Role?

Underlying the two contrasting images of a barn-raising versus a vending machine are the two roles of municipal government: representative/political and administrative/service delivery – and they are also in conflict. If the first role is emphasized, the municipality is seen as a vehicle used by the community to address its collective concerns. This role conveys the notion of collective action to deal with shared problems and challenges (consistent with the image of the barn-raising). Municipalities are viewed as local democratic institutions that respond to collective public concerns by providing public services financed from taxes. The ultimate measure of their performance is how effectively they respond to the elusive public interest.

If the administrative role is emphasized, as has certainly been the case in recent years, the municipality is seen as but one of many players in a competitive market place in which individuals are free to pursue their personal interests by seeking out the services that they find most attractive. The image is manifestly not one of the collective

---

[17] Michael Keating, *Comparative Urban Politics*, Aldershot, Edward Elgar, 1991, p. 108.

identification of issues and collective responses. A variety of alternative service providers is seen as offering the range of choice needed for individual consumers of services to pursue their best interests. Charging user fees for these services is favoured over payment through taxes, because the former allows individuals to select only those services they want to use, and to pay accordingly (as in the vending machine analogy). The ultimate measurement of performance is how efficiently municipalities deliver services as reflected in their bottom line. The figure that follows depicts the key characteristics of these two contrasting views.

Figure 11.1 The Contrasting Characteristics

Representative role/
Political institution

Administrative role/
Servicing agent

Collective responsibility
Provision of public goods
Financed by taxes
Focused on effectiveness

Individual self-interest
Varied service providers
Financed by user fees
Focused on efficiency

The second role, of municipality as servicing agent, contains within it both positive elements and potential dangers, depending on the extent to which its key features are pushed. The benefits of a competitive atmosphere have long been evident in the public sector, and public choice proponents are persuasive when they contend that the choice for citizens is enhanced when there are multiple local service providers and when there is freedom to access a service or not by paying a user fee or not. As noted elsewhere in this text, there is considerable evidence to suggest that a fragmented municipal structure provides services less expensively than one large, consolidated unit. It is also well documented that "what gets measured, gets done,"[18] and that concerted efforts to promote and reward productivity improvements bear fruit.

On the other hand, we have also noted in this text that whatever efficiency benefits there may be from a fragmented municipal structure are potentially offset by problems caused by the lack of a unified approach to intermunicipal issues and by the perpetuation of servicing and financing inequities. With a number of separate municipalities, individuals are free to choose the one which provides whatever combination of services and charges best meet their needs –

---

[18] Osborne and Gaebler, *Reinventing Government*, p. 146.

assuming that they have both knowledge of the choices available and the mobility to act upon this knowledge. But this structural arrangement may also allow the creation or preservation of communities of relatively well-to-do individuals who need minimal government services and are taxed accordingly, and who aren't obliged to contribute, thanks to their separate governing jurisdiction, to the costs of the many government services needed by the less fortunate in society, who are located in other jurisdictions. Carried to an extreme, this can result in a kind of social apartheid, in which the elite "feel increasingly justified in paying only what is necessary to insure that everyone in their community is sufficiently well educated and has access to the public services they need to succeed."[19] It is clear that the pursuit of individual self-interest can work better for some individuals than it does for others. Along with what is best for the individual, as measured in strictly financial terms, there has to be some consideration of what is best for the broader community and region in which one moves and interacts.

Similarly, an over-preoccupation with the efficiency of service delivery, a tendency to measure municipal operations in the same way as a business, can lead to some harmful distortions. It must be remembered that many of the services provided by government are not provided by the private sector because they do not, and cannot, generate a profit or even come close to operating at break-even. This bad bottom line doesn't make such services a candidate for termination; it is why they belong in the public domain. User charges have their benefits, when applied selectively, but any widespread expansion of their use can be self-defeating. Once again, the self-interested individual will attempt to minimize costs. The wealthier citizens have no need of services such as public transit. They can forego public parks in favour of cottages and private resorts, and may even feel less need for police services thanks to their secure access high rise or gated community. Indeed, there are now far more private security forces than there are public police. But public programs and services certainly cannot be financed solely from user charges paid by the less wealthy in society.

Consider the example of municipal bus or transit services. These services never operate at break-even, a fact which seems to cause

---

[19] Robert Reich, "Secession of the Successful," *New York Times Magazine*, January 6, 1991, as quoted in Murray Dobbin, *The Myth of the Good Corporate Citizen*, Toronto, Stoddart, 1998, pp. 128-129.

great controversy – even though the public roads provided for the convenience of the motor car and which are much more heavily subsidized by government also never come close to operating at break-even. Yet the typical response to a transit deficit is to increase the fees and to reduce the service, actions hardly conducive to an improvement in the situation. A totally different way at looking at public transit would be to view it as an essential public good which is also cost-effective when one factors in the costs which would arise without it, in the form of increased air pollution and traffic congestion, greater traffic control costs, time and money lost in commuting, more "fender-benders" and other accidents, and more associated police and court costs. When everything is taken into consideration, it might even be that the much-maligned municipal transit system is a bargain. But when the focus is only on the bottom line, rather than on the broader benefits to society, we are likely to be guilty of shortsighted bookkeeping.

Concluding Comments

The contrasting images and roles that we have been examining are not, or need not be, either/or options for municipalities. They represent gradations of behaviour and orientation, and it is certainly possible (and highly desirable) to combine the best of both. Our favoured combination would keep the vending machine in the back of the barn. In other words, we believe that the representative/political role should be paramount, but that features of the service delivery role are also valuable in moderation and within the framework of the first role. Efficient and economical use of municipal resources is a desirable objective, provided that such measures are balanced by considerations of effectiveness. The pursuit of the bottom line cannot be allowed to take precedence over pursuit of the public interest.

Under different circumstances, it should not be that difficult to add business-like, competitive features to local democratic institutions. Presently, however, we face the added challenge that the institutions of government (at all levels) seem to be under attack, as a result of the global economy, the dictates of international capitalism, and the neoconservative or neoliberal ideology that has held sway for the past couple of decades. Not content to have government act in a more business-like manner, there are many who wish to go further and downgrade the role and significance of government in our society, while elevating the importance of the private sector.

One manifestation of this viewpoint is the widespread attitude that virtually all spending by government is inherently less desirable than spending by and on the private sector, and that no further tax increases can be tolerated. To put things in perspective, various published reports suggest that some $6 billion was spent on products related to the Pokémon craze during the last three years of the 20th century, even as we continue to debate whether or not we can afford welfare, public housing, public health, environmental programs, and other services that form part of a basic standard of living in a civilized society. Obviously we can afford public services if we believe in them and are prepared to support them with our taxes.[20]

Moreover, the bill for local government services is something of a bargain, as vividly illustrated by Jim Sharpe's comment that:

> ...although the local government bill is not small, it provides education, public health, social services, highways, libraries, fire, police, refuse collection, and a whole range of other public services which most people need and demand, at a total cost that is no larger than the amount we collectively spend on such things as wine and beer, cigarettes, eye shadow, tennis rackets and a flutter on the horses.[21]

It is highly unlikely that paying taxes will ever become a popular pastime in Canada. But it is through such taxes that a society provides the goods and services that serve and enhance the public good. This community need and collective responsibility provide a marked contrast to the emphasis on individual preferences and choices that has been receiving growing attention. Unless and until citizens show more commitment to governments and to their responsibilities within the governmental system, municipalities will remain vulnerable to the pressures to convert them into quasi-businesses. To resist these pressures, therefore, municipalities need to do as much as possible to demonstrate their value and relevance to their communities.

---

[20] This discussion is based on C. Richard Tindal, *A Citizen's Guide to Government*, 2nd Edition, Whitby, McGraw-Hill Ryerson Limited, 2000, p. 7.

[21] L. J. Sharpe (ed.), *The Local Fiscal Crisis in Western Europe, Myths and Realities*, London, Sage Publications, 1981, p. 224.

There is an additional, and compelling, reason for municipalities to reassert their political role and to reforge links with their
citizens. As noted earlier in this chapter, this relationship represents
the best hope for municipalities in the future. Experience has shown
that there is little to be gained by relying on the provincial and federal
levels and waiting to see what may trickle down from above. Far
better to build strength upward from the community, from the
citizens municipalities exist to serve. That means taking into account
the views and concerns of all citizens, not just propertied or business
interests. It means being efficient where possible, but also being
prepared to provide services or programs which aren't necessarily cost-
effective, if they are required to address a public need. It means being
mindful of the bottom line but also dedicated to the public interest.

Select Bibliography

Advisory Commission on Intergovernmental Relations, *A Look to the North: Canadian Regional Experience*, Washington, 1974.

Anderson, Wayne, Chester Newland, and Richard J. Stillman, *The Effective Local Government Manager*, Washington, International City Management Association, 1983.

Andrew, Caroline, "The shame of (ignoring) the cities," *Journal of Canadian Studies*, Winter 2001.

_____, "Federal Urban Activity: Intergovernmental Relations in an Age of Restraint," in Frances Frisken (ed.), *The Changing Canadian Metropolis: A Public Policy Perspective*, Vol. 2, Toronto, Canadian Urban Institute, 1994.

_____, "Recasting Political Analysis for Canadian Cities," in Vered Amit-Talia and Henri Lustiger-Thaler (eds.), *Urban Lives*, Toronto, McClelland and Stewart Limited, 1994.

_____, Katherine A. Graham, and Susan D. Phillips (eds.), *Urban Affairs: Back on the Policy Agenda*, Kingston, McGill-Queen's University Press, 2002.

Antoft, Kell, and Jack Novack, *Grassroots Democracy: Local Government in the Maritimes*, Halifax, Centre for Public Management, Dalhousie University, 1998.

Association of Municipalities of Ontario, *Local Governance in the Future: Issues and Trends*, Toronto, 1994.

_____, *Ontario Charter: A Proposed Bill of Rights for Local Government*, Toronto, 1994.

Aucoin, Peter, *The New Public Management in Canada in Comparative Perspective*, Montreal, Institute for Research on Public Policy, 1995.

Banfield, Edward C., *The Unheavenly City*, Boston, Little, Brown and Company, 1968.

_____. and James Q. Wilson, *City Politics*, New York, Random House, 1963.

Bird, R. M., and N. E. Slack, *Urban Public Finance in Canada*, Toronto, Butterworths, 1983 and Toronto, John Wiley & Sons, 1993.

Bish, Robert L., *Local Government Amalgamations: Discredited Nineteenth-Century Ideals Alive in the Twenty-First*, Commentary No. 150, C. D. Howe Institute, March 2001.

_____, "Evolutionary Alternatives for Metropolitan Areas: The Capital Region of British Columbia," *Canadian Journal of Regional Science*, Special Issue, Spring 2000.

_____, *The Public Economy of Metropolitan Areas*, Chicago, Markham Publishing Company, 1971.

_____, and Eric Clemens, *Local Government in British Columbia*, 3rd Edition, Richmond, Union of British Columbia Municipalities, 1999.

_____, and Vincent Ostrom, *Understanding Urban Government: Metropolitan Reform Reconsidered*, Washington, American Enterprise Institute for Public Policy Research, 1973.

Blais, Pamela, *Inching Toward Sustainability: The Evolving Urban Structure of the GTA*, Report to the Neptis Foundation, March 2000.

Borins, Sandford, "The new public management is here to stay," *Canadian Public Administration*, Spring 1995.

Bourne, Larry, *People and Times: A Portrait of the Evolving Social Character of the Greater Toronto Region*, Toronto, Neptis Foundation, 2000.

_____, (ed.), *Internal Structure of the City*, Toronto, Oxford University Press, 1971.

_____, and Jim Simmons, "New Fault Lines" Recent Trends in the Canadian Urban System and Their Implications for Planning and Public Policy, *Canadian Journal of Urban Research*, Volume 12, Issue 1, Summer 2003.

Boyer, J. Patrick, *Lawmaking by the People: Referendums and Plebiscites in Canada*, Toronto, Butterworths, 1982.

Bradford, Neil, *Why Cities Matter: Policy Research Perspective for Canada*, CPRN Discussion Paper F\23, Canadian Policy Research Networks, June 2002.

Broadbent, Alan, *The Place of Cities in Canada: Inside the Constitutional Box and Out*, Ottawa, Calendon Institute of Social Policy, June 2002.

Bunting, Trudi and Pierre Filion (eds.), *Canadian Cities in Transition*, 2nd Edition, Toronto, Oxford University Press, 2000.

Burke, Mike, Colin Mooers, and John Shields, *Restructuring and Resistance: Canadian Public Policy in an Age of Global Capitalism*, Halifax, Fernwood Publishing, 2000.

Cameron, David M., "Provincial responsibilities for municipal government," *Canadian Public Administration*, Summer 1980.

Cameron, John R., *Provincial-Municipal Relations in the Maritime Provinces*, Fredericton, Maritime Union Study, 1970.

Canada West Foundation, *Big City Revenues: A Canada-U.S. Comparison of Municipal Tax Tools and Revenue Levers* (Casey G. Vander Ploeg), September 2002.

_____, *Cities at the Crossroads: Addressing Intergovernmental Structures for Western Canada's Cities* (Denis Wong), August 2002.

_____, *Regional Approaches to Services in the West: Health, Social Services and Education* (Evan Jones and Susan McFarlane), February 2002.

_____, *Framing a Fiscal Fix-Up: Options for Strengthening the Finances of Western Canada's Big Cities* (Casey G. Vander Ploeg), January 2002.

Canadian Federation of Mayors and Municipalities, *Puppets on a Shoestring*, Ottawa, April 28, 1976.

Canadian Urban Institute, *Smart Growth in Canada*, Toronto, March 2001.

_____, *The Future of Greater Montreal: Lessons for the Greater Toronto Area?*, Conference Proceedings, Toronto, 1994.

_____, *Disentangling Local Government Responsibilities: International Comparisons*, Toronto, 1993.

Carrel, André, *Citizen's Hall*, Toronto, Between the Lines, 2001.

Caufield, Jon, *The Tiny Perfect Mayor*, Toronto, James Lorimer and Co., 1974.

Charlton, Mark and Paul Barker (eds.), *Crosscurrents: Contemporary Political Issues*, 3rd Edition, Toronto, Nelson, 1998.

Chirah, Mohamed, and Arthur Daniels (eds.), *New Public Management and Public Administration in Canada*, Toronto, Institute of Public Administration of Canada, 1997.

Clarke, Michael and John Stewart, *The Choices for Local Government*, Harlow, Longman, 1991.

Clarke, Terry Nichols, and Michael Rempel (eds.), *Citizen Politics in Post Industrial Societies*, Boulder, Westview Press, 1997.

Clarkson, Stephen, *Uncle Sam and Us, Globalization, Neoconservatism, and the Canadian State*, Toronto, University of Toronto Press, 2002.

_____, *City Lib*, Toronto, Hakkert, 1972.

Cochrane, Allan, *Whatever Happened to Local Government?*, Buckingham, Open University Press, 1993.

Colton, Timothy J., *Big Daddy*, Toronto, University of Toronto Press, 1980.

Courchene, Thomas J., *A State of Minds*, Montreal, Institute of Research on Public Policy, 2001.

_____, and C. R. Telmer, *From Heartland to North American Region-State: The Social, Fiscal, and Federal Evolution of Ontario*, Toronto, Faculty of Management, University of Toronto, 1998.

Craig, Gerald M. (ed.), *Lord Durham's Report*, Toronto, McClelland and Stewart Limited, 1963.

Crawford, K. G., *Canadian Municipal Government*, Toronto, University of Toronto Press, 1954.

Diamant, Peter, and Amy Pike, *The Structure of Local Government and the Small Municipality*, Rural Development Institute, Brandon University, 1994.

Dickerson, M. O., S. Drabek, and J. T. Woods (eds.), *Problems of Change in Urban Government*, Waterloo, Wilfrid Laurier University Press, 1980.

Downey, T. J. and R. J. Williams, "Provincial agendas, local responses: the 'common sense' restructuring of Ontario's municipal governments," *Canadian Public Administration*, Summer 1998.

Dreier, Peter, John Mollenkopf, and Todd Swanstrom, *Place Matters: Metropolitics for the Twenty-First Century*, Lawrence, University Press of Kansas, 2001.

Dunn, Christopher (ed.), *The Handbook of Canadian Public Administration*, Toronto, Oxford University Press, 2002.

Dupre, J. Stefan, *Intergovernmental Finance in Ontario: A Provincial- Local Perspective*, Toronto, Queen's Printer, 1968.

d'Entremont, Harley and Patrick Robardet, "More Reform in New Brunswick: Rural Municipalities," *Canadian Public Administration*, Fall 1997.

Fainstein, Susan, and Scott Campbell (eds.), *Readings in Urban Theory*, Cambridge, Blackwell Publishers Inc., 1996.

Federation of Canadian Municipalities, *Early Warning: Will Canadian Cities Compete?*, May 2001.

_____, *Quality of Life in Canadian Communities 2001 Report*, March 2001.

_____, *Brief to the Royal Commission on the Economic Union and Development Prospects for Canada*, October 1983.

_____, *Municipal Government in a New Canadian Federal System, Report of the Task Force on Constitutional Reform*, Ottawa, FCM, 1980.

Feldman, Lionel D., *Ontario 1945-1973: The Municipal Dynamic*, Toronto, Ontario Economic Council, 1974.

_____, "Tribunals, Politics and the Public Interest: The Edmonton Annexation Case – A Response," *Canadian Public Policy*, Spring 1982.

_____ (ed.), *Politics and Government of Urban Canada*, Toronto, Methuen, 1981.

_____ and Katherine Graham, *Bargaining for Cities*, Toronto, Butterworths, 1979.

Final Report of the Capital Region Review Panel, Manitoba, 1999.

Final Report, Prime Minister's Caucus Task Force on Urban Issues (Judy Sgro, Chair), *Canada's Urban Strategy: A Blueprint for Action*, November 2002.

Final Report, *Task Force on Municipal Regionalization*, St. John's, September 1997.

Florida, Richard, *The Rise of the Creative Class*, New York, Basic Books, 2002.

_____, *The Economic Geography of Talent*, Pittsburgh, Carnegie Mellon University, 2001.

_____, *Technology and Tolerance: The Importance of Diversity to High-Technology Growth*, Washington, The Brookings Institution, June 2001.

Foot, David K., with Daniel Stoffman, *Boom, Bust & Echo*, Toronto, Macfarlane Walter & Ross, 1996.

Fowler, Edmund P., *Building Cities That Work*, Kingston, McGill-Queen's University Press, 1992.

_____, and David Siegel, *Urban Policy Issues*, 2nd Edition, Toronto, Oxford University Press, 2002.

Fraser, Graham, *Fighting Back*, Toronto, Hakkert, 1972.

Frisken, Frances (ed.), *The Changing Canadian Metropolis: A Public Policy Perspective*, 2 vol., Toronto, Canadian Urban Institute, 1994.

_____, *City Policy-Making in Theory and Practice: The Case of Toronto's Downtown Plan*, Local Government Case Study No. 3, London, University of Western Ontario, 1988.

_____, "Canadian Cities and the American Example: A Prologue to Urban Policy Analysis," *Canadian Public Administration*, Fall 1986.

Garreau, Joel, *Edge City: Life on the New Frontier*, New York, Doubleday, 1991.

Gertler, L. O. and R. W. Crowley, *Changing Canadian Cities: The Next 25 Years*, Toronto, McClelland and Stewart Limited, 1977.

Gertler, Meric S., "City-Regions in the Global Economy: Choices Facing Toronto," *Policy Options*, September 1996.

Gillham, Oliver, *The Limitless City: A Primer on the Urban Sprawl Debate*, Washington, Island Press, 2002.

Goetz, Edward G. and Susan E. Clarke (eds.), *The New Localism*, Newbury Park, Sage Publications, 1993.

Goldrick, Michael, "The Anatomy of Urban Reform in Toronto," in Dimitrios Roussopoulos (ed.), *The City and Radical Social Change*, Montreal, Black Rose Books, 1982.

Gottdiener, M., *The Decline of Urban Politics: Political Theory and the Crisis of the Local State*, Newbury Park, Sage Publications, 1987.

Gould, Ellen, *International Trade and Investment Agreements: A Primer for Local Governments*, Richmond, Union of British Columbia Municipalities, June 2001.

Graham, Katherine A., Susan D. Phillips, and Allan M. Maslove, *Urban Governance in Canada*, Toronto, Harcourt Brace & Company, 1998.

Graham, Katherine A. and Susan D. Phillips, *Citizen Engagement: Lessons in Participation from Local Government*, Toronto, Institute of Public Administration of Canada, 1998.

_____, "Who Does What in Ontario: The Process of Provincial-Municipal Disentanglement," *Canadian Public Administration*, Summer 1998.

_____, "Customer engagement: beyond the customer revolution," *Canadian Public Administration*, Summer 1997.

Granatstein, J. L., *Marlborough Marathon*, Toronto, Hakkert and James Lewis and Samuel, 1971.

Gutstein, Donald, *Vancouver Ltd.*, Toronto, James Lorimer and Co., 1975.

Gyford, John, *Local Politics in Britain*, London, Croom Helm Ltd., 1976.

_____, Steve Leach, and Chris Game, *The Changing Politics of Local Government*, London, Unwin Hyman, 1989.

Hambleton, Robin, Hank V. Savitch, and Murray Stewart (eds.), *Globalism and Local Democracy*, London, Palgrave Macmillan, 2002.

Headrick, T. E., *The Town Clerk in English Local Government*, London, George Allen & Unwin, 1962.

Herland, Karen, *People, Potholes and City Politics*, Montreal, Black Rose Books, 1992.

Higgins, Donald J. H., *Local and Urban Politics in Canada*, Toronto, Gage, 1986.

_____, *Urban Canada: Its Government and Politics*, Toronto, Macmillan, 1977.

Hill, Dilys, *Citizens and Cities*, Hemel Hempstead, Harvester Wheatsheaf, 1994.

Hobson, Paul A. R., *The Economic Effects of the Property Tax: A Survey*, Ottawa, Economic Council of Canada, 1987.

_____, and France St-Hilaire (eds.), *Urban Governance and Finance*, Montreal, Institute of Research on Public Policy, 1997.

Hodge, Gerald, *Planning Canadian Communities*, Toronto, Methuen, 1986 and Scarborough, Nelson Canada, 1991.

_____, and Ira M. Robinson, *Planning Canadian Regions*, Vancouver, UBC Press, 2001.

Hollick, Thomas R., and David Siegel, *Evolution, Revolution, Amalgamation: Restructuring in Three Ontario Municipalities*, Local Government Case Studies No. 10, London, University of Western Ontario, 2001.

Isin, Engin F. (ed.), *Democracy, Citizenship and the Global City*, London, Routledge, 2000.

_____, *Cities Without Citizens*, Montreal, Black Rose Books, 1992.

Jacobs, Jane, *The Death and Life of Great American Cities*, New York, Random House, 1961.

Jones, George and John Stewart, *The Case for Local Government*, London, Allen & Unwin Inc., 1985.

Judge, David, Gerry Stoker, and Harold Wolman (eds.), *Theories of Urban Politics*, London, Sage Publications, 1995.

Kaplan, Harold, *Urban Political Systems: A Functional Analysis of Metro Toronto*, New York, Columbia University Press, 1967.

_____, *Reform, Planning and City Politics: Montreal, Winnipeg, Toronto*, Toronto, University of Toronto Press, 1982.

Keating, Michael, *Comparative Urban Politics*, Aldershot, Edward Elgar, 1991.

Kernaghan, Kenneth, Brian Marson, and Sandford Borins, *The New Public Organization*, Toronto, Institute of Public Administration of Canada, 2000.

King, Desmond, and Jon Pierre (eds.), *Challenges to Local Government*, London, Sage Publications, 1990.

_____, and Gerry Stoker (eds.), *Rethinking Local Democracy*, Houndmills, Macmillan Press Ltd, 1996.

Kitchen, Harry, *Municipal Revenue and Expenditure Issues in Canada*, CanadianTax Paper No. 107, Toronto, Canadian Tax Foundation, 2002.

_____, *Municipal Finance in a New Fiscal Environment*, Commentary No. 147, C. D. Howe Institute, November 2000.

Klos, Nancy (ed.), *The State of Unicity – 25 Years Later*, Winnipeg, Institute of Urban Studies, 1998.

Kushner, Joseph, I. Masse, T. Peters, and L. Soroka, "The determinants of municipal expenditures in Ontario," *Canadian Tax Journal* (1996), vol. 44, no. 2.

Laffin, Martin, and Ken Young, *Professionalism in Local Government*, Harlow, Longman, 1990.

Landon, Fred, *Western Ontario and the American Frontier*, Toronto, McClelland and Stewart Limited, 1967.

Lang, Vernon, *The Service State Emerges in Ontario*, Toronto, Ontario Economic Council, 1974.

Lennon, Richard, and Christopher Leo, *Stopping the Sprawl: How Winnipeg Could Benefit From Metropolitan Growth Strategies for a Slow-Growth Region*, Canadian Centre for Policy Alternatives, January 2001.

Leo, Christopher, "The Urban Economy and the Power of the Local State," in Frances Frisken (ed.), *The Changing Canadian Metropolis: A Public Policy Perspective*, Vol. 2, Toronto, Canadian Urban Institute, 1994.

_____, *The Politics of Urban Development: Canadian Urban Expressway Disputes*, Monographs on Canadian Urban Government, No. 3, Toronto, Institute of Public Administration, 1977

_____, with Susan Mulligan, "Rethinking Urban Governance in the 21st Century," paper presented at the Canadian Political Science Association conference, Halifax, May 2003.

LeSage, Edward, *Municipal Reform in Alberta: A Review of Statutory, Financial and Structural Changes Over the Past Decade*, paper presented at the Canadian Political Science Association annual meeting, Quebec City, May 28, 2001.

Levine, Allan (ed.), *Your Worship: The Lives of Eight of Canada's Most Unforgettable Mayors*, Toronto, James Lorimer, 1989.

Lidstone, Donald, "Municipal Acts of the Provinces and Territories: A Report Card," Ottawa, Federation of Canadian Municipalities, Summer 2003.

Lightbody, James, "A new perspective on clothing the emperor: Canadian metropolitan form, function and frontiers," in *Canadian Public Administration*, Fall 1997.

_____ (ed.), *Canadian Metropolitics: Governing Our Cities*, Toronto, Copp Clark Ltd., 1995.

Lindblom, Charles E., *The Policy Making Process*, Englewood Cliffs, Prentice-Hall Inc., 1980.

Lithwick, N. H., *Urban Canada: Problems and Prospects*, Ottawa, Central Mortgage and Housing Corporation, 1970.

Lorimer, James, *The Developers*, Toronto, James Lorimer, 1978.

_____, *A Citizen's Guide to City Politics*, Toronto, James Lewis and Samuel, 1972.

_____, *The Real World of City Politics*, Toronto, James Lewis and Samuel, 1970.

_____, and Carolyn MacGregor (eds.), *After the Developers*, Toronto, James Lorimer, 1981.

_____, and E. Ross (eds.), *The City Book: The Planning and Politics of Canada's Cities*, Toronto, James Lorimer and Company, 1976.

Lowi, Theodore, *The End of Liberalism*, 2nd Edition, New York, W. W. Norton, 1979.

Lustiger-Thaler, Henri (ed.), *Political Arrangements: Power and the City*, Montreal, Black Rose Books, 1992.

Lyons, W. E., David Lowery, and Ruth Hoogland DeHoog, *The Politics of Dissatisfaction*, Armonk, M. E. Sharpe, Inc., 1992.

Magnusson, Warren, *The Search for Political Space*, Toronto, University of Toronto Press, 1996.

_____, "The Local State in Canada: Theoretical Perspectives," *Canadian Public Administration*, Winter 1985.

_____, "Urban Politics and the Local State," *Studies in Political Economy*, 16, 1985.

_____ and Andrew Sancton (eds.), *City Politics in Canada*, Toronto, University of Toronto Press, 1983.

Mancuso, Maureen, Richard Price, and Ronald Wagenberg (eds.), *Leaders and Leadership in Canada*, Toronto, Oxford University Press, 1994.

Manitoba, Government of, *Proposals for Urban Reorganization in the Greater Winnipeg Area (White Paper)*, Winnipeg, Queen's Printer, 1970.

Masson, Jack, with Edward C. Lesage, Jr., *Alberta's Local Governments: Politics and Democracy*, Edmonton, University of Alberta Press, 1994.

_____, and James D. Anderson (eds.), *Emerging Party Politics in Urban Canada*, Toronto, McClelland and Stewart Limited, 1972.

McDavid, James, "The impacts of amalgamation on police services in the Halifax Regional Municipality," *Canadian Public Administration*, Winter 2002.

_____, and Brian Marson (eds.), *The Well-Performing Government Organization*, Toronto, Institute of Public Administration, 1991.

McEvoy, John M., *The Ontario Township*, University of Toronto, Political Studies, 1st Series No. 1, 1889.

McIver, J. M., "Survey of the City Manager Plan in Canada," *Canadian Public Administration*, Fall 1960.

Mellon, Hugh, "Reforming the Electoral System of Metropolitan Toronto," *Canadian Public Administration*, Toronto, Spring 1993.

Milner, Henry, "The Montreal Citizens' Movement: Then and Now," Hanover, *Quebec Studies*, No. 6, 1988.

Minister of Urban Affairs, *Strengthening Local Government in Winnipeg: Proposals for Changes to the City of Winnipeg Act, Discussion Paper*, Winnipeg, February 27, 1987.

Ministry of Municipal Affairs (Ont.), *Study of Innovative Financing Approaches for Ontario Municipalities* (Price Waterhouse), March 31, 1993.

_____, *Joint Services in Municipalities: Five Case Studies*, Toronto, April 1983.

Mollenkopf, John H., *The Contested City*, Princeton, Princeton University Press, 1983.

Municipal Finance Officers Association of Ontario and Association of Municipal Clerks and Treasurers of Ontario, *Innovative Financing: A Collection of Stories from Ontario Municipalities*, Toronto, 1993.

New Brunswick, Government of, *Local Government Review Panel, Miramichi City: Our Future – Strength Through Unicity*, and *Greater Moncton Urban Community: Strength Through Cooperation*, April 1994.

_____, *The Commission on Land Use and the Rural Environment: Summary Report*, Fredericton, April 1993.

_____, *Strengthening Municipal Government in New Brunswick's Urban Centres*, Ministry of Municipalities, Culture and Housing, December 1992.

Nova Scotia, Government of, *Interim Report of the Municipal Reform Commissioner, Cape Breton County*, Department of Municipal Affairs, July 8, 1993.

_____, *Task Force on Local Government*, April 1992.

O'Brien, Allan, *Municipal Consolidation in Canada and Its Alternatives*, Toronto, ICURR Publications, May 1993.

_____, "Holding Pattern: A Look at the Provincial-Municipal Relationship," in Donald C. MacDonald (ed.), *Government and Politics of Ontario*, Toronto, Nelson, 1985.

_____, "The Ministry of State for Urban Affairs: A Municipal Perspective," *The Canadian Journal of Regional Science*, Halifax, Spring 1982.

_____, "Local Government Priorities for the Eighties," *Canadian Public Administration*, Spring 1976.

Orfield, Myron, *Metropolitics: A Regional Agenda for Community and Stability*, Washington, Brookings Institution Press, 1997.

Osborne, David and Ted Gaebler, *Reinventing Government*, New York, Penguin Books, 1993.

Ostrom, Vincent, Robert Bish, and Elinor Ostrom, *Local Government in the United States*, San Francisco, Institute for Contemporary Analysis, 1988.

Peirce, Neil R., *Citi-States: How Urban America Can Prosper in a Competitive World*, Washington, Seven Locks Press, 1993.

Peters, Thomas J., *Thriving on Chaos*, New York, HarperCollins Publishers, 1988.

_____, and Nancy Austin, *A Passion for Excellence*, New York, Random House, 1985.

_____, and Robert H. Waterman, Jr., *In Search of Excellence*, New York, Warner Books, 1982.

Peterson, Paul E., *City Limits*, Chicago, University of Chicago Press, 1981.

Plunkett, T. J., *City Management in Canada: The Role of the Chief Administrative Officer*, Toronto, Institute of Public Administration, 1992.

_____, *Urban Canada and Its Government*, Toronto, Macmillan, 1968.

_____, and Meyer Brownstone, *Metropolitan Winnipeg: Politics and Reform of Local Government*, Berkeley, University of California Press, 1983.

_____, and Katherine Graham, "Whither Municipal Government," *Canadian Public Administration*, Winter 1982.

_____, and James Lightbody, "Tribunals, Politics and the Public Interest: The Edmonton Annexation Case," in *Canadian Public Policy*, Spring 1982.

_____, and G. M. Betts, *The Management of Canadian Urban Government*, Kingston, Queen's University, 1978.

Poel, Dale H., "Amalgamation Perspectives: Citizen Responses to Municipal Consolidation," *Canadian Journal of Regional Science*, Special Issue, Spring 2000.

Polese, Mario, and Richard Stren (eds.), *Social Sustainability of Cities: Diversity and the Management of Change*, Toronto, University of Toronto Press, 2000.

Prior, David, John Stewart, and Kieron Walsh, *Citizenship: Rights, Community & Participation*, London, Pitman Publishing, 1995.

Quesnel, Louise, *Public Consultations: A Tool for Democracy*, Toronto, ICURR Publications, August 2000.

Regional District Survey Committee, *Summary Report of the Regional District Survey Committee*, Victoria, Queen's Printer, 1986.

Report and Recommendations, Committee of Review, City of Winnipeg Act, Winnipeg, Queen's Printer, October 1976.

Report of the Advisory Committee to the Minister of Municipal Affairs, on the Provincial-Municipal Relationship (Hopcroft Report), Toronto, January 1991.

Report of the GTA Task Force, *Greater Toronto*, Queen's Printer, January 1996.

Report of the Municipal Study Commission (Parizeau Report), Montreal, Union of Quebec Municipalities, December 1986.

Report of the Special Representative (Drury Report), *Constitutional Development in the Northwest Territories*, Ottawa, 1980.

Report of the Task Force on Nonincorporated Areas in New Brunswick, Fredericton, Queen's Printer, 1976.

Report to the Government of Nova Scotia, *Task Force on Local Government*, April 1992.

Richardson, Boyce, *The Future of Canadian Cities*, Toronto, New Press, 1972.

Richmond, Dale, and David Siegel (eds.), *Agencies, Boards and Commissions in Canadian Local Government*, Toronto, Institute of Public Administration of Canada, 1994.

Rothblatt, Donald N. and Andrew Sancton (eds.), *Metropolitan Governance: American/Canadian Intergovernmental Perspectives*, Berkeley, Institute of Governmental Studies Press, 1993.

Roussopoulos, Dimitri (ed.), *The City and Radical Social Change*, Montreal, Black Rose Books Ltd., 1982.

Rowe, Mary, *Toronto: Considering Self-Government*, Owen Sound, The Ginger Press, Inc., 2000.

Royal Commission on Education, Public Services, and Provincial-Munic-pal Relations in Nova Scotia. Report (John Graham, Commissioner), Halifax, Queen's Printer, 1974.

Royal Commission on Metropolitan Toronto. Report (H. Carl Goldenberg, Commissioner), Toronto, Queen's Printer, 1965.

Royal Commission on Metropolitan Toronto. Report (John Robarts, Commissioner), Toronto, Queen's Printer, June 1977.

Royal Commission on Municipal Government in Newfoundland and Labrador. Report (H. Whalen, Commissioner), St. John's, Queen's Printer, 1974.

Rusk, David, *Inside Game Outside Game*, Washington, Brookings Institution Press, 1999.

_____, *Cities Without Suburbs*, Washington, Woodrow Wilson Centre Press, 1993.

Rutherford, Paul (ed.), *Saving the Canadian City: The First Phase 1880-1920*, Toronto, University of Toronto Press, 1974.

Sancton, Andrew, "Canadian Cities and the New Regionalism," *Journal of Urban Affairs*, 2001, Volume 23, Number 5.

_____, *Merger Mania*, Kingston, McGill-Queen's University Press, 2000.

_____, "Globalization Does Not Require Amalgamation," *Policy Options*, November 1999.

_____, "Reducing costs by consolidating municipalities: New Brunswick, Nova Scotia and Ontario," *Canadian Public Administration*, Fall 1996.

_____, *Governing Canada's City Regions: Adapting Form to Function*, Montreal, Institute for Research on Public Policy, 1994.

_____, "Canada as a Highly Urbanized Nation," *Canadian Public Administration*, Fall 1992.

_____, *Local Government Reorganization in Canada Since 1975*, Toronto, ICURR Press, April 1991.

_____, "Montreal's Metropolitan Government," Hanover, *Quebec Studies*, No. 6, 1988.

_____, Rebecca James, and Rick Ramsay, *Amalgamation vs. Inter-Municipal Cooperation: Financing Local and Infrastructure Services*, Toronto, ICURR Press, July 2000.

_____, and Paul Woolner, "Full-time municipal councillors: a strategic challenge for Canadian urban government," *Canadian Public Administration*, Winter 1990.

Savitch, H. V., and Paul Kantor, *Cities in the International Marketplace*, Princeton, Princeton University Press, 2002.

Savoie, Donald J., "What is wrong with the new public management?" *Canadian Public Administration*, Spring 1995.

Schneider, Mark, *The Competitive City*, Pittsburgh, University of Pittsburgh Press, 1989.

Scott, Allen J. (ed.), *Global City Regions, Trends, Theory, Policy*, Oxford, Oxford University Press, 2001.

Seidle, Leslie, *The Federal Role in Canada's Cities: Overview of Issues and Proposed Actions*, Ottawa, Canadian Policy Research Network Inc., December 2002.

_____, (ed.), *Rethinking the Delivery of Public Services to Citizens*, Montreal, Institute for Research on Public Policy, 1995.

_____, *Rethinking Government: Reform or Revolution?*, Montreal, Institute for Research on Public Policy, 1993.

Sewell, John, *The Shape of the City*, Toronto, University of Toronto Press, 1993.

_____, *Up Against City Hall*, Toronto, James Lewis and Samuel, 1972.

Sharpe, L. J., *The Government of World Cities: The Future of the Metropolitan Model*, Chicester, John Wiley & Sons, 1995.

_____, "Failure of Local Government Modernization in Britain," *Canadian Public Administration*, Spring 1981.

_____ (ed.), *The Local Fiscal Crisis in Western Europe, Myths and Realities*, London, Sage Publications, 1981.

_____, and K. Newton, *Does Politics Matter?*, Oxford, Clarendon Press, 1984.

Shields, John and B. Mitchell Evans, *Shrinking the State: Globalization and Public Administration "Reform,"* Halifax, Fernwood Publishing, 1998.

Shortt, Adam, *Municipal Government in Ontario, An Historical Sketch*, Toronto, University of Toronto Studies, History and Economics, Vol. II, No. 2, undated.

_____ and Arthur G. Doughty (eds.), *Canada and Its Provinces: A History of the Canadian People and Their Institutions*, Toronto, Glasgow, Brook and Company, 1914, Vol. XVIII.

Siegel, David, "Politics, politicians, and public servants in non-partisan local governments," *Canadian Public Administration*, Spring 1994.

_____, "City Hall Doesn't Need Parties," *Policy Options*, June 1987.

_____, "Provincial-Municipal Relations in Canada: An Overview," *Canadian Public Administration*, Summer 1980.

Slack, Enid, *Municipal Finance and the Pattern of Urban Growth*, Commentary No. 160, C. D. Howe Institute, February 2002.

Smith, Patrick, "Restructuring Metropolitan Governance: Vancouver and BC Reforms," *Policy Options*, September 1996.

_____, "Regional Governance in British Columbia," *Planning and Administration*, 13, 1986.

_____ and Kennedy Stewart, *Making Accountability Work in British Columbia*, Report for the Ministry of Municipal Affairs and Housing, June 1998.

Stein, David Lewis, *Toronto for Sale: The Destruction of a City*, Toronto, New Press, 1972.

Stelter, Gilbert A. and Alan F. Artibise (eds.), *Power and Place: Canadian Urban Development in the North American City*, Vancouver, University of British Columbia Press, 1986.

_____, *Shaping the Urban Landscape: Aspects of the Canadian City-Building Process*, Ottawa, Carleton University Press, 1982.

_____, *The Canadian City: Essays in Urban History*, Toronto, Mc-Clelland and Stewart Limited, 1977.

Stephens, G. Ross, and Nelson Wikstrom, *Metropolitan Government and Governance*, Oxford, Oxford University Press, 2000.

Stewart, John, *The Responsive Local Authority*, London, Charles Knight and Co. Ltd., 1974.

_____, and Gerry Stoker (eds.), *Local Government in the 1990s*, Houndmills, The Macmillan Press Ltd., 1995.

Stewart, Kennedy, *Think Democracy: Options for Local Democratic Reform in Vancouver*, Vancouver, Institute of Governance Studies, Simon Fraser University, 2003.

Stoker, Gerry, *The Politics of Local Government*, London, Macmillan Education Ltd., 1988.

_____, and Stephen Young, *Cities in the 1990s*, Harlow, Longman, 1993.

Stone, Clarence N. and Heywood T. Sanders (eds.), *The Politics of Urban Development*, Lawrence, University Press of Kansas, 1987.

Swenarchuk, Michelle, *From Global to Local: GATS Impacts on Canadian Municipalities*, Ottawa, Canadian Centre for Policy Alternatives, May 2002.

Task Force on Housing and Urban Development. Report, Ottawa, Queen's Printer, 1969.

Task Force on Municipal Legislative Renewal, *Municipal Governance for Saskatchewan in the 21ˢᵗ Century, Options 2000: A Framework for Municipal Renewal – Summary of Final Report*, August 2000.

Task Force on Nonincorporated Areas in New Brunswick. Report, Fredericton, Queen's Printer, 1976.

Tennant, Paul and David Zirnhelt, "Metropolitan Government in Vancouver: the strategy of gentle imposition," *Canadian Public Administration*, Spring 1973.

Thomas, Timothy L. (ed.), *The Politics of the City*, Toronto, ITP Nelson, 1997.

_____, *A City With a Difference*, Montreal, Véhicule Press, 1997.

Tiebout, Charles, "A Pure Theory of Local Expenditures," *Journal of Political Economy*, Vol. 64.

Tindal, C. Richard, *A Citizen's Guide to Government*, 2nd Edition, Whitby, McGraw-Hill Ryerson Limited, 1997.

_____, *Structural Changes in Local Government: Government for Urban Regions*, Monographs on Canadian Urban Government, No. 2, Toronto, Institute of Public Administration of Canada, 1977.

Tomalty, Ray, *The Compact Metropolis: Growth Management and Intensification in Vancouver, Toronto and Montreal*, Toronto, ICURR Press, 1997.

_____, and Andrejs Skaburskis, "Development Charges and City Planning Objectives: The Ontario Disconnect," *Canadian Journal of Urban Research*, Volume 12, Issue 1, Summer 2003.

Toronto Dominion Bank, *The Greater Toronto Area (GTA): Canada's Primary Economic Locomotive In Need of Repairs*, May 2002.

_____, *A Choice Between Investing in Canada's Cities or Disinvesting in Canada's Future*, April 2002.

Vaillancourt, F., "Financing Local Governments in Quebec: New Arrangements for the 1990s," *Canadian Tax Journal*, Vol. 40, No. 5, 1992.

Vojnovic, Igor, "Municipal Consolidation, Regional Planning and Fiscal Accountability: The Recent Experiences in Two Maritime Provinces," *Canadian Journal of Regional Science*, Special Edition, Spring 2000.

_____, "The fiscal distribution of the provincial-municipal service exchange in Nova Scotia," *Canadian Public Administration*, Winter 1999.

_____, *Municipal Consolidation in the 1990s: An Analysis of Five Canadian Municipalities*, Toronto, ICURR Press, 1997.

Weaver, John C., *Shaping the Canadian City: Essays on Urban Politics and Policy, 1890-1920*, Monographs on Canadian Urban Government, No. 1, Toronto, Institute of Public Administration of Canada, 1977.

Whalen, H. J., *The Development of Local Government in New Brunswick*, Fredericton, 1963.

Wichern, Phil H., Jr., *Evaluating Winnipeg's Unicity: Citizen Participation and Resident Advisory Groups*, Research and Working Paper No. 11, Winnipeg, Institute of Urban Studies, University of Winnipeg, 1984.

_____, *Evaluating Winnipeg's Unicity: The City of Winnipeg Act Review Committee, 1984-1986*, Research and Working Paper No. 26, Winnipeg, Institute of Urban Studies, University of Winnipeg, 1986.

Wolfe, Jeanne M., "A National Urban Policy for Canada? Prospects and Challenges," *Canadian Journal of Urban Research*, Volume 12, Issue 1, Summer 2003.

Wolman, Harold, and Michael Goldsmith, *Urban Politics and Policy: A Comparative Approach*, Cambridge, Blackwell Publishers, 1992.

Yates, Douglas, *The Ungovernable City*, Cambridge, M.I.T. Press, 1977.

Using the Internet

Listing all of the web sites pertinent to local government would require as many entries as the preceding "hard copy" items. The brief annotated list that follows brings together, for convenient reference, the main web addresses cited in footnotes in this book. It also contains information on a few general sites that deal with broad categories or contain numerous links to other sites. The main municipal associations are listed separately below. All of these sites were active at the time this book was written.

www.gov.gc.ca	Web site for government of Canada with links to provincial and territorial governments. Using this site, you can access any provincial department of municipal affairs, or comparable organization.
www.canlii.org.	Canadian Legal Information Institute site, containing statutes from all 10 provinces and the three territories as well as from the federal government.
www.acjnet.org	Access to Justice Network also contains federal and provincial statutes, and case law as well.
www.municipalworld.com	*Municipal World* Magazine. This site also has extensive links to other local government web sites.
www.munimall.net	Source of clippings on municipal developments across Canada, updated weekly, plus links and other features.
www.cwf.ca	Canada West Foundation, which publishes reports on a variety of local government topics, some cited earlier in this book.
www.cprn.org	Canadian Policy Research Networks, another source of reports on various topics, including local government.
www.cdhowe.org	C. D. Howe Institute, which publishes on a wide variety of topics, including a local government series.

Municipal addresses follow a standard format consisting of the type of municipality followed by its name, the provincial short form, and ca. For example, the address for Edmonton, Alberta, is www.city.edmonton.ab.ca. and that of Oakville, Ontario, is www.town.oakville.on.ca.

Municipal Associations in Canada

Most of the municipal associations in the various provinces have their own web sites. These are usually cited in the links in the entries noted above, but are also listed in the table that follows.

Association	Web Address
Alberta Association of Municipal Districts & Counties (AAMD & C)	www.aamdc.com
Alberta Urban Municipalities Association (AUMA)	www.munilink.net/sitemap.asp
Association of Manitoba Municipalities	www.amm.mb.ca
Association of Municipal Administrators of New Brunswick AMANB/ AAMNB	www.munisource.org/amanb
Association of Municipal Administrators, Nova Scotia (AMANS)	www.amans.ca
Association of Municipal Managers, Clerks and Treasurers of Ontario (AMCTO)	www.acmto.com
Association of Municipalities of Ontario	www.amo.on.ca
Association of Yukon Communities (AYC)	www.ayc.yk.ca
Canadian Association of Municipal Administrators	www.camacam.ca
Federation of Canadian Municipalities	www.fcm.ca
Federation of Prince Edward Island Municipalities	www.fpeim.ca
Local Government Administration Association of Alberta (LGAA)	www.lgaa.ab.ca
Local Government Management Association of British Columbia	www.lgma.ca
Manitoba Municipal Administrators Association (MMAA)	www.mmaa.mb.ca
Municipal Finance Officers Association of Ontario	www.mfoa.on.ca
Newfoundland and Labrador Federation of Municipalities (NLFM)	www.nlfm.nf.ca/
North West Territories Association of Municipalities	www.nwtac.com
Ontario Municipal Administrators' Association	www.omaa.on.ca
Ontario Municipal Management Institute	www.ommi.on.ca
Rural Municipal Administrators' Association of Saskatchewan	www.rmaa.ca
Rural Ontario Municipal Association	www.roma.on.ca
Saskatchewan Association of Rural Municipalities	www.quantumlynx.com/sarm
Society of Local Government Managers of Alberta	www.clgm.net
Urban Municipalities Administrators Association of Saskatchewan (UMAAS)	www.quantumlynx.com/umaas

Index

A
Accountability, 199, 200, 201, 202-203, 286, 338
Adams, Thomas, 49-50
Administrative role, 7, 19, 302, 383-384
Agencies, boards and commissions, 4-5, 42, 56-57, 82, 86, 94-85, 131-132, 144
  348-349
Alberta, 226, 237, 333
  history of local government, 39
  local government reforms, 92-96
Alberta Capital Region Alliance, 93, 173
Alberta Capital Region Forum, 93
Alberta Capital Region Governance Review Report (2002), 93-94
Alternative service delivery, 19, 170, 379-380, 384
Annexations and amalgamations, 3, 21, 83, 84, 92, 93, 96, 97, 113-114, 115,
  117, 118, 124, 133, 137, 146, 151, 152, 153, 154, 164, 165
Assessment. *See* Property tax
Association of Municipalities of Ontario (AMO), 186, 188, 193, 197, 299, 204
At large elections. *See* Ward elections
Axworthy, Lloyd, 210

B
Baldwin Act. *See* Municipal Act (Ont)
Baldwin, Robert, 30
Bedard Commission, 118, 24
Belleville, 27
Benchmarking. *See* Performance measurement
Best practices. *See* Performance measurement
Board of control, 54-55, 274-275. *See also* Executive committee
Board of police, 27
Bourque, Pierre, 165, 319, 330
British Columbia,
  history of local government, 39-40
  local government reforms, 86-91
British North America Act (Constitution Act), 10, 29, 360
Brockville, 27
Budgeting process, 372-373, 375
Burlington, 306
Business models of government and governing, 18-19, 59, 203, 294-297, 336-
  337, 385-386
Byrne Commission (Royal Commission on Finance and Municipal Taxation,
  NB, 1963), 127

405

C